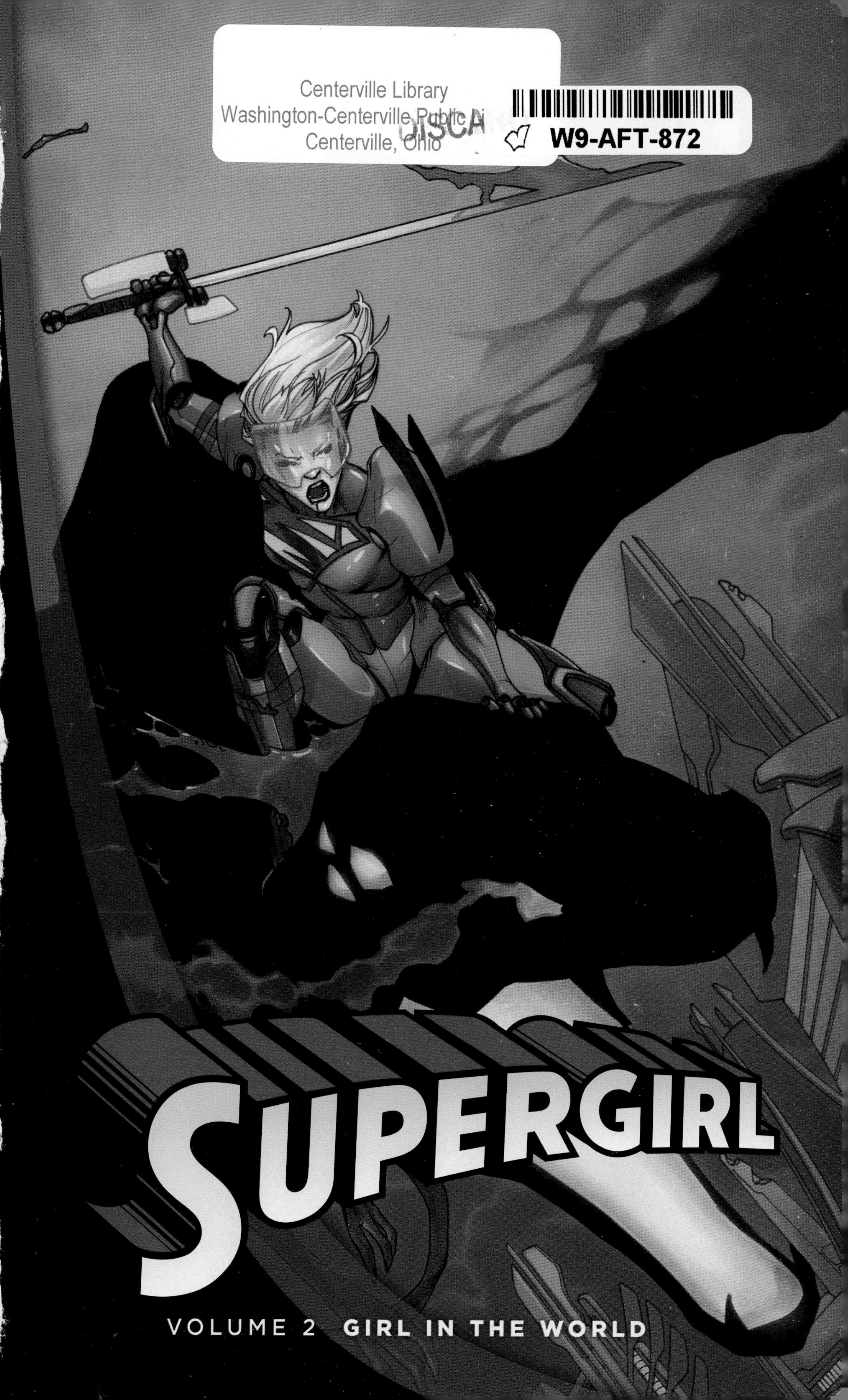

SUPERGIRL

VOLUME 2 **GIRL IN THE WORLD**

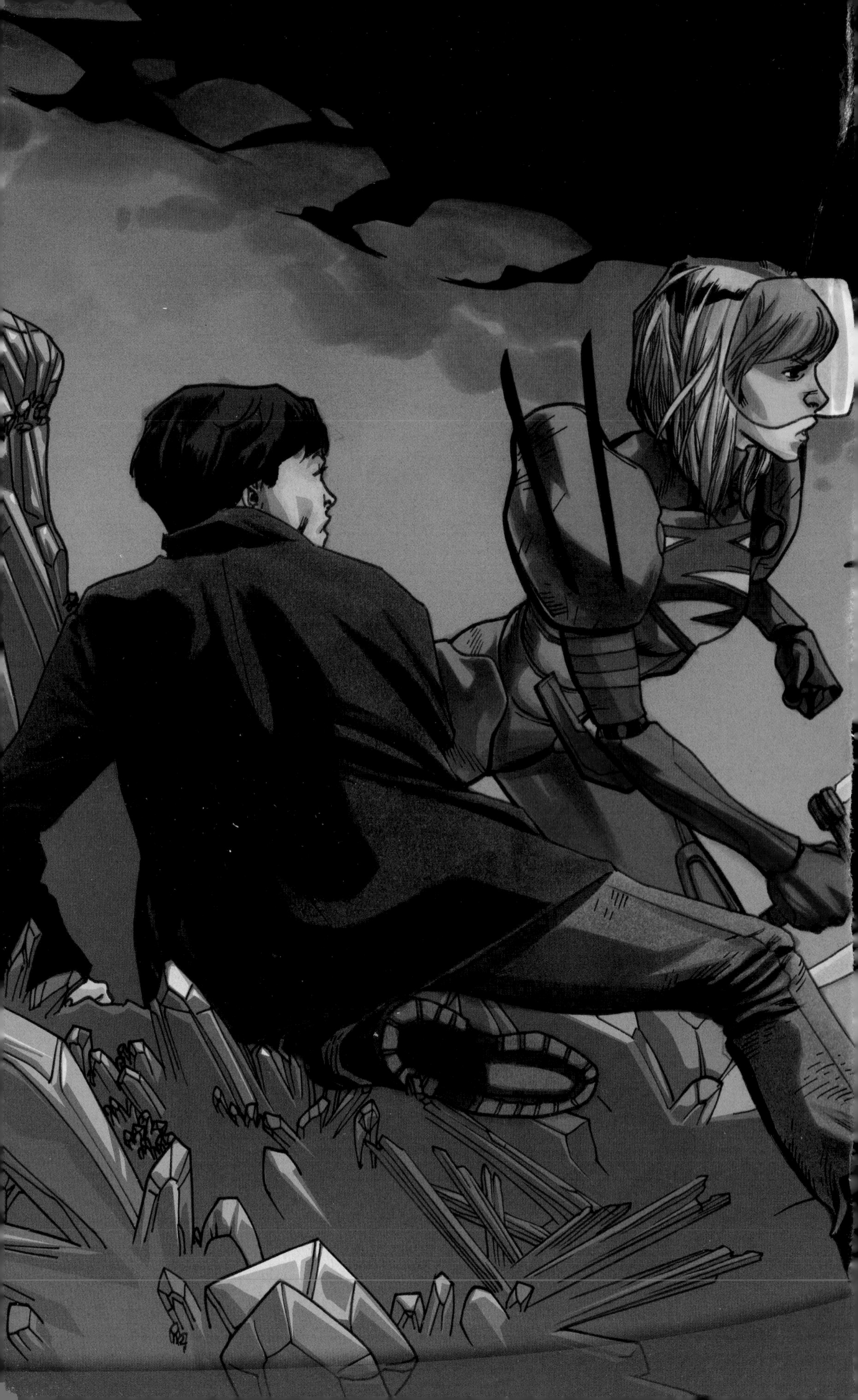

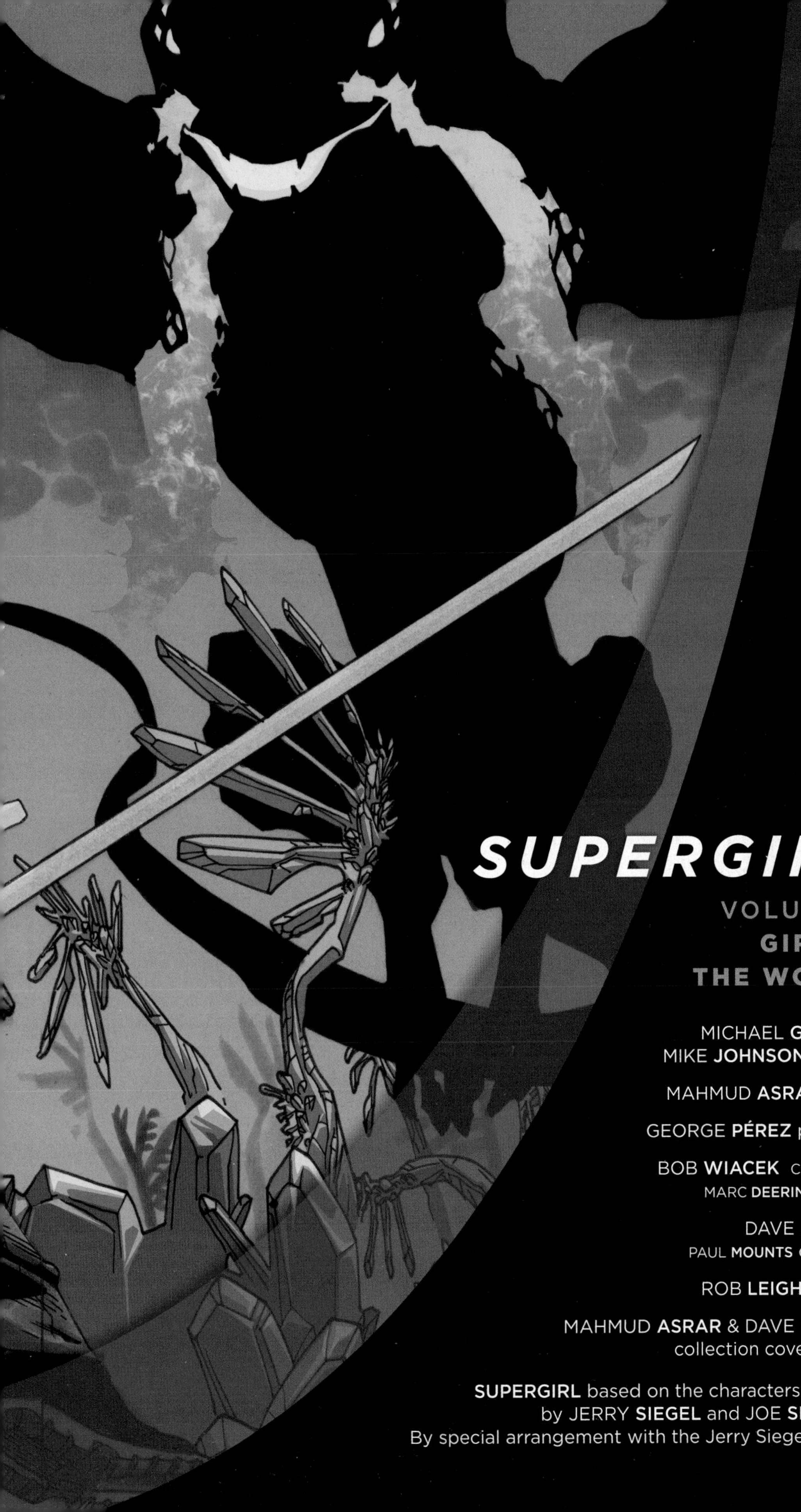

SUPERGIRL

VOLUME 2
GIRL IN THE WORLD

MICHAEL **GREEN** &
MIKE **JOHNSON** writers

MAHMUD **ASRAR** artist

GEORGE **PÉREZ** penciller

BOB **WIACEK** CAM **SMITH**
MARC **DEERING** inkers

DAVE **McCAIG**
PAUL **MOUNTS** colorists

ROB **LEIGH** letterer

MAHMUD **ASRAR** & DAVE **McCAIG**
collection cover artists

SUPERGIRL based on the characters created
by JERRY **SIEGEL** and JOE **SHUSTER**
By special arrangement with the Jerry Siegel Family

WIL MOSS Editor – Original Series RACHEL PINNELAS Editor
ROBBIN BROSTERMAN Design Director – Books ROBBIE BIEDERMAN Publication Design

BOB HARRAS Senior VP – Editor-in-Chief, DC Comics

DIANE NELSON President DAN DIDIO and JIM LEE Co-Publishers GEOFF JOHNS Chief Creative Officer
JOHN ROOD Executive VP – Sales, Marketing and Business Development AMY GENKINS Senior VP – Business and Legal Affairs
NAIRI GARDINER Senior VP – Finance JEFF BOISON VP – Publishing Planning
MARK CHIARELLO VP – Art Direction and Design JOHN CUNNINGHAM VP – Marketing
TERRI CUNNINGHAM VP – Editorial Administration ALISON GILL Senior VP – Manufacturing and Operations
HANK KANALZ Senior VP – Vertigo & Integrated Publishing JAY KOGAN VP – Business and Legal Affairs, Publishing
JACK MAHAN VP – Business Affairs, Talent NICK NAPOLITANO VP – Manufacturing Administration
SUE POHJA VP – Book Sales COURTNEY SIMMONS Senior VP – Publicity BOB WAYNE Senior VP – Sales

SUPERGIRL VOLUME 2: GIRL IN THE WORLD

DC Comics, 1700 Broadway, New York, NY 10019
A Warner Bros. Entertainment Company.
Printed by RR Donnelley, Salem, VA, USA. 6/7/13. First Printing.

ISBN: 978-1-4012-4087-5

Library of Congress Cataloging-in-Publication Data

Green, Michael, 1943-
Supergirl. Volume 2, Girl in the world / Michael Green, Mike Johnson, Mahmud Asrar.
pages cm. — (Supergirl)
"Originally published in single magazine form in Supergirl 0, 8-12."
ISBN 978-1-4012-4087-5
1. Graphic novels. I. Johnson, Mike. II. Asrar, Mahmud A. III. Title. IV. Title: Girl in the world.
PN6728.S89G75 2013
741.5'973—dc23
2013009139

SUSTAINABLE FORESTRY INITIATIVE
Certified Chain of Custody
At Least 20% Certified Forest Content
www.sfiprogram.org
SFI-01042
APPLIES TO TEXT STOCK ONLY

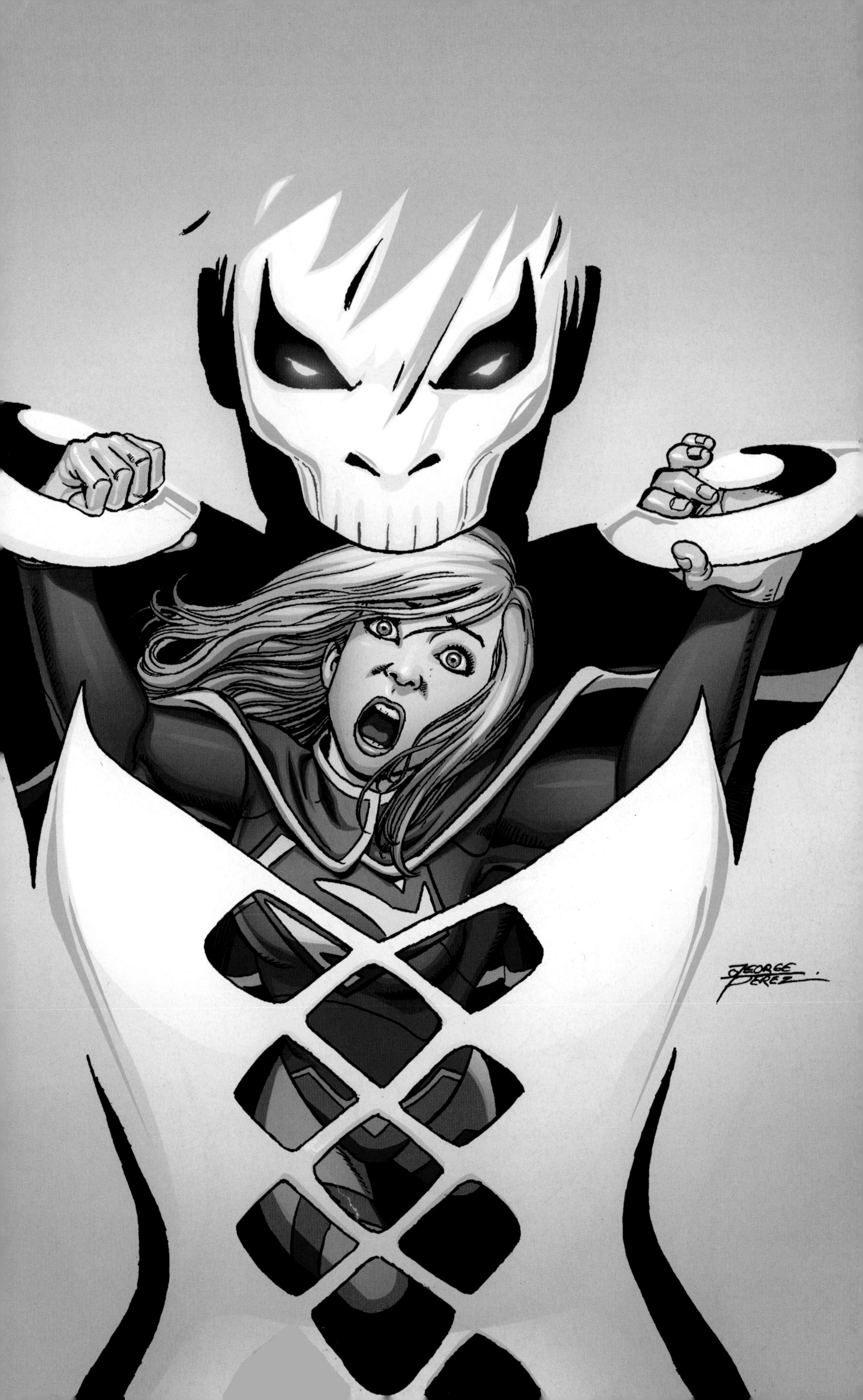
GEORGE PEREZ

GIRL IN THE WORLD

MICHAEL GREEN & MIKE JOHNSON writers **GEORGE PÉREZ** penciller **BOB WIACEK** inker cover art by **GEORGE PÉREZ & DAVE McCAIG**

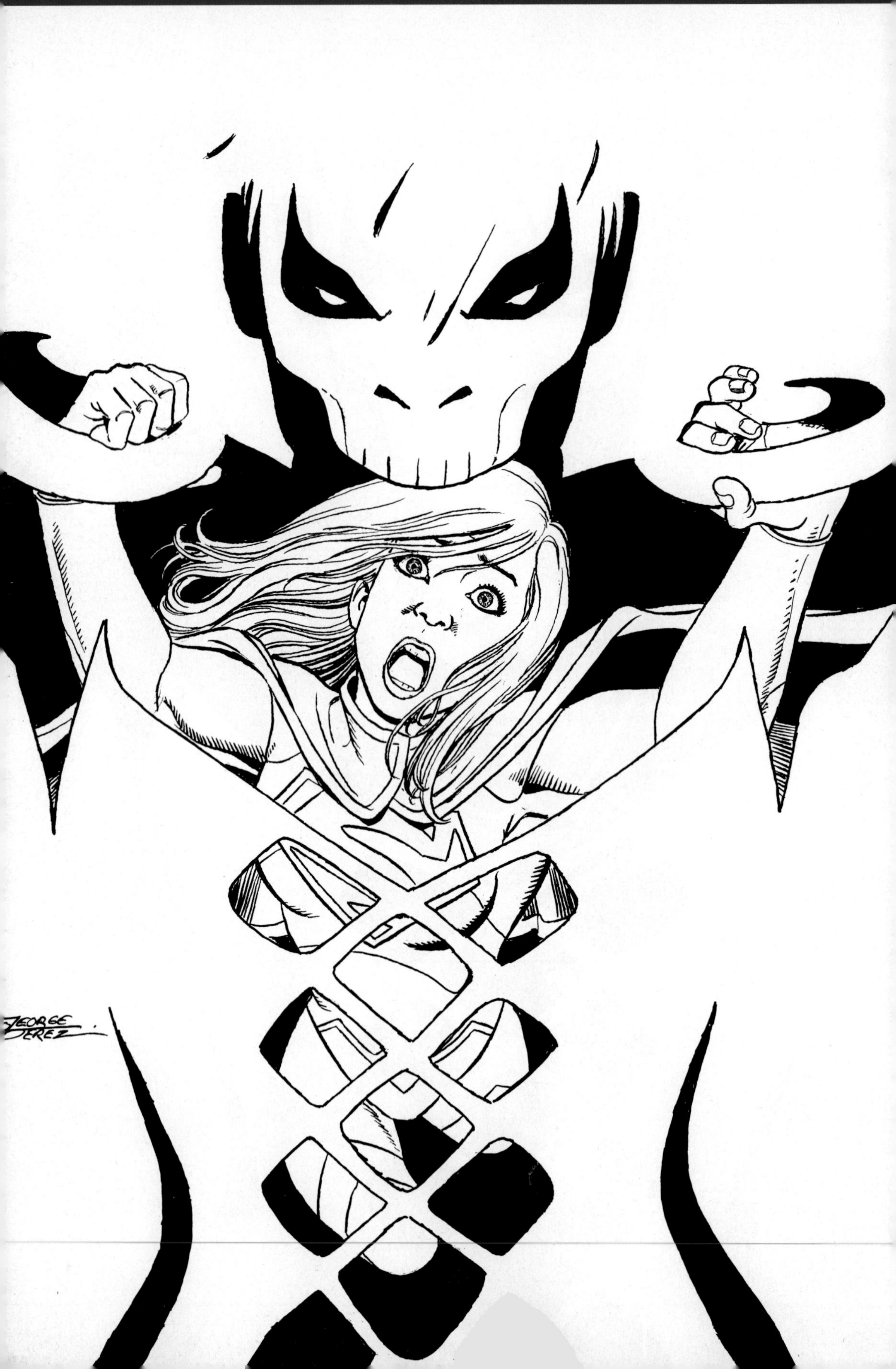
GEORGE PEREZ

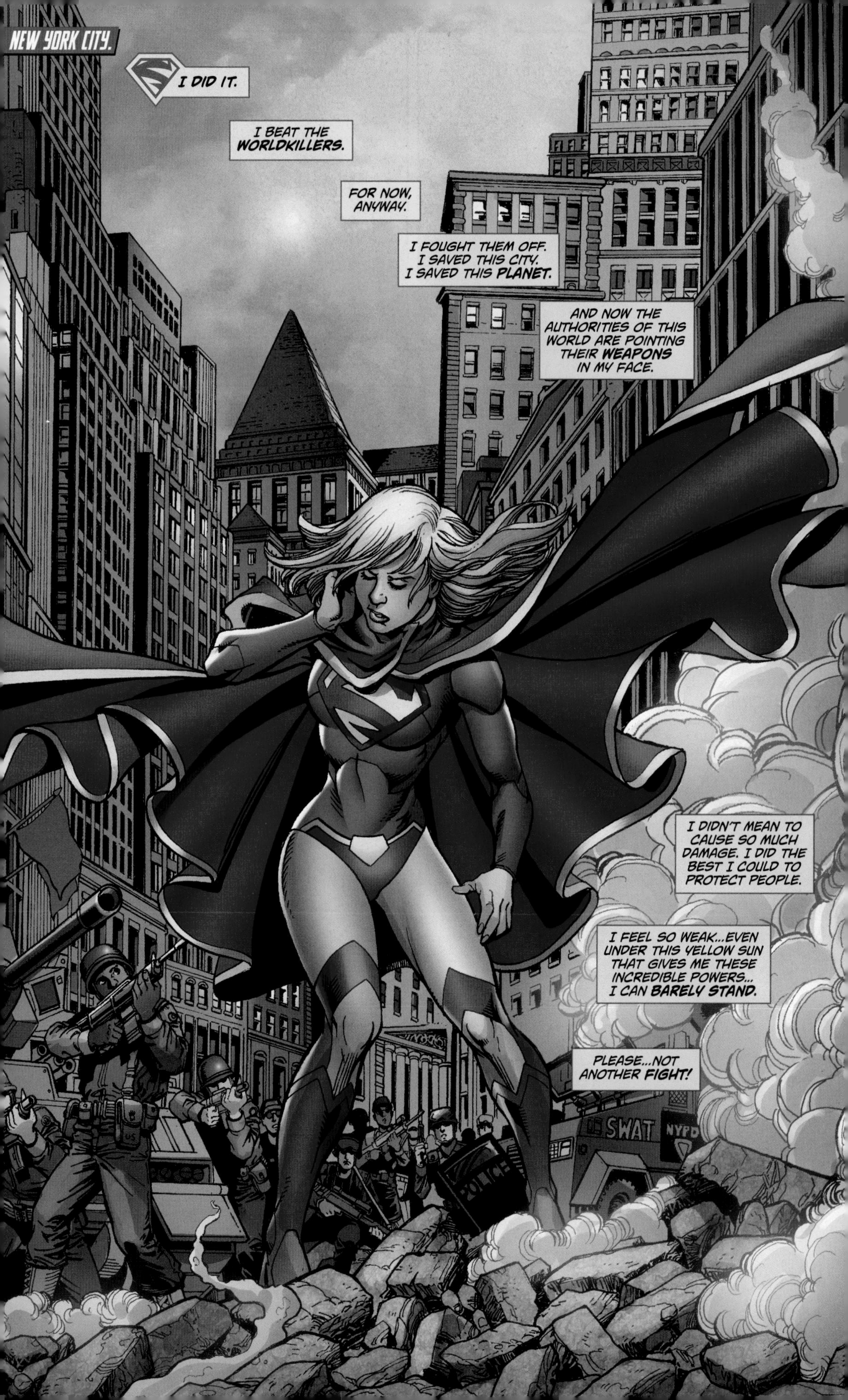
NEW YORK CITY.
I DID IT.
I BEAT THE WORLDKILLERS.
FOR NOW, ANYWAY.
I FOUGHT THEM OFF. I SAVED THIS CITY. I SAVED THIS PLANET.
AND NOW THE AUTHORITIES OF THIS WORLD ARE POINTING THEIR WEAPONS IN MY FACE.
I DIDN'T MEAN TO CAUSE SO MUCH DAMAGE. I DID THE BEST I COULD TO PROTECT PEOPLE.
I FEEL SO WEAK...EVEN UNDER THIS YELLOW SUN THAT GIVES ME THESE INCREDIBLE POWERS... I CAN BARELY STAND.
PLEASE...NOT ANOTHER FIGHT!
SWAT
NYPD
POLICE

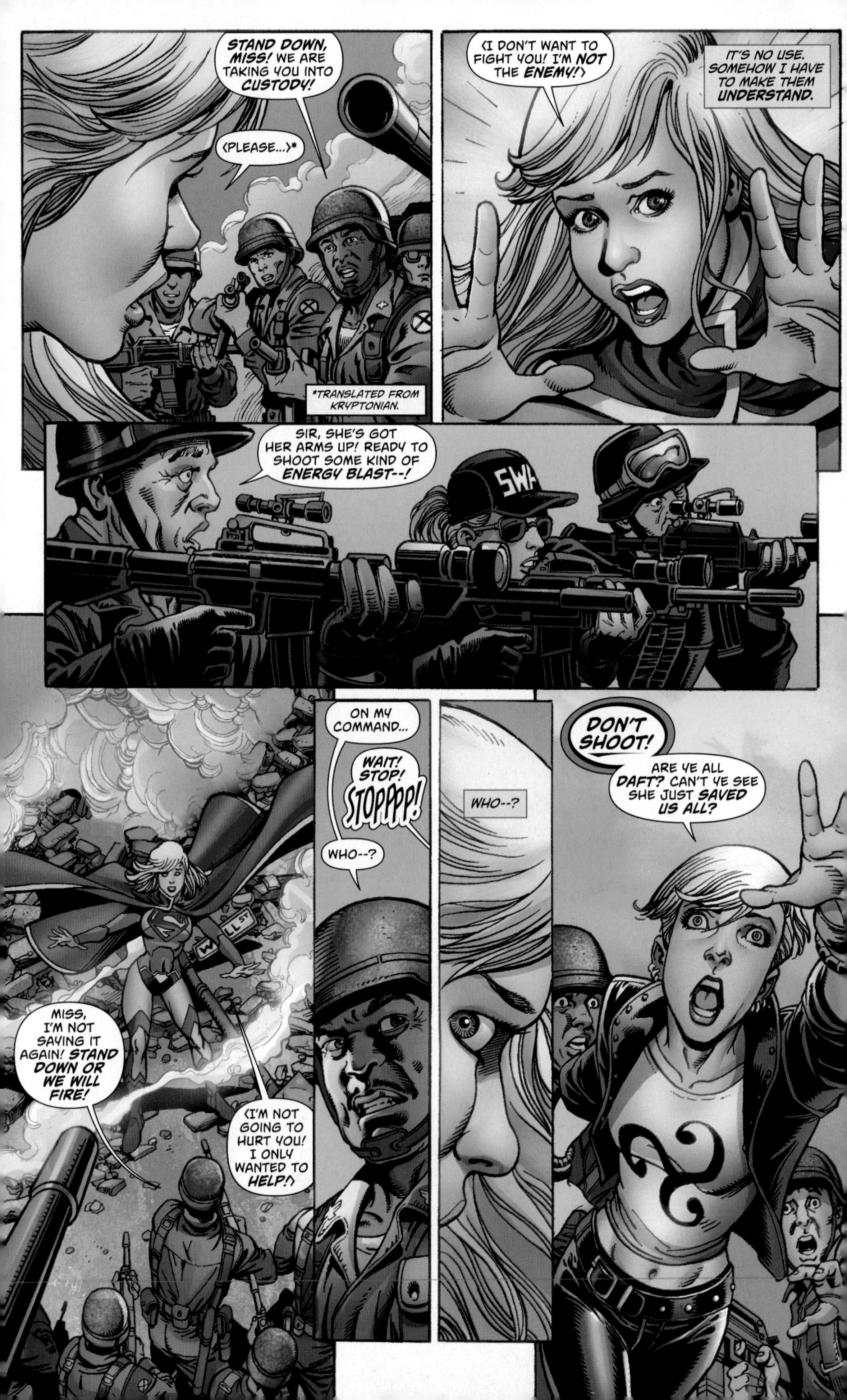

STAND DOWN, MISS! WE ARE TAKING YOU INTO CUSTODY!
‹PLEASE...›*
*TRANSLATED FROM KRYPTONIAN.
‹I DON'T WANT TO FIGHT YOU! I'M NOT THE ENEMY!›
IT'S NO USE. SOMEHOW I HAVE TO MAKE THEM UNDERSTAND.
SIR, SHE'S GOT HER ARMS UP! READY TO SHOOT SOME KIND OF ENERGY BLAST--!
MISS, I'M NOT SAYING IT AGAIN! STAND DOWN OR WE WILL FIRE!
‹I'M NOT GOING TO HURT YOU! I ONLY WANTED TO HELP!›
ON MY COMMAND...
WAIT! STOP! STOPPPP!
WHO--?
WHO--?
DON'T SHOOT!
ARE YE ALL DAFT? CAN'T YE SEE SHE JUST SAVED US ALL?

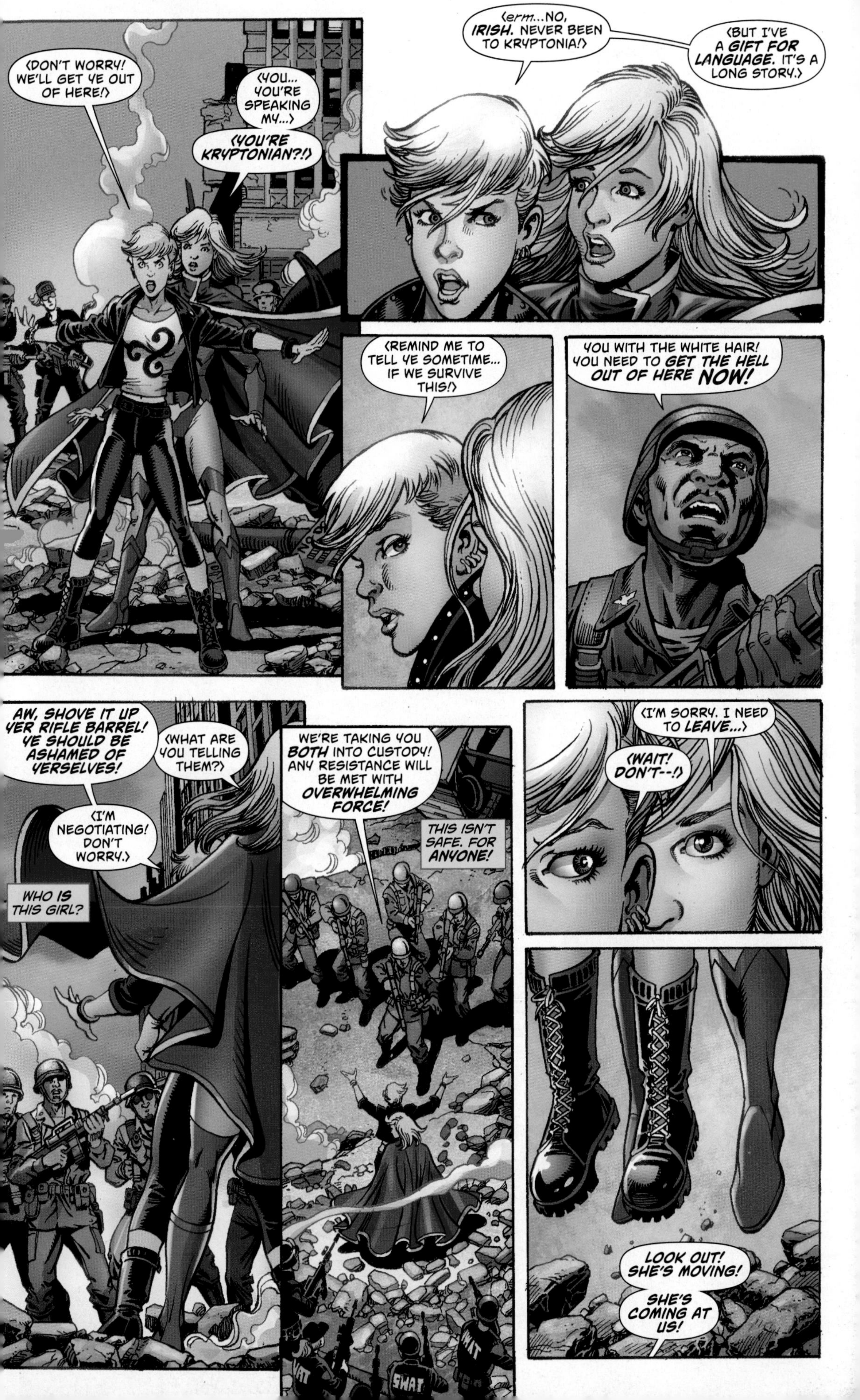

‹DON'T WORRY! WE'LL GET YE OUT OF HERE!›
‹YOU... YOU'RE SPEAKING MY...›
‹YOU'RE KRYPTONIAN?!›
‹erm...NO, IRISH. NEVER BEEN TO KRYPTONIA!›
‹BUT I'VE A GIFT FOR LANGUAGE. IT'S A LONG STORY.›
‹REMIND ME TO TELL YE SOMETIME... IF WE SURVIVE THIS!›
YOU WITH THE WHITE HAIR! YOU NEED TO GET THE HELL OUT OF HERE NOW!
AW, SHOVE IT UP YER RIFLE BARREL! YE SHOULD BE ASHAMED OF YERSELVES!
‹WHAT ARE YOU TELLING THEM?›
‹I'M NEGOTIATING! DON'T WORRY.›
WHO IS THIS GIRL?
WE'RE TAKING YOU BOTH INTO CUSTODY! ANY RESISTANCE WILL BE MET WITH OVERWHELMING FORCE!
THIS ISN'T SAFE. FOR ANYONE!
‹I'M SORRY. I NEED TO LEAVE...›
‹WAIT! DON'T--!›
LOOK OUT! SHE'S MOVING!
SHE'S COMING AT US!

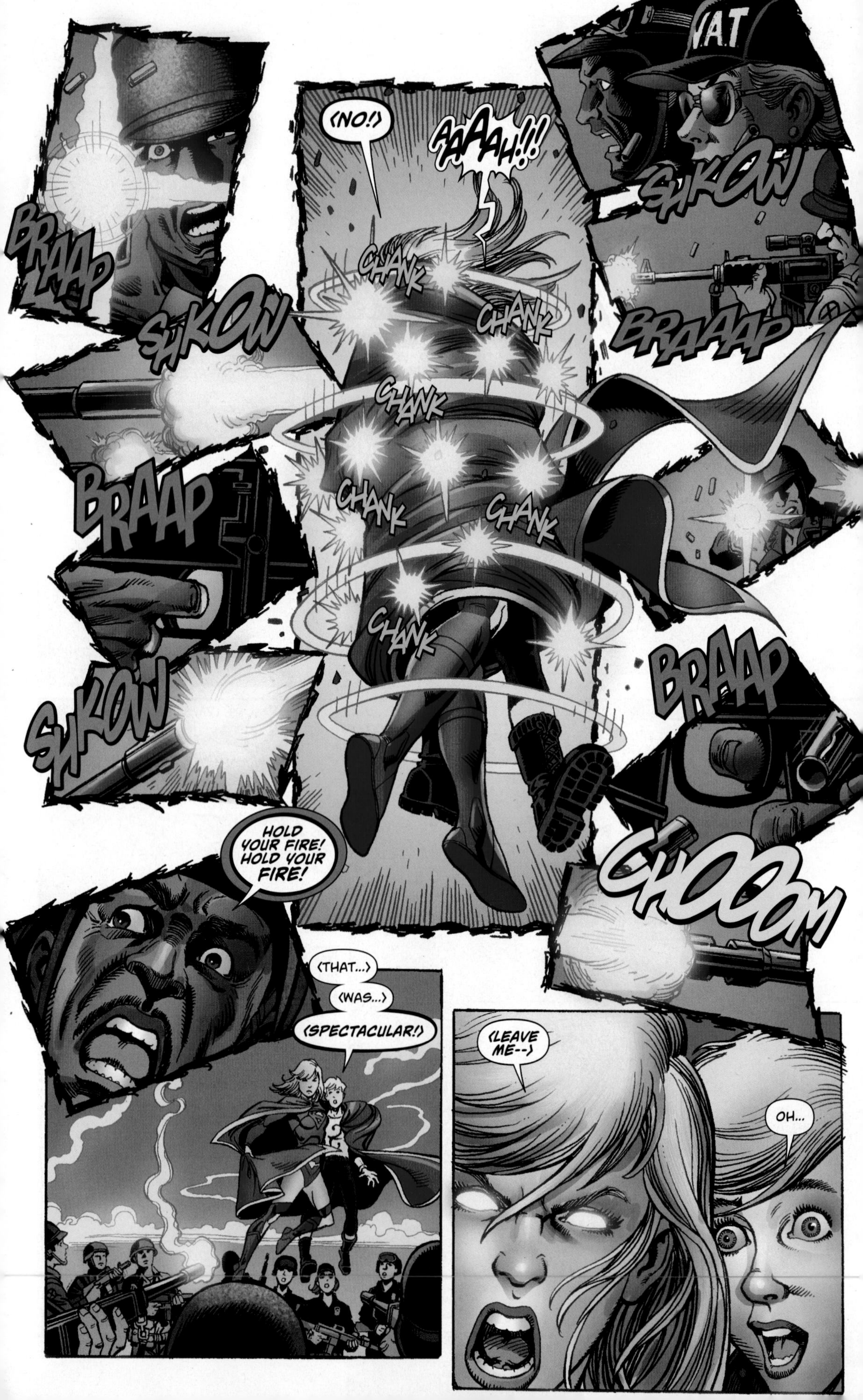
BRAAAP
SHKOW
⟨NO!⟩
AAAAAH!!!
CHANK
CHANK
CHANK
CHANK
CHANK
CHANK
SHKOW
BRAAAP
BRAAP
SHKOW
BRAAP
HOLD YOUR FIRE! HOLD YOUR FIRE!
CHOOOM
⟨THAT...⟩
⟨WAS...⟩
⟨SPECTACULAR!⟩
⟨LEAVE ME--⟩
OH...

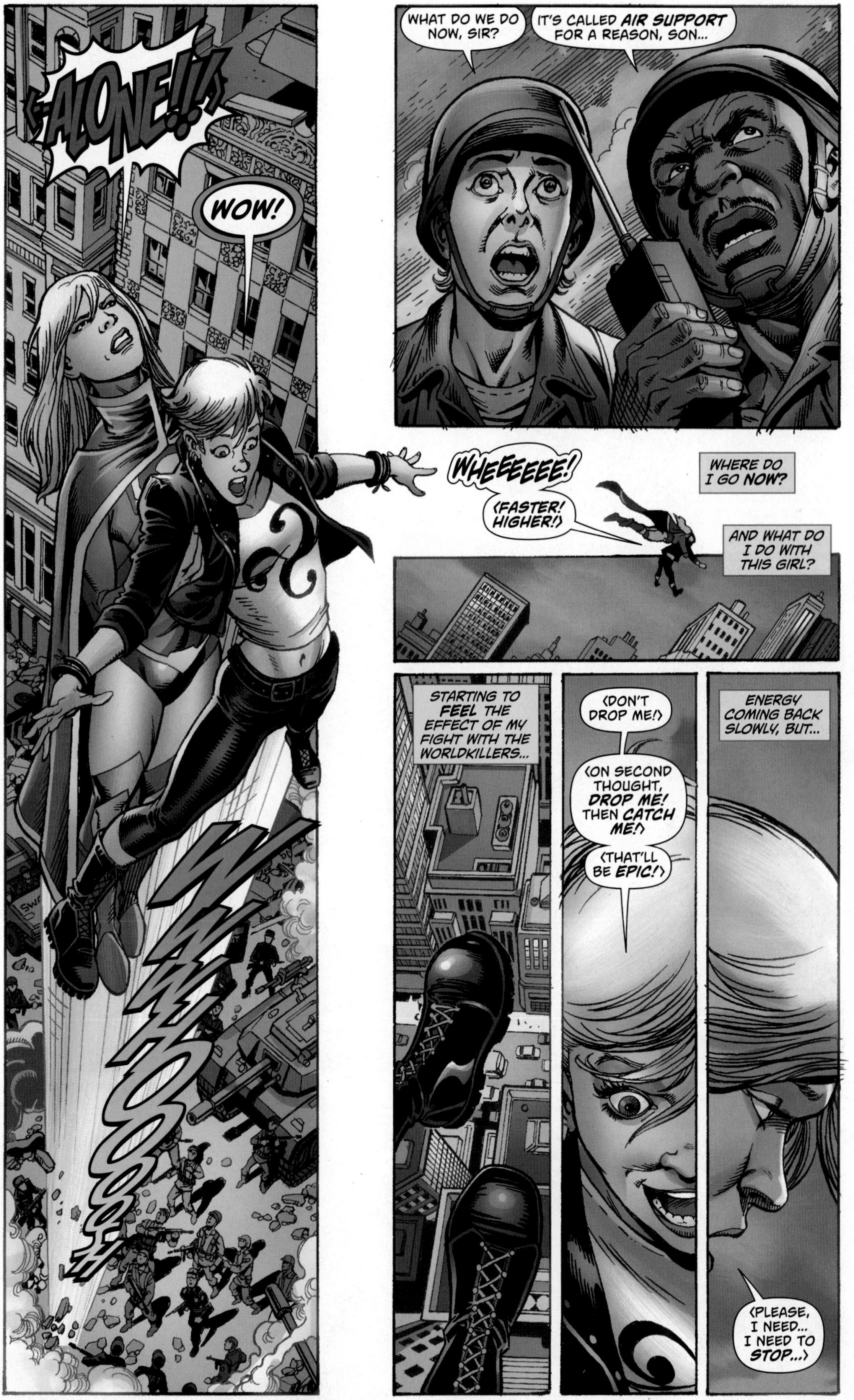
‹–ALONE!!›
WOW!
WHOOOOOOOSH!
WHAT DO WE DO NOW, SIR?
IT'S CALLED AIR SUPPORT FOR A REASON, SON...
WHEEEEEEE!
‹FASTER! HIGHER!›
WHERE DO I GO NOW?
AND WHAT DO I DO WITH THIS GIRL?
STARTING TO FEEL THE EFFECT OF MY FIGHT WITH THE WORLDKILLERS...
‹DON'T DROP ME!›
‹ON SECOND THOUGHT, DROP ME! THEN CATCH ME!›
‹THAT'LL BE EPIC!›
ENERGY COMING BACK SLOWLY, BUT...
‹PLEASE, I NEED... I NEED TO STOP...›

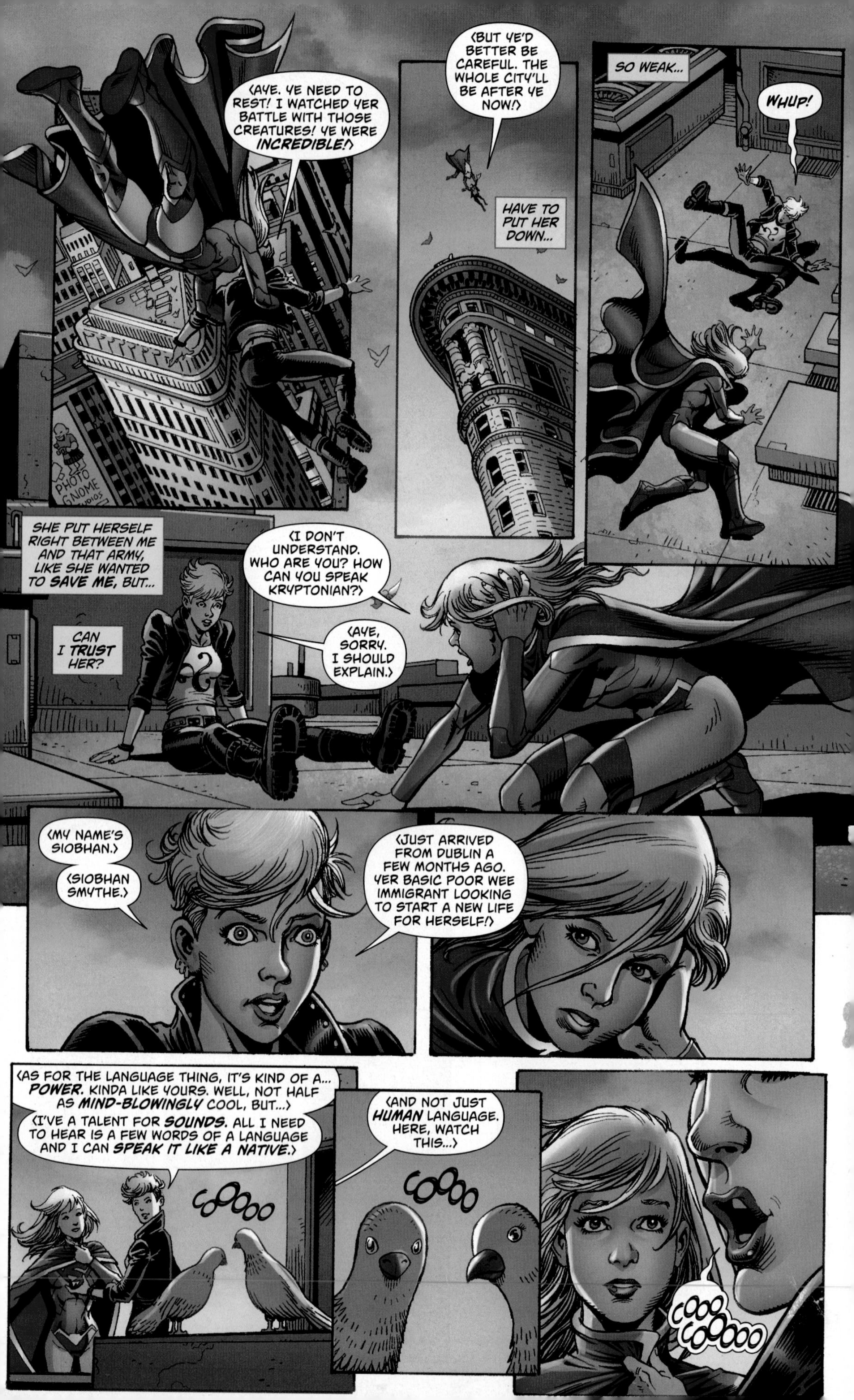

⟨AYE. YE NEED TO REST! I WATCHED YER BATTLE WITH THOSE CREATURES! YE WERE INCREDIBLE!⟩
PHOTO GNOME STUDIOS
⟨BUT YE'D BETTER BE CAREFUL. THE WHOLE CITY'LL BE AFTER YE NOW!⟩
HAVE TO PUT HER DOWN...
SO WEAK...
WHUP!
SHE PUT HERSELF RIGHT BETWEEN ME AND THAT ARMY, LIKE SHE WANTED TO SAVE ME, BUT...
⟨I DON'T UNDERSTAND. WHO ARE YOU? HOW CAN YOU SPEAK KRYPTONIAN?⟩
CAN I TRUST HER?
⟨AYE, SORRY. I SHOULD EXPLAIN.⟩
⟨MY NAME'S SIOBHAN.⟩
⟨SIOBHAN SMYTHE.⟩
⟨JUST ARRIVED FROM DUBLIN A FEW MONTHS AGO. YER BASIC POOR WEE IMMIGRANT LOOKING TO START A NEW LIFE FOR HERSELF!⟩
⟨AS FOR THE LANGUAGE THING, IT'S KIND OF A... POWER. KINDA LIKE YOURS. WELL, NOT HALF AS MIND-BLOWINGLY COOL, BUT...⟩
⟨I'VE A TALENT FOR SOUNDS. ALL I NEED TO HEAR IS A FEW WORDS OF A LANGUAGE AND I CAN SPEAK IT LIKE A NATIVE.⟩
COOOOO
⟨AND NOT JUST HUMAN LANGUAGE. HERE, WATCH THIS...⟩
COOOO
COOO COOOOO

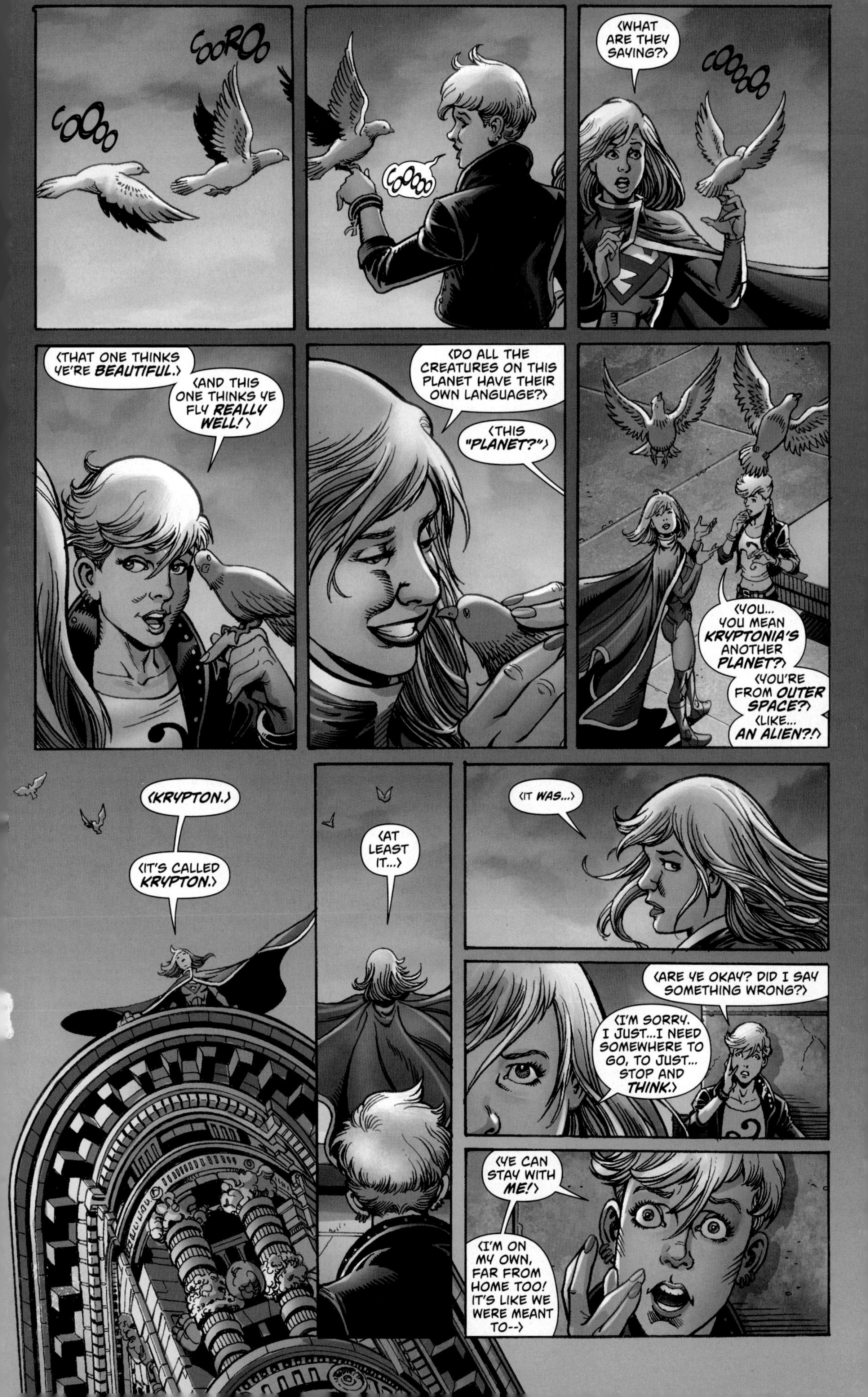

COOOO
COOROO
COOOOO
‹WHAT ARE THEY SAYING?›
COOOOO
‹THAT ONE THINKS YE'RE BEAUTIFUL.›
‹AND THIS ONE THINKS YE FLY REALLY WELL!›
‹DO ALL THE CREATURES ON THIS PLANET HAVE THEIR OWN LANGUAGE?›
‹THIS "PLANET?"›
‹YOU... YOU MEAN KRYPTONIA'S ANOTHER PLANET?›
‹YOU'RE FROM OUTER SPACE?›
‹LIKE... AN ALIEN?!›
‹KRYPTON.›
‹IT'S CALLED KRYPTON.›
‹AT LEAST IT...›
‹IT WAS...›
‹ARE YE OKAY? DID I SAY SOMETHING WRONG?›
‹I'M SORRY. I JUST...I NEED SOMEWHERE TO GO, TO JUST... STOP AND THINK.›
‹YE CAN STAY WITH ME!›
‹I'M ON MY OWN, FAR FROM HOME TOO! IT'S LIKE WE WERE MEANT TO--›

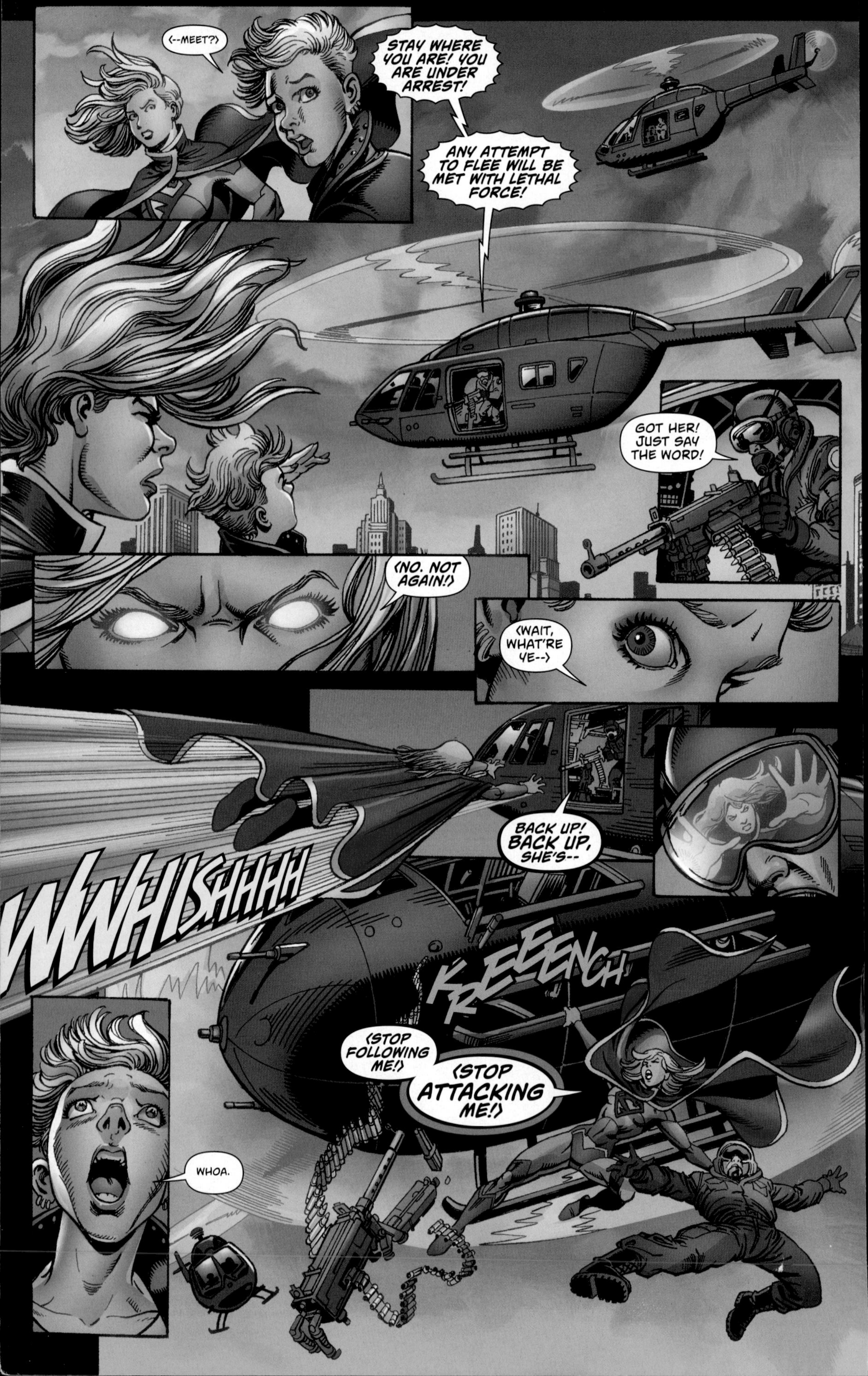

‹--MEET?›
STAY WHERE YOU ARE! YOU ARE UNDER ARREST!
ANY ATTEMPT TO FLEE WILL BE MET WITH LETHAL FORCE!
GOT HER! JUST SAY THE WORD!
‹NO. NOT AGAIN!›
‹WAIT, WHAT'RE YE--›
BACK UP! BACK UP, SHE'S--
WWHISHHHH
KREEEENCH
‹STOP FOLLOWING ME!›
‹STOP ATTACKING ME!›
WHOA.

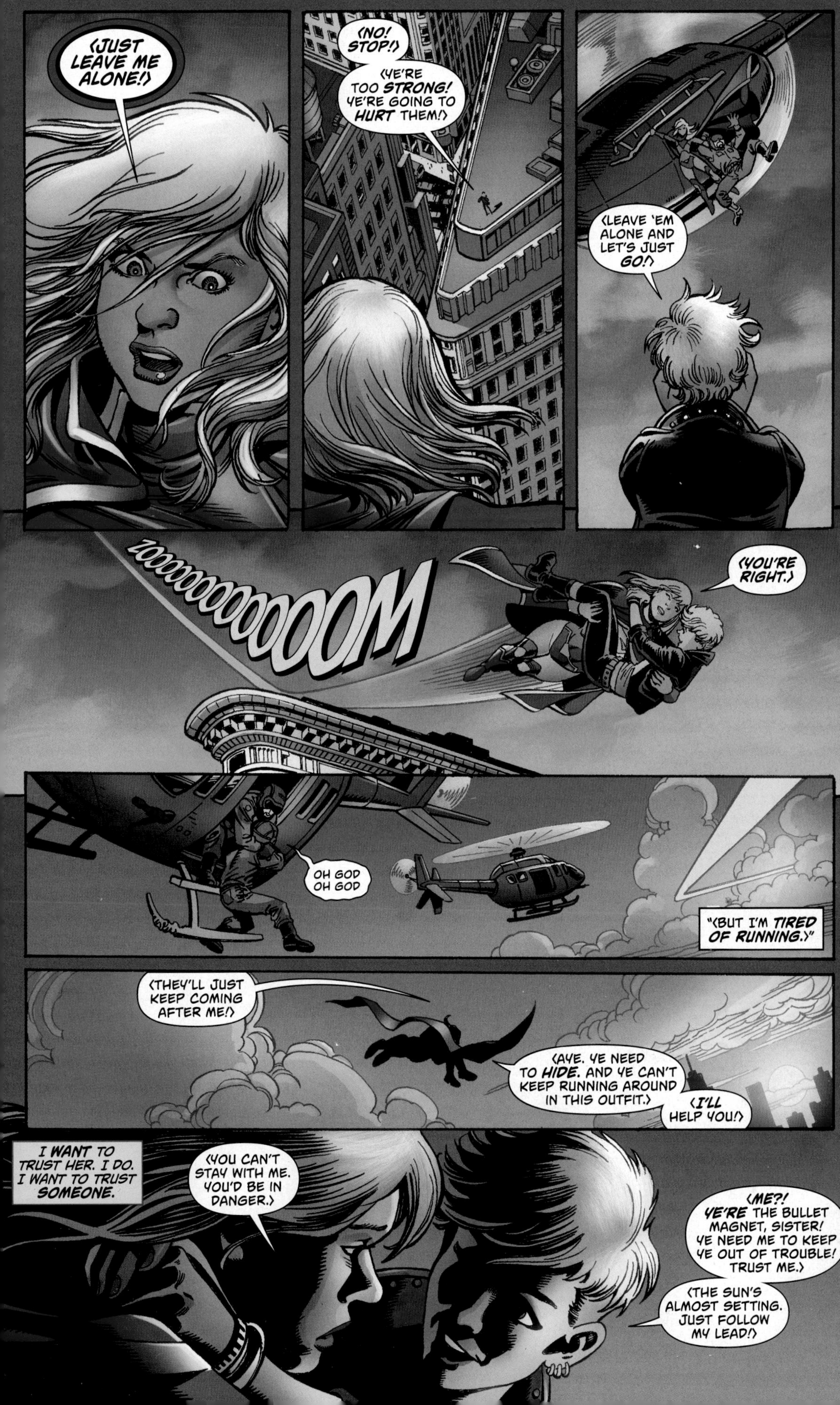
‹JUST LEAVE ME ALONE!›
‹NO! STOP!›
‹YE'RE TOO STRONG! YE'RE GOING TO HURT THEM!›
‹LEAVE 'EM ALONE AND LET'S JUST GO!›
ZOOOOOOOOOOOOOM
‹YOU'RE RIGHT.›
OH GOD OH GOD
"‹BUT I'M TIRED OF RUNNING.›"
‹THEY'LL JUST KEEP COMING AFTER ME!›
‹AYE. YE NEED TO HIDE. AND YE CAN'T KEEP RUNNING AROUND IN THIS OUTFIT.›
‹I'LL HELP YOU!›
I WANT TO TRUST HER. I DO. I WANT TO TRUST SOMEONE.
‹YOU CAN'T STAY WITH ME. YOU'D BE IN DANGER.›
‹ME?! YE'RE THE BULLET MAGNET, SISTER! YE NEED ME TO KEEP YE OUT OF TROUBLE! TRUST ME.›
‹THE SUN'S ALMOST SETTING. JUST FOLLOW MY LEAD!›

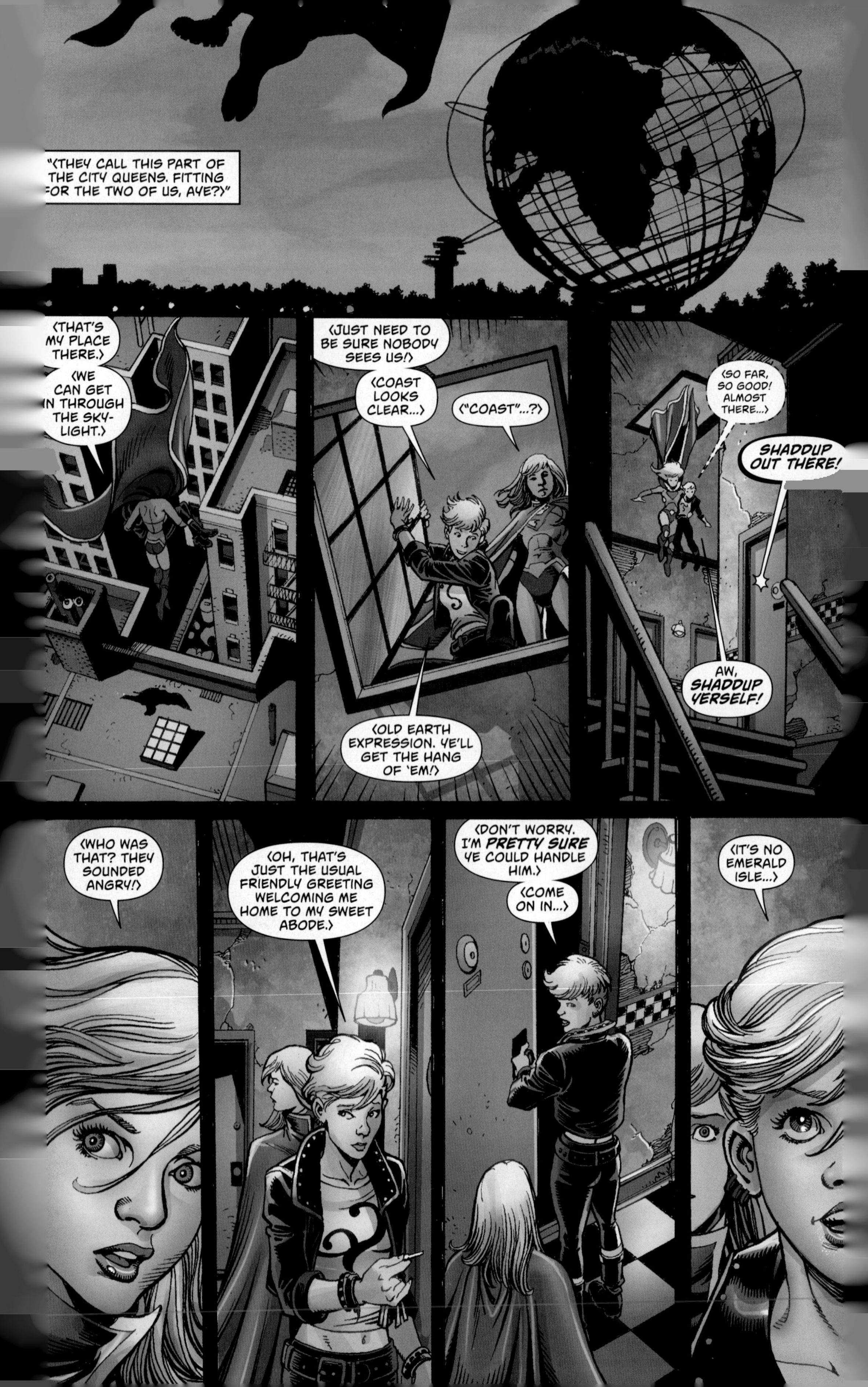
"‹THEY CALL THIS PART OF THE CITY QUEENS. FITTING FOR THE TWO OF US, AYE?›"
‹THAT'S MY PLACE THERE.›
‹WE CAN GET IN THROUGH THE SKY-LIGHT.›
‹JUST NEED TO BE SURE NOBODY SEES US!›
‹COAST LOOKS CLEAR...›
‹"COAST"...?›
‹OLD EARTH EXPRESSION. YE'LL GET THE HANG OF 'EM!›
‹SO FAR, SO GOOD! ALMOST THERE...›
SHADDUP OUT THERE!
AW, SHADDUP YERSELF!
‹WHO WAS THAT? THEY SOUNDED ANGRY!›
‹OH, THAT'S JUST THE USUAL FRIENDLY GREETING WELCOMING ME HOME TO MY SWEET ABODE.›
‹DON'T WORRY. I'M PRETTY SURE YE COULD HANDLE HIM.›
‹COME ON IN...›
‹IT'S NO EMERALD ISLE...›

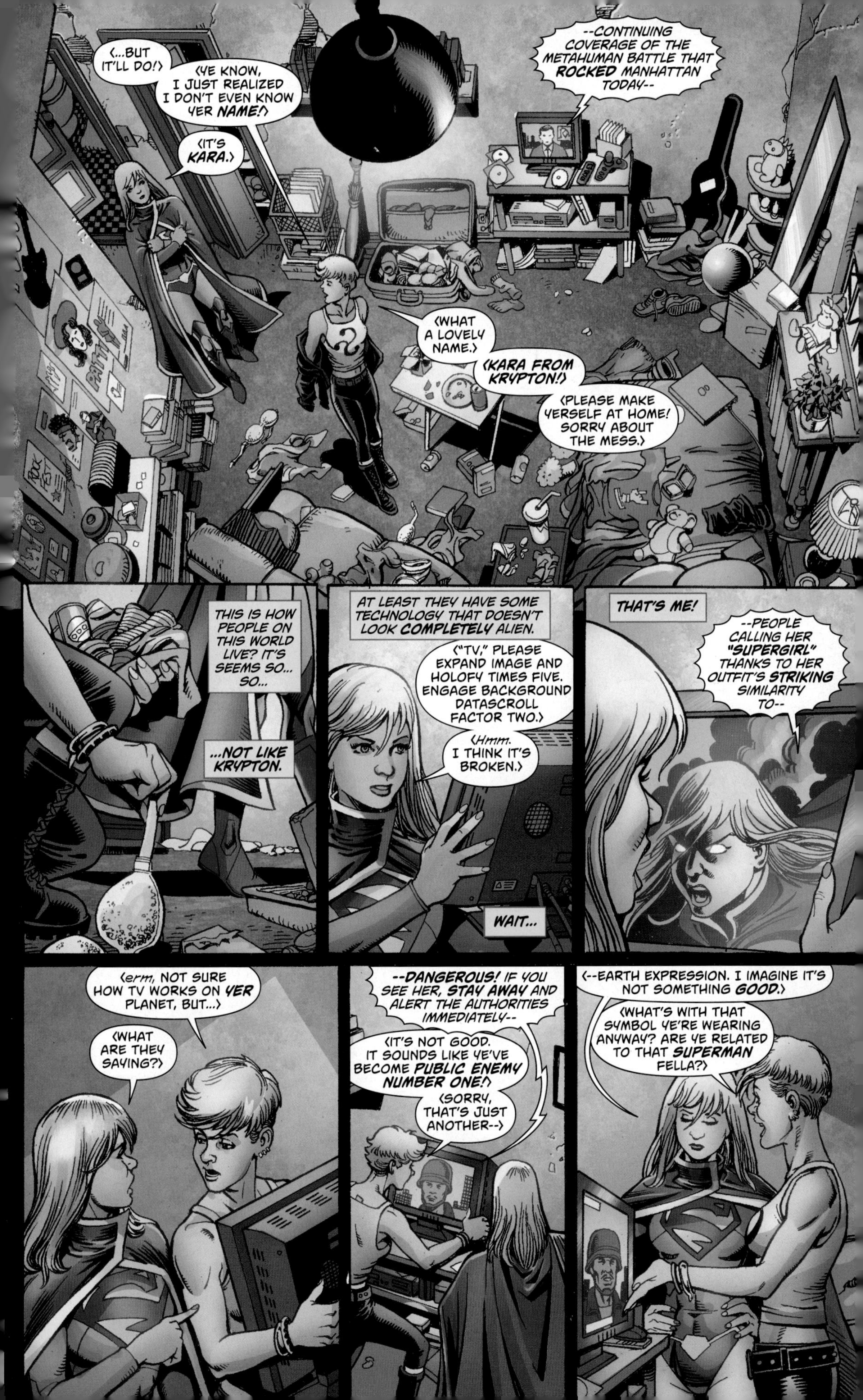

<...BUT IT'LL DO!>
<YE KNOW, I JUST REALIZED I DON'T EVEN KNOW YER NAME!>
<IT'S KARA.>
--CONTINUING COVERAGE OF THE METAHUMAN BATTLE THAT ROCKED MANHATTAN TODAY--
<WHAT A LOVELY NAME.>
<KARA FROM KRYPTON!>
<PLEASE MAKE YERSELF AT HOME! SORRY ABOUT THE MESS.>
THIS IS HOW PEOPLE ON THIS WORLD LIVE? IT'S SEEMS SO... SO...
...NOT LIKE KRYPTON.
AT LEAST THEY HAVE SOME TECHNOLOGY THAT DOESN'T LOOK COMPLETELY ALIEN.
<"TV," PLEASE EXPAND IMAGE AND HOLOFY TIMES FIVE. ENGAGE BACKGROUND DATASCROLL FACTOR TWO.>
<Hmm. I THINK IT'S BROKEN.>
WAIT...
THAT'S ME!
--PEOPLE CALLING HER "SUPERGIRL" THANKS TO HER OUTFIT'S STRIKING SIMILARITY TO--
<erm, NOT SURE HOW TV WORKS ON YER PLANET, BUT...>
<WHAT ARE THEY SAYING?>
--DANGEROUS! IF YOU SEE HER, STAY AWAY AND ALERT THE AUTHORITIES IMMEDIATELY--
<IT'S NOT GOOD. IT SOUNDS LIKE YE'VE BECOME PUBLIC ENEMY NUMBER ONE!>
<SORRY, THAT'S JUST ANOTHER-->
<--EARTH EXPRESSION. I IMAGINE IT'S NOT SOMETHING GOOD.>
<WHAT'S WITH THAT SYMBOL YE'RE WEARING ANYWAY? ARE YE RELATED TO THAT SUPERMAN FELLA?>

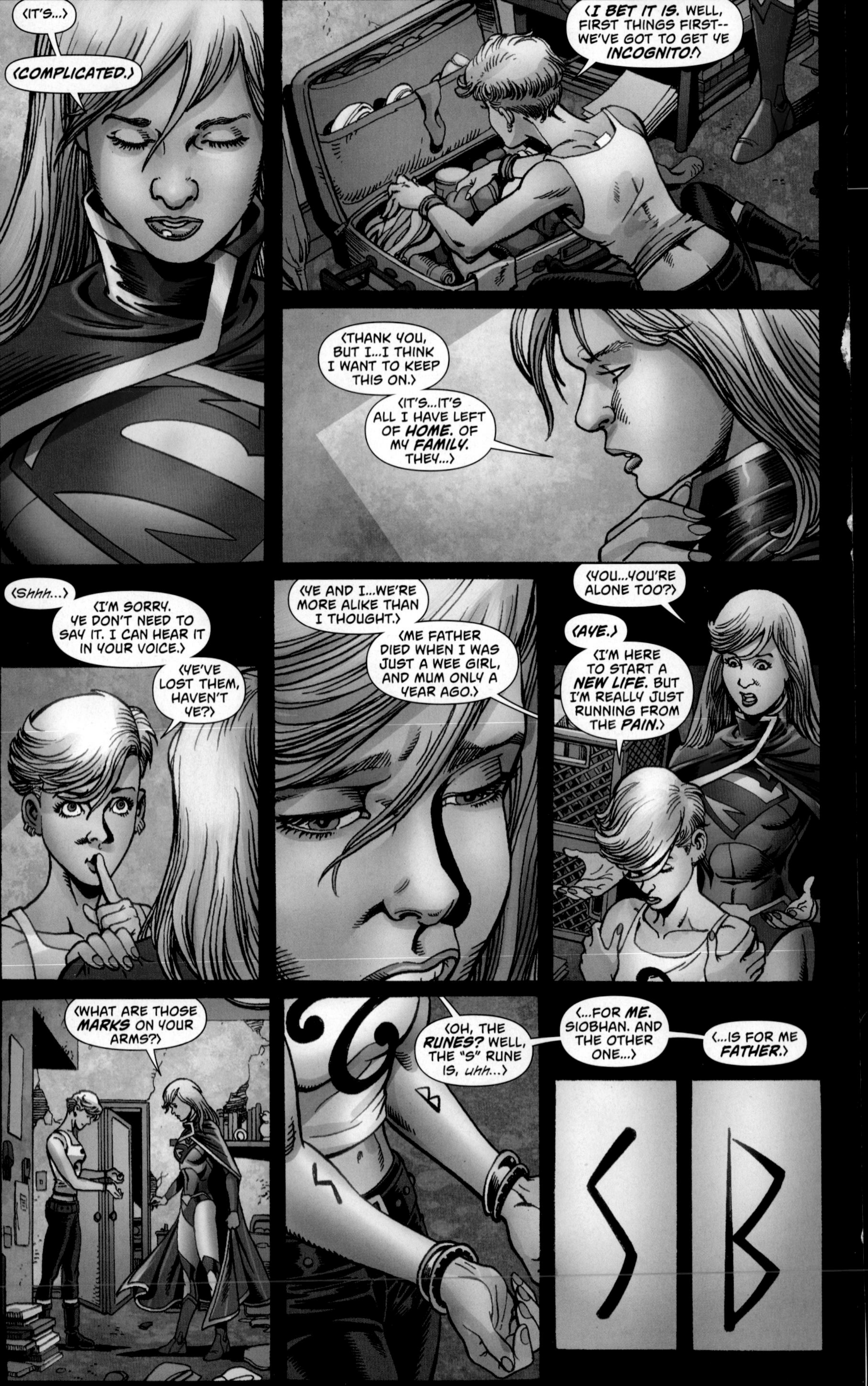

‹IT'S...›
‹COMPLICATED.›
‹I BET IT IS. WELL, FIRST THINGS FIRST--WE'VE GOT TO GET YE INCOGNITO!›
‹THANK YOU, BUT I...I THINK I WANT TO KEEP THIS ON.›
‹IT'S...IT'S ALL I HAVE LEFT OF HOME. OF MY FAMILY. THEY...›
‹Shhh...›
‹I'M SORRY. YE DON'T NEED TO SAY IT. I CAN HEAR IT IN YOUR VOICE.›
‹YE'VE LOST THEM, HAVEN'T YE?›
‹YE AND I...WE'RE MORE ALIKE THAN I THOUGHT.›
‹ME FATHER DIED WHEN I WAS JUST A WEE GIRL, AND MUM ONLY A YEAR AGO.›
‹YOU...YOU'RE ALONE TOO?›
‹AYE.›
‹I'M HERE TO START A NEW LIFE. BUT I'M REALLY JUST RUNNING FROM THE PAIN.›
‹WHAT ARE THOSE MARKS ON YOUR ARMS?›
‹OH, THE RUNES? WELL, THE "S" RUNE IS, uhh...›
‹...FOR ME. SIOBHAN. AND THE OTHER ONE...›
‹...IS FOR ME FATHER.›

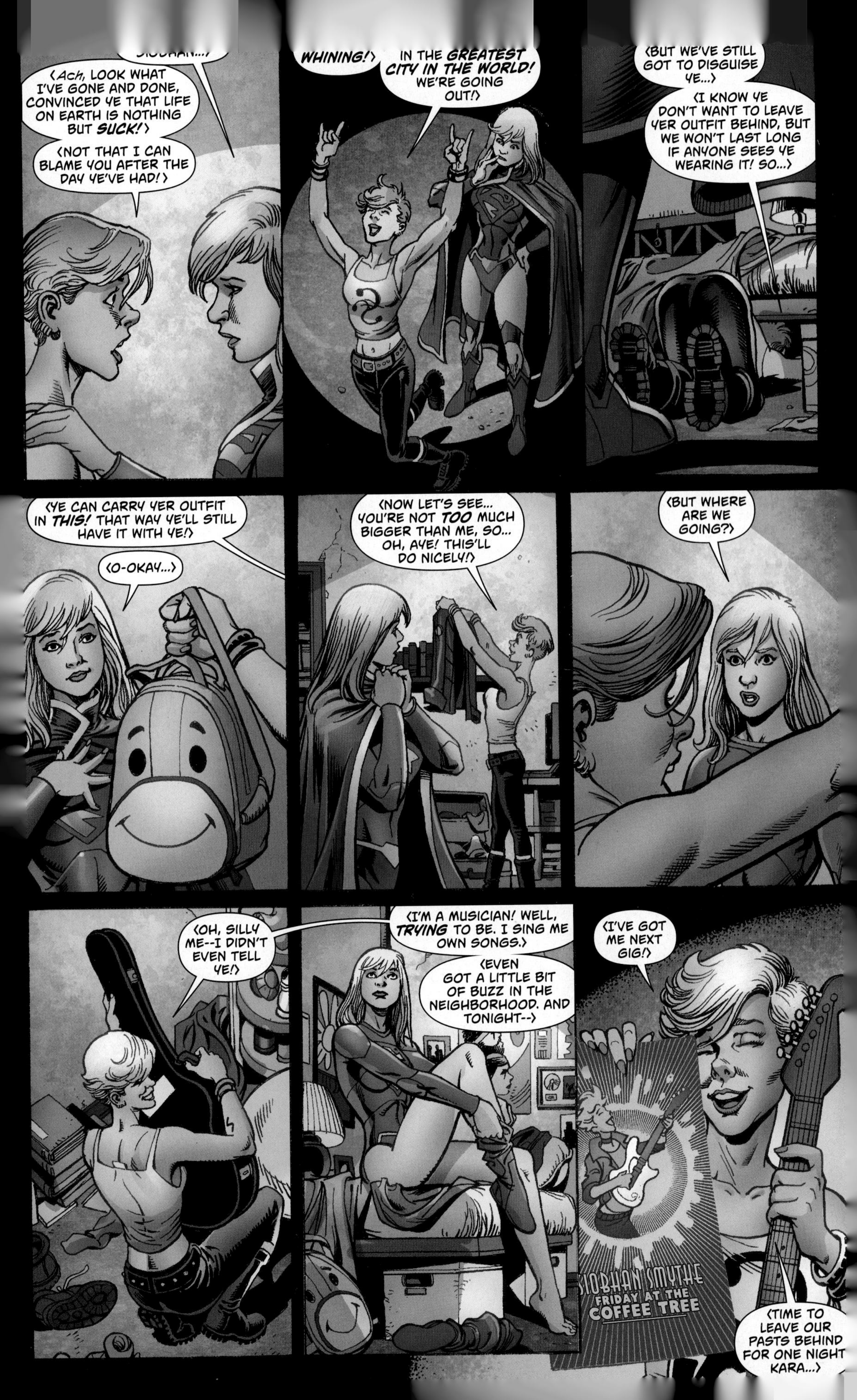
‹Ach, LOOK WHAT I'VE GONE AND DONE, CONVINCED YE THAT LIFE ON EARTH IS NOTHING BUT SUCK!›
‹NOT THAT I CAN BLAME YOU AFTER THE DAY YE'VE HAD!›
WHINING!›
IN THE GREATEST CITY IN THE WORLD! WE'RE GOING OUT!›
‹BUT WE'VE STILL GOT TO DISGUISE YE...›
‹I KNOW YE DON'T WANT TO LEAVE YER OUTFIT BEHIND, BUT WE WON'T LAST LONG IF ANYONE SEES YE WEARING IT! SO...›
‹YE CAN CARRY YER OUTFIT IN THIS! THAT WAY YE'LL STILL HAVE IT WITH YE!›
‹O-OKAY...›
‹NOW LET'S SEE... YOU'RE NOT TOO MUCH BIGGER THAN ME, SO... OH, AYE! THIS'LL DO NICELY!›
‹BUT WHERE ARE WE GOING?›
‹OH, SILLY ME--I DIDN'T EVEN TELL YE!›
‹I'M A MUSICIAN! WELL, TRYING TO BE. I SING ME OWN SONGS.›
‹EVEN GOT A LITTLE BIT OF BUZZ IN THE NEIGHBORHOOD. AND TONIGHT--›
‹I'VE GOT ME NEXT GIG!›
SIOBHAN SMYTHE
FRIDAY AT THE
COFFEE TREE
‹TIME TO LEAVE OUR PASTS BEHIND FOR ONE NIGHT KARA...›

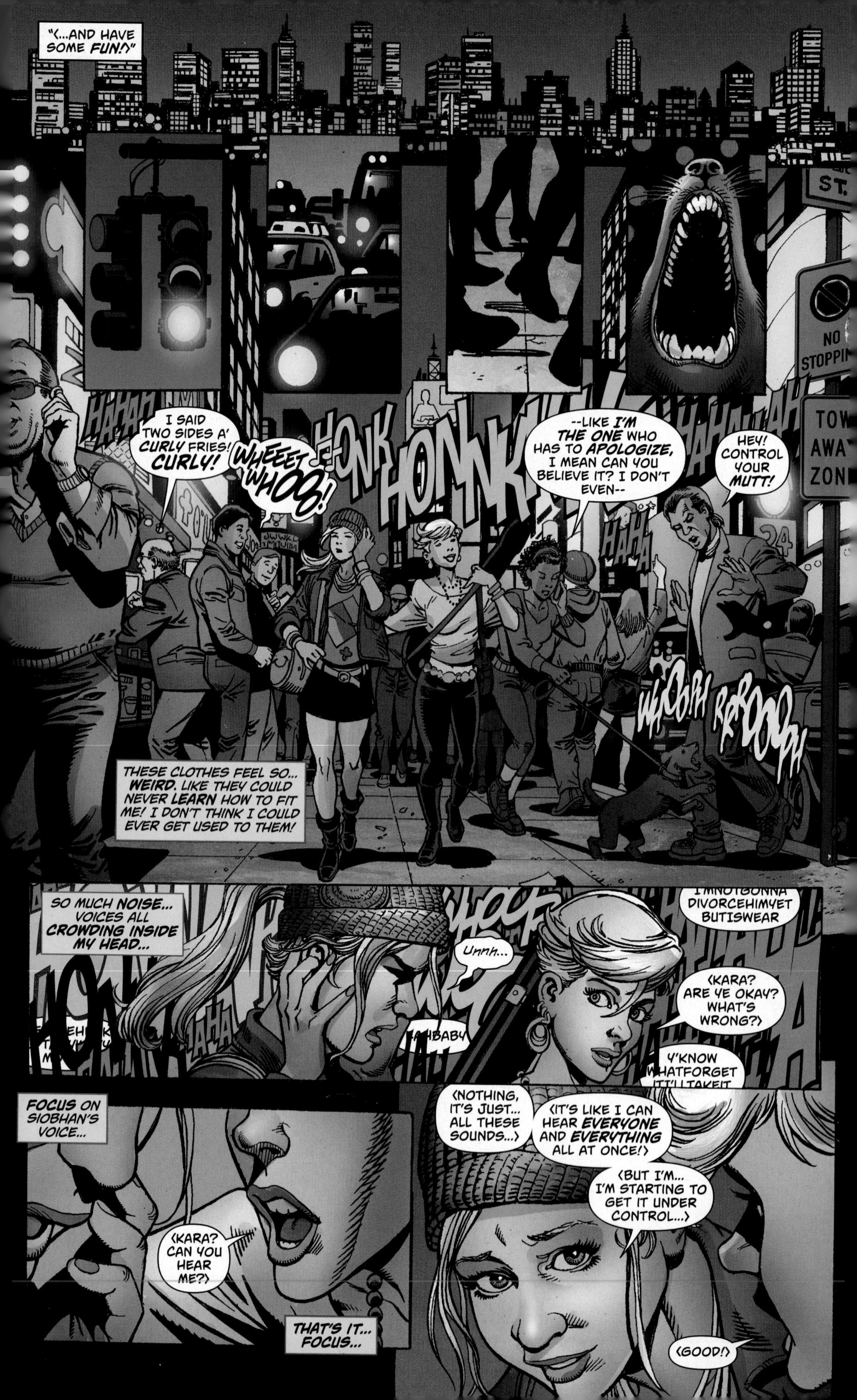

‹...AND HAVE SOME FUN!›"
ST.
NO STOPPIN
TOW AWAY ZONE
HAHAH
I SAID TWO SIDES A' CURLY FRIES! CURLY!
WHEEEET WHOO!
HONK HONNK
--LIKE I'M THE ONE WHO HAS TO APOLOGIZE, I MEAN CAN YOU BELIEVE IT? I DON'T EVEN--
HAHAHAHAH
HEY! CONTROL YOUR MUTT!
HAHA
WHOOOH RRROOOH
THESE CLOTHES FEEL SO... WEIRD. LIKE THEY COULD NEVER LEARN HOW TO FIT ME! I DON'T THINK I COULD EVER GET USED TO THEM!
SO MUCH NOISE... VOICES ALL CROWDING INSIDE MY HEAD...
IMNOTGONNA DIVORCEHIMYET BUTISWEAR
Unnh...
‹KARA? ARE YE OKAY? WHAT'S WRONG?›
Y'KNOW WHATFORGET
FOCUS ON SIOBHAN'S VOICE...
‹NOTHING, IT'S JUST... ALL THESE SOUNDS...›
‹IT'S LIKE I CAN HEAR EVERYONE AND EVERYTHING ALL AT ONCE!›
‹BUT I'M... I'M STARTING TO GET IT UNDER CONTROL...›
‹KARA? CAN YOU HEAR ME?›
THAT'S IT... FOCUS...
‹GOOD!›

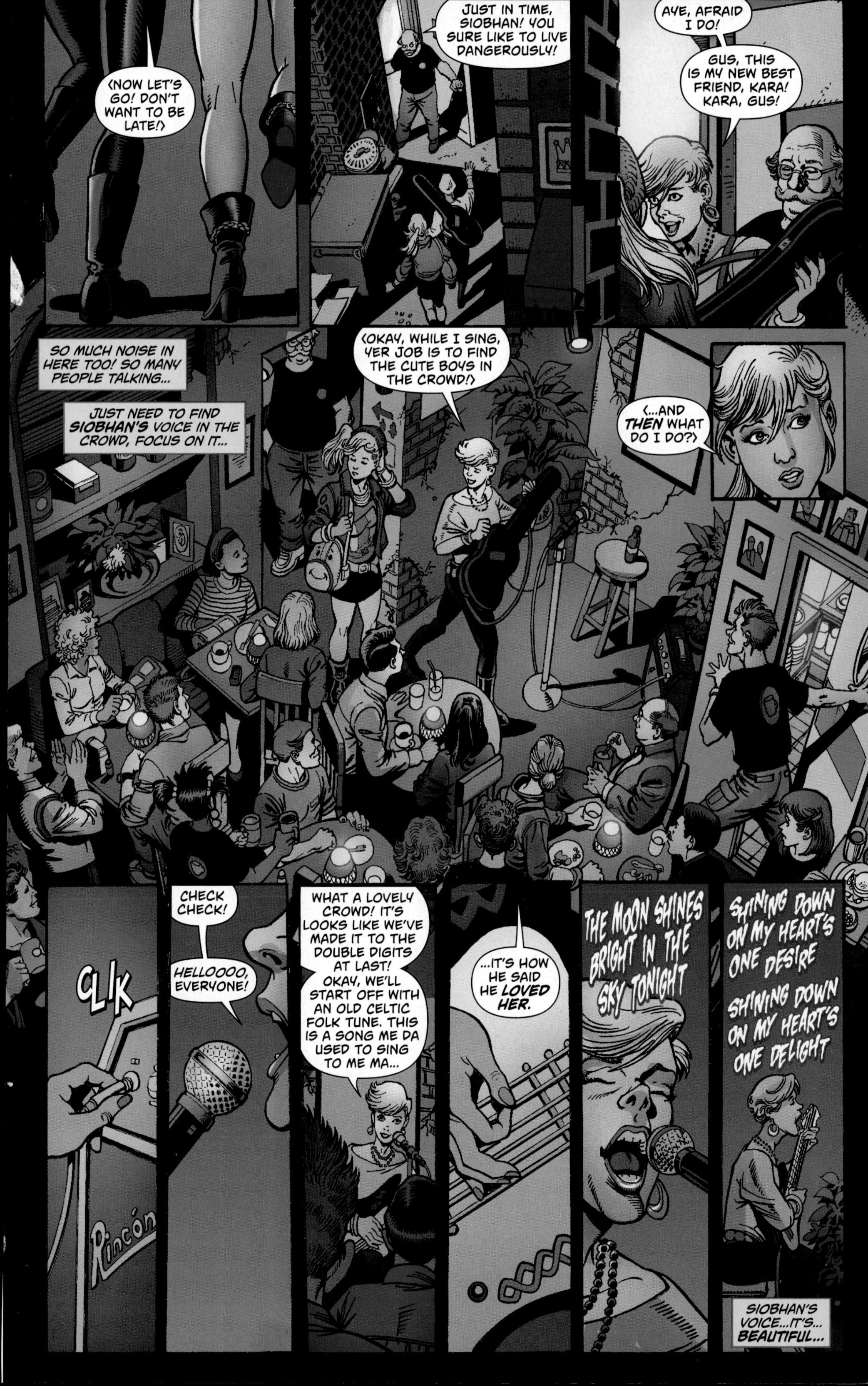
⟨NOW LET'S GO! DON'T WANT TO BE LATE!⟩
JUST IN TIME, SIOBHAN! YOU SURE LIKE TO LIVE DANGEROUSLY!
AYE, AFRAID I DO!
GUS, THIS IS MY NEW BEST FRIEND, KARA! KARA, GUS!
SO MUCH NOISE IN HERE TOO! SO MANY PEOPLE TALKING...
JUST NEED TO FIND SIOBHAN'S VOICE IN THE CROWD, FOCUS ON IT...
⟨OKAY, WHILE I SING, YER JOB IS TO FIND THE CUTE BOYS IN THE CROWD!⟩
⟨...AND THEN WHAT DO I DO?⟩
CLIK
CHECK CHECK!
HELLOOOO, EVERYONE!
WHAT A LOVELY CROWD! IT'S LOOKS LIKE WE'VE MADE IT TO THE DOUBLE DIGITS AT LAST! OKAY, WE'LL START OFF WITH AN OLD CELTIC FOLK TUNE. THIS IS A SONG ME DA USED TO SING TO ME MA...
...IT'S HOW HE SAID HE LOVED HER.
THE MOON SHINES BRIGHT IN THE SKY TONIGHT
SHINING DOWN ON MY HEART'S ONE DESIRE
SHINING DOWN ON MY HEART'S ONE DELIGHT
SIOBHAN'S VOICE...IT'S... BEAUTIFUL...
Rincón

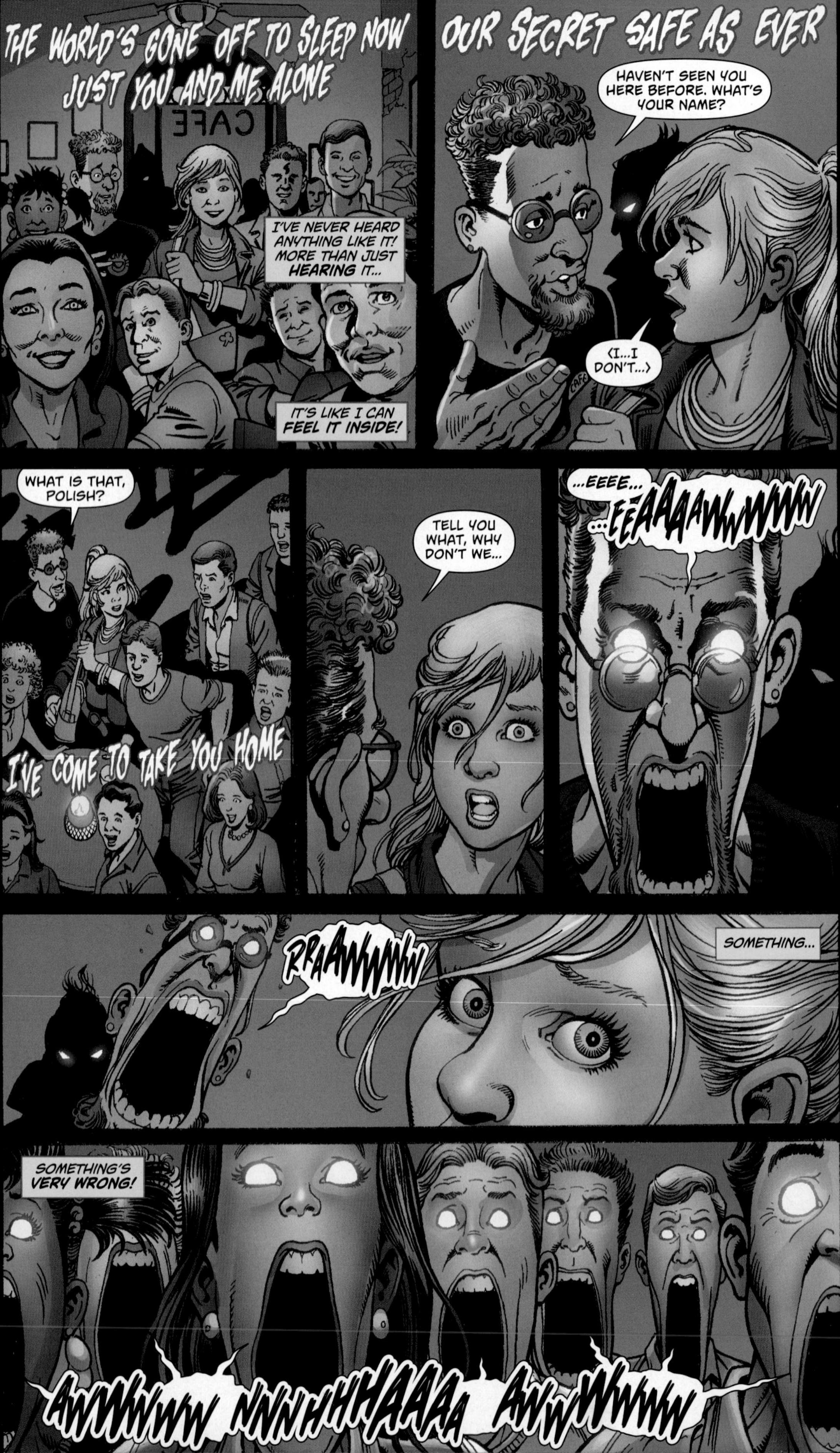
THE WORLD'S GONE OFF TO SLEEP NOW
JUST YOU AND ME ALONE
CAFE
I'VE NEVER HEARD ANYTHING LIKE IT! MORE THAN JUST HEARING IT...
IT'S LIKE I CAN FEEL IT INSIDE!
OUR SECRET SAFE AS EVER
HAVEN'T SEEN YOU HERE BEFORE. WHAT'S YOUR NAME?
‹I...I DON'T...›
WHAT IS THAT, POLISH?
I'VE COME TO TAKE YOU HOME
TELL YOU WHAT, WHY DON'T WE...
...EEEE...
...EEAAAAAWWWWW
RRAAWWWW
SOMETHING...
SOMETHING'S VERY WRONG!
AWWWWW NNHHHHAAAAA AWWWWWW

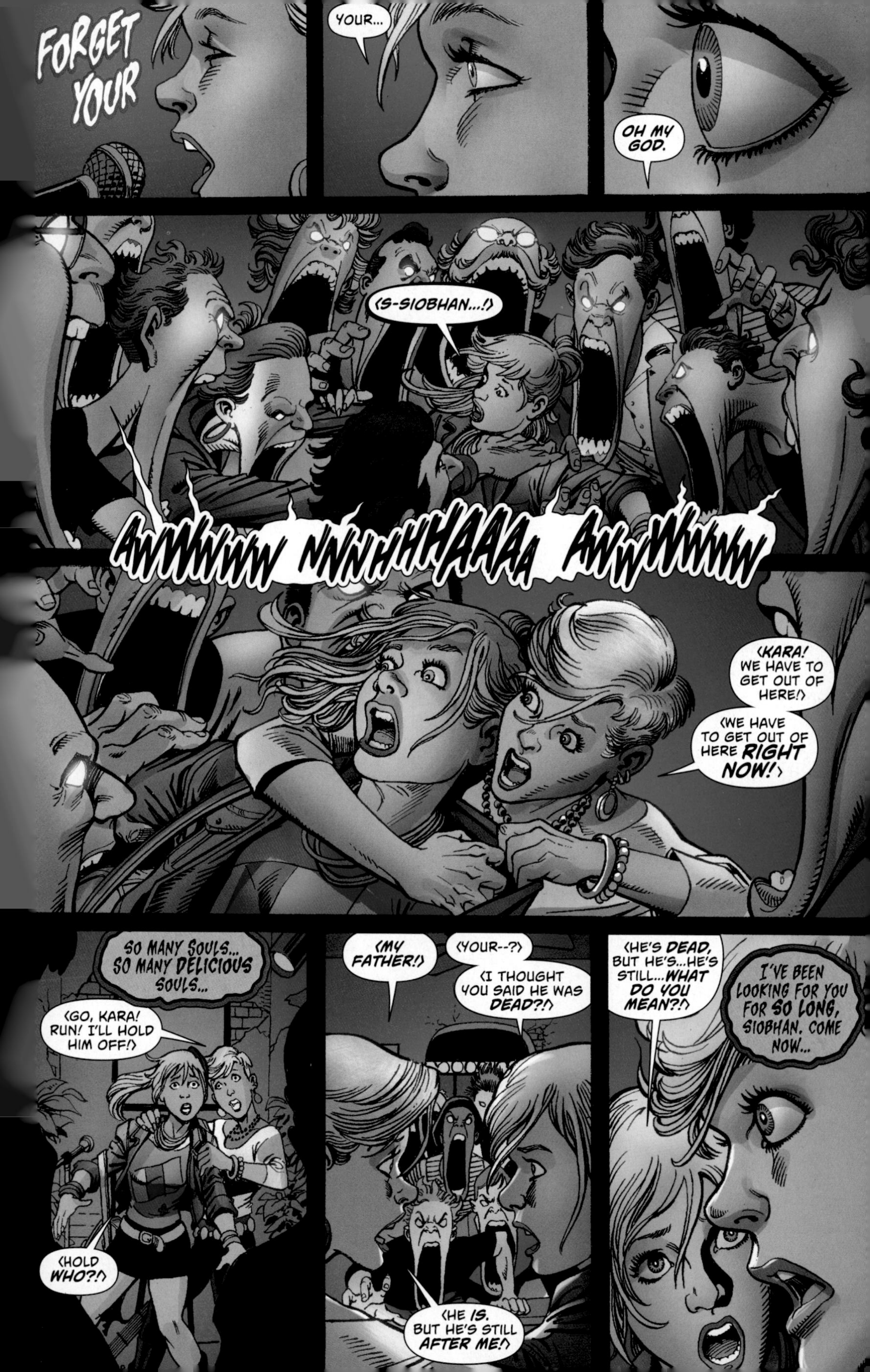
FORGET YOUR
YOUR...
OH MY GOD.
‹S-SIOBHAN...!›
AWWWWWW NNNHHHAAAA AWWWWWW
‹KARA! WE HAVE TO GET OUT OF HERE!›
‹WE HAVE TO GET OUT OF HERE RIGHT NOW!›
SO MANY SOULS... SO MANY DELICIOUS SOULS...
‹GO, KARA! RUN! I'LL HOLD HIM OFF!›
‹HOLD WHO?!›
‹MY FATHER!›
‹YOUR--?›
‹I THOUGHT YOU SAID HE WAS DEAD?!›
‹HE IS. BUT HE'S STILL AFTER ME!›
‹HE'S DEAD, BUT HE'S...HE'S STILL...WHAT DO YOU MEAN?!›
I'VE BEEN LOOKING FOR YOU FOR SO LONG, SIOBHAN. COME NOW...

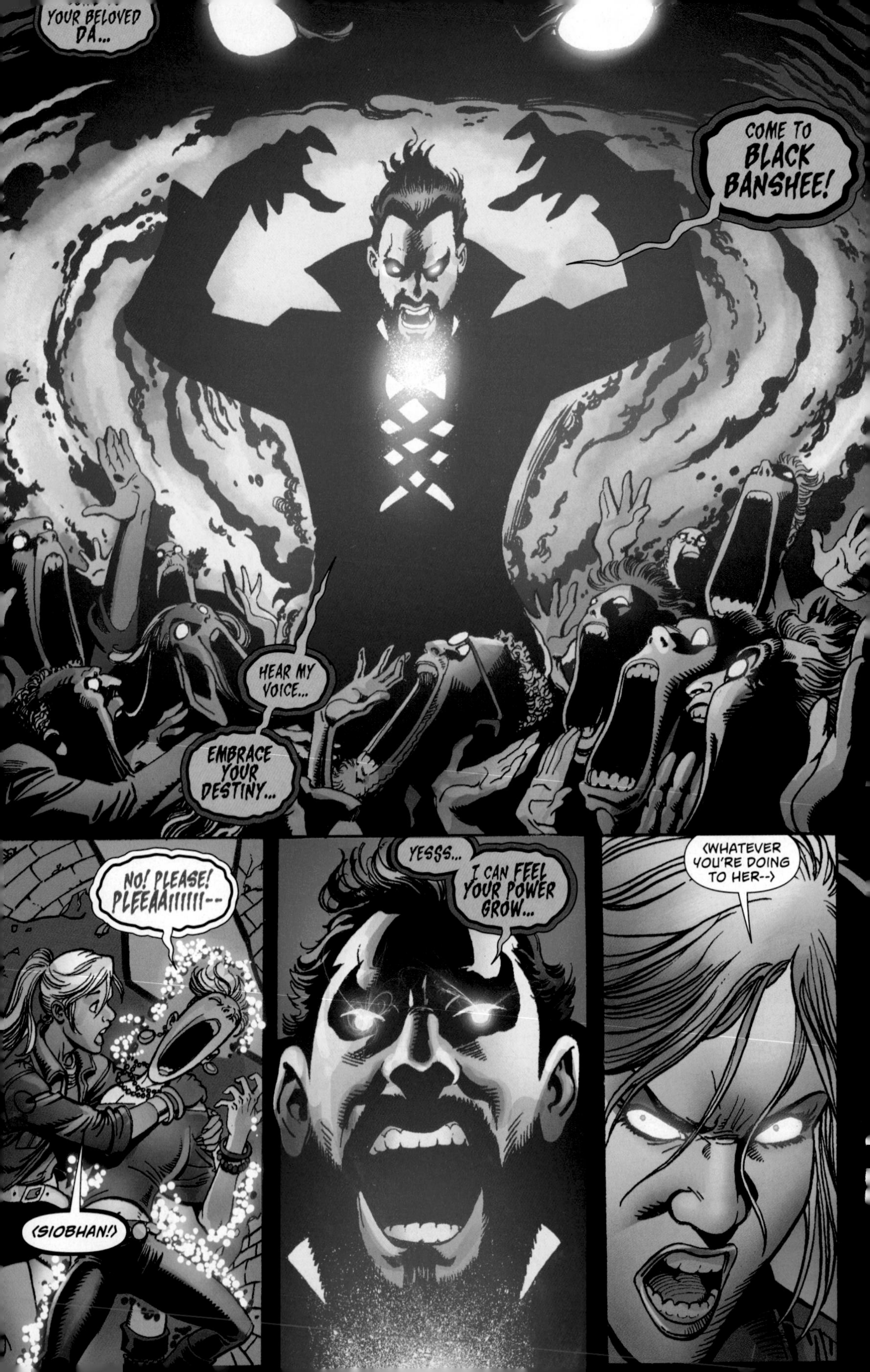
YOUR BELOVED DA...
COME TO BLACK BANSHEE!
HEAR MY VOICE...
EMBRACE YOUR DESTINY...
NO! PLEASE! PLEEAAIIIIII--
(SIOBHAN!)
YESSS...
I CAN FEEL YOUR POWER GROW...
(WHATEVER YOU'RE DOING TO HER--)

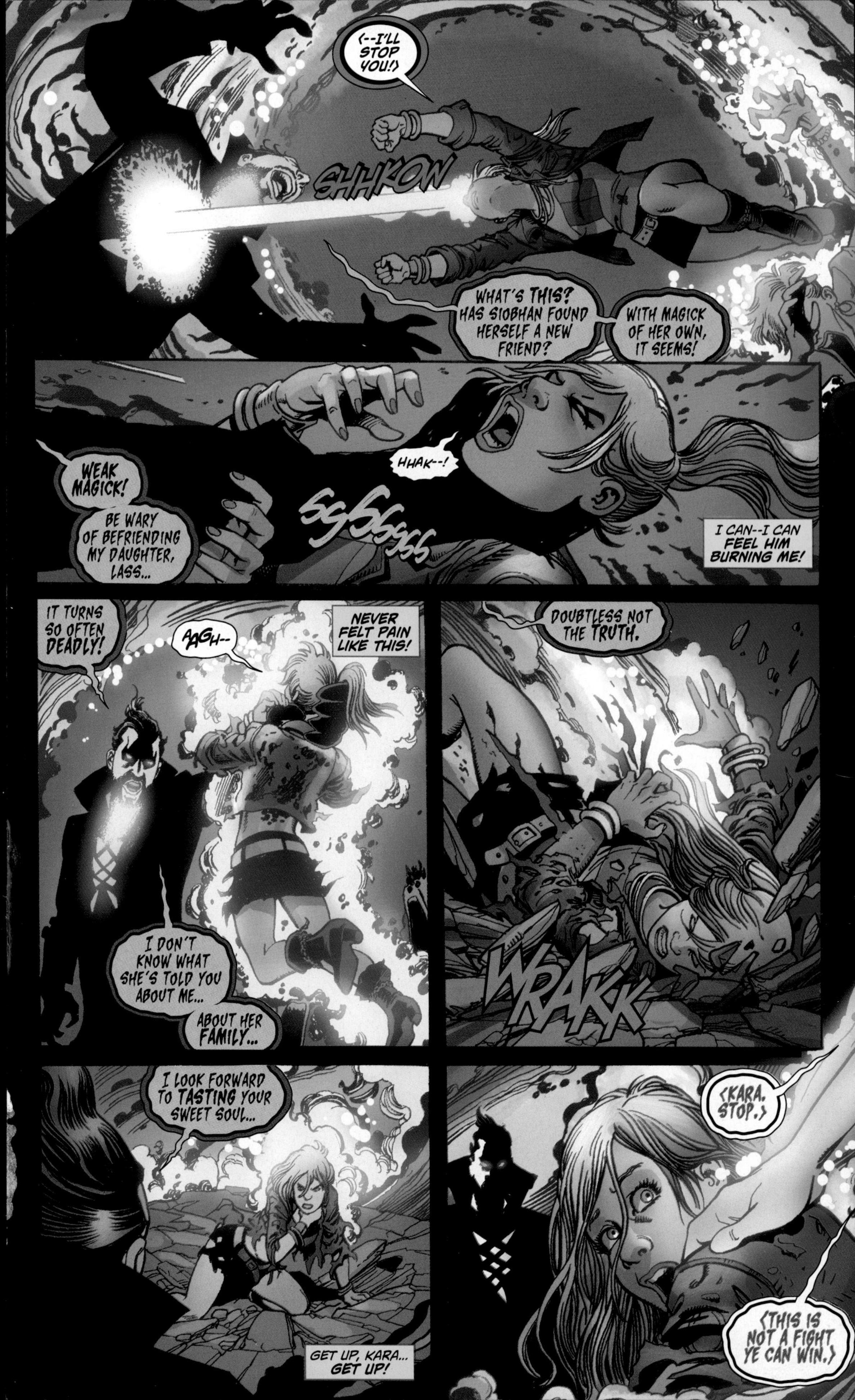

<--I'LL STOP YOU!>
SHHKOW
WHAT'S THIS? HAS SIOBHAN FOUND HERSELF A NEW FRIEND?
WITH MAGICK OF HER OWN, IT SEEMS!
HHAK--!
WEAK MAGICK!
BE WARY OF BEFRIENDING MY DAUGHTER, LASS...
SSSSSSSS
I CAN--I CAN FEEL HIM BURNING ME!
IT TURNS SO OFTEN DEADLY!
AAGH--
NEVER FELT PAIN LIKE THIS!
I DON'T KNOW WHAT SHE'S TOLD YOU ABOUT ME...
ABOUT HER FAMILY...
DOUBTLESS NOT THE TRUTH.
WRAKK
I LOOK FORWARD TO TASTING YOUR SWEET SOUL...
GET UP, KARA... GET UP!
<KARA. STOP.>
<THIS IS NOT A FIGHT YE CAN WIN.>

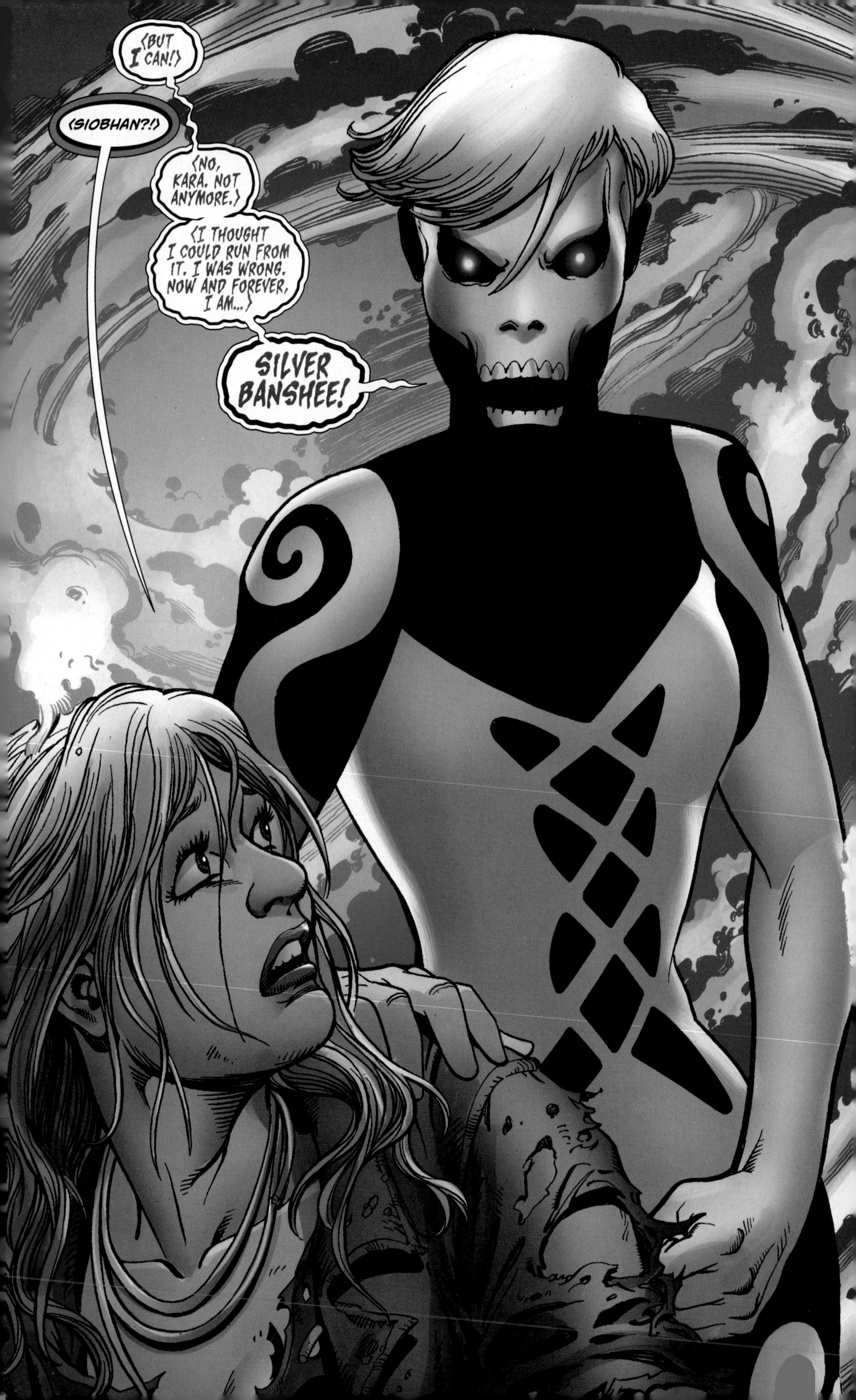

‹SIOBHAN?!›
‹BUT I CAN!›
‹NO, KARA. NOT ANYMORE.›
‹I THOUGHT I COULD RUN FROM IT. I WAS WRONG. NOW AND FOREVER, I AM...›
SILVER BANSHEE!

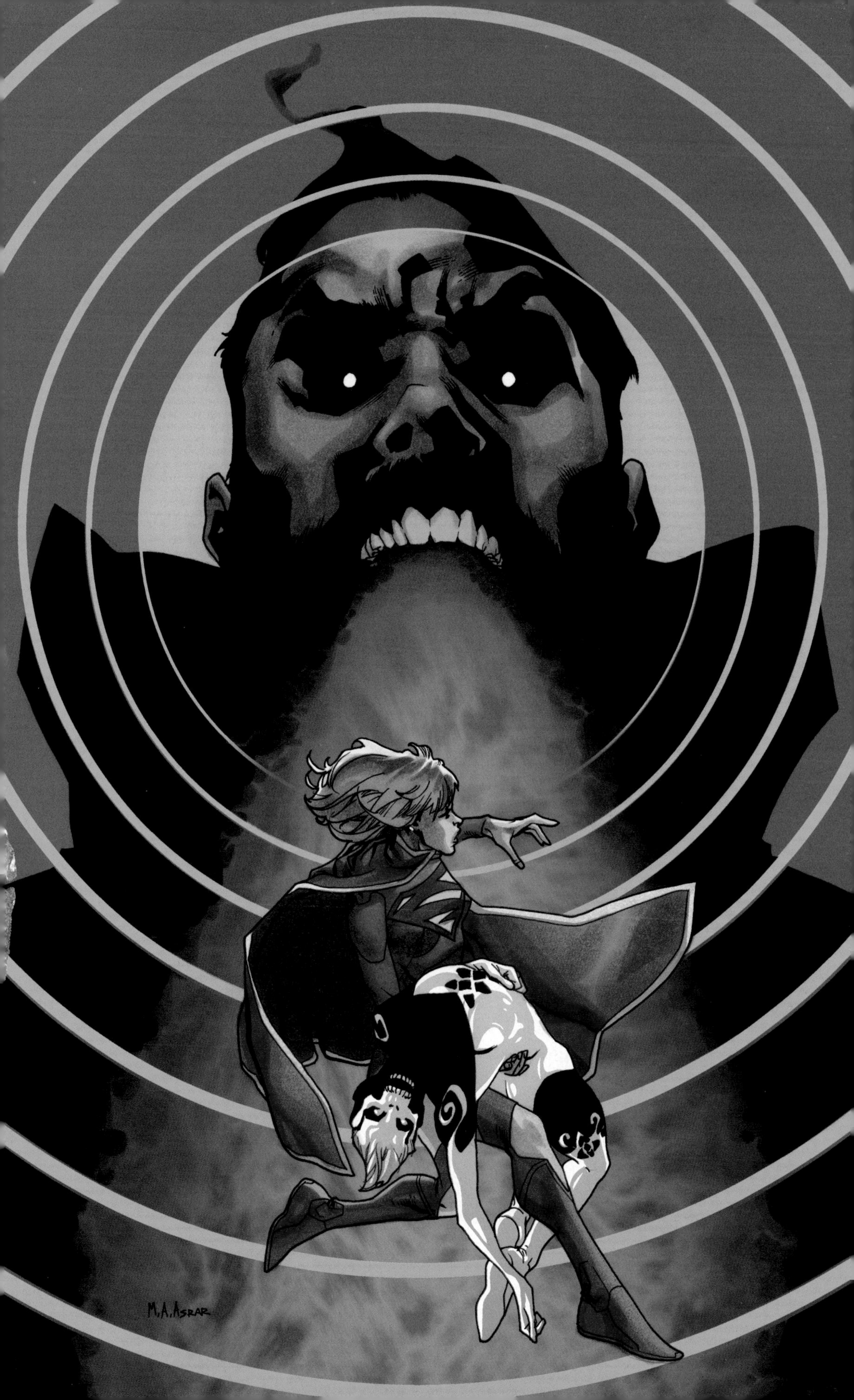
M.A.Asrar

LIKE DAUGHTER

MICHAEL GREEN & MIKE JOHNSON writers **MAHMUD ASRAR** artist cover art by **MAHMUD ASRAR & DAVE McCAIG**

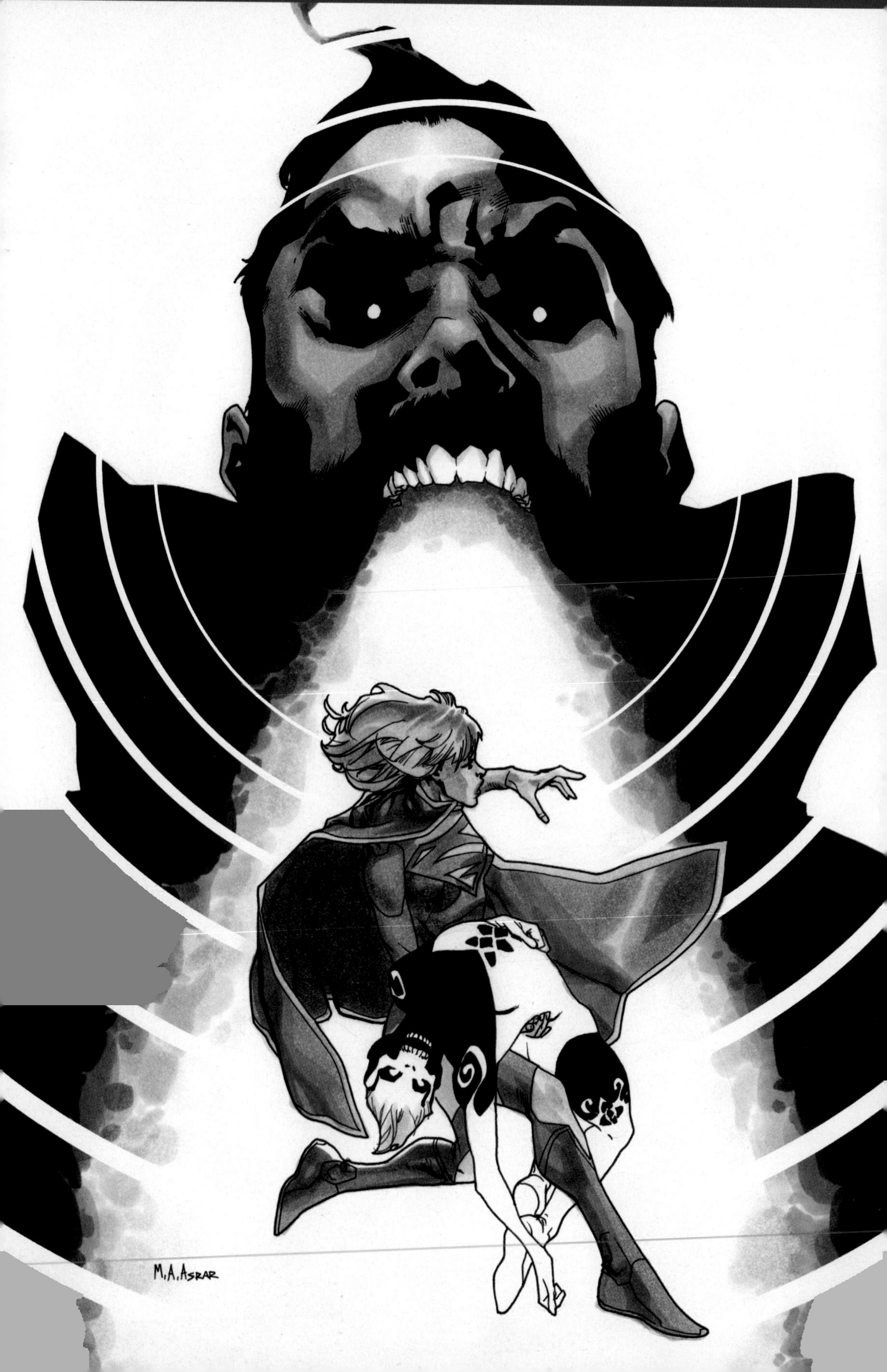
M.A.Asrar

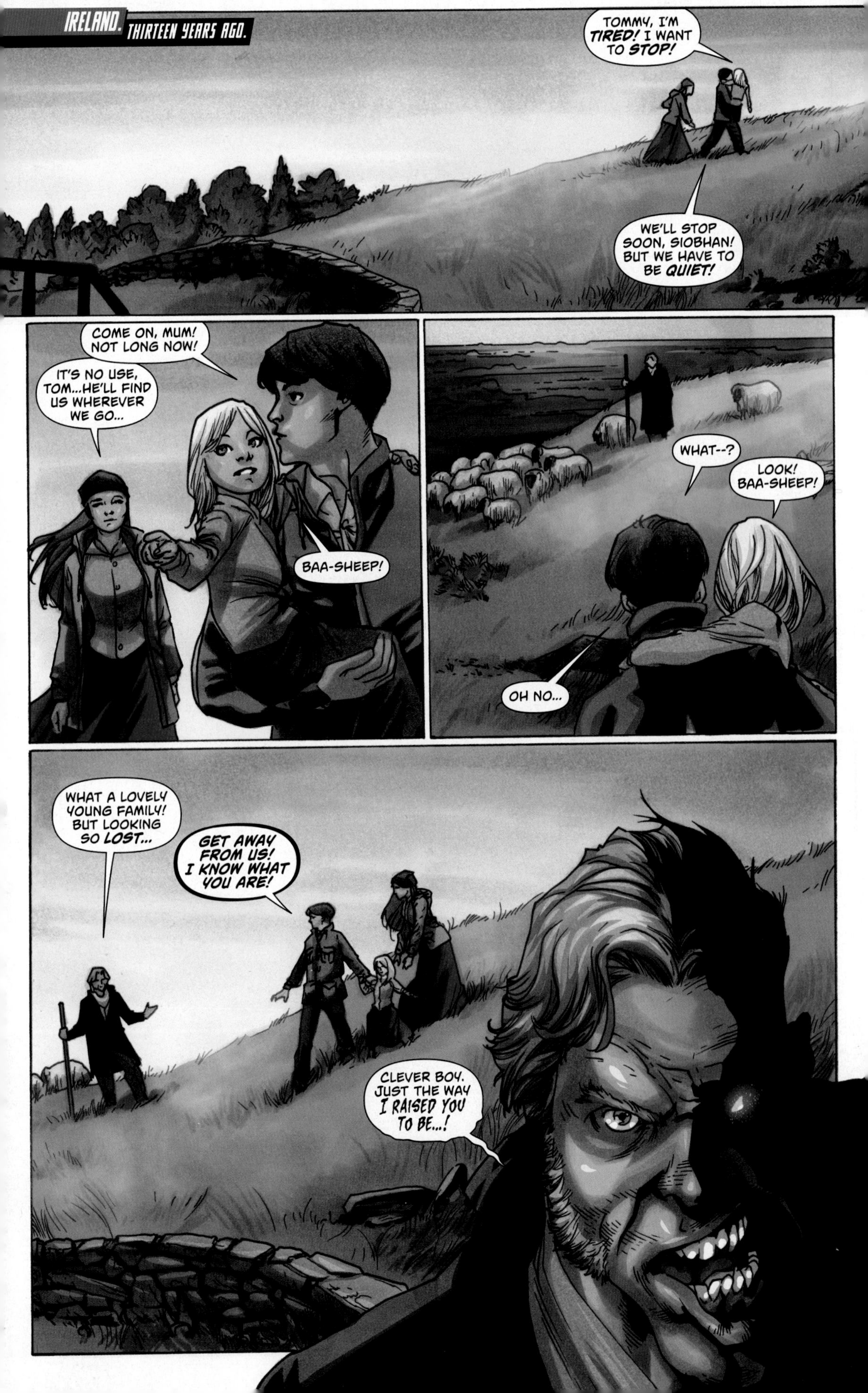
IRELAND. THIRTEEN YEARS AGO.
TOMMY, I'M TIRED! I WANT TO STOP!
WE'LL STOP SOON, SIOBHAN! BUT WE HAVE TO BE QUIET!
COME ON, MUM! NOT LONG NOW!
IT'S NO USE, TOM...HE'LL FIND US WHEREVER WE GO...
BAA-SHEEP!
WHAT--?
LOOK! BAA-SHEEP!
OH NO...
WHAT A LOVELY YOUNG FAMILY! BUT LOOKING SO LOST...
GET AWAY FROM US! I KNOW WHAT YOU ARE!
CLEVER BOY. JUST THE WAY I RAISED YOU TO BE...!

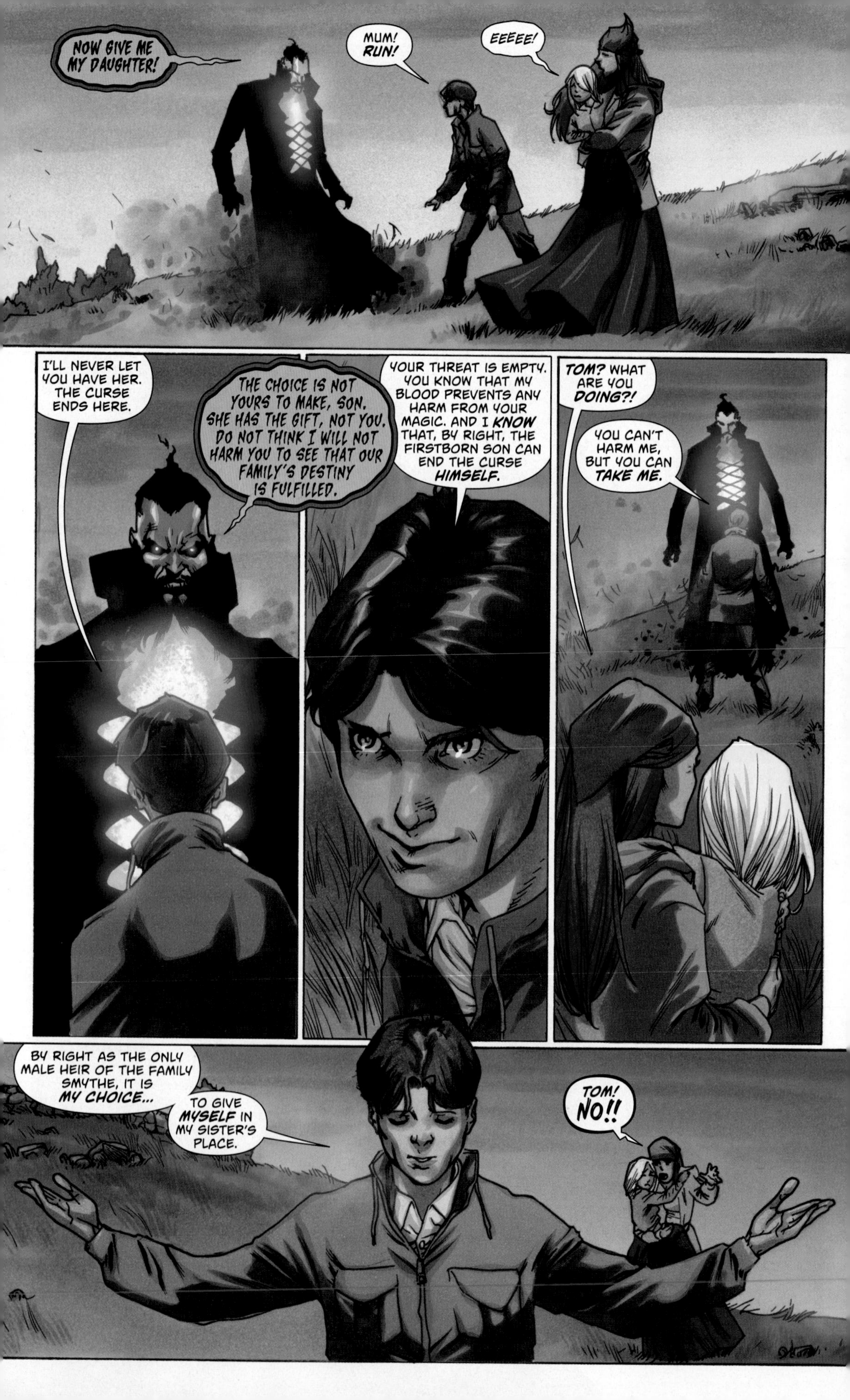
NOW GIVE ME MY DAUGHTER!
MUM! RUN!
EEEEE!
I'LL NEVER LET YOU HAVE HER. THE CURSE ENDS HERE.
THE CHOICE IS NOT YOURS TO MAKE, SON. SHE HAS THE GIFT, NOT YOU. DO NOT THINK I WILL NOT HARM YOU TO SEE THAT OUR FAMILY'S DESTINY IS FULFILLED.
YOUR THREAT IS EMPTY. YOU KNOW THAT MY BLOOD PREVENTS ANY HARM FROM YOUR MAGIC. AND I KNOW THAT, BY RIGHT, THE FIRSTBORN SON CAN END THE CURSE HIMSELF.
TOM? WHAT ARE YOU DOING?!
YOU CAN'T HARM ME, BUT YOU CAN TAKE ME.
BY RIGHT AS THE ONLY MALE HEIR OF THE FAMILY SMYTHE, IT IS MY CHOICE...
TO GIVE MYSELF IN MY SISTER'S PLACE.
TOM! NO!!

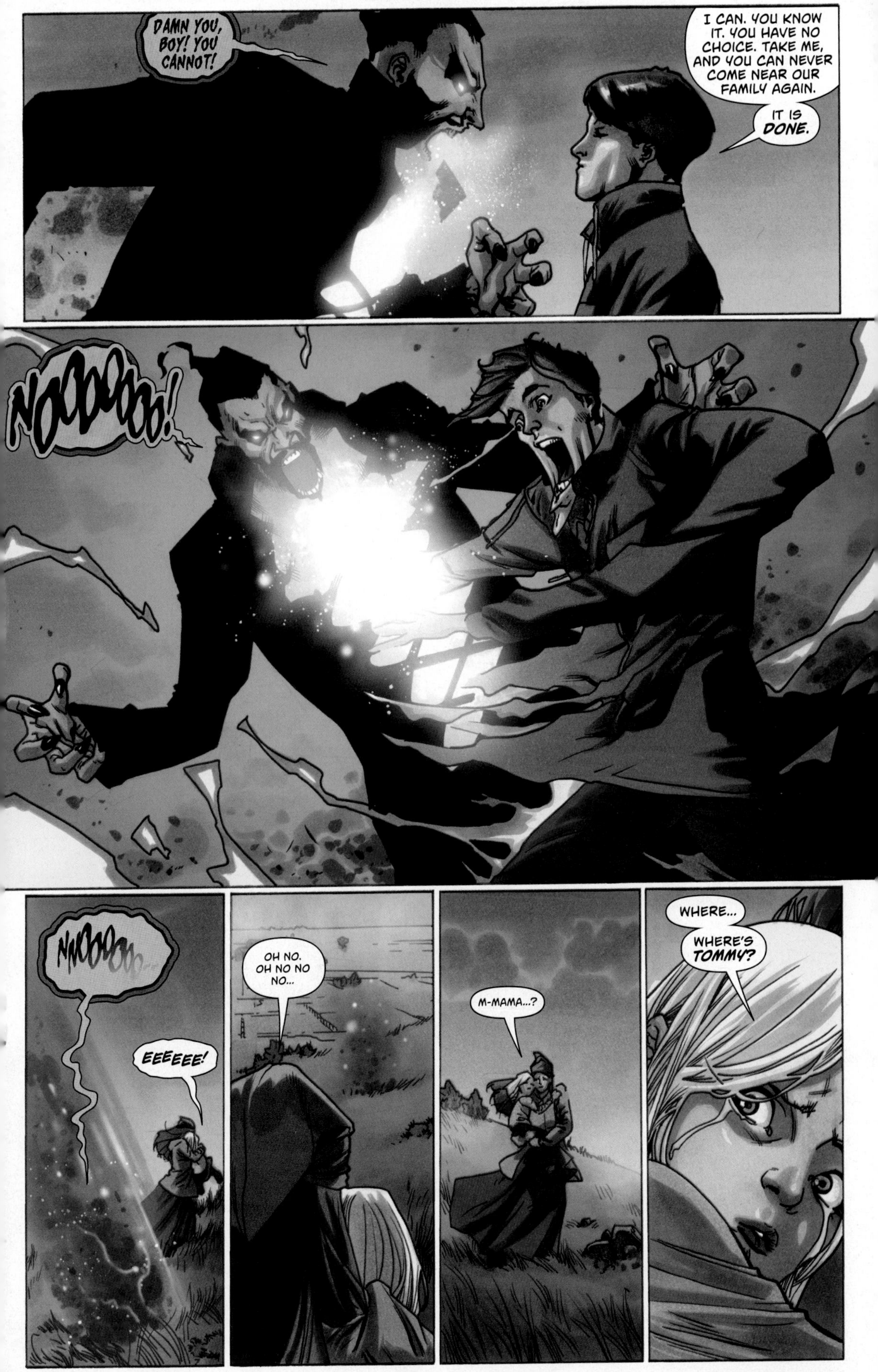
DAMN YOU, BOY! YOU CANNOT!
I CAN. YOU KNOW IT. YOU HAVE NO CHOICE. TAKE ME, AND YOU CAN NEVER COME NEAR OUR FAMILY AGAIN.
IT IS DONE.
NOOOOOOO!
NNOOOOOO...
EEEEEE!
OH NO. OH NO NO NO...
M-MAMA...?
WHERE...
WHERE'S TOMMY?

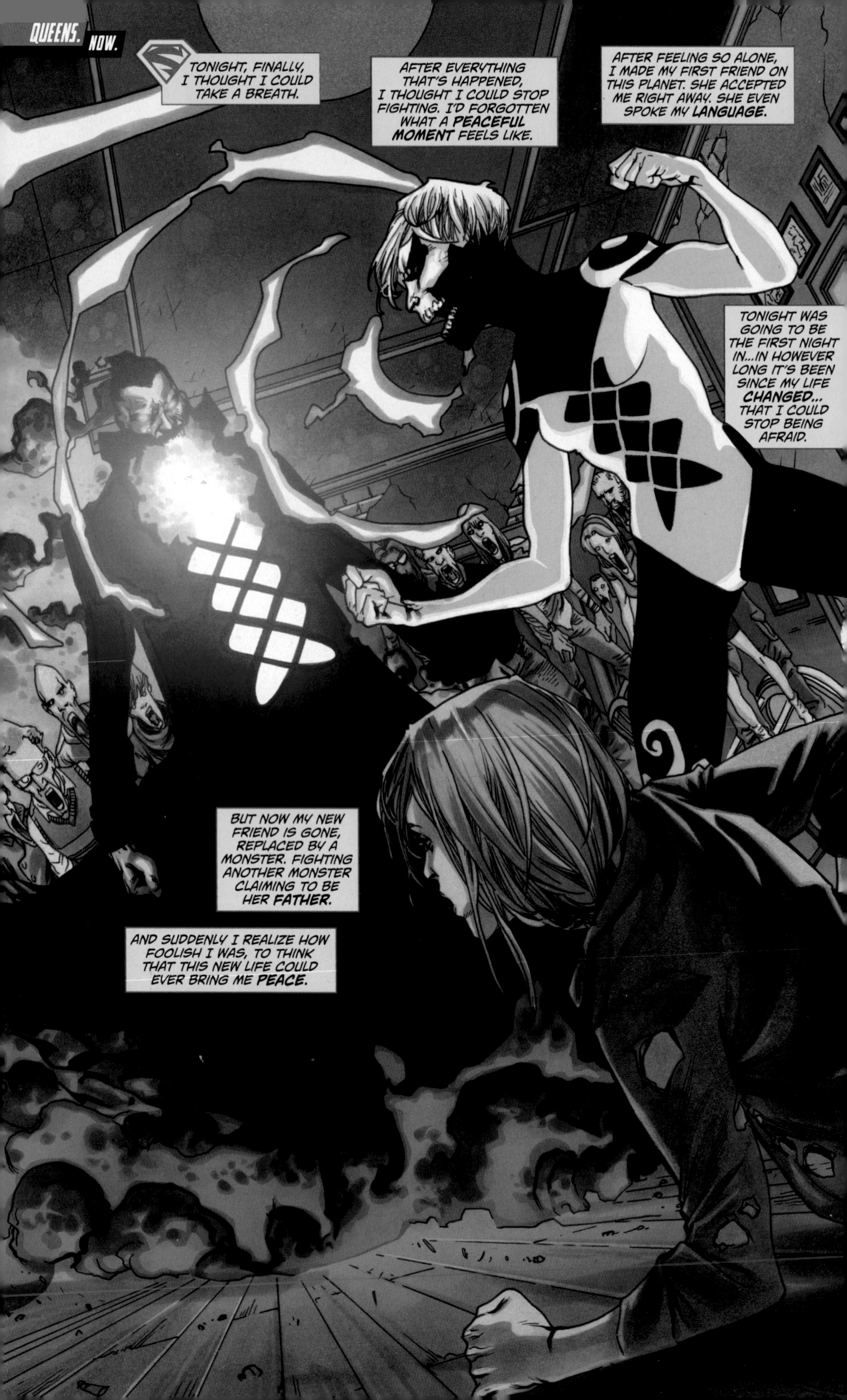
QUEENS. NOW.
TONIGHT, FINALLY, I THOUGHT I COULD TAKE A BREATH.
AFTER EVERYTHING THAT'S HAPPENED, I THOUGHT I COULD STOP FIGHTING. I'D FORGOTTEN WHAT A PEACEFUL MOMENT FEELS LIKE.
AFTER FEELING SO ALONE, I MADE MY FIRST FRIEND ON THIS PLANET. SHE ACCEPTED ME RIGHT AWAY. SHE EVEN SPOKE MY LANGUAGE.
TONIGHT WAS GOING TO BE THE FIRST NIGHT IN...IN HOWEVER LONG IT'S BEEN SINCE MY LIFE CHANGED... THAT I COULD STOP BEING AFRAID.
BUT NOW MY NEW FRIEND IS GONE, REPLACED BY A MONSTER. FIGHTING ANOTHER MONSTER CLAIMING TO BE HER FATHER.
AND SUDDENLY I REALIZE HOW FOOLISH I WAS, TO THINK THAT THIS NEW LIFE COULD EVER BRING ME PEACE.

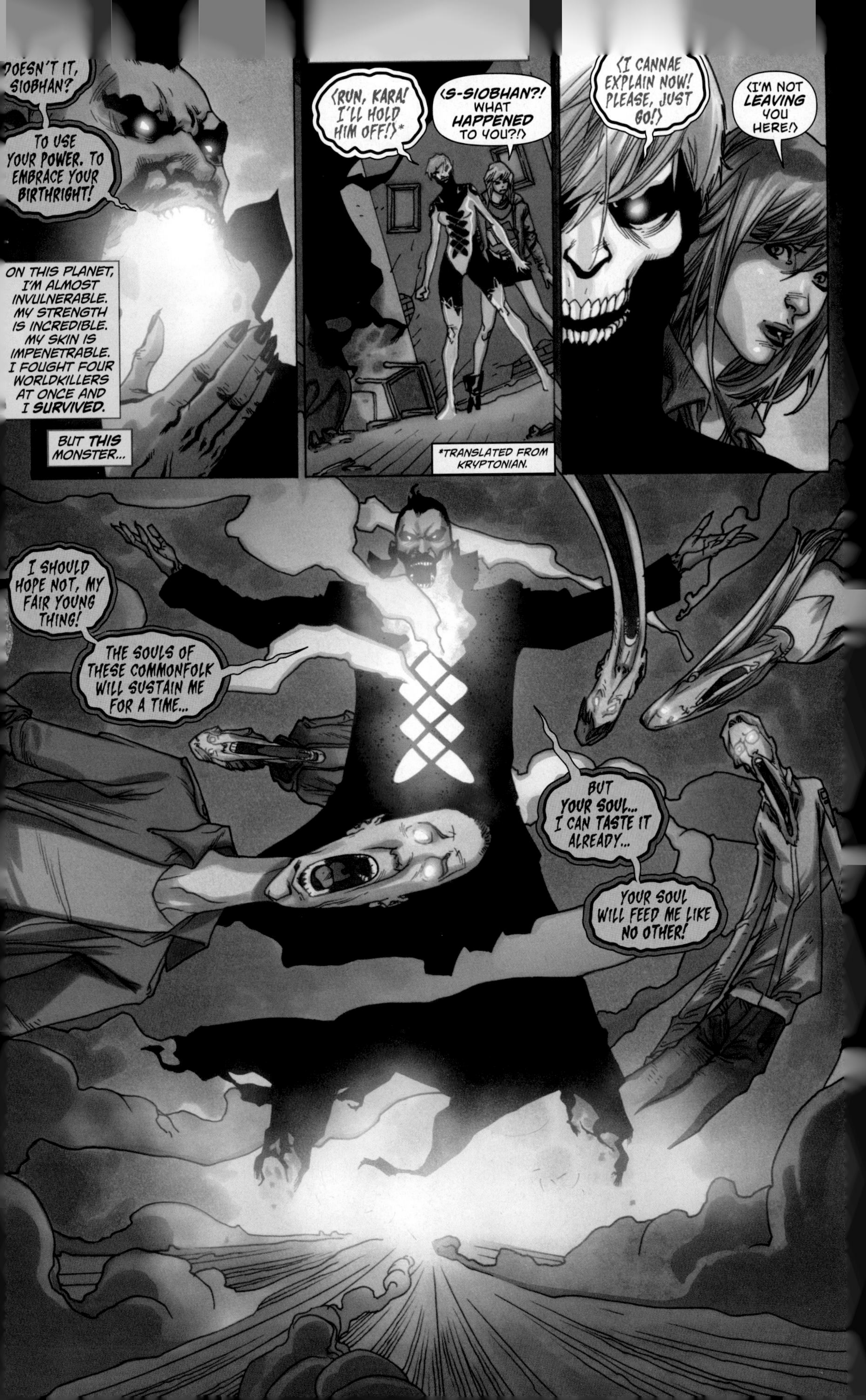
DOESN'T IT, SIOBHAN?
TO USE YOUR POWER. TO EMBRACE YOUR BIRTHRIGHT!
ON THIS PLANET, I'M ALMOST INVULNERABLE. MY STRENGTH IS INCREDIBLE. MY SKIN IS IMPENETRABLE. I FOUGHT FOUR WORLDKILLERS AT ONCE AND I SURVIVED.
BUT THIS MONSTER...
‹RUN, KARA! I'LL HOLD HIM OFF!›*
‹S-SIOBHAN?! WHAT HAPPENED TO YOU?!›
*TRANSLATED FROM KRYPTONIAN.
‹I CANNAE EXPLAIN NOW! PLEASE, JUST GO!›
‹I'M NOT LEAVING YOU HERE!›
I SHOULD HOPE NOT, MY FAIR YOUNG THING!
THE SOULS OF THESE COMMONFOLK WILL SUSTAIN ME FOR A TIME...
BUT YOUR SOUL... I CAN TASTE IT ALREADY...
YOUR SOUL WILL FEED ME LIKE NO OTHER!

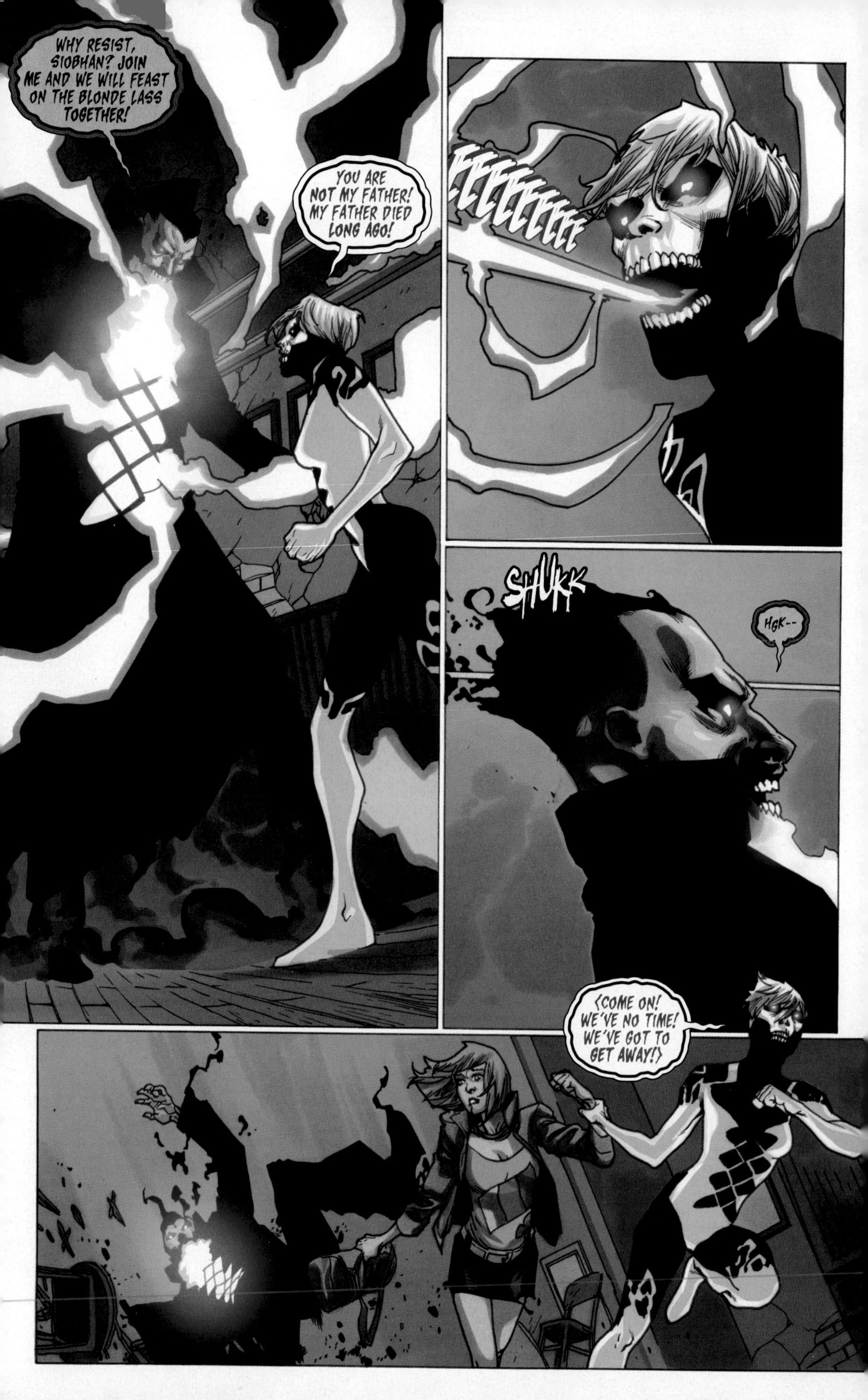
WHY RESIST, SIOBHAN? JOIN ME AND WE WILL FEAST ON THE BLONDE LASS TOGETHER!
YOU ARE NOT MY FATHER! MY FATHER DIED LONG AGO!
EEEEEEEEEEEE
SHUKK
HGK--
⟨COME ON! WE'VE NO TIME! WE'VE GOT TO GET AWAY!⟩

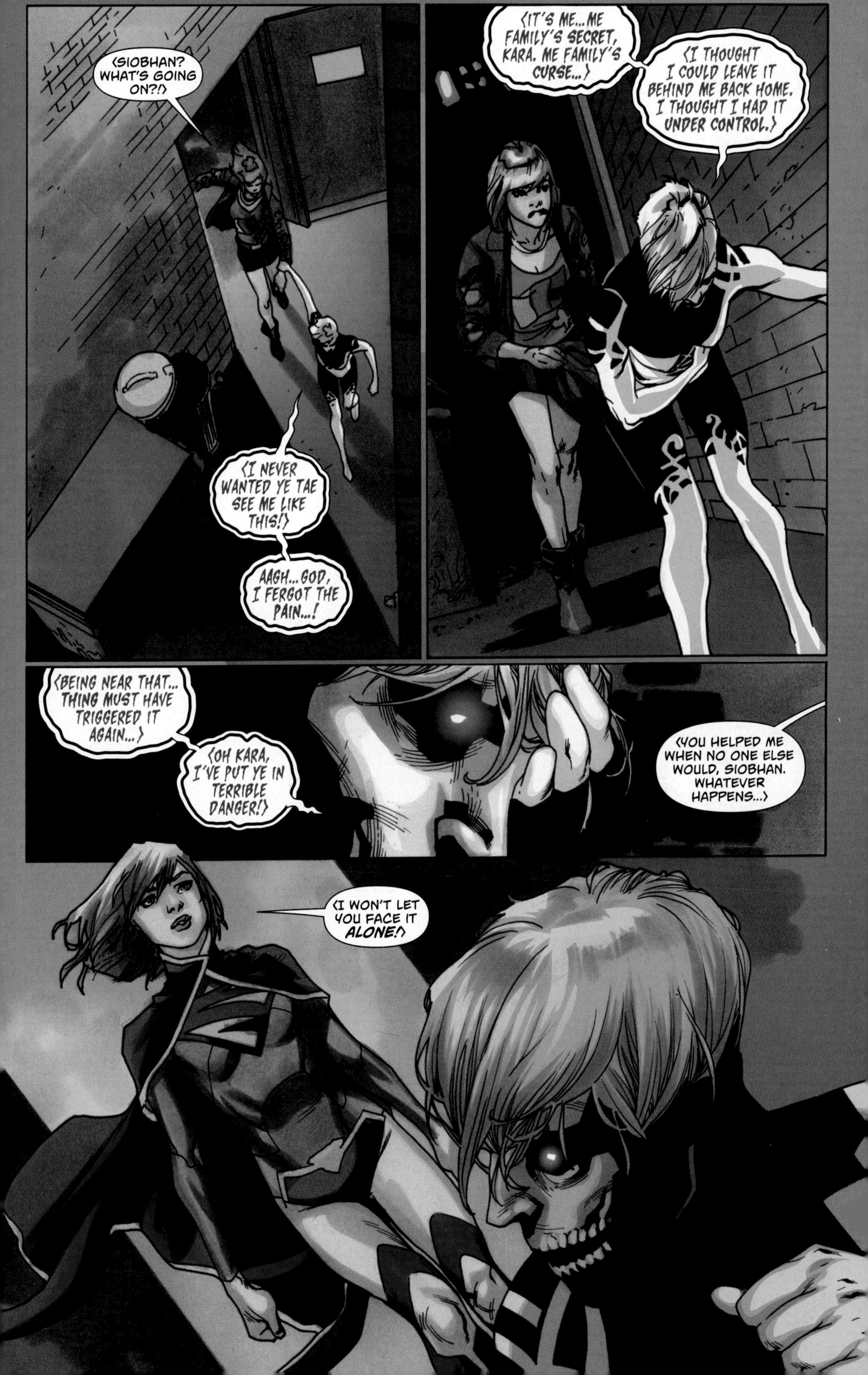

‹SIOBHAN? WHAT'S GOING ON?!›
‹I NEVER WANTED YE TAE SEE ME LIKE THIS!›
AAGH...GOD, I FERGOT THE PAIN...!
‹IT'S ME...ME FAMILY'S SECRET, KARA. ME FAMILY'S CURSE...›
‹I THOUGHT I COULD LEAVE IT BEHIND ME BACK HOME. I THOUGHT I HAD IT UNDER CONTROL.›
‹BEING NEAR THAT... THING MUST HAVE TRIGGERED IT AGAIN...›
‹OH KARA, I'VE PUT YE IN TERRIBLE DANGER!›
‹YOU HELPED ME WHEN NO ONE ELSE WOULD, SIOBHAN. WHATEVER HAPPENS...›
‹I WON'T LET YOU FACE IT ALONE!›

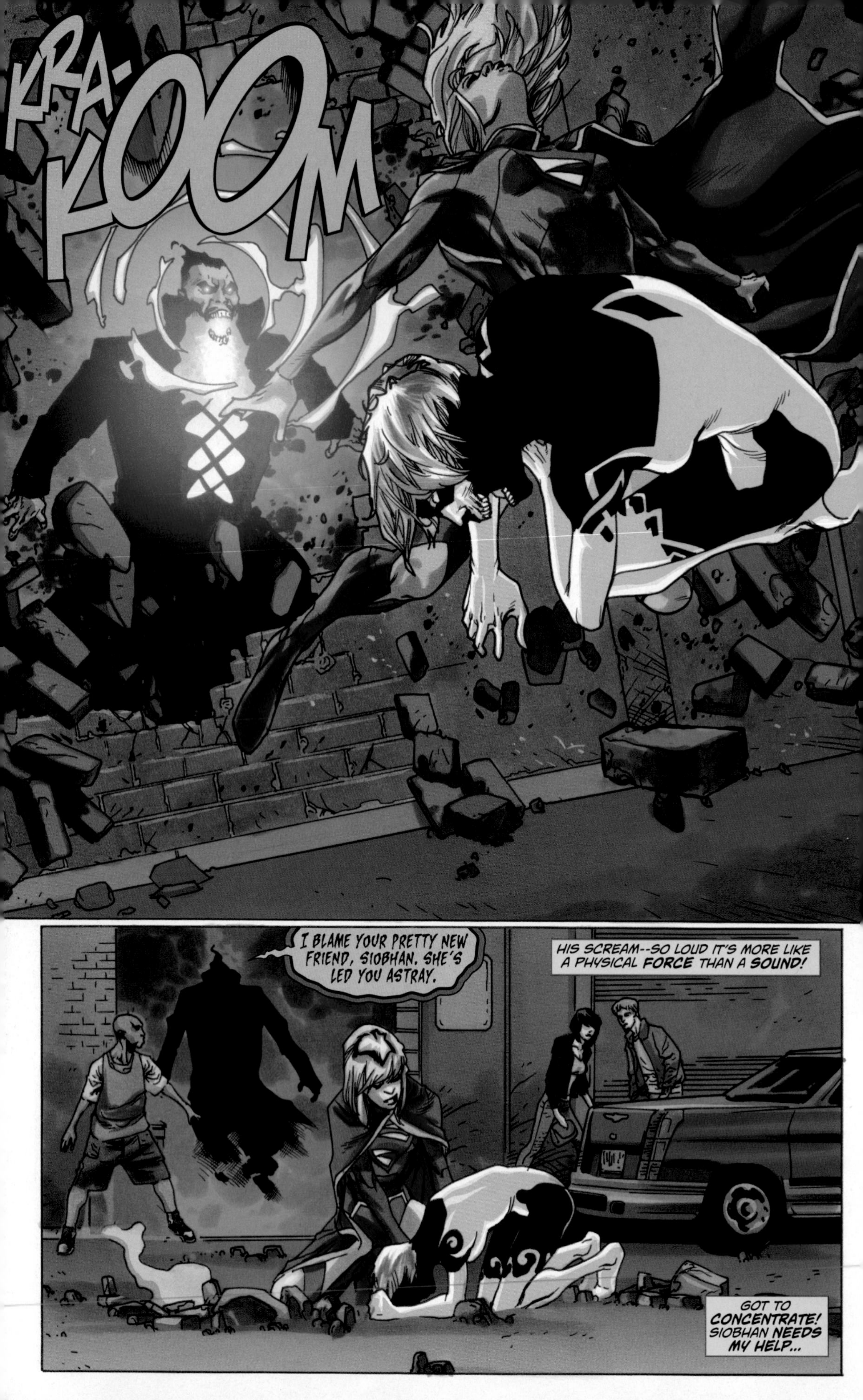
KRA-KOOM
I BLAME YOUR PRETTY NEW FRIEND, SIOBHAN. SHE'S LED YOU ASTRAY.
HIS SCREAM--SO LOUD IT'S MORE LIKE A PHYSICAL FORCE THAN A SOUND!
GOT TO CONCENTRATE! SIOBHAN NEEDS MY HELP...

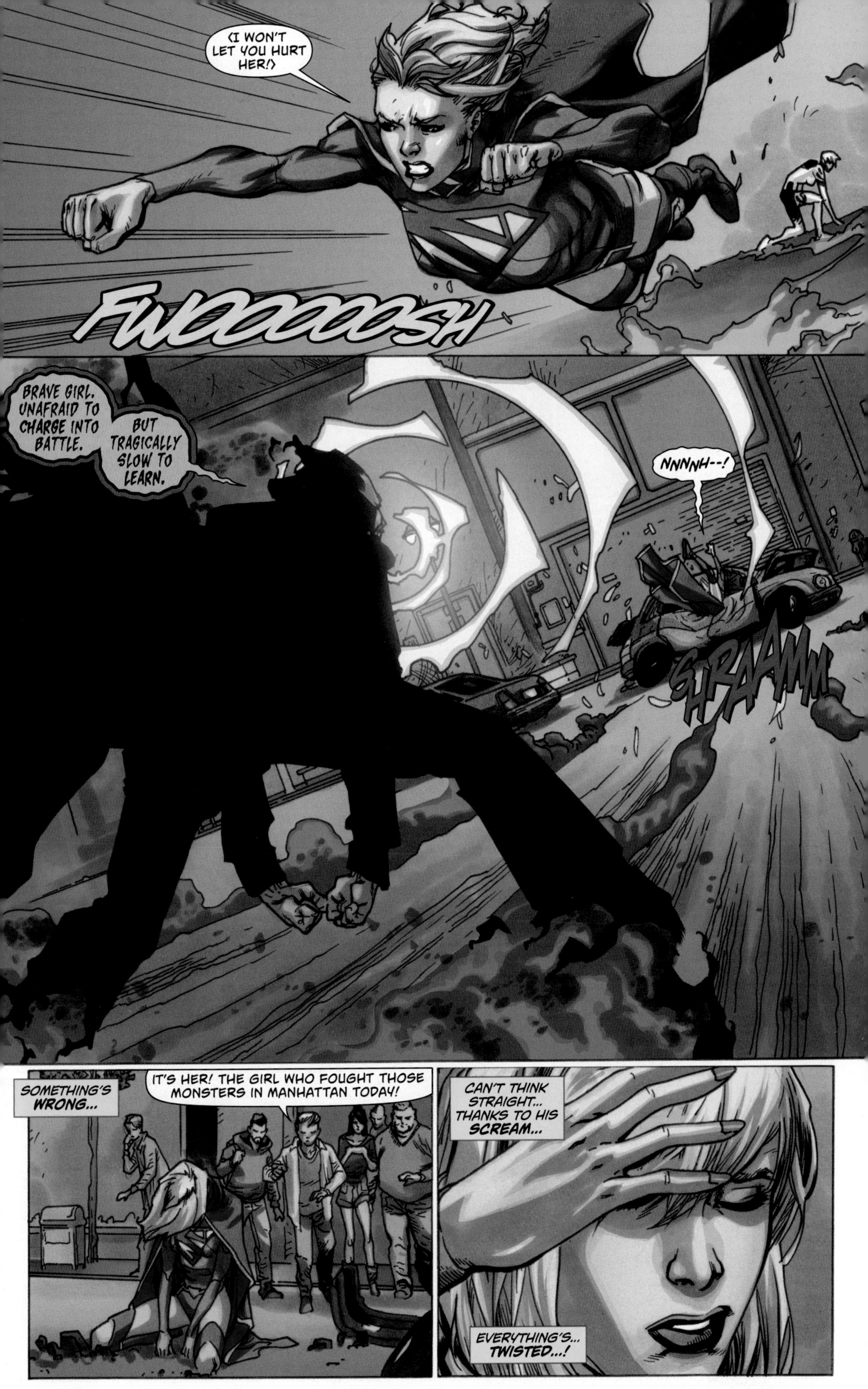
‹I WON'T LET YOU HURT HER!›
FWOOOOOSH
BRAVE GIRL. UNAFRAID TO CHARGE INTO BATTLE.
BUT TRAGICALLY SLOW TO LEARN.
NNNNH--!
SHRAAMM
SOMETHING'S WRONG...
IT'S HER! THE GIRL WHO FOUGHT THOSE MONSTERS IN MANHATTAN TODAY!
CAN'T THINK STRAIGHT... THANKS TO HIS SCREAM...
EVERYTHING'S... TWISTED...!

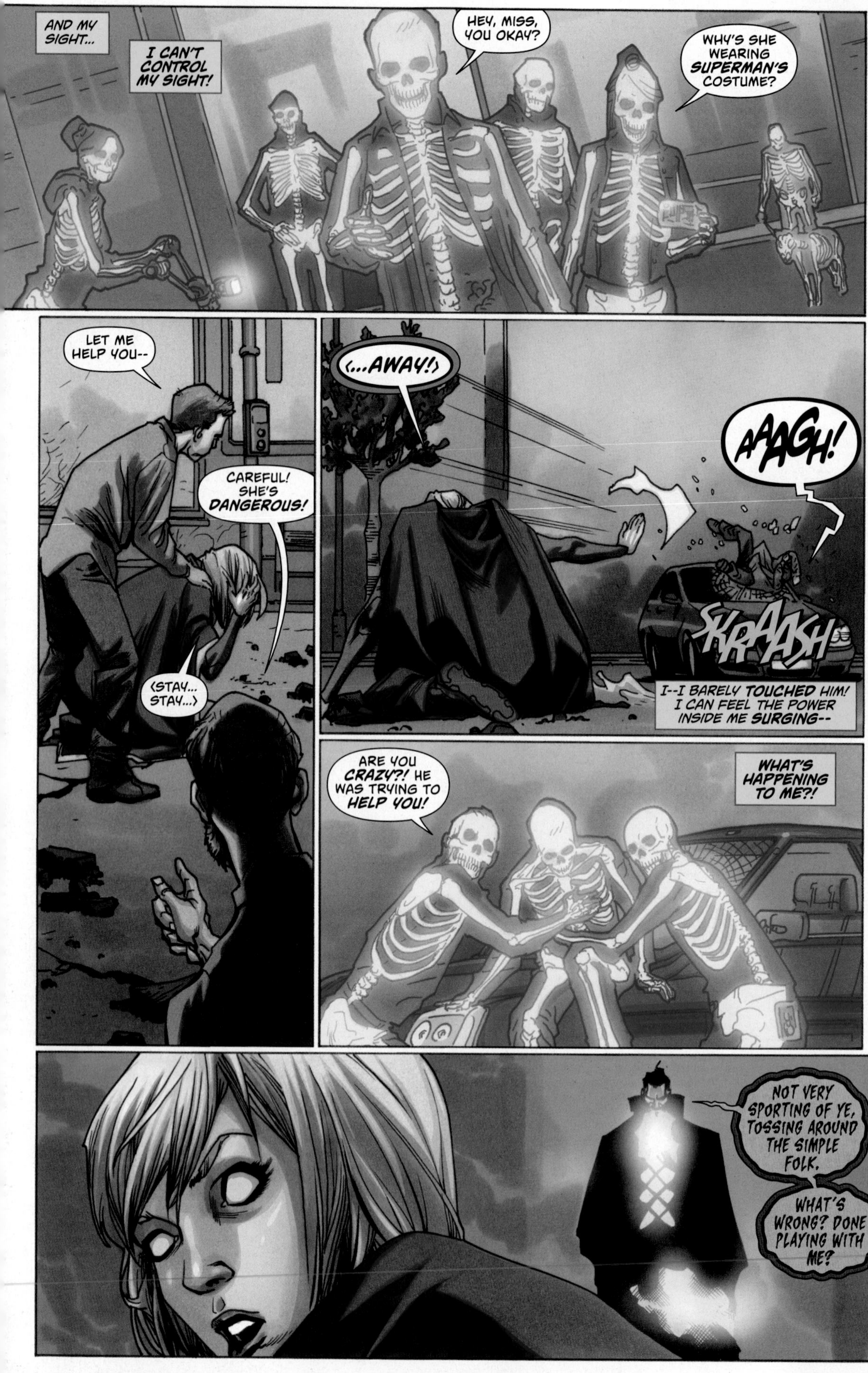

AND MY SIGHT...
I CAN'T CONTROL MY SIGHT!
HEY, MISS, YOU OKAY?
WHY'S SHE WEARING SUPERMAN'S COSTUME?
LET ME HELP YOU--
CAREFUL! SHE'S DANGEROUS!
<STAY... STAY...>
<...AWAY!>
AAAGH!
SKRAAASH
I--I BARELY TOUCHED HIM! I CAN FEEL THE POWER INSIDE ME SURGING--
ARE YOU CRAZY?! HE WAS TRYING TO HELP YOU!
WHAT'S HAPPENING TO ME?!
NOT VERY SPORTING OF YE, TOSSING AROUND THE SIMPLE FOLK.
WHAT'S WRONG? DONE PLAYING WITH ME?

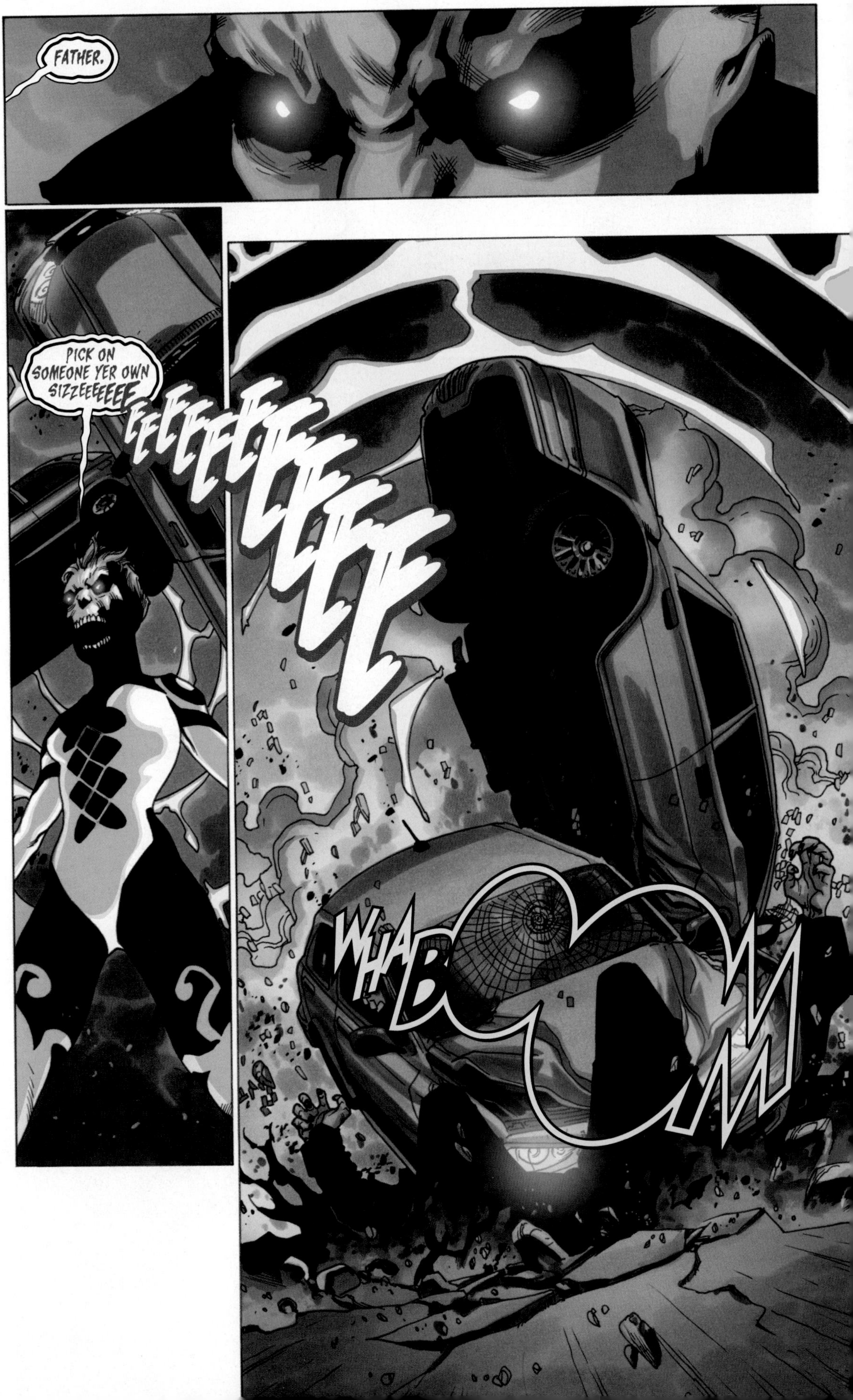
FATHER.
PICK ON SOMEONE YER OWN SIZZEEEEEEE
EEEEEEEEEEEE
WHABOOM

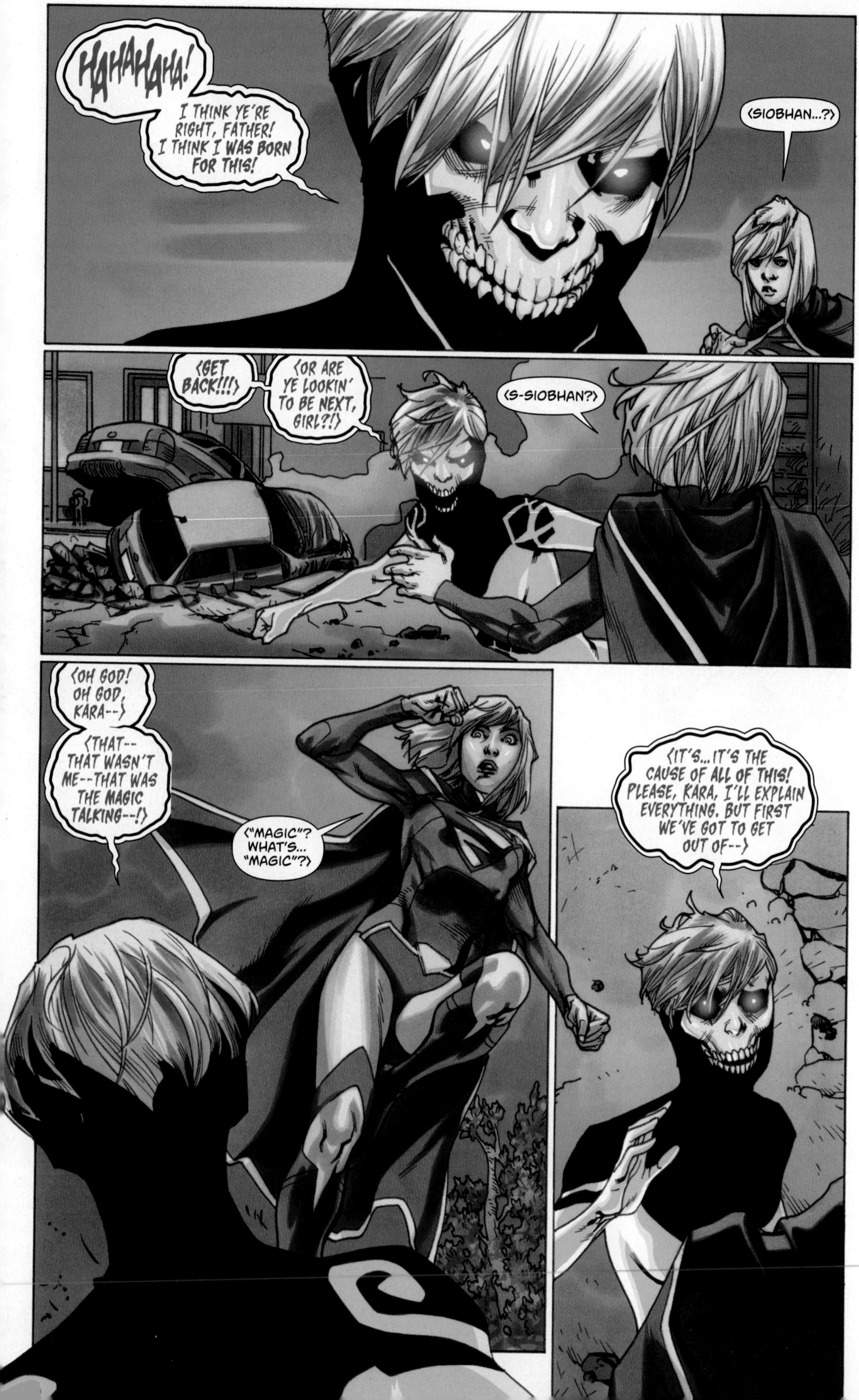
HAHAHAHA!
I THINK YE'RE RIGHT, FATHER! I THINK I WAS BORN FOR THIS!
⟨SIOBHAN...?⟩
⟨GET BACK!!!⟩
⟨OR ARE YE LOOKIN' TO BE NEXT, GIRL?!⟩
⟨S-SIOBHAN?⟩
⟨OH GOD! OH GOD, KARA--⟩
⟨THAT-- THAT WASN'T ME--THAT WAS THE MAGIC TALKING--!⟩
⟨"MAGIC"? WHAT'S... "MAGIC"?⟩
⟨IT'S...IT'S THE CAUSE OF ALL OF THIS! PLEASE, KARA, I'LL EXPLAIN EVERYTHING. BUT FIRST WE'VE GOT TO GET OUT OF--⟩

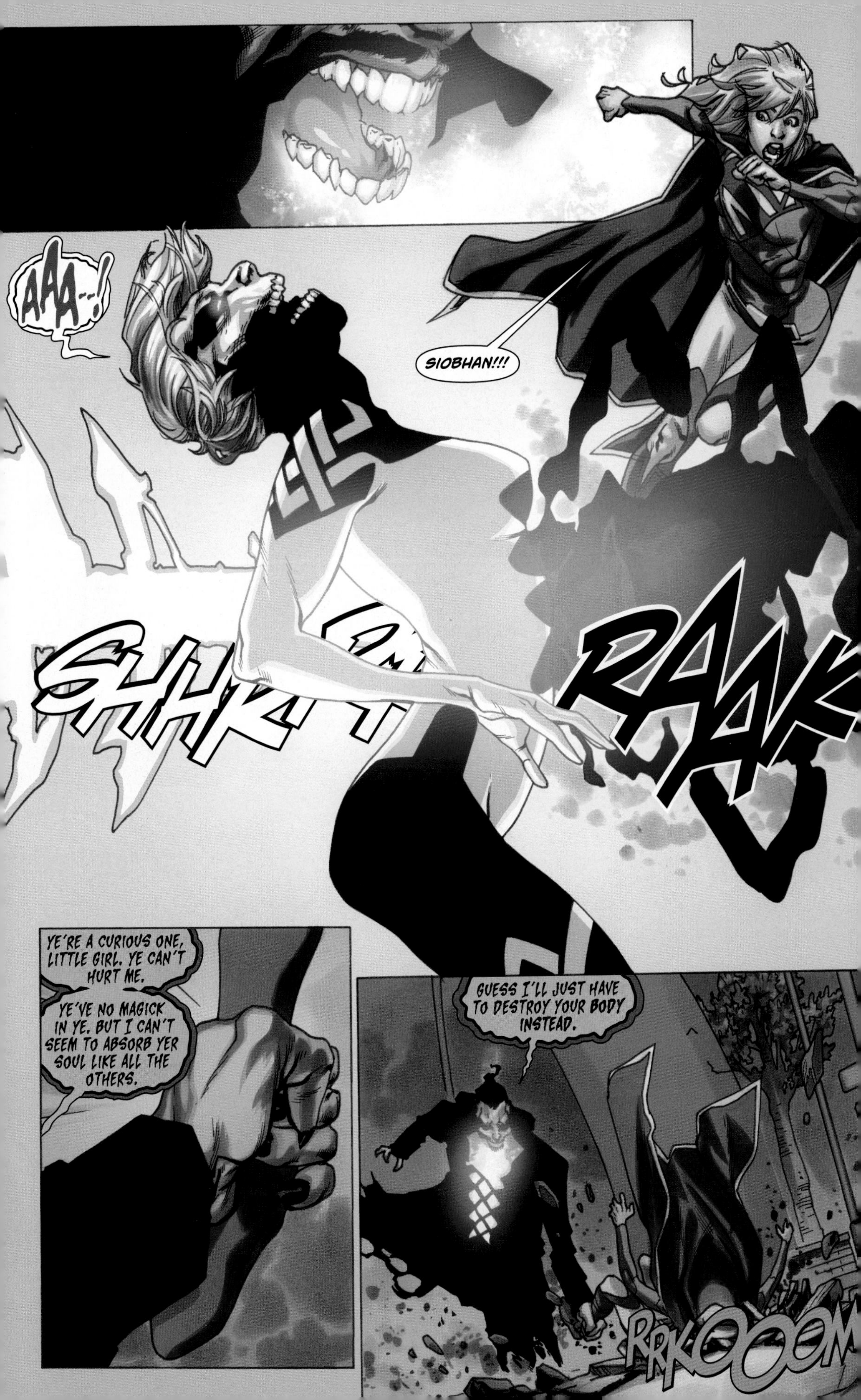
AAA--!
SIOBHAN!!!
SHHK
RAAK
YE'RE A CURIOUS ONE, LITTLE GIRL. YE CAN'T HURT ME.
YE'VE NO MAGICK IN YE. BUT I CAN'T SEEM TO ABSORB YER SOUL LIKE ALL THE OTHERS.
GUESS I'LL JUST HAVE TO DESTROY YOUR BODY INSTEAD.
RRKOOOM

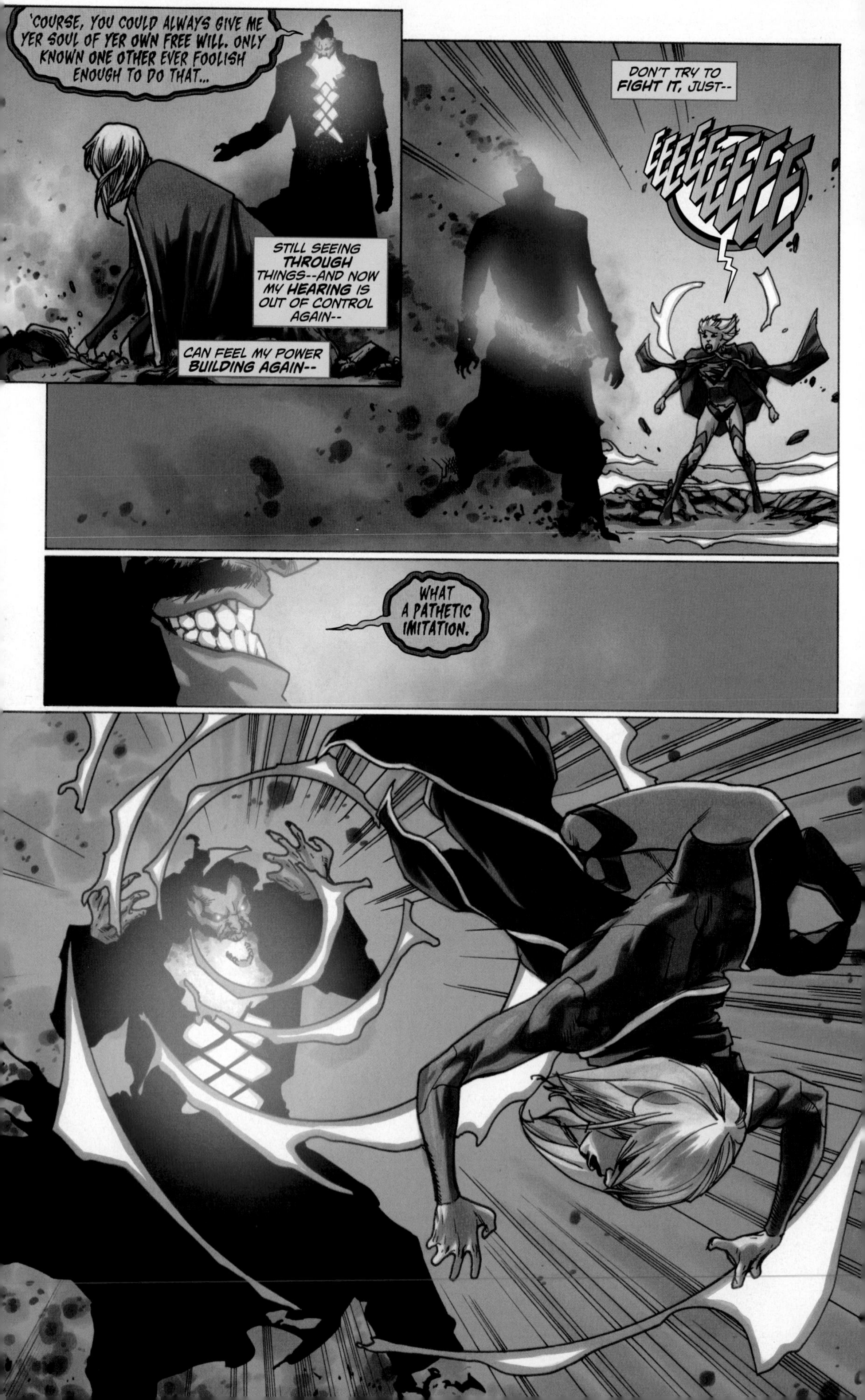
'COURSE, YOU COULD ALWAYS GIVE ME YER SOUL OF YER OWN FREE WILL. ONLY KNOWN ONE OTHER EVER FOOLISH ENOUGH TO DO THAT...
STILL SEEING THROUGH THINGS--AND NOW MY HEARING IS OUT OF CONTROL AGAIN--
CAN FEEL MY POWER BUILDING AGAIN--
DON'T TRY TO FIGHT IT, JUST--
EEEEEEEEEEE
WHAT A PATHETIC IMITATION.

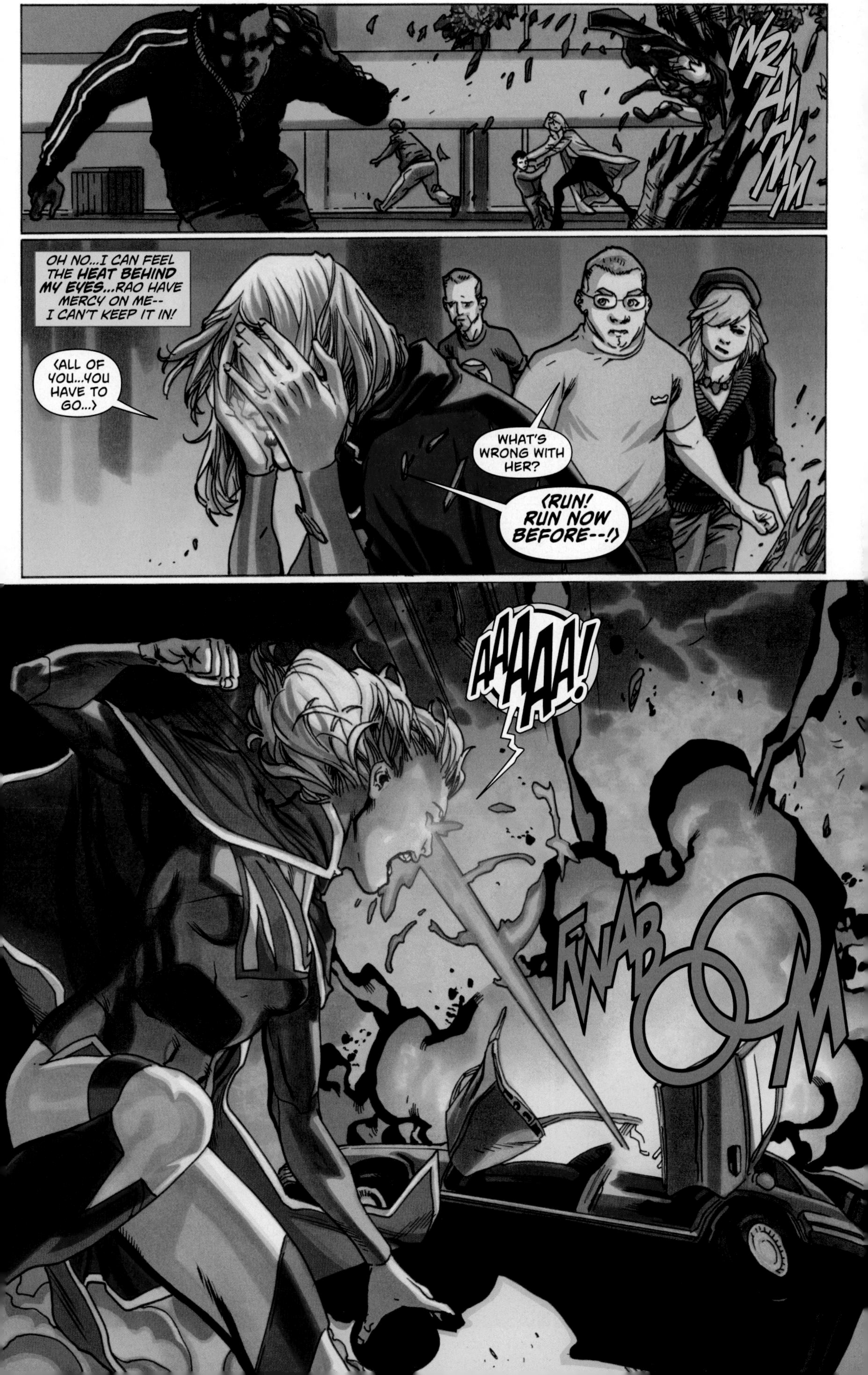
WRAAAMM
OH NO...I CAN FEEL THE HEAT BEHIND MY EYES...RAO HAVE MERCY ON ME-- I CAN'T KEEP IT IN!
‹ALL OF YOU...YOU HAVE TO GO...›
WHAT'S WRONG WITH HER?
‹RUN! RUN NOW BEFORE--!›
AAAAA!
FWABOOM

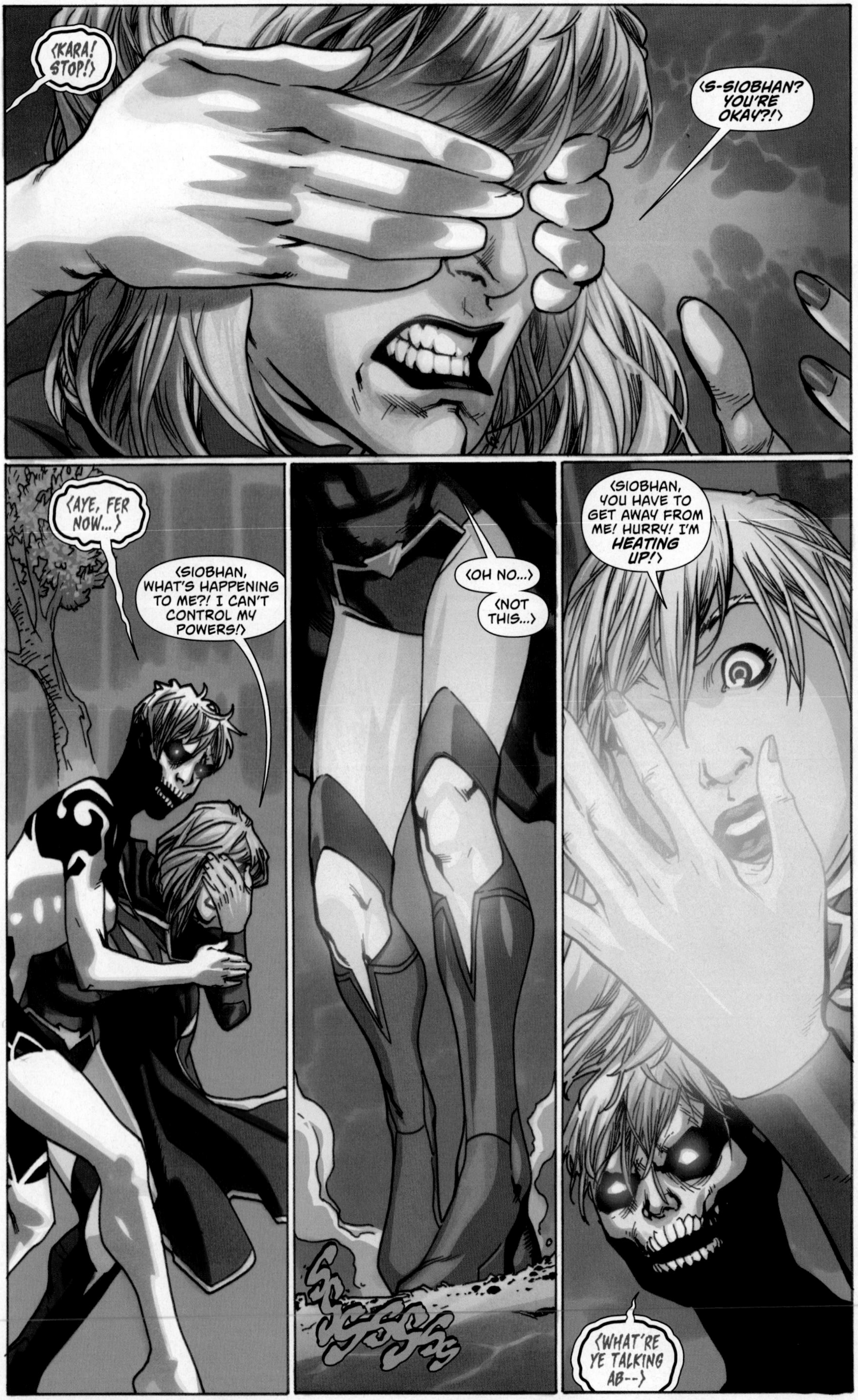

⟨KARA! STOP!⟩
⟨S-SIOBHAN? YOU'RE OKAY?!⟩
⟨AYE, FER NOW...⟩
⟨SIOBHAN, WHAT'S HAPPENING TO ME?! I CAN'T CONTROL MY POWERS!⟩
⟨OH NO...⟩
⟨NOT THIS...⟩
⟨SIOBHAN, YOU HAVE TO GET AWAY FROM ME! HURRY! I'M **HEATING UP!**⟩
⟨WHAT'RE YE TALKING AB--⟩

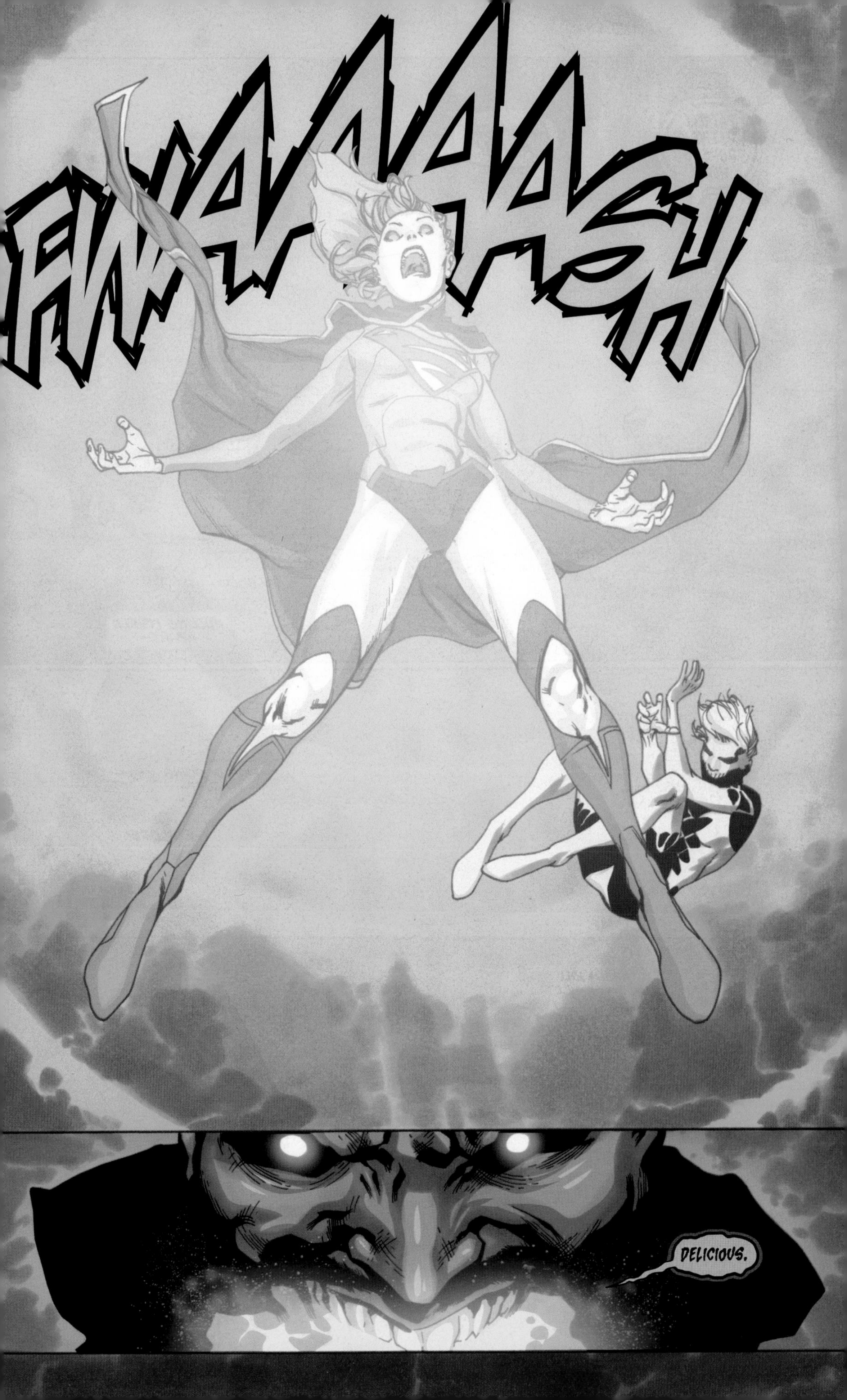
FWAAAASH
DELICIOUS.

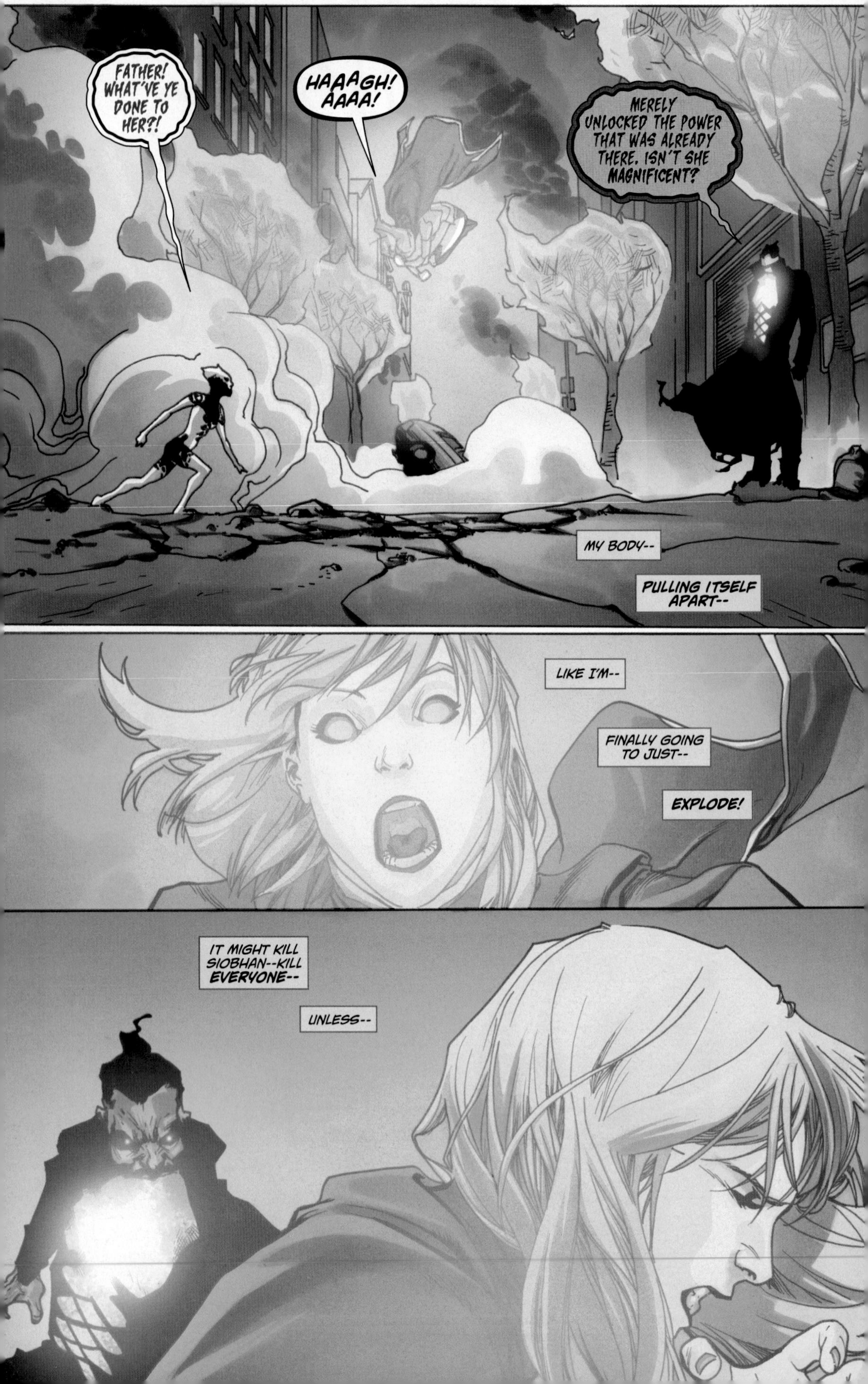
FATHER! WHAT'VE YE DONE TO HER?!
HAAAGH! AAAA!
MERELY UNLOCKED THE POWER THAT WAS ALREADY THERE. ISN'T SHE MAGNIFICENT?
MY BODY--
PULLING ITSELF APART--
LIKE I'M--
FINALLY GOING TO JUST--
EXPLODE!
IT MIGHT KILL SIOBHAN--KILL EVERYONE--
UNLESS--

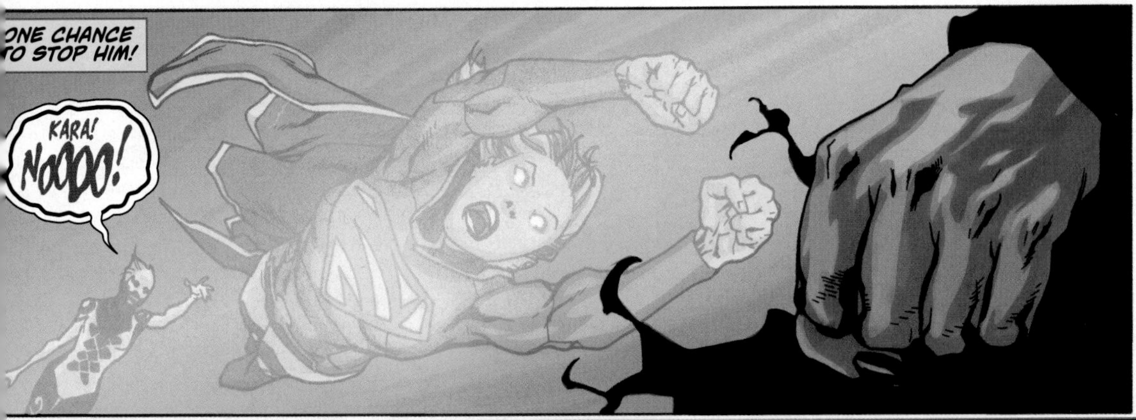
ONE CHANCE TO STOP HIM!
KARA! NOOOO!

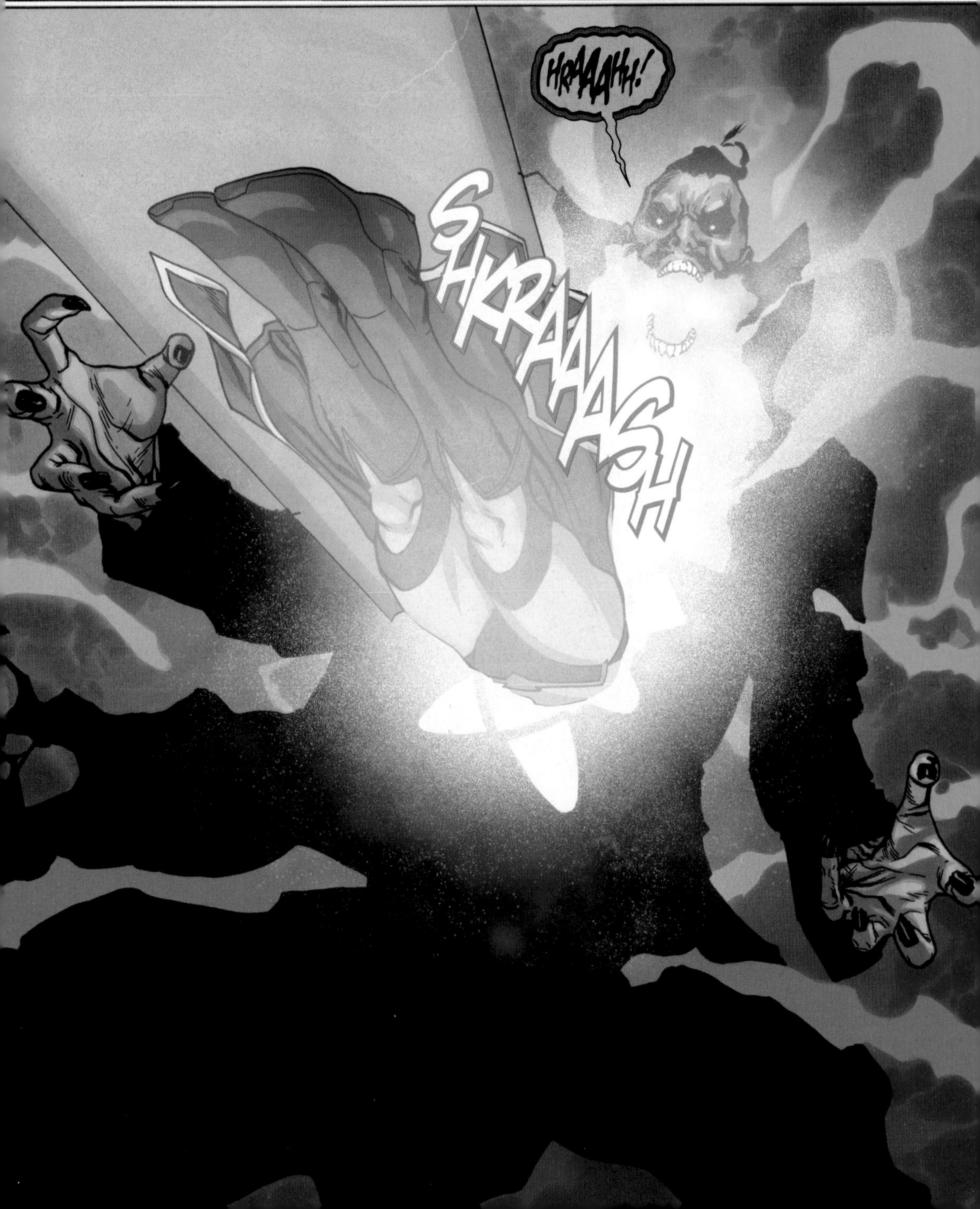
HRAAAAHH!
SHKRAAAASH

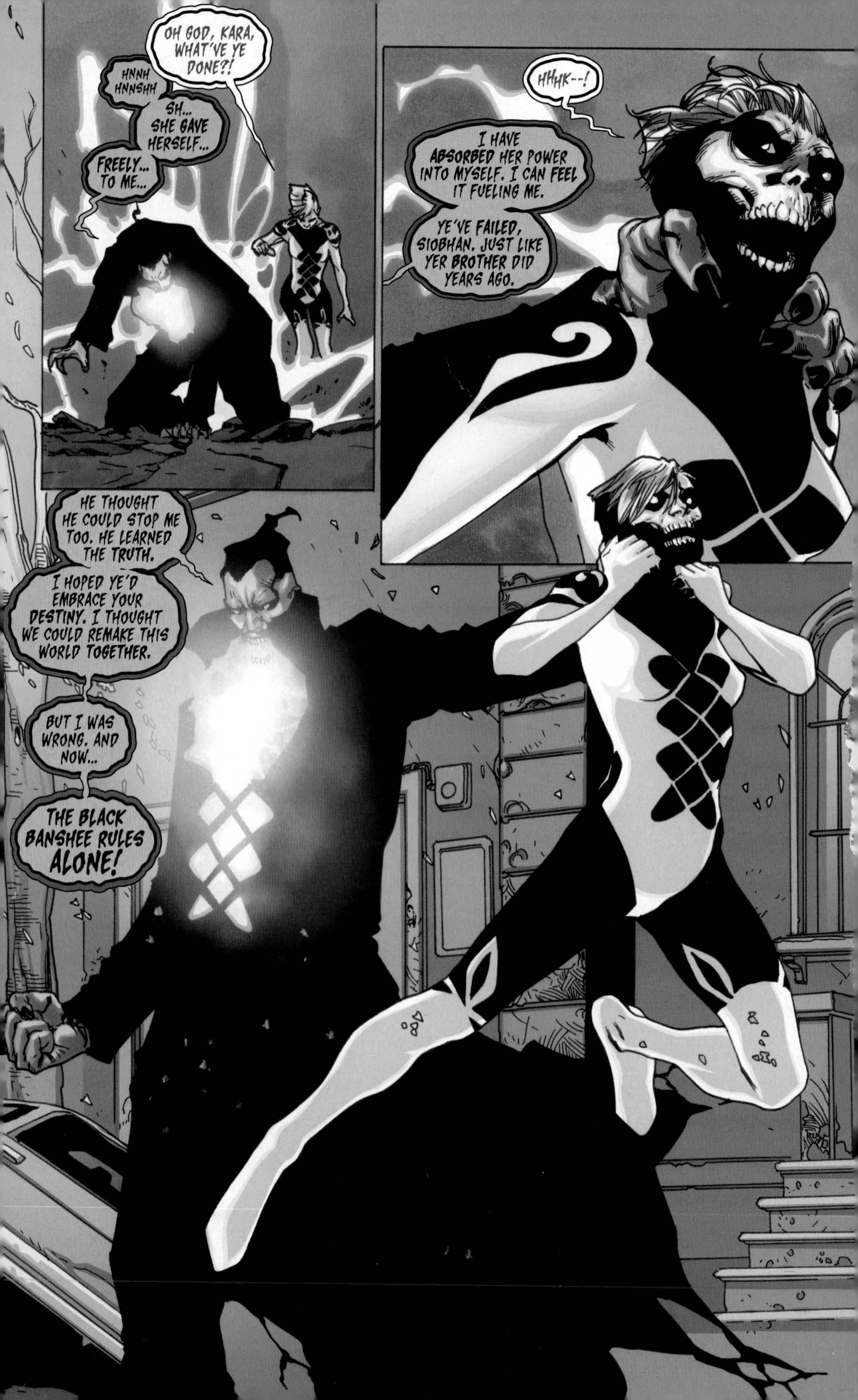
OH GOD, KARA, WHAT'VE YE DONE?!
HNNH HNNSHH
SH... SHE GAVE HERSELF...
FREELY... TO ME...
HHHK--!
I HAVE ABSORBED HER POWER INTO MYSELF. I CAN FEEL IT FUELING ME.
YE'VE FAILED, SIOBHAN. JUST LIKE YER BROTHER DID YEARS AGO.
HE THOUGHT HE COULD STOP ME TOO. HE LEARNED THE TRUTH.
I HOPED YE'D EMBRACE YOUR DESTINY. I THOUGHT WE COULD REMAKE THIS WORLD TOGETHER.
BUT I WAS WRONG. AND NOW...
THE BLACK BANSHEE RULES ALONE!

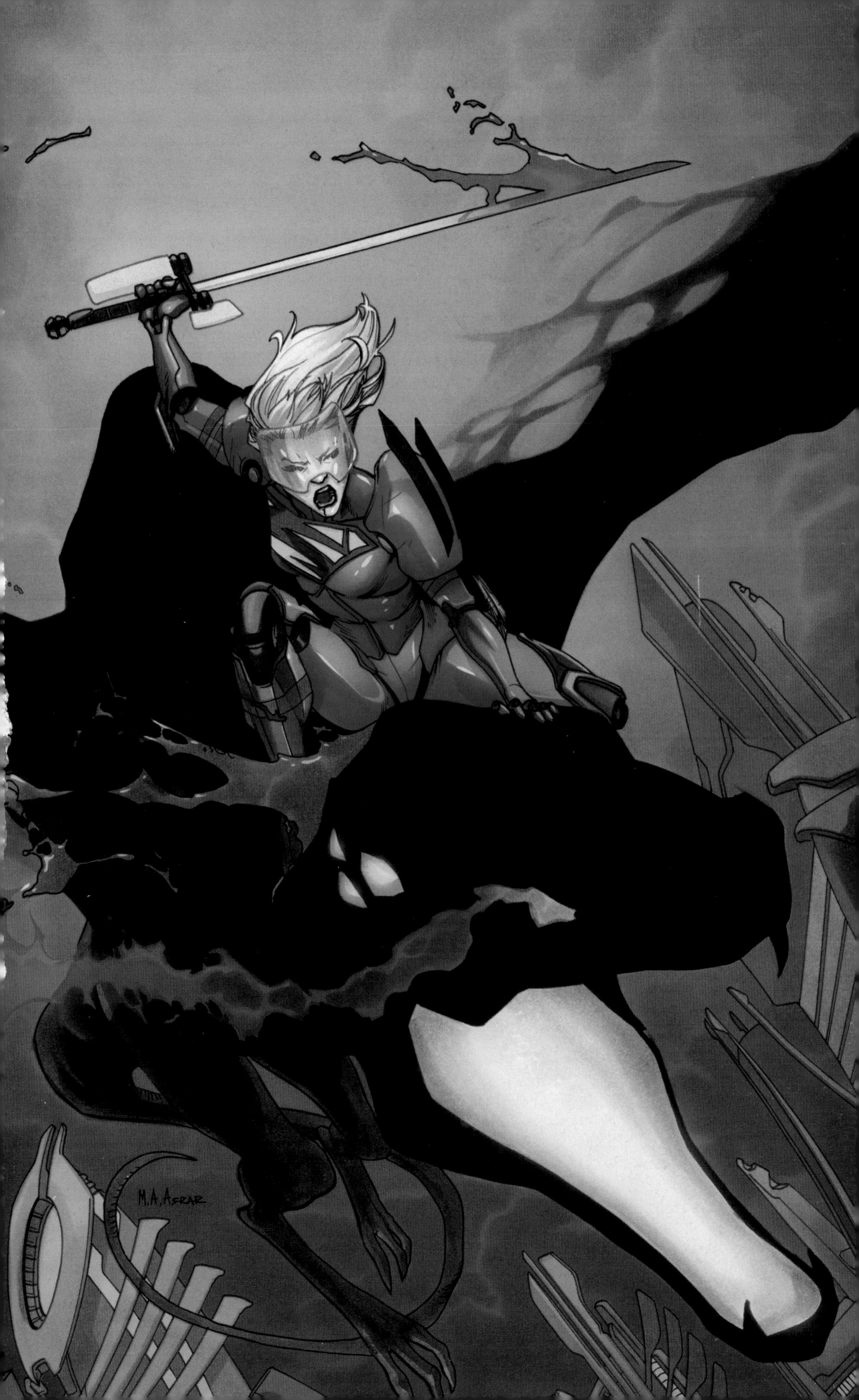
M.A.ASRAR

RESCUER

MICHAEL GREEN & MIKE JOHNSON writers **MAHMUD ASRAR** artist cover art by **MAHMUD ASRAR & DAVE McCAIG**

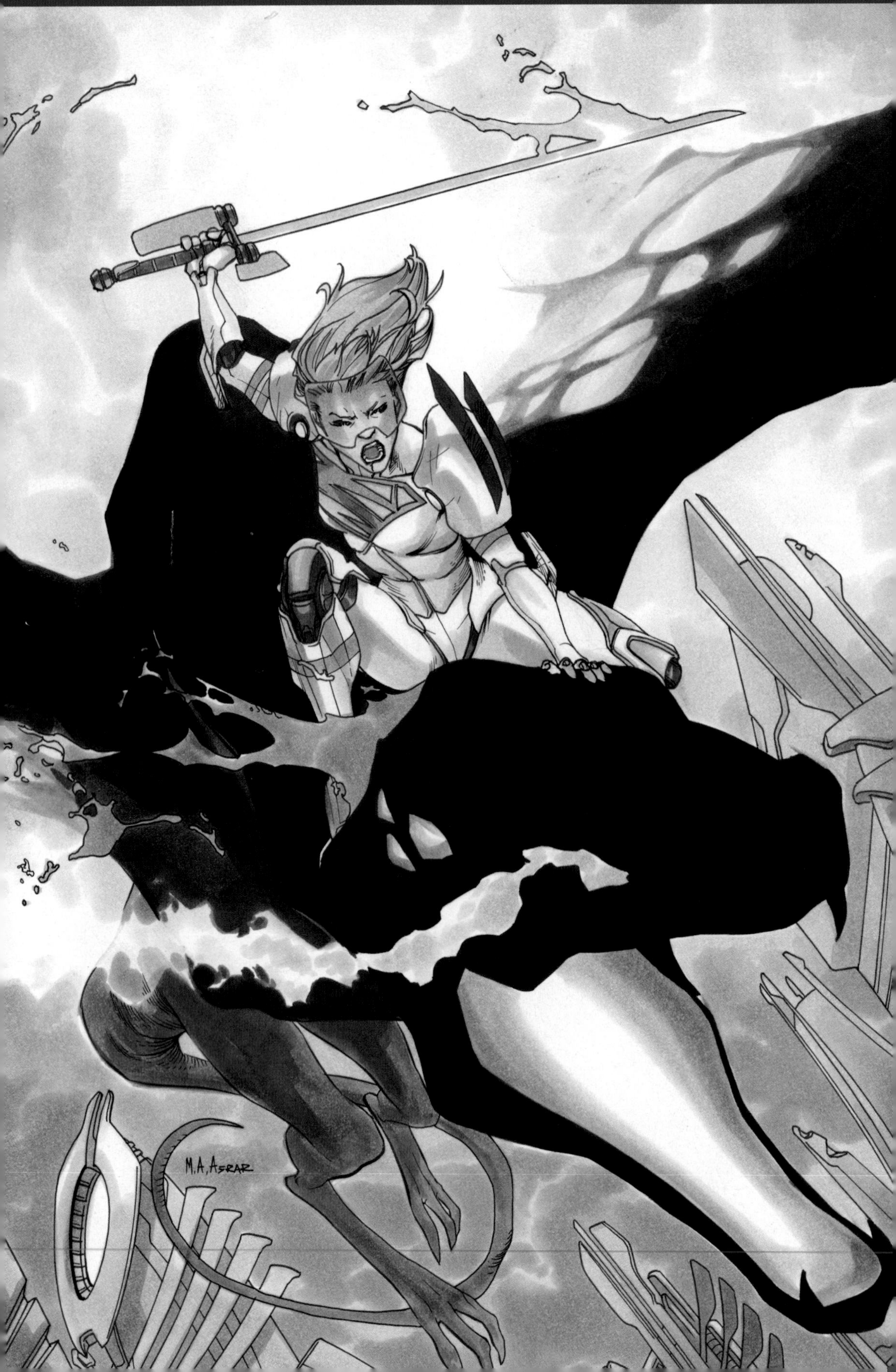
M.A. ASRAR

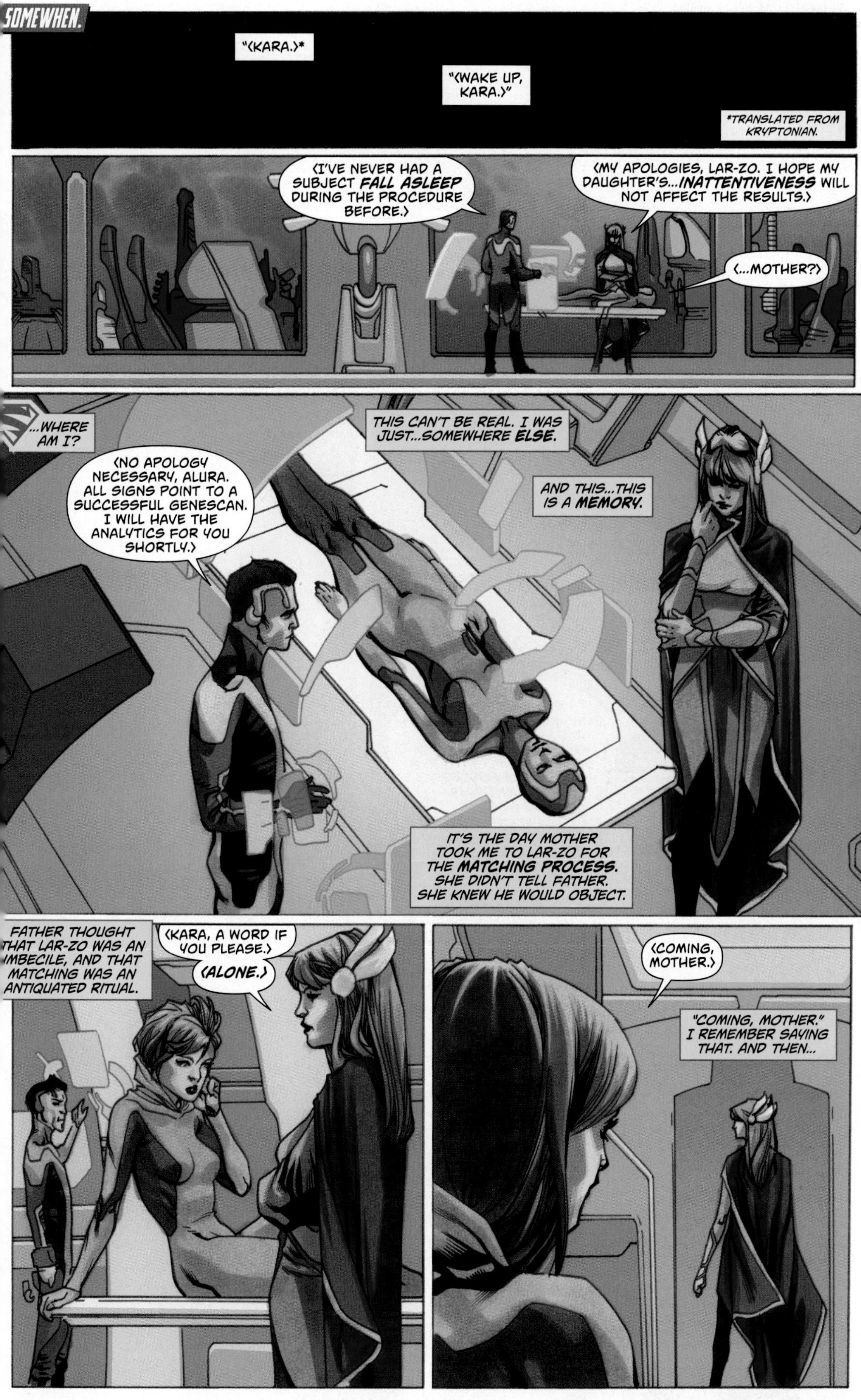
SOMEWHEN.
"‹KARA.›*
"‹WAKE UP, KARA.›"
*TRANSLATED FROM KRYPTONIAN.
‹I'VE NEVER HAD A SUBJECT FALL ASLEEP DURING THE PROCEDURE BEFORE.›
‹MY APOLOGIES, LAR-ZO. I HOPE MY DAUGHTER'S...INATTENTIVENESS WILL NOT AFFECT THE RESULTS.›
‹...MOTHER?›
...WHERE AM I?
THIS CAN'T BE REAL. I WAS JUST...SOMEWHERE ELSE.
‹NO APOLOGY NECESSARY, ALURA. ALL SIGNS POINT TO A SUCCESSFUL GENESCAN. I WILL HAVE THE ANALYTICS FOR YOU SHORTLY.›
AND THIS...THIS IS A MEMORY.
IT'S THE DAY MOTHER TOOK ME TO LAR-ZO FOR THE MATCHING PROCESS. SHE DIDN'T TELL FATHER. SHE KNEW HE WOULD OBJECT.
FATHER THOUGHT THAT LAR-ZO WAS AN IMBECILE, AND THAT MATCHING WAS AN ANTIQUATED RITUAL.
‹KARA, A WORD IF YOU PLEASE.›
‹ALONE.›
‹COMING, MOTHER.›
"COMING, MOTHER." I REMEMBER SAYING THAT. AND THEN...

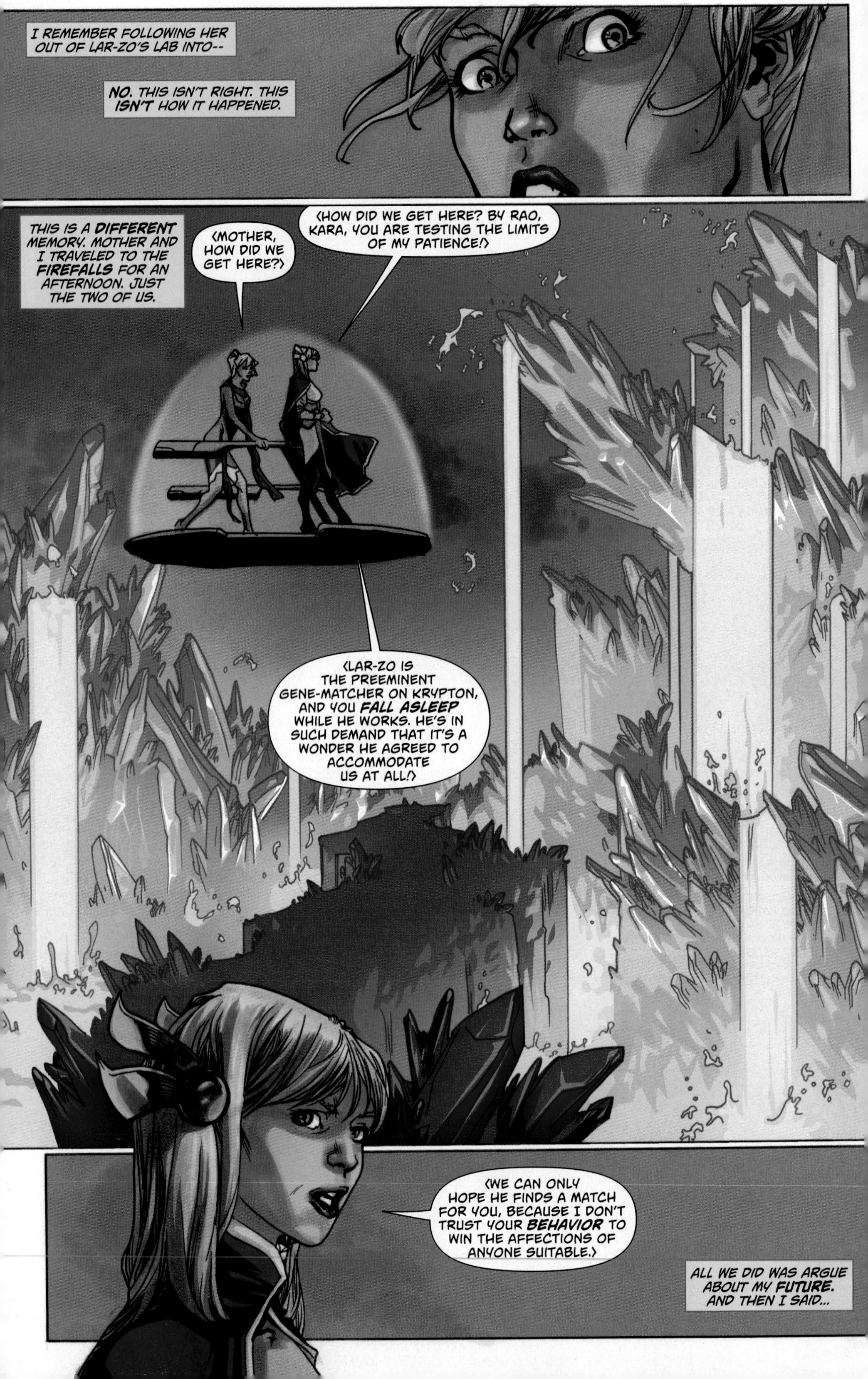
I REMEMBER FOLLOWING HER OUT OF LAR-ZO'S LAB INTO--
NO. THIS ISN'T RIGHT. THIS ISN'T HOW IT HAPPENED.
THIS IS A DIFFERENT MEMORY. MOTHER AND I TRAVELED TO THE FIREFALLS FOR AN AFTERNOON. JUST THE TWO OF US.
‹MOTHER, HOW DID WE GET HERE?›
‹HOW DID WE GET HERE? BY RAO, KARA, YOU ARE TESTING THE LIMITS OF MY PATIENCE!›
‹LAR-ZO IS THE PREEMINENT GENE-MATCHER ON KRYPTON, AND YOU FALL ASLEEP WHILE HE WORKS. HE'S IN SUCH DEMAND THAT IT'S A WONDER HE AGREED TO ACCOMMODATE US AT ALL!›
‹WE CAN ONLY HOPE HE FINDS A MATCH FOR YOU, BECAUSE I DON'T TRUST YOUR BEHAVIOR TO WIN THE AFFECTIONS OF ANYONE SUITABLE.›
ALL WE DID WAS ARGUE ABOUT MY FUTURE. AND THEN I SAID...

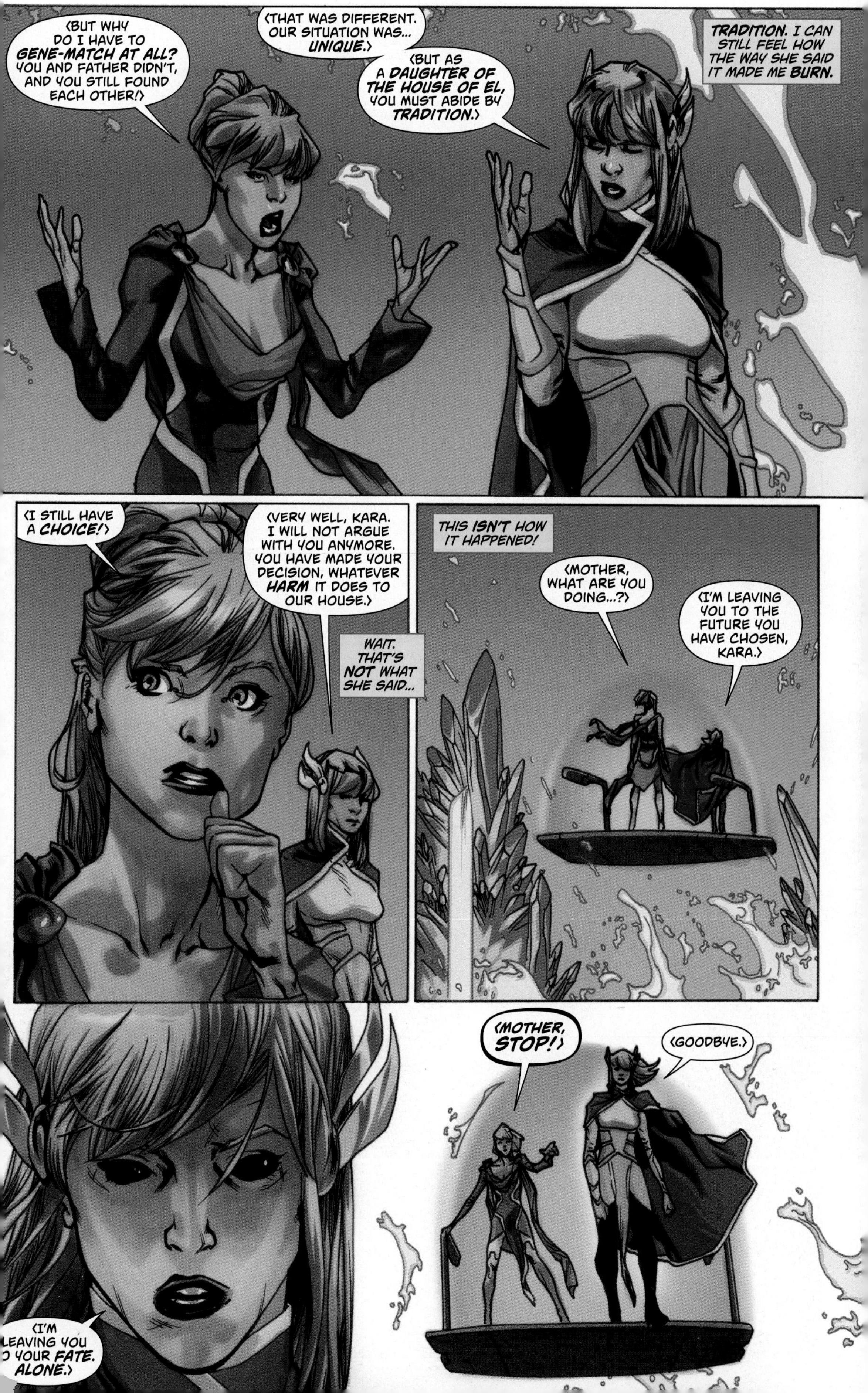
‹BUT WHY DO I HAVE TO GENE-MATCH AT ALL? YOU AND FATHER DIDN'T, AND YOU STILL FOUND EACH OTHER!›
‹THAT WAS DIFFERENT. OUR SITUATION WAS... UNIQUE.›
‹BUT AS A DAUGHTER OF THE HOUSE OF EL, YOU MUST ABIDE BY TRADITION.›
TRADITION. I CAN STILL FEEL HOW THE WAY SHE SAID IT MADE ME BURN.
‹I STILL HAVE A CHOICE!›
‹VERY WELL, KARA. I WILL NOT ARGUE WITH YOU ANYMORE. YOU HAVE MADE YOUR DECISION, WHATEVER HARM IT DOES TO OUR HOUSE.›
WAIT. THAT'S NOT WHAT SHE SAID...
THIS ISN'T HOW IT HAPPENED!
‹MOTHER, WHAT ARE YOU DOING...?›
‹I'M LEAVING YOU TO THE FUTURE YOU HAVE CHOSEN, KARA.›
‹MOTHER, STOP!›
‹GOODBYE.›
‹I'M LEAVING YOU O YOUR FATE. ALONE.›

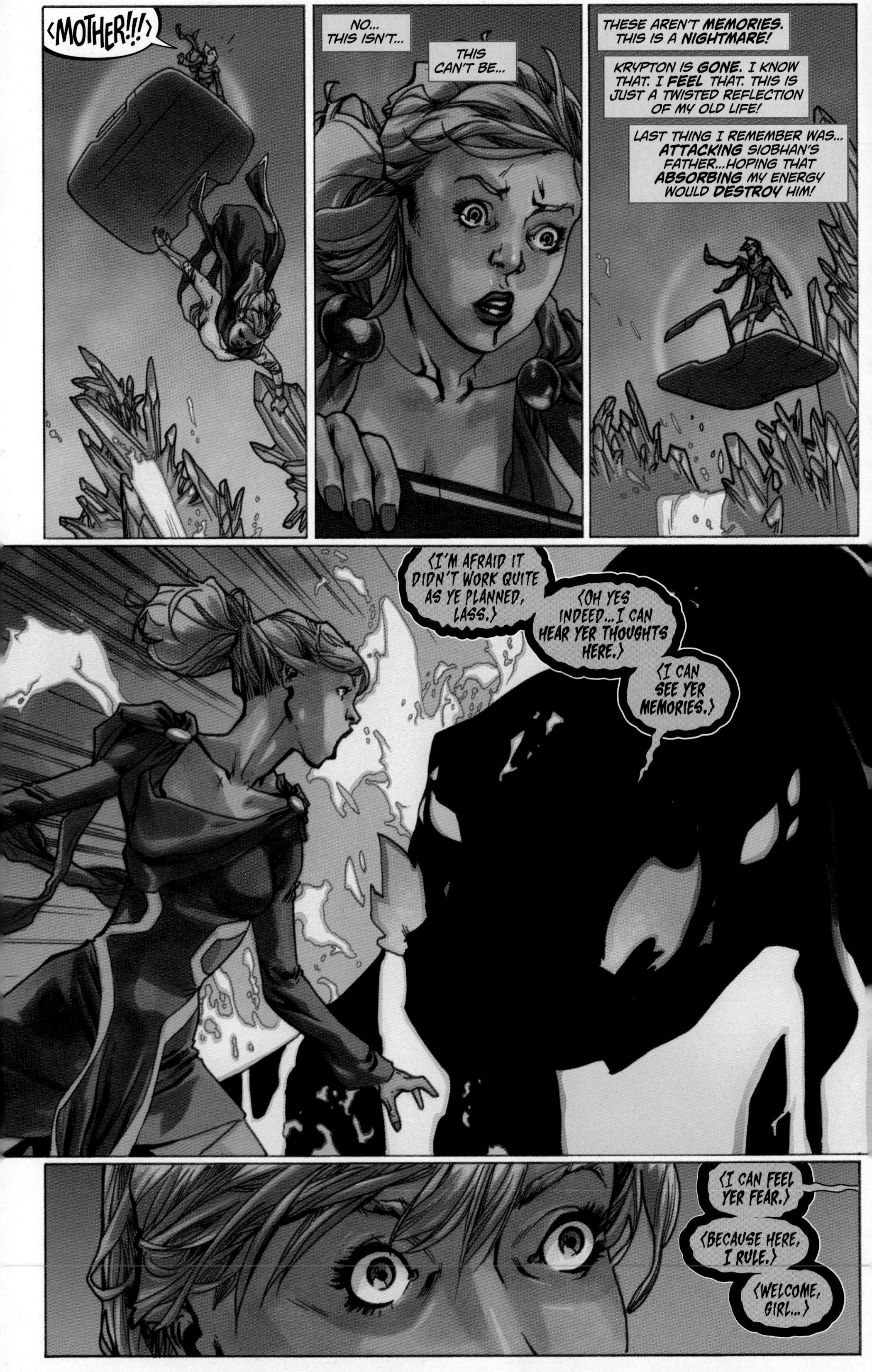
<MOTHER!!!>
NO... THIS ISN'T...
THIS CAN'T BE...
THESE AREN'T MEMORIES. THIS IS A NIGHTMARE!
KRYPTON IS GONE. I KNOW THAT. I FEEL THAT. THIS IS JUST A TWISTED REFLECTION OF MY OLD LIFE!
LAST THING I REMEMBER WAS... ATTACKING SIOBHAN'S FATHER...HOPING THAT ABSORBING MY ENERGY WOULD DESTROY HIM!
<I'M AFRAID IT DIDN'T WORK QUITE AS YE PLANNED, LASS.>
<OH YES INDEED...I CAN HEAR YER THOUGHTS HERE.>
<I CAN SEE YER MEMORIES.>
<I CAN FEEL YER FEAR.>
<BECAUSE HERE, I RULE.>
<WELCOME, GIRL...>

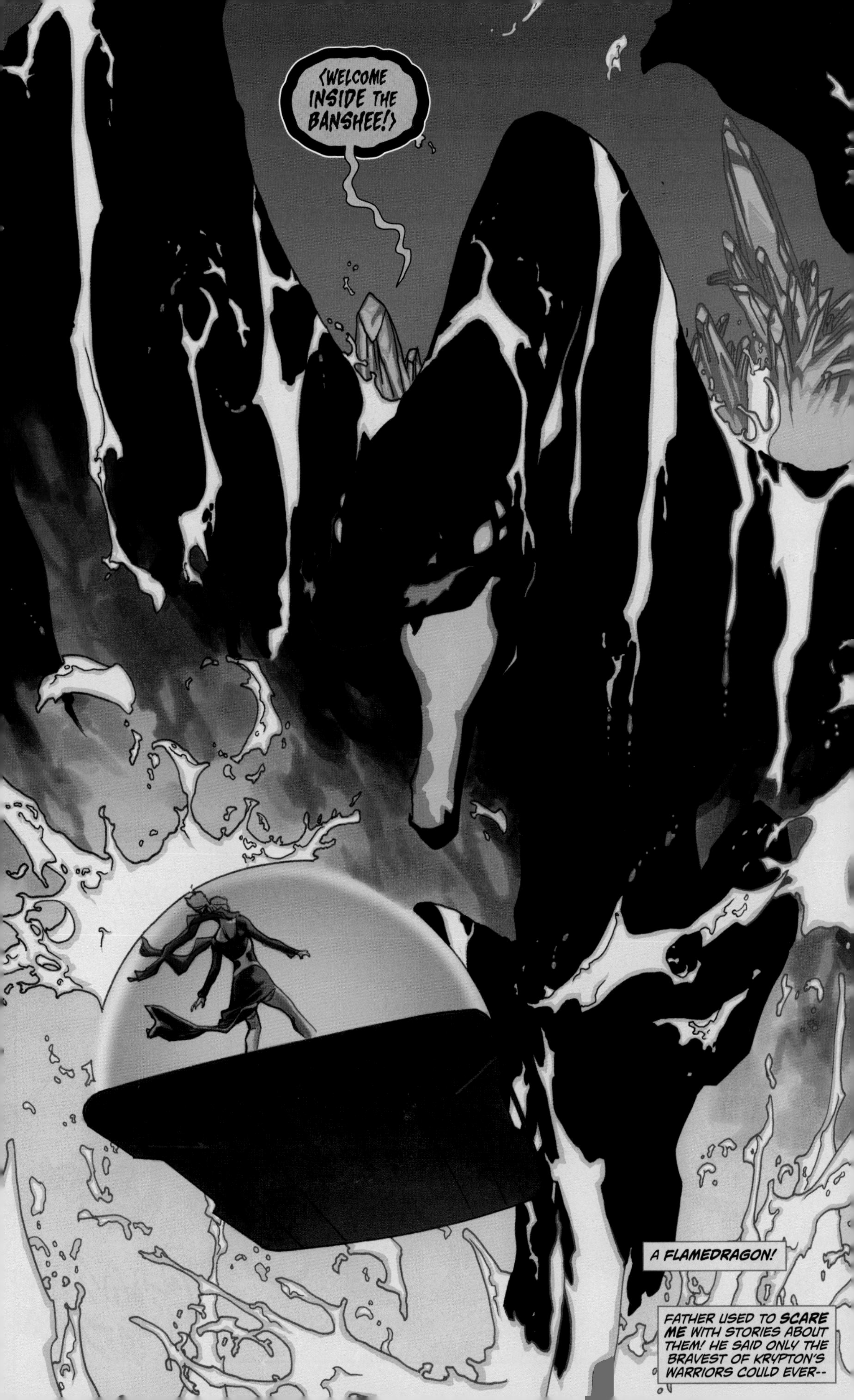

‹WELCOME INSIDE THE BANSHEE!›
A FLAMEDRAGON!
FATHER USED TO SCARE ME WITH STORIES ABOUT THEM! HE SAID ONLY THE BRAVEST OF KRYPTON'S WARRIORS COULD EVER--

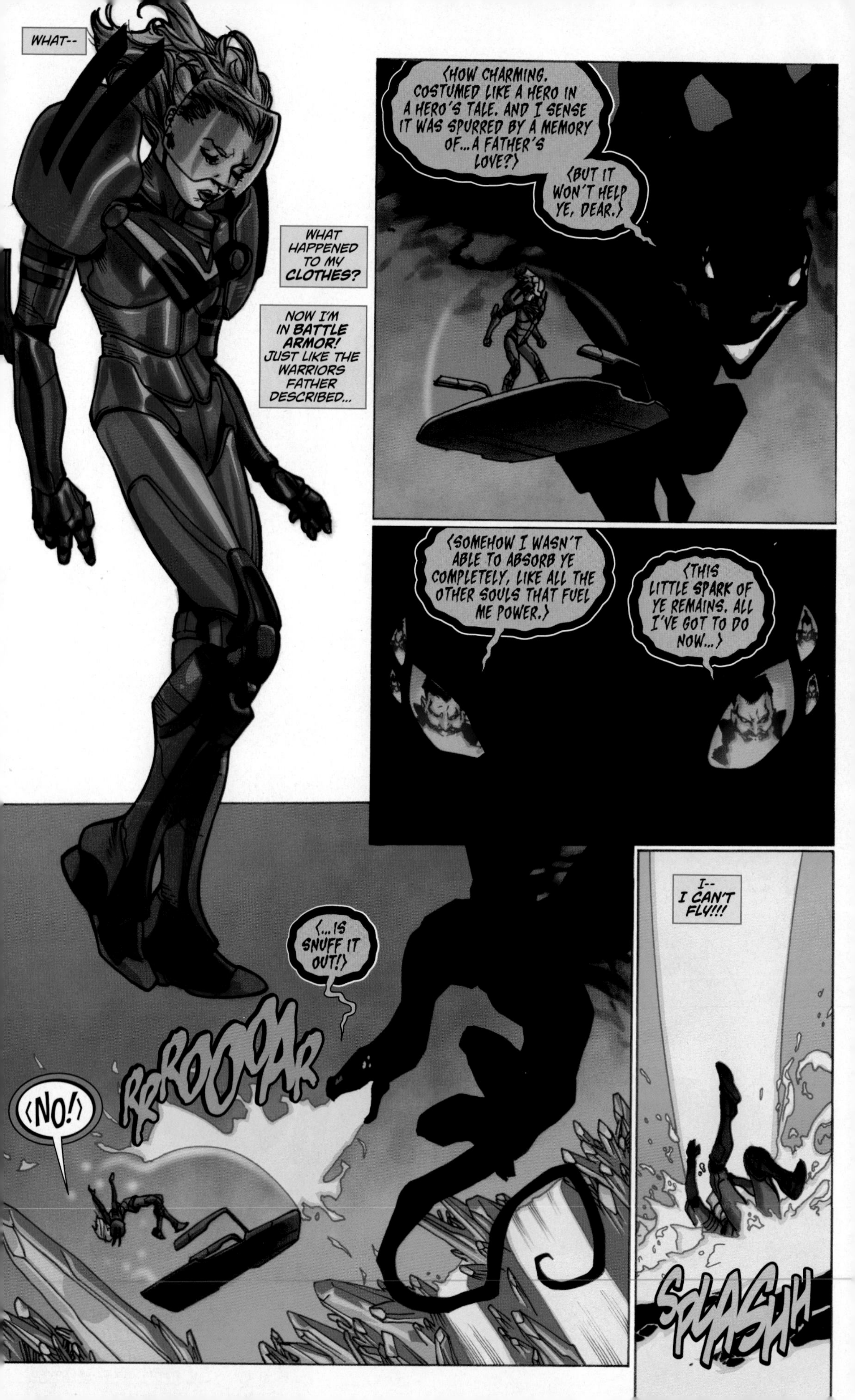
WHAT--
WHAT HAPPENED TO MY CLOTHES?
NOW I'M IN BATTLE ARMOR! JUST LIKE THE WARRIORS FATHER DESCRIBED...
⟨HOW CHARMING. COSTUMED LIKE A HERO IN A HERO'S TALE. AND I SENSE IT WAS SPURRED BY A MEMORY OF...A FATHER'S LOVE?⟩
⟨BUT IT WON'T HELP YE, DEAR.⟩
⟨SOMEHOW I WASN'T ABLE TO ABSORB YE COMPLETELY, LIKE ALL THE OTHER SOULS THAT FUEL ME POWER.⟩
⟨THIS LITTLE SPARK OF YE REMAINS. ALL I'VE GOT TO DO NOW...⟩
⟨...IS SNUFF IT OUT!⟩
RRROOOAR
⟨NO!⟩
I-- I CAN'T FLY!!!
SPLASHH

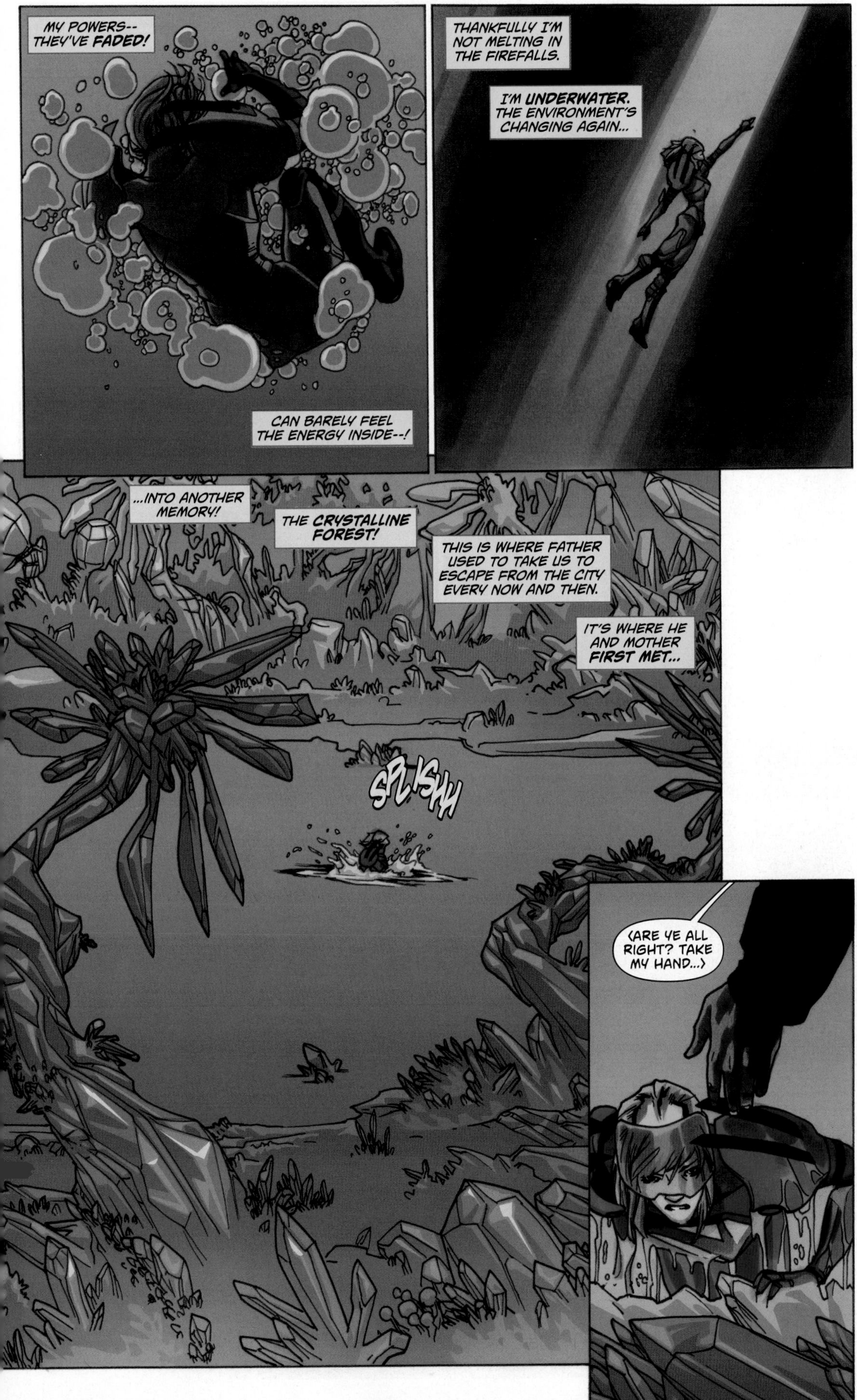
MY POWERS-- THEY'VE FADED!
CAN BARELY FEEL THE ENERGY INSIDE--!
THANKFULLY I'M NOT MELTING IN THE FIREFALLS.
I'M UNDERWATER. THE ENVIRONMENT'S CHANGING AGAIN...
...INTO ANOTHER MEMORY!
THE CRYSTALLINE FOREST!
THIS IS WHERE FATHER USED TO TAKE US TO ESCAPE FROM THE CITY EVERY NOW AND THEN.
IT'S WHERE HE AND MOTHER FIRST MET...
SPLISHH
<ARE YE ALL RIGHT? TAKE MY HAND...>

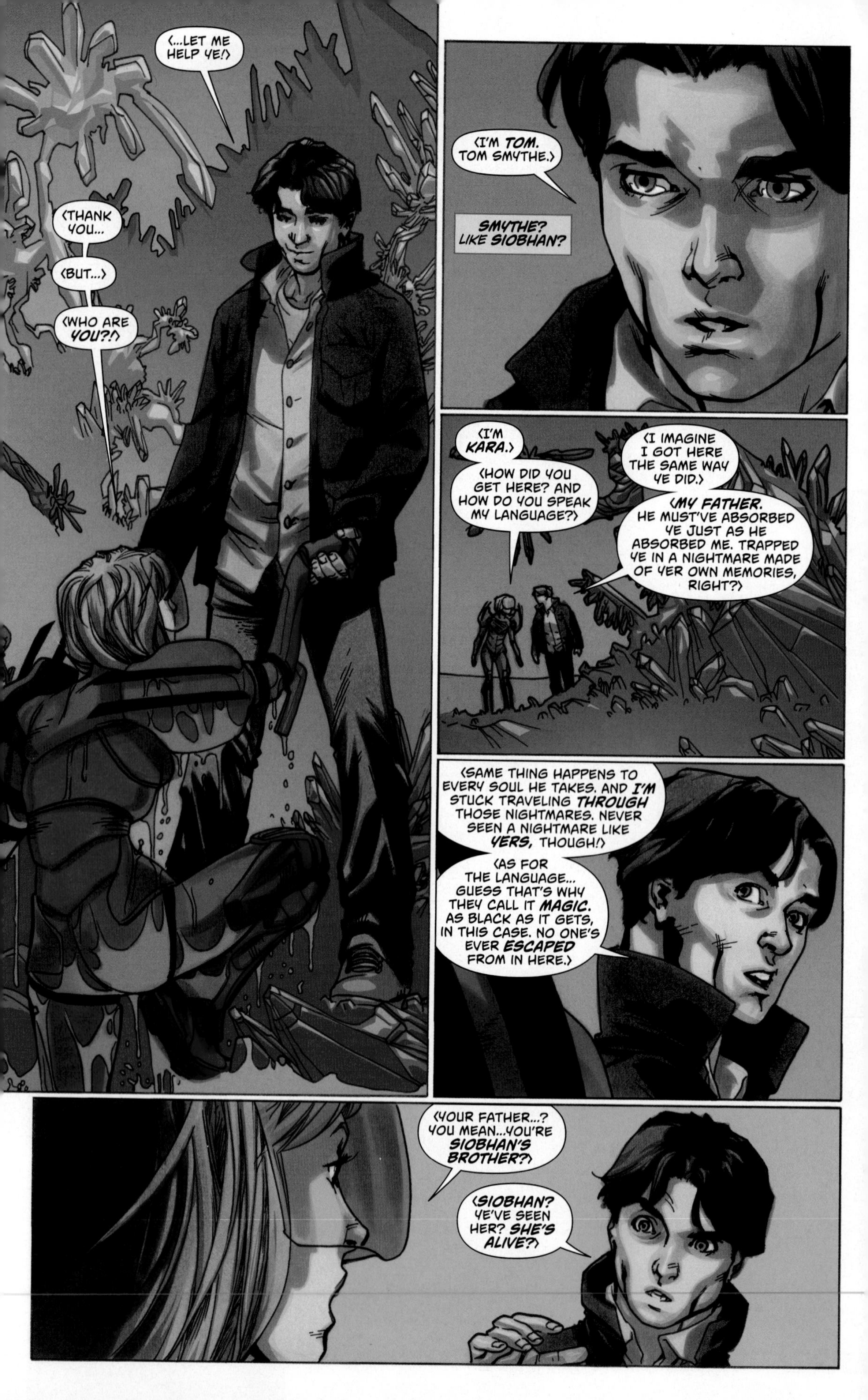

⟨...LET ME HELP YE!⟩
⟨THANK YOU...
⟨BUT...⟩
⟨WHO ARE YOU?!⟩
⟨I'M TOM. TOM SMYTHE.⟩
SMYTHE? LIKE SIOBHAN?
⟨I'M KARA.⟩
⟨HOW DID YOU GET HERE? AND HOW DO YOU SPEAK MY LANGUAGE?⟩
⟨I IMAGINE I GOT HERE THE SAME WAY YE DID.⟩
⟨MY FATHER. HE MUST'VE ABSORBED YE JUST AS HE ABSORBED ME. TRAPPED YE IN A NIGHTMARE MADE OF YER OWN MEMORIES, RIGHT?⟩
⟨SAME THING HAPPENS TO EVERY SOUL HE TAKES. AND I'M STUCK TRAVELING THROUGH THOSE NIGHTMARES. NEVER SEEN A NIGHTMARE LIKE YERS, THOUGH!⟩
⟨AS FOR THE LANGUAGE... GUESS THAT'S WHY THEY CALL IT MAGIC. AS BLACK AS IT GETS, IN THIS CASE. NO ONE'S EVER ESCAPED FROM IN HERE.⟩
⟨YOUR FATHER...? YOU MEAN...YOU'RE SIOBHAN'S BROTHER?⟩
⟨SIOBHAN? YE'VE SEEN HER? SHE'S ALIVE?⟩

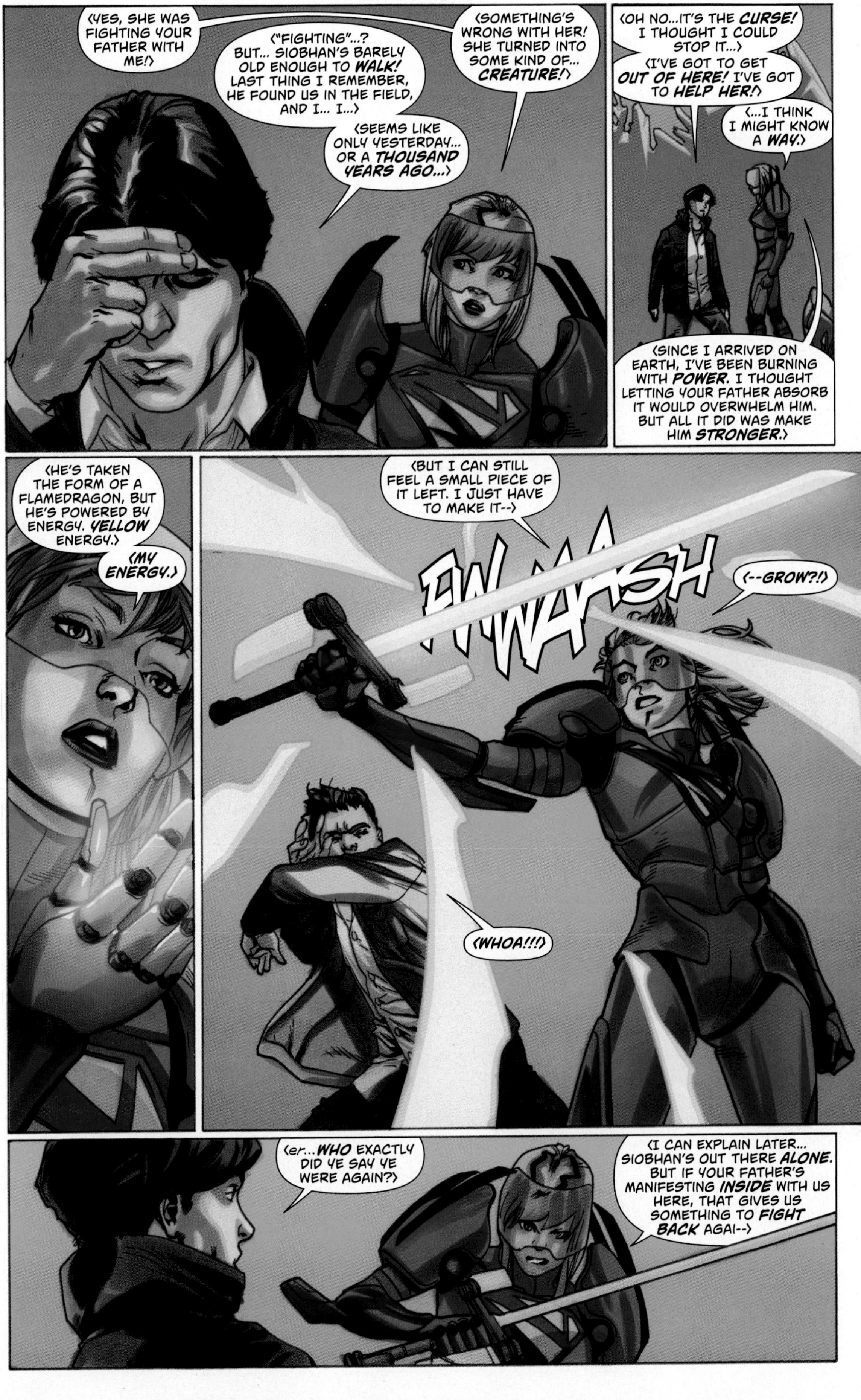

‹YES, SHE WAS FIGHTING YOUR FATHER WITH ME!›
‹"FIGHTING"...? BUT... SIOBHAN'S BARELY OLD ENOUGH TO WALK! LAST THING I REMEMBER, HE FOUND US IN THE FIELD, AND I... I...›
‹SEEMS LIKE ONLY YESTERDAY... OR A THOUSAND YEARS AGO...›
‹SOMETHING'S WRONG WITH HER! SHE TURNED INTO SOME KIND OF... CREATURE!›
‹OH NO...IT'S THE CURSE! I THOUGHT I COULD STOP IT...›
‹I'VE GOT TO GET OUT OF HERE! I'VE GOT TO HELP HER!›
‹...I THINK I MIGHT KNOW A WAY.›
‹SINCE I ARRIVED ON EARTH, I'VE BEEN BURNING WITH POWER. I THOUGHT LETTING YOUR FATHER ABSORB IT WOULD OVERWHELM HIM. BUT ALL IT DID WAS MAKE HIM STRONGER.›
‹HE'S TAKEN THE FORM OF A FLAMEDRAGON, BUT HE'S POWERED BY ENERGY. YELLOW ENERGY.›
‹MY ENERGY.›
‹BUT I CAN STILL FEEL A SMALL PIECE OF IT LEFT. I JUST HAVE TO MAKE IT--›
FWAASH
‹--GROW?!›
‹WHOA!!!›
‹er...WHO EXACTLY DID YE SAY YE WERE AGAIN?›
‹I CAN EXPLAIN LATER... SIOBHAN'S OUT THERE ALONE. BUT IF YOUR FATHER'S MANIFESTING INSIDE WITH US HERE, THAT GIVES US SOMETHING TO FIGHT BACK AGAI--›

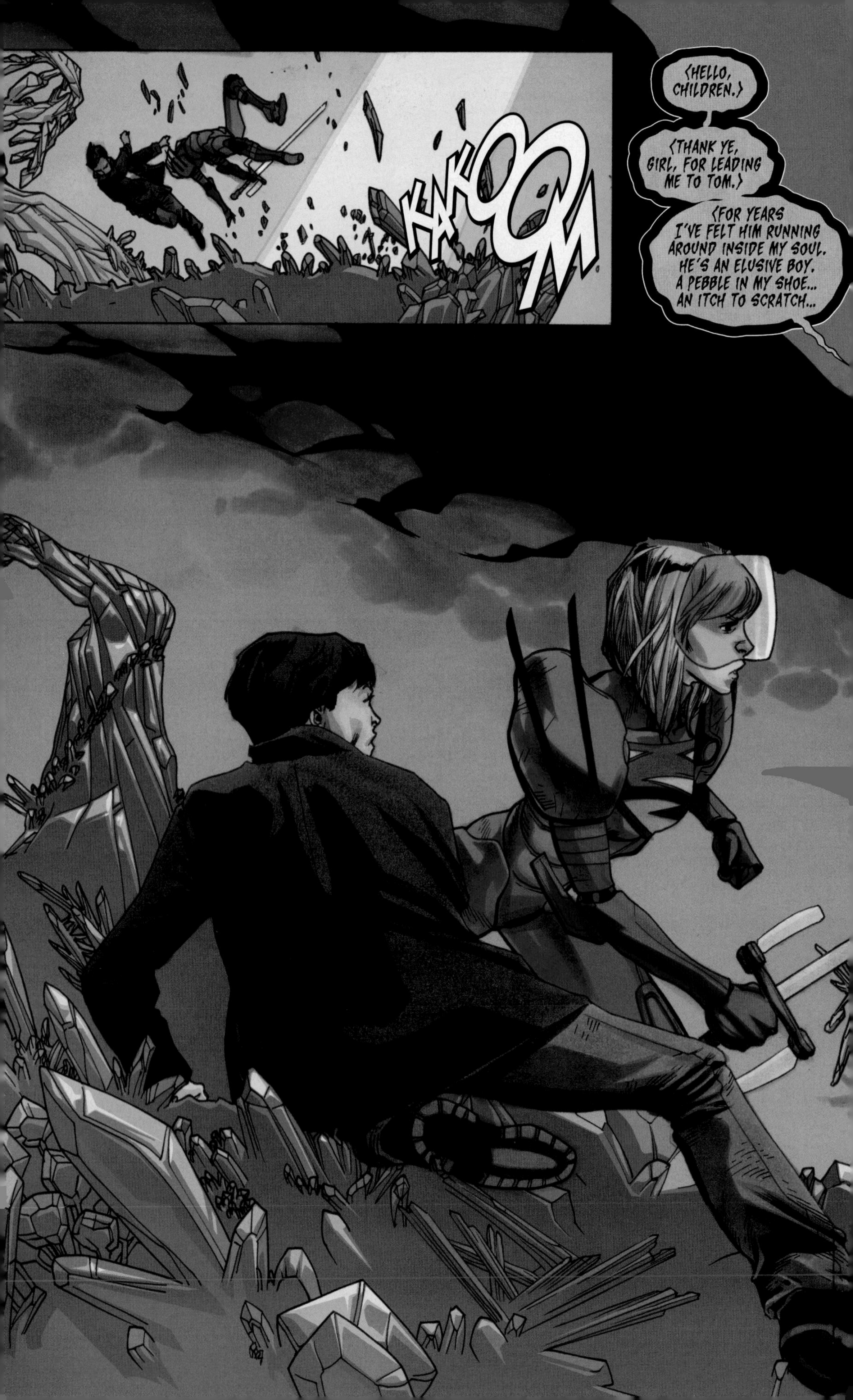
KAKOOM
<HELLO, CHILDREN.>
<THANK YE, GIRL, FOR LEADING ME TO TOM.>
<FOR YEARS I'VE FELT HIM RUNNING AROUND INSIDE MY SOUL. HE'S AN ELUSIVE BOY. A PEBBLE IN MY SHOE... AN ITCH TO SCRATCH...

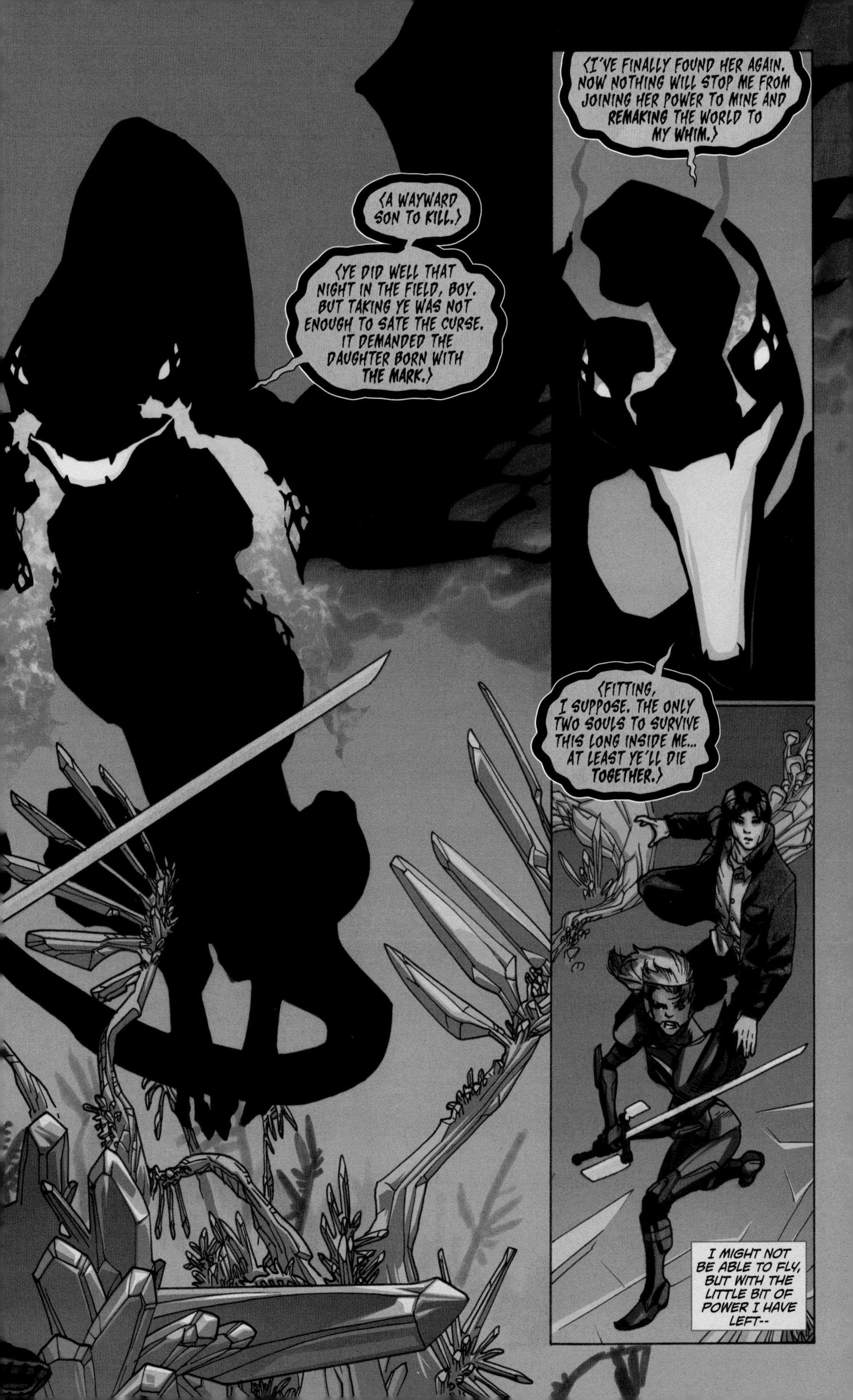
<A WAYWARD SON TO KILL.>
<YE DID WELL THAT NIGHT IN THE FIELD, BOY. BUT TAKING YE WAS NOT ENOUGH TO SATE THE CURSE. IT DEMANDED THE DAUGHTER BORN WITH THE MARK.>
<I'VE FINALLY FOUND HER AGAIN. NOW NOTHING WILL STOP ME FROM JOINING HER POWER TO MINE AND REMAKING THE WORLD TO MY WHIM.>
<FITTING, I SUPPOSE. THE ONLY TWO SOULS TO SURVIVE THIS LONG INSIDE ME... AT LEAST YE'LL DIE TOGETHER.>
I MIGHT NOT BE ABLE TO FLY, BUT WITH THE LITTLE BIT OF POWER I HAVE LEFT--

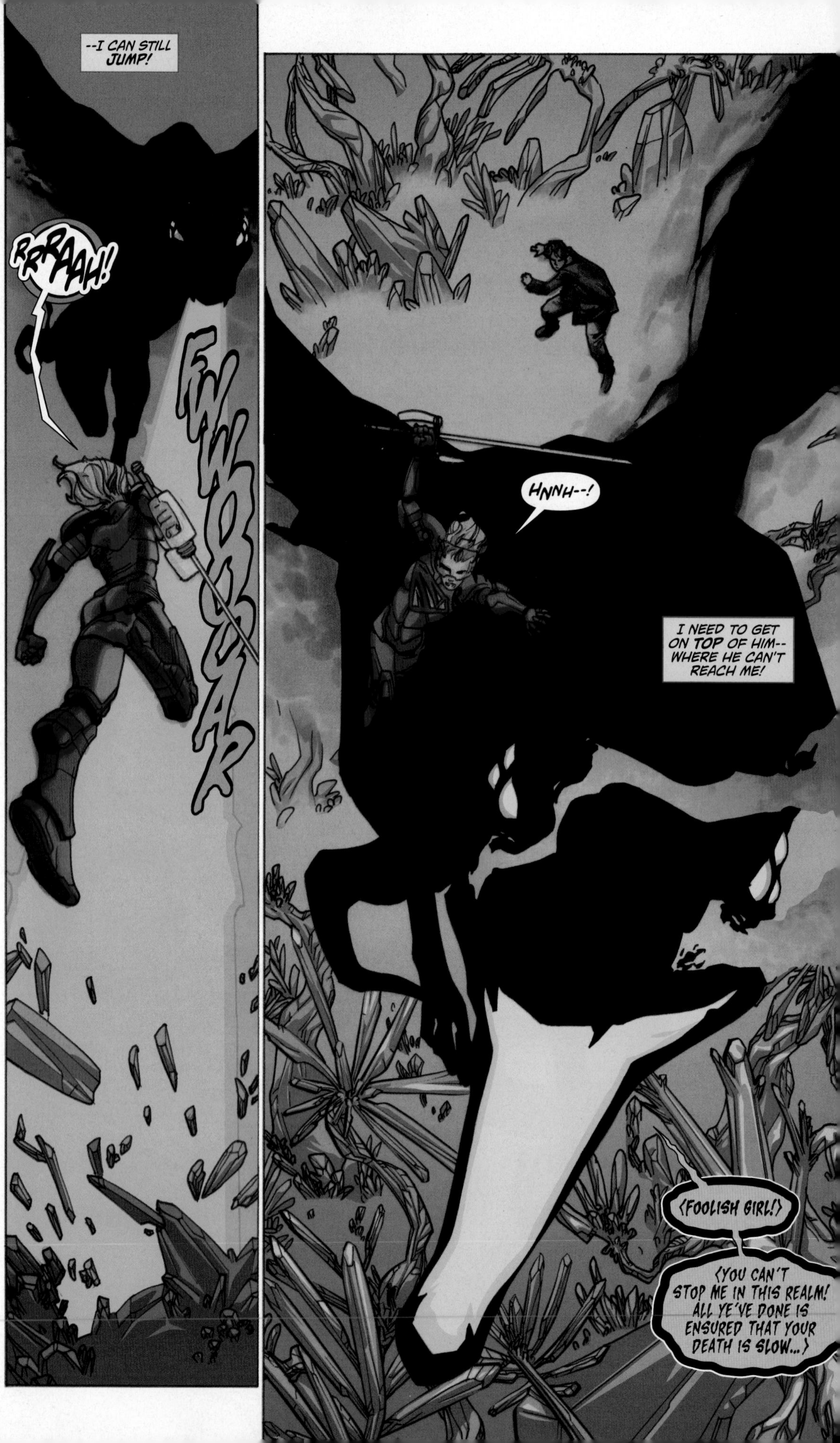
--I CAN STILL JUMP!
RRRAAAH!
FWOOSHAR
HNNH--!
I NEED TO GET ON TOP OF HIM-- WHERE HE CAN'T REACH ME!
⟨FOOLISH GIRL!⟩
⟨YOU CAN'T STOP ME IN THIS REALM! ALL YE'VE DONE IS ENSURED THAT YOUR DEATH IS SLOW...⟩

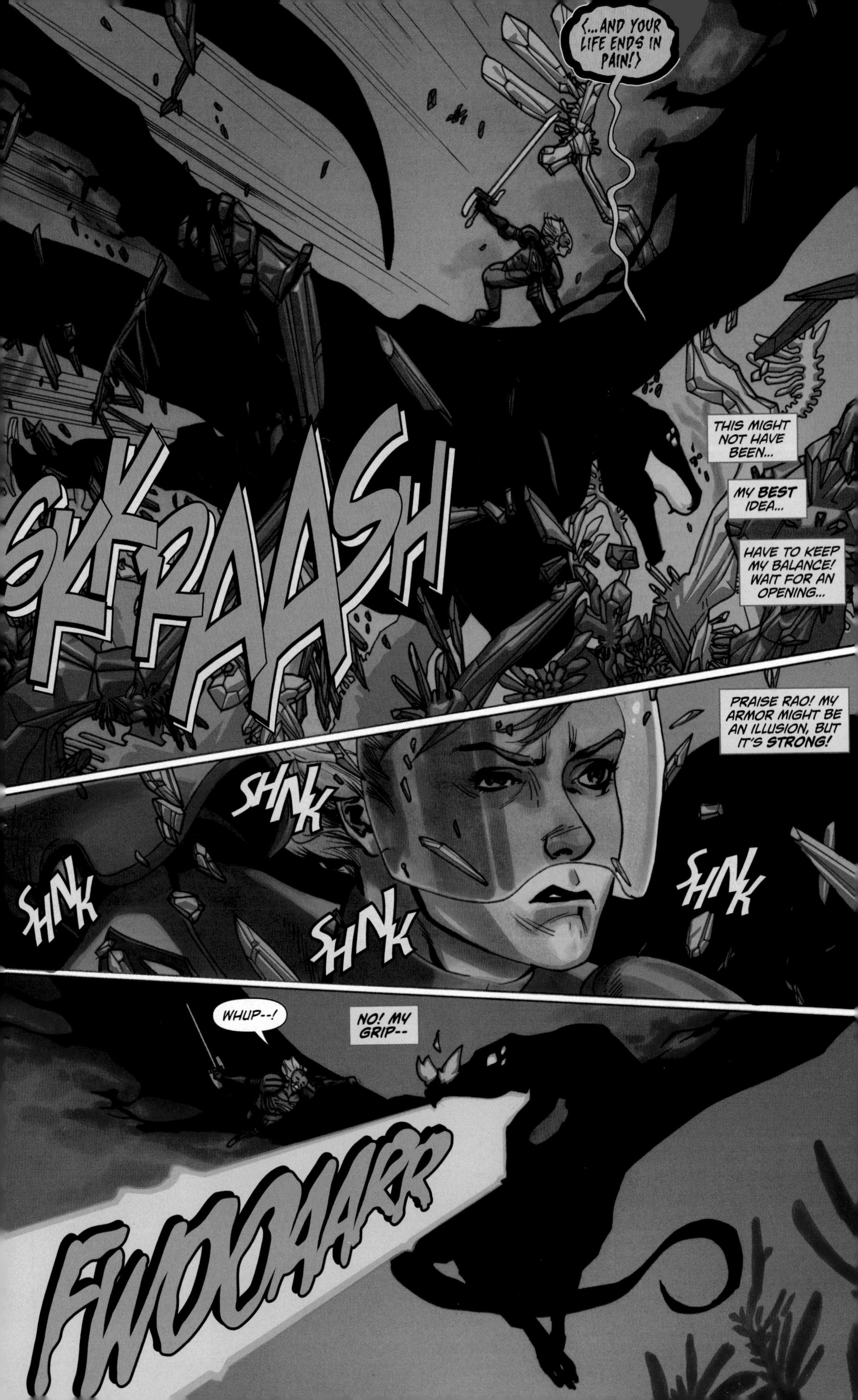

⟨...AND YOUR LIFE ENDS IN PAIN!⟩
SKKRAASH
THIS MIGHT NOT HAVE BEEN...
MY BEST IDEA...
HAVE TO KEEP MY BALANCE! WAIT FOR AN OPENING...
PRAISE RAO! MY ARMOR MIGHT BE AN ILLUSION, BUT IT'S STRONG!
SHNK
SHNK
SHNK
SHNK
WHUP--!
NO! MY GRIP--
FWOOAARR

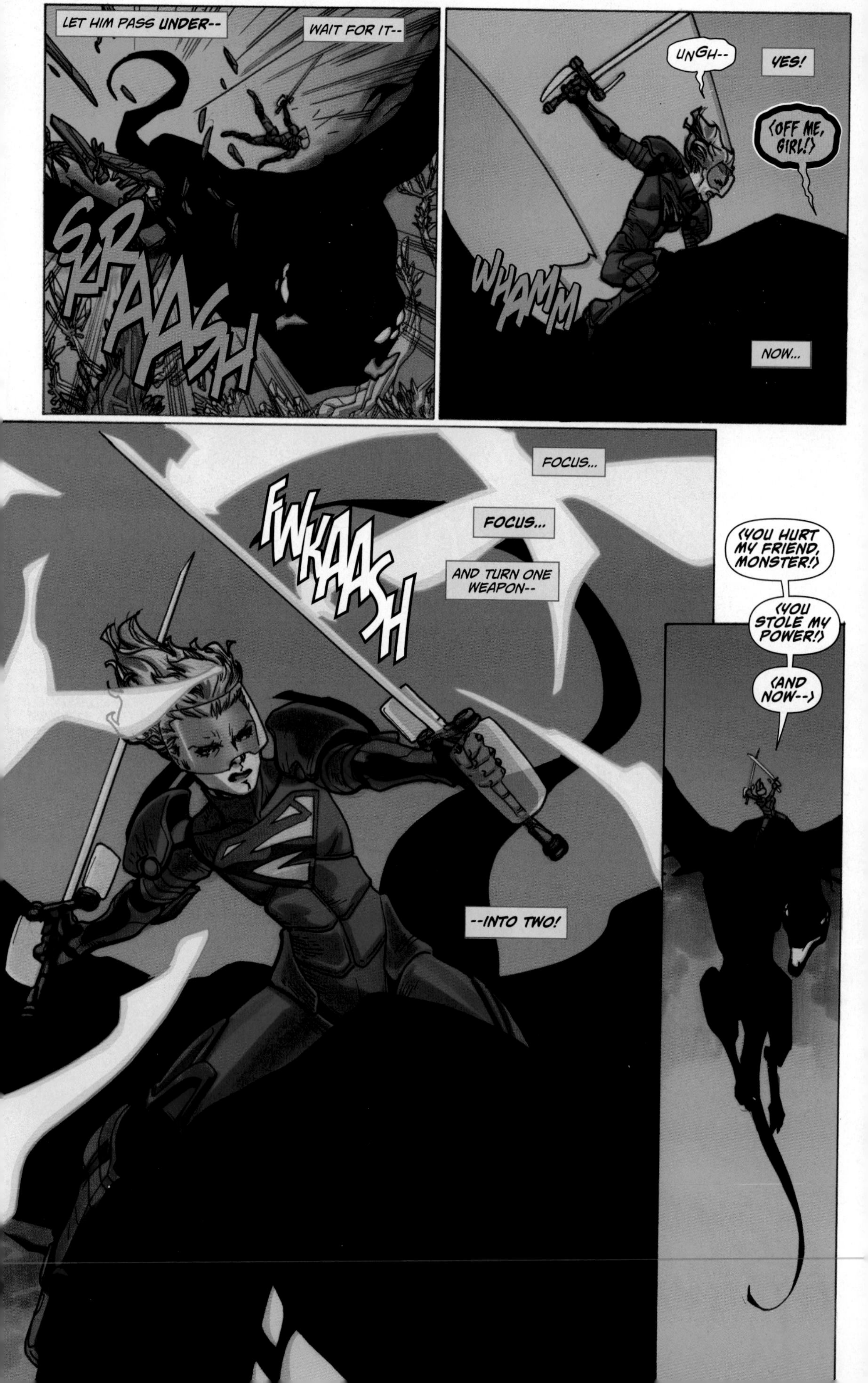
LET HIM PASS UNDER--
WAIT FOR IT--
SKRAASH
UNGH--
YES!
‹OFF ME, GIRL!›
WHAMM
NOW...
FOCUS...
FWKAASH
FOCUS...
AND TURN ONE WEAPON--
--INTO TWO!
‹YOU HURT MY FRIEND, MONSTER!›
‹YOU STOLE MY POWER!›
‹AND NOW--›

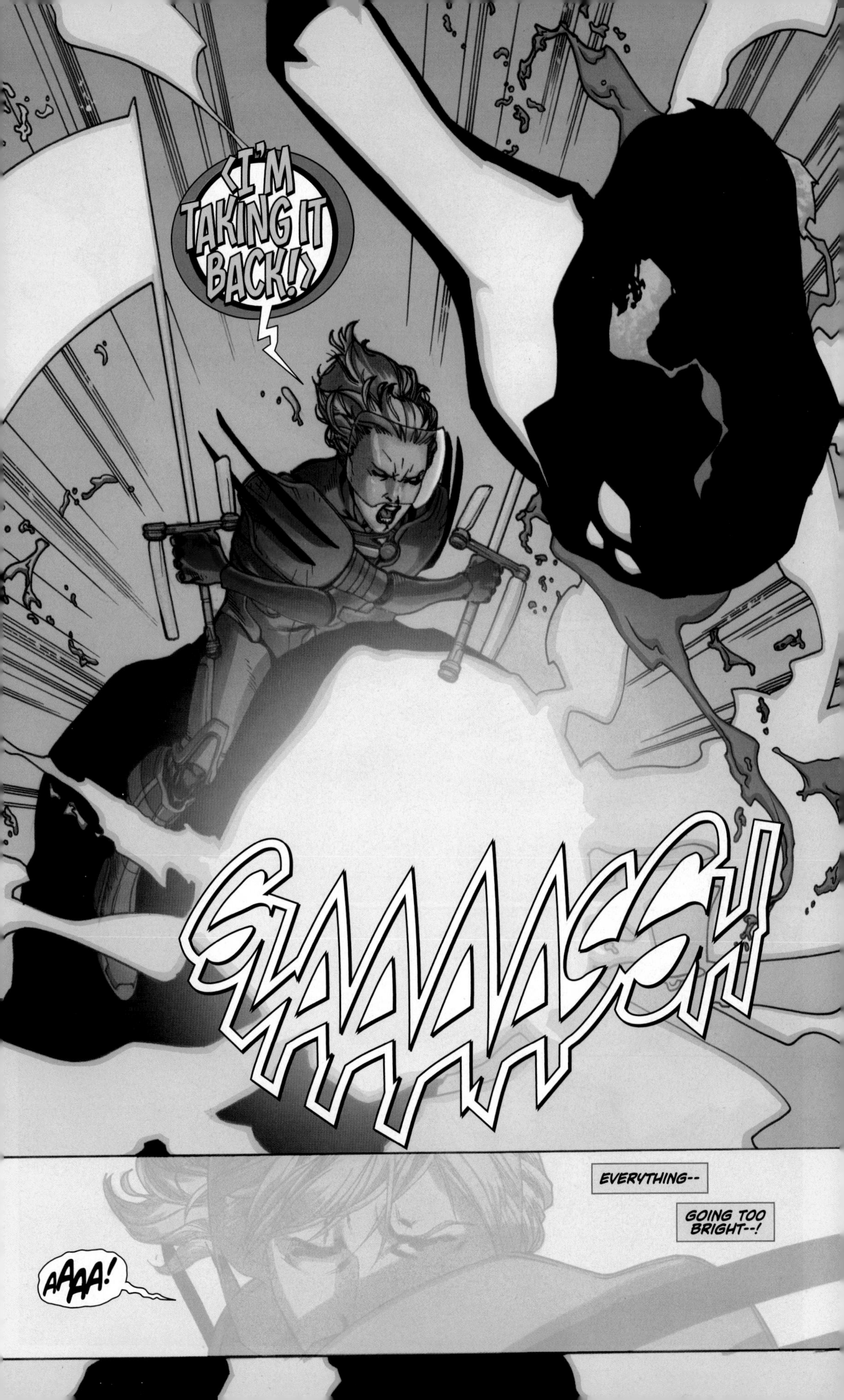
‹I'M TAKING IT BACK!›
SHAAAACCH
EVERYTHING--
GOING TOO BRIGHT--!
AAAA!

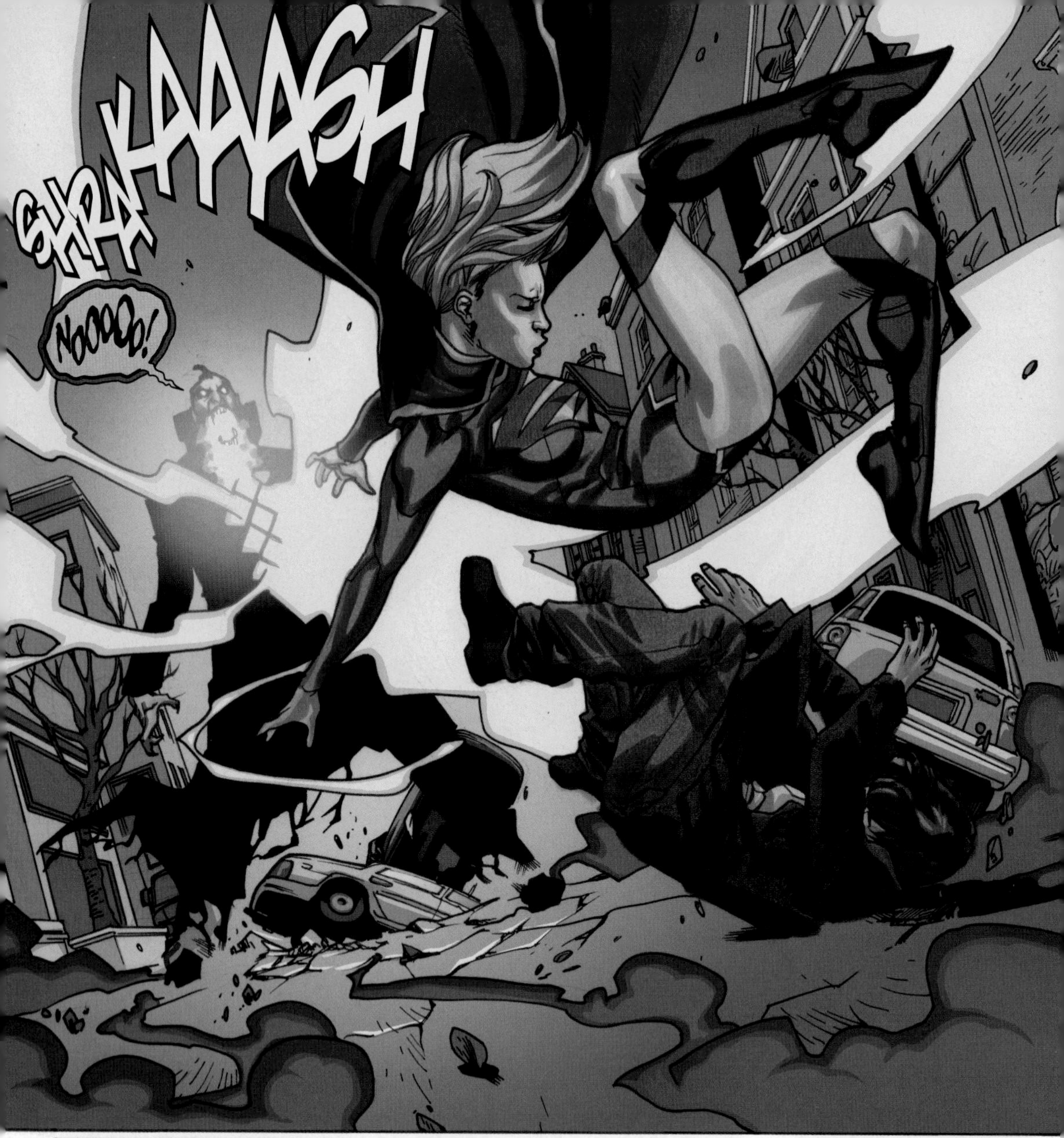
SHRAKAAASH
NOOOOO!
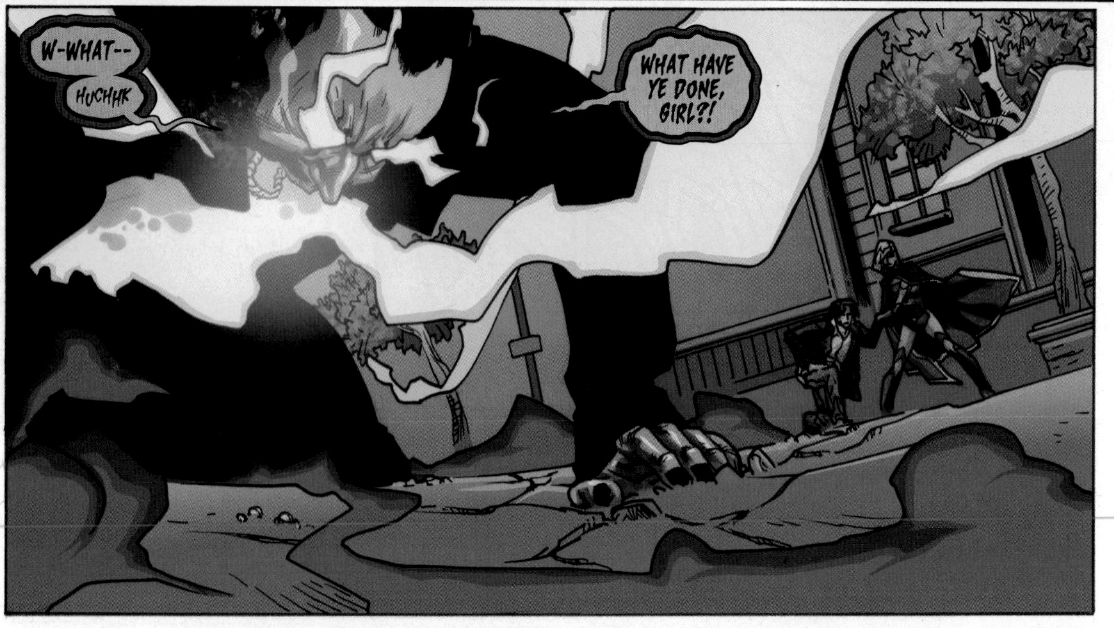
W-WHAT--
HUCHHK
WHAT HAVE YE DONE, GIRL?!

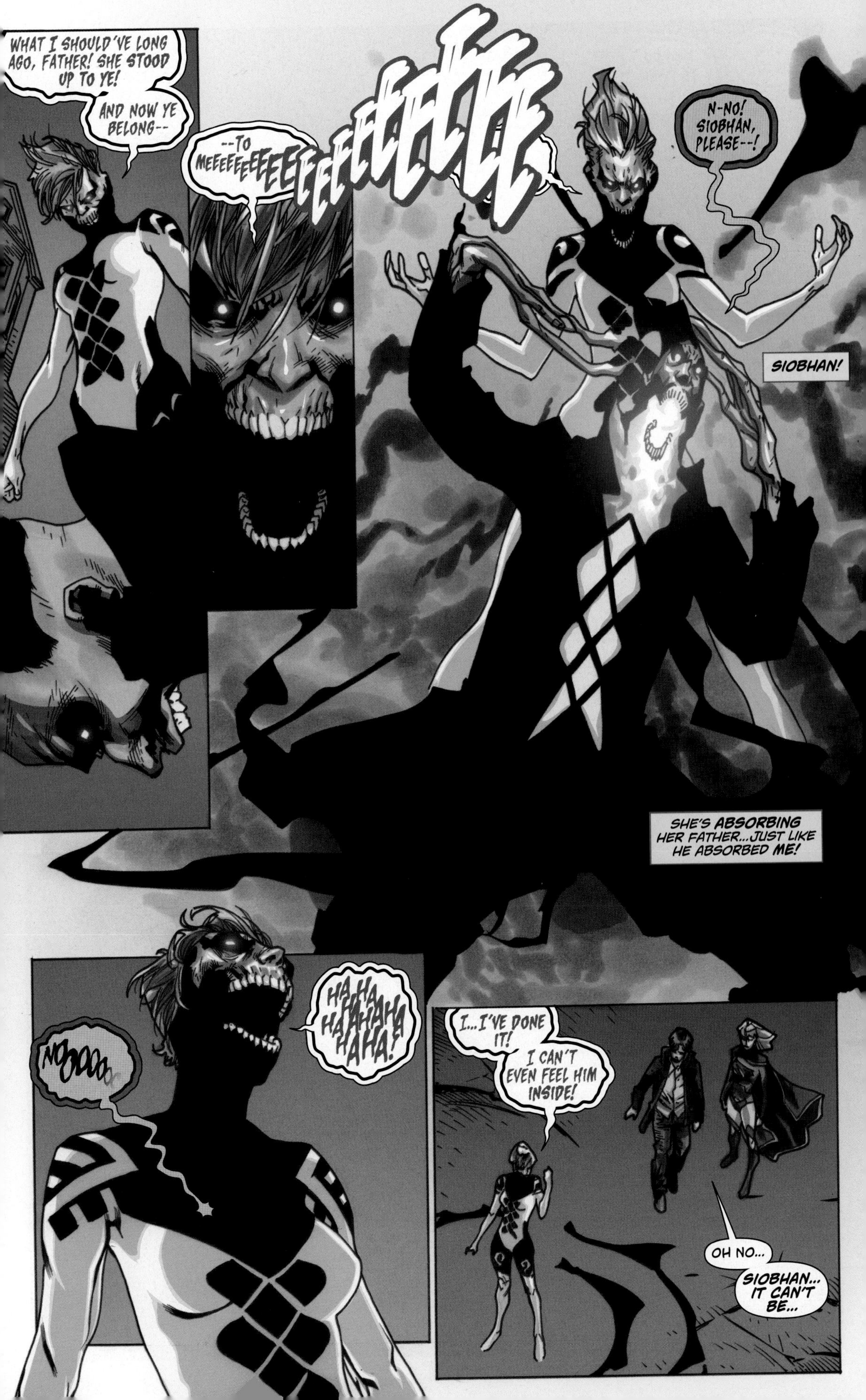
WHAT I SHOULD'VE LONG AGO, FATHER! SHE STOOD UP TO YE!
AND NOW YE BELONG--
--TO MEEEEEEEEEEEEEEEEEEEEE
N-NO! SIOBHAN, PLEASE--!
SIOBHAN!
SHE'S ABSORBING HER FATHER...JUST LIKE HE ABSORBED ME!
HA HA HAHAHAHA HAHA!
NOOOOOO
I...I'VE DONE IT!
I CAN'T EVEN FEEL HIM INSIDE!
OH NO...
SIOBHAN... IT CAN'T BE...

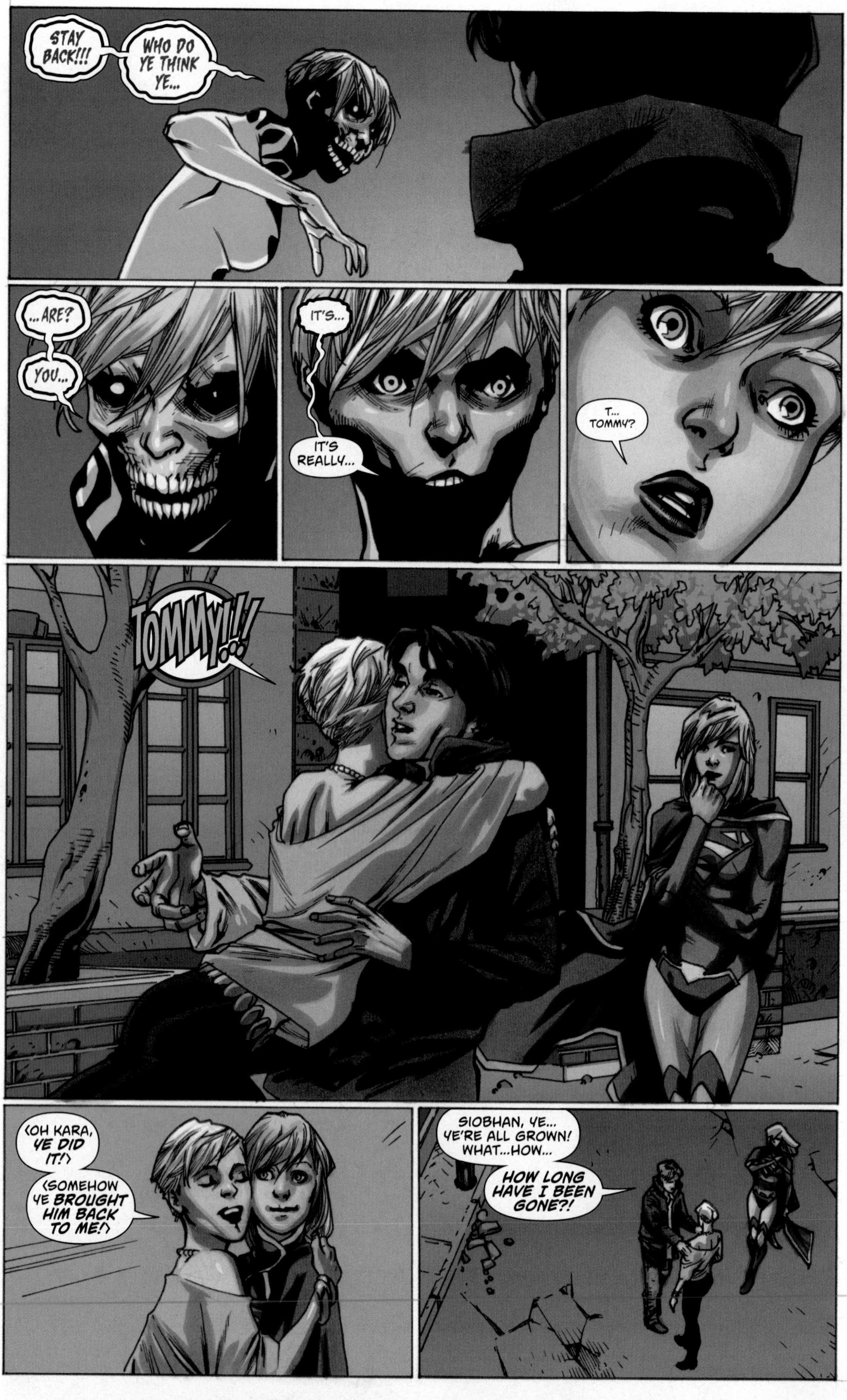
STAY BACK!!!
WHO DO YE THINK YE...
...ARE?
YOU...
IT'S...
IT'S REALLY...
T... TOMMY?
TOMMY!!!
‹OH KARA, YE DID IT!›
‹SOMEHOW YE BROUGHT HIM BACK TO ME!›
SIOBHAN, YE... YE'RE ALL GROWN! WHAT...HOW...
HOW LONG HAVE I BEEN GONE?!

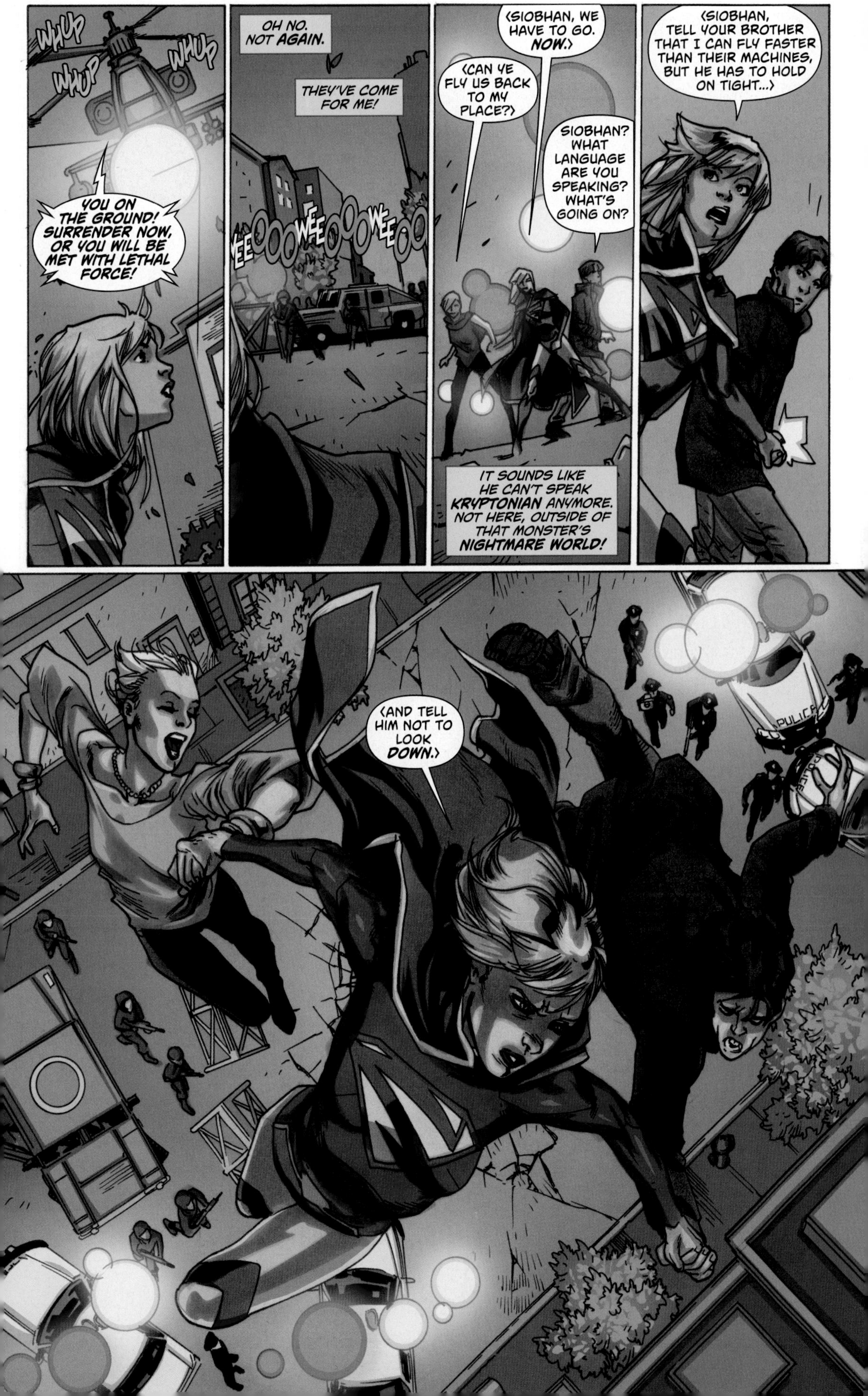
WHUP
WHUP
WHUP
YOU ON THE GROUND! SURRENDER NOW, OR YOU WILL BE MET WITH LETHAL FORCE!
OH NO. NOT AGAIN.
THEY'VE COME FOR ME!
WEEOOOO WEEOOOO WEEOOOO
‹SIOBHAN, WE HAVE TO GO. NOW.›
‹CAN YE FLY US BACK TO MY PLACE?›
SIOBHAN? WHAT LANGUAGE ARE YOU SPEAKING? WHAT'S GOING ON?
IT SOUNDS LIKE HE CAN'T SPEAK KRYPTONIAN ANYMORE. NOT HERE, OUTSIDE OF THAT MONSTER'S NIGHTMARE WORLD!
‹SIOBHAN, TELL YOUR BROTHER THAT I CAN FLY FASTER THAN THEIR MACHINES, BUT HE HAS TO HOLD ON TIGHT...›
‹AND TELL HIM NOT TO LOOK DOWN.›
POLICE
POLICE

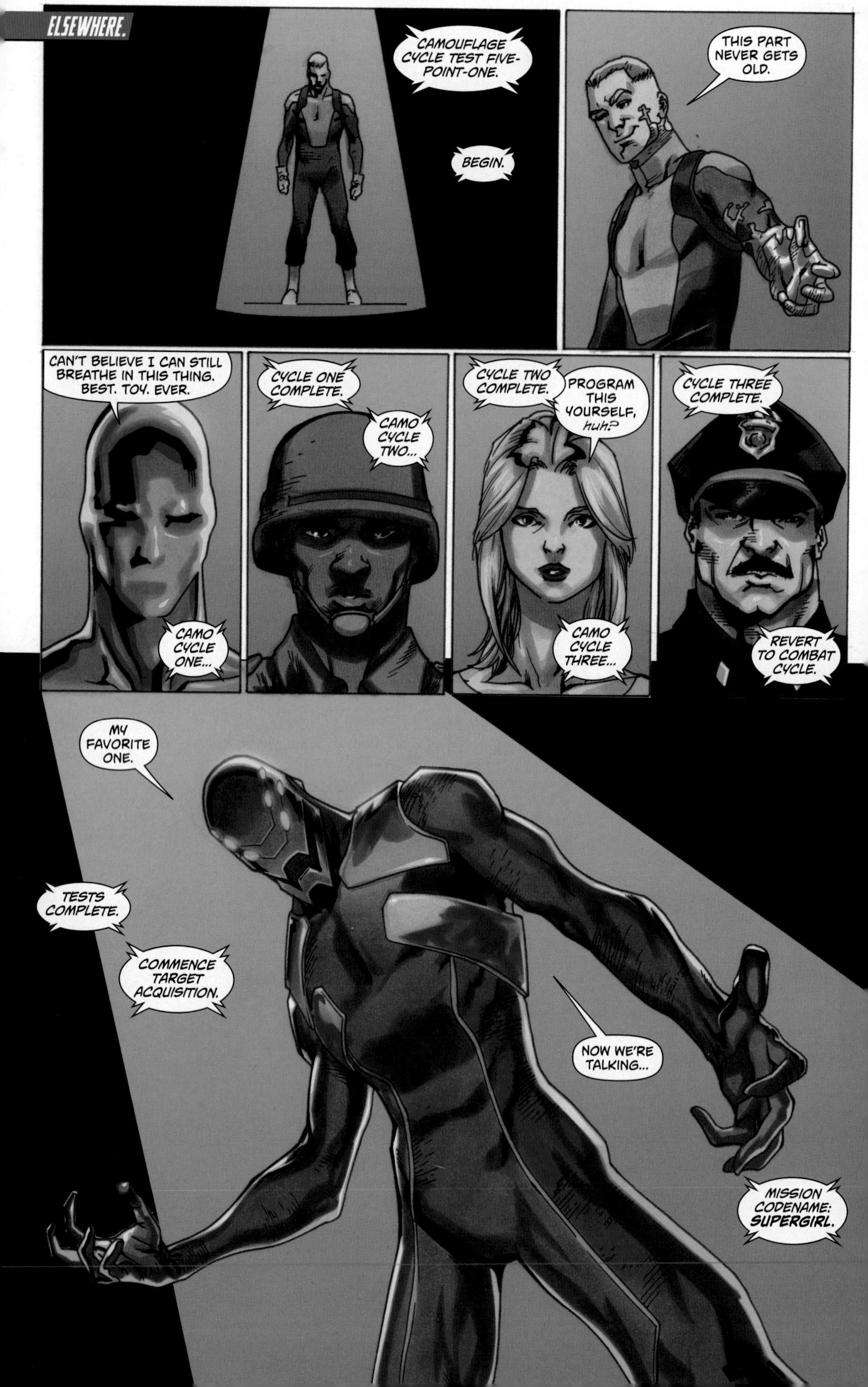
ELSEWHERE.
CAMOUFLAGE CYCLE TEST FIVE-POINT-ONE.
BEGIN.
THIS PART NEVER GETS OLD.
CAN'T BELIEVE I CAN STILL BREATHE IN THIS THING. BEST. TOY. EVER.
CAMO CYCLE ONE...
CYCLE ONE COMPLETE.
CAMO CYCLE TWO...
CYCLE TWO COMPLETE.
PROGRAM THIS YOURSELF, *huh?*
CAMO CYCLE THREE...
CYCLE THREE COMPLETE.
REVERT TO COMBAT CYCLE.
MY FAVORITE ONE.
TESTS COMPLETE.
COMMENCE TARGET ACQUISITION.
NOW WE'RE TALKING...
MISSION CODENAME: **SUPERGIRL.**

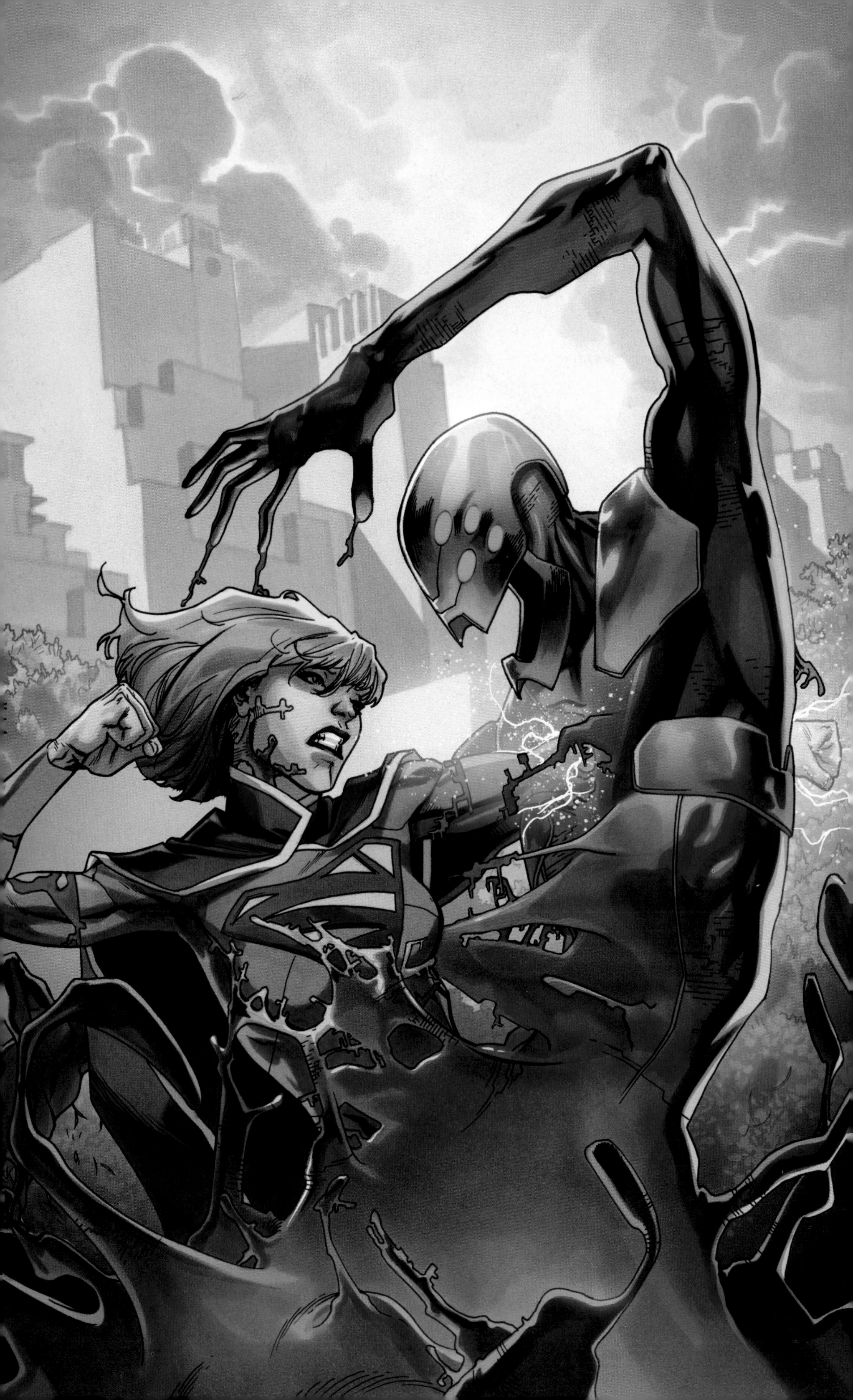

OUTSIDER

MICHAEL GREEN & MIKE JOHNSON writers MAHMUD ASRAR artist cover art by MAHMUD ASRAR & DAVE McCAIG

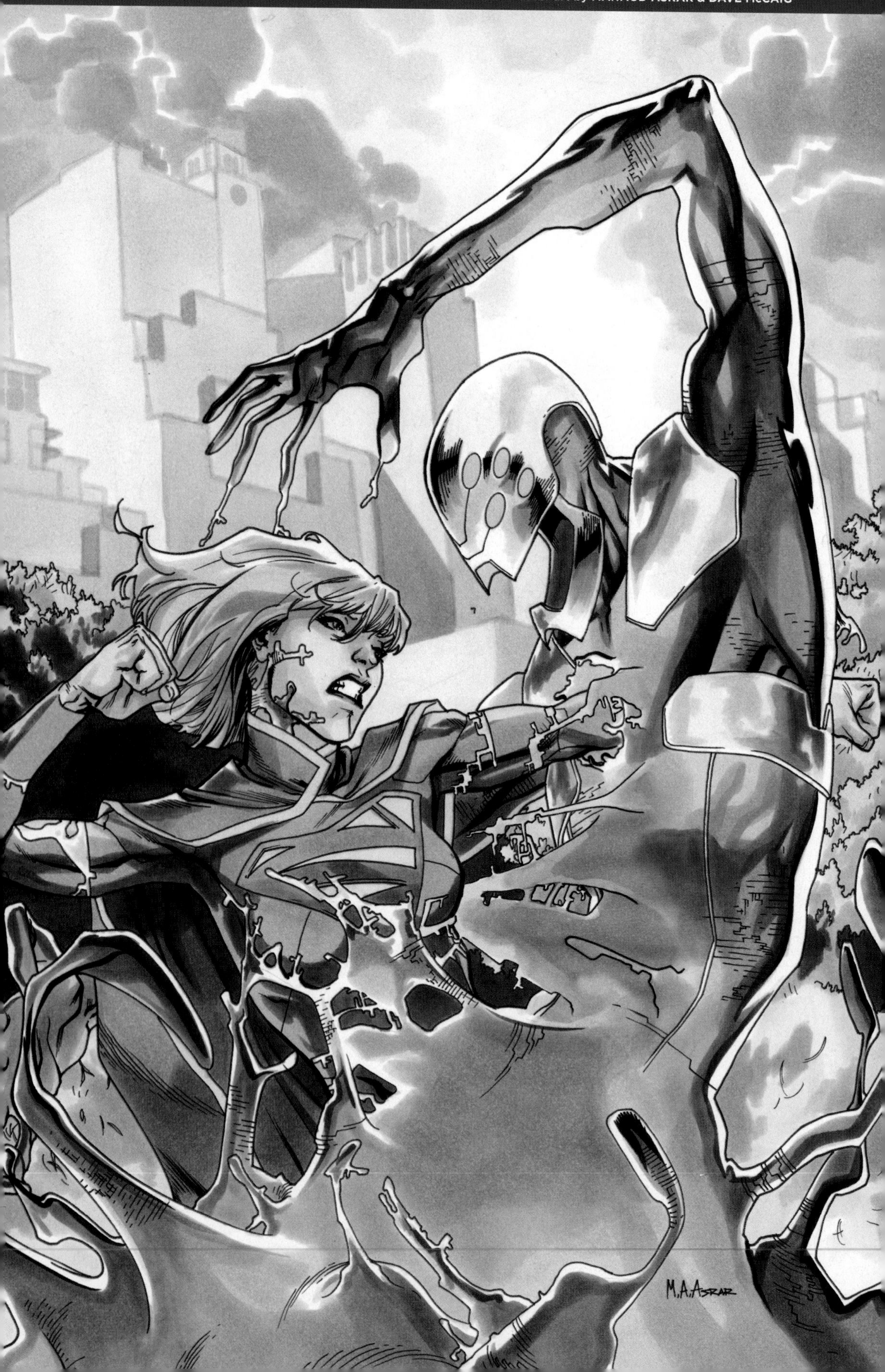
M.A.ASRAR

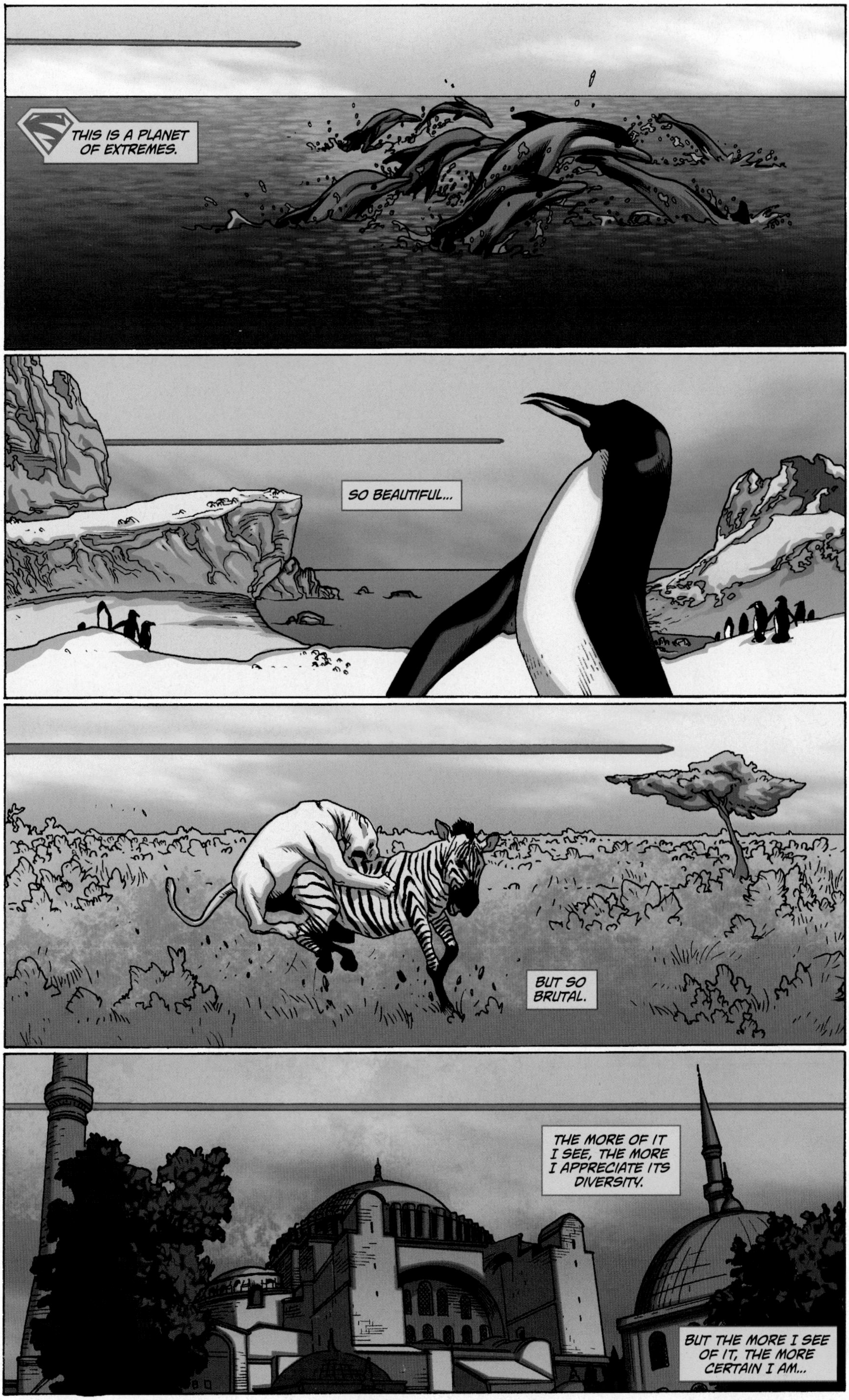
THIS IS A PLANET OF EXTREMES.
SO BEAUTIFUL...
BUT SO BRUTAL.
THE MORE OF IT I SEE, THE MORE I APPRECIATE ITS DIVERSITY.
BUT THE MORE I SEE OF IT, THE MORE CERTAIN I AM...

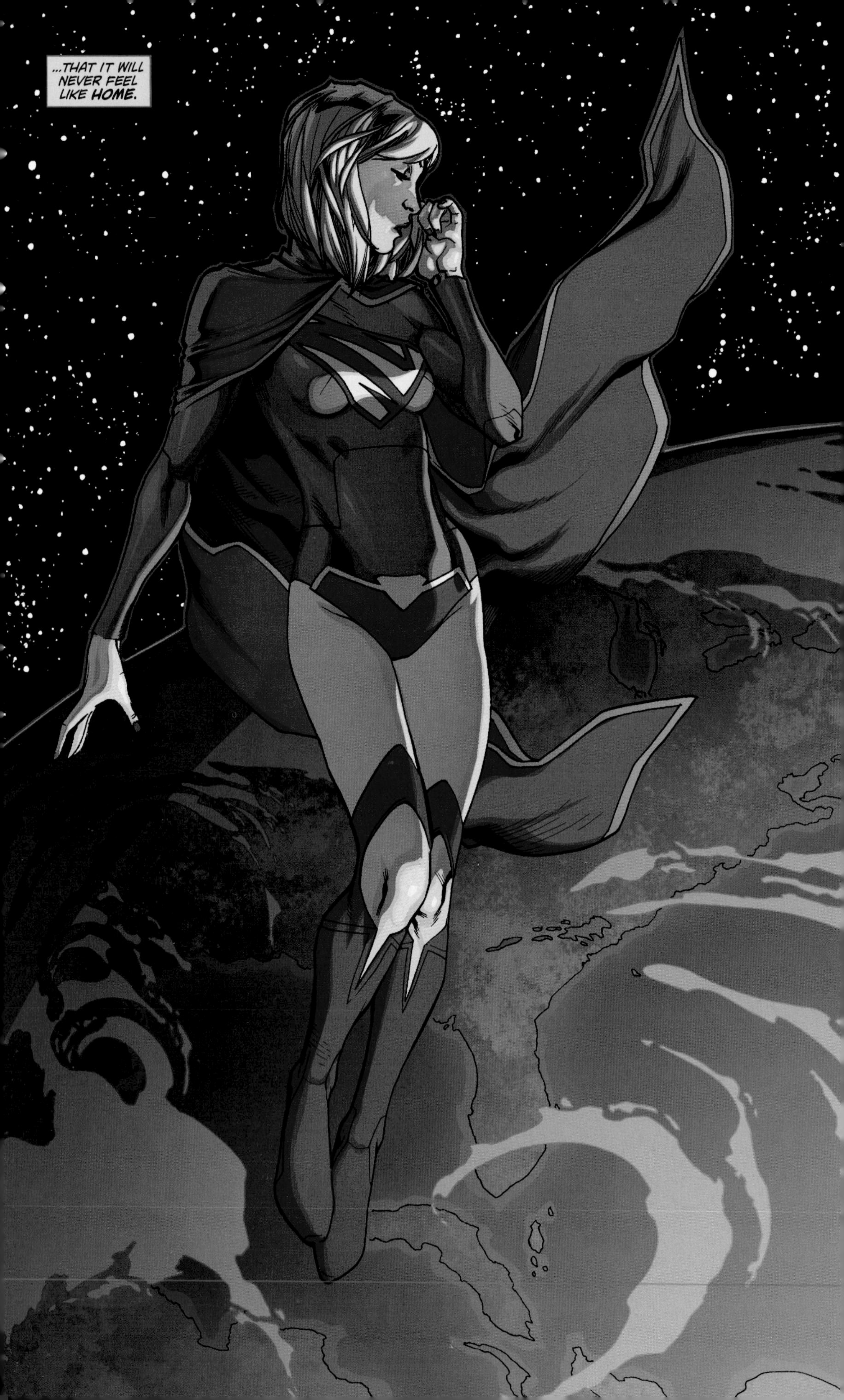
...THAT IT WILL NEVER FEEL LIKE HOME.

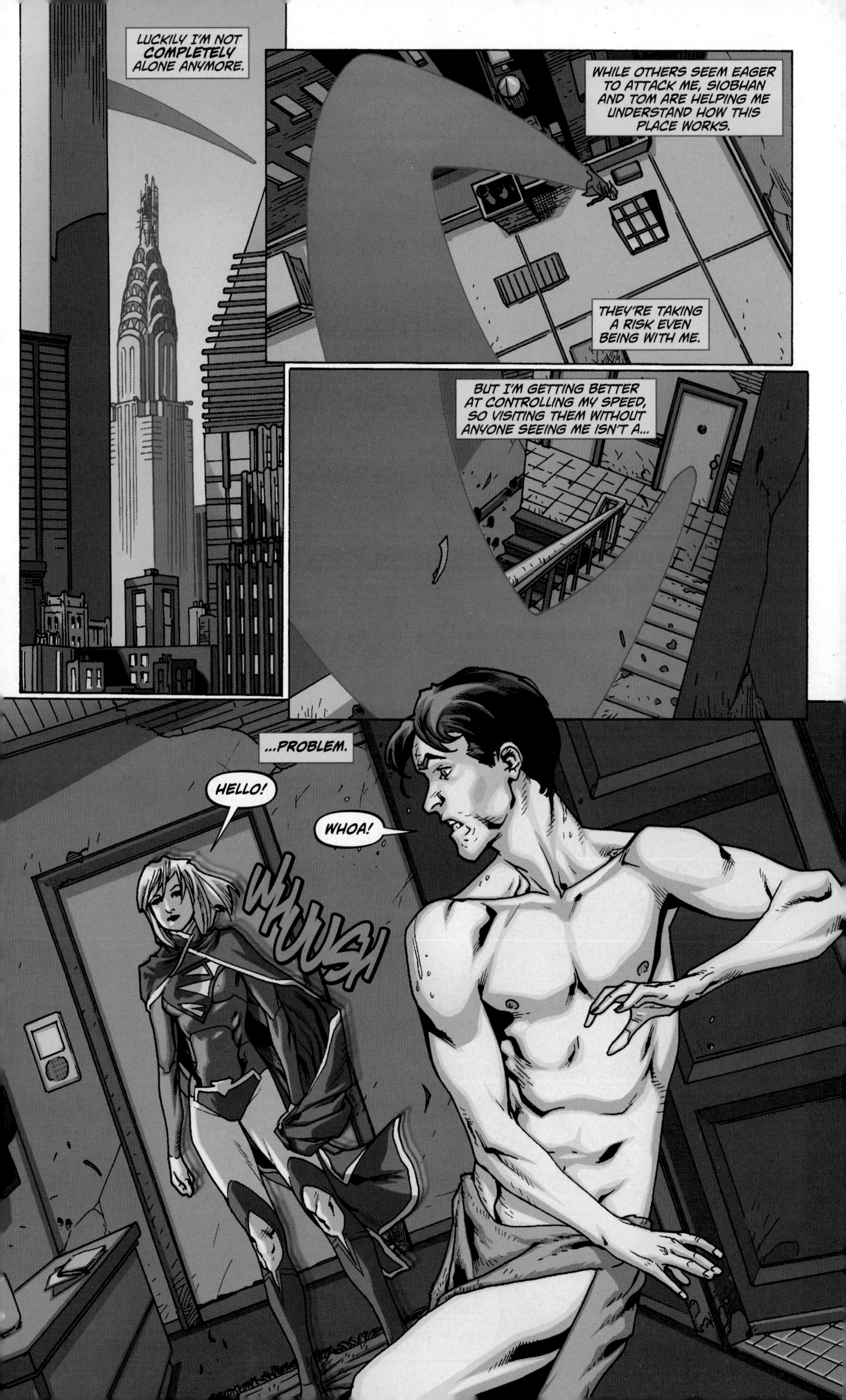
LUCKILY I'M NOT COMPLETELY ALONE ANYMORE.
WHILE OTHERS SEEM EAGER TO ATTACK ME, SIOBHAN AND TOM ARE HELPING ME UNDERSTAND HOW THIS PLACE WORKS.
THEY'RE TAKING A RISK EVEN BEING WITH ME.
BUT I'M GETTING BETTER AT CONTROLLING MY SPEED, SO VISITING THEM WITHOUT ANYONE SEEING ME ISN'T A...
...PROBLEM.
HELLO!
WHOA!
WHUUSH

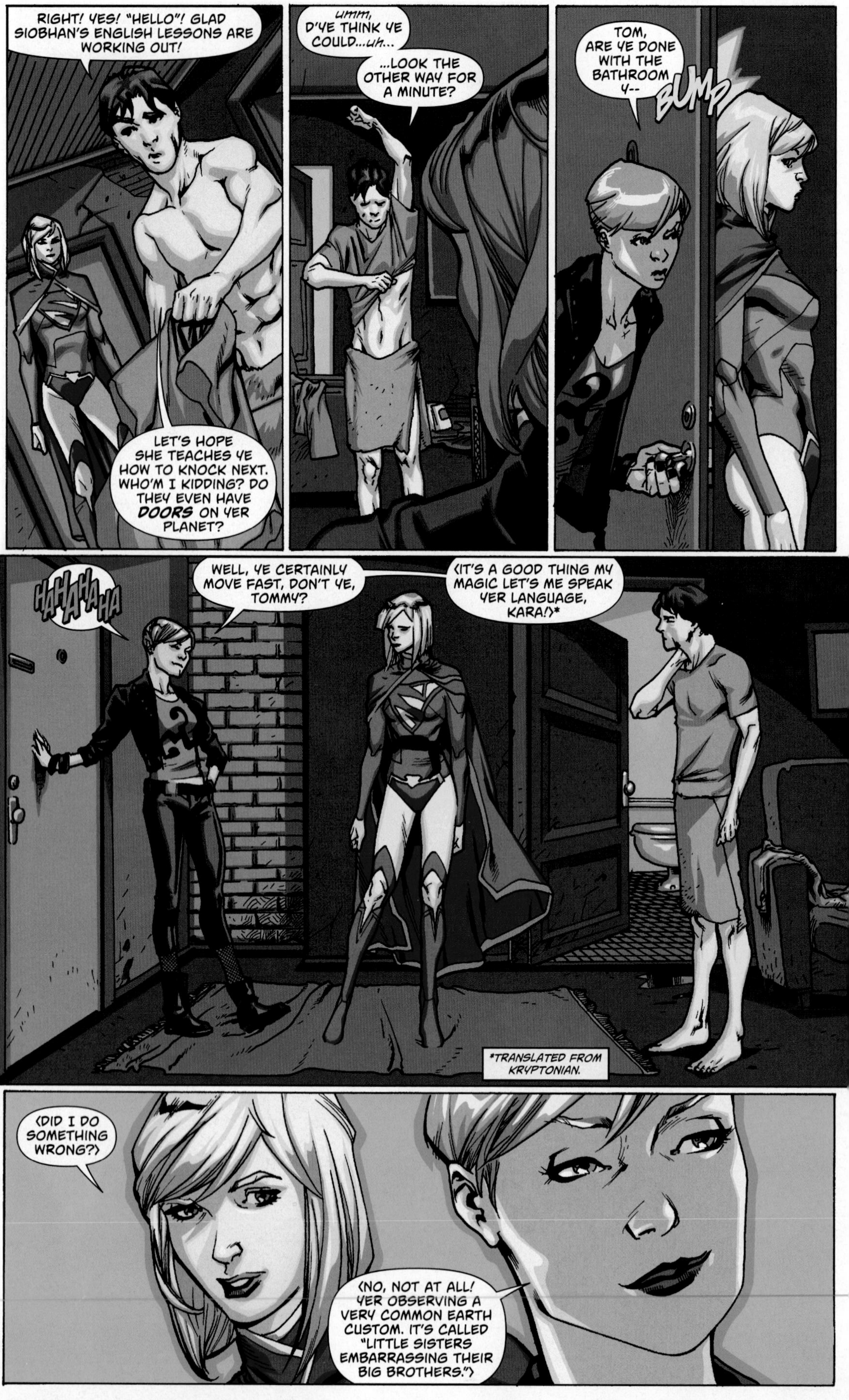
RIGHT! YES! "HELLO"! GLAD SIOBHAN'S ENGLISH LESSONS ARE WORKING OUT!
LET'S HOPE SHE TEACHES YE HOW TO KNOCK NEXT. WHO'M I KIDDING? DO THEY EVEN HAVE **DOORS** ON YER PLANET?
UMM, D'YE THINK YE COULD...UH...
...LOOK THE OTHER WAY FOR A MINUTE?
TOM, ARE YE DONE WITH THE BATHROOM Y--
BUMP
HAHAHAHAHA
WELL, YE CERTAINLY MOVE FAST, DON'T YE, TOMMY?
‹IT'S A GOOD THING MY MAGIC LET'S ME SPEAK YER LANGUAGE, KARA!›*
*TRANSLATED FROM KRYPTONIAN.
‹DID I DO SOMETHING WRONG?›
‹NO, NOT AT ALL! YER OBSERVING A VERY COMMON EARTH CUSTOM. IT'S CALLED "LITTLE SISTERS EMBARRASSING THEIR BIG BROTHERS."›

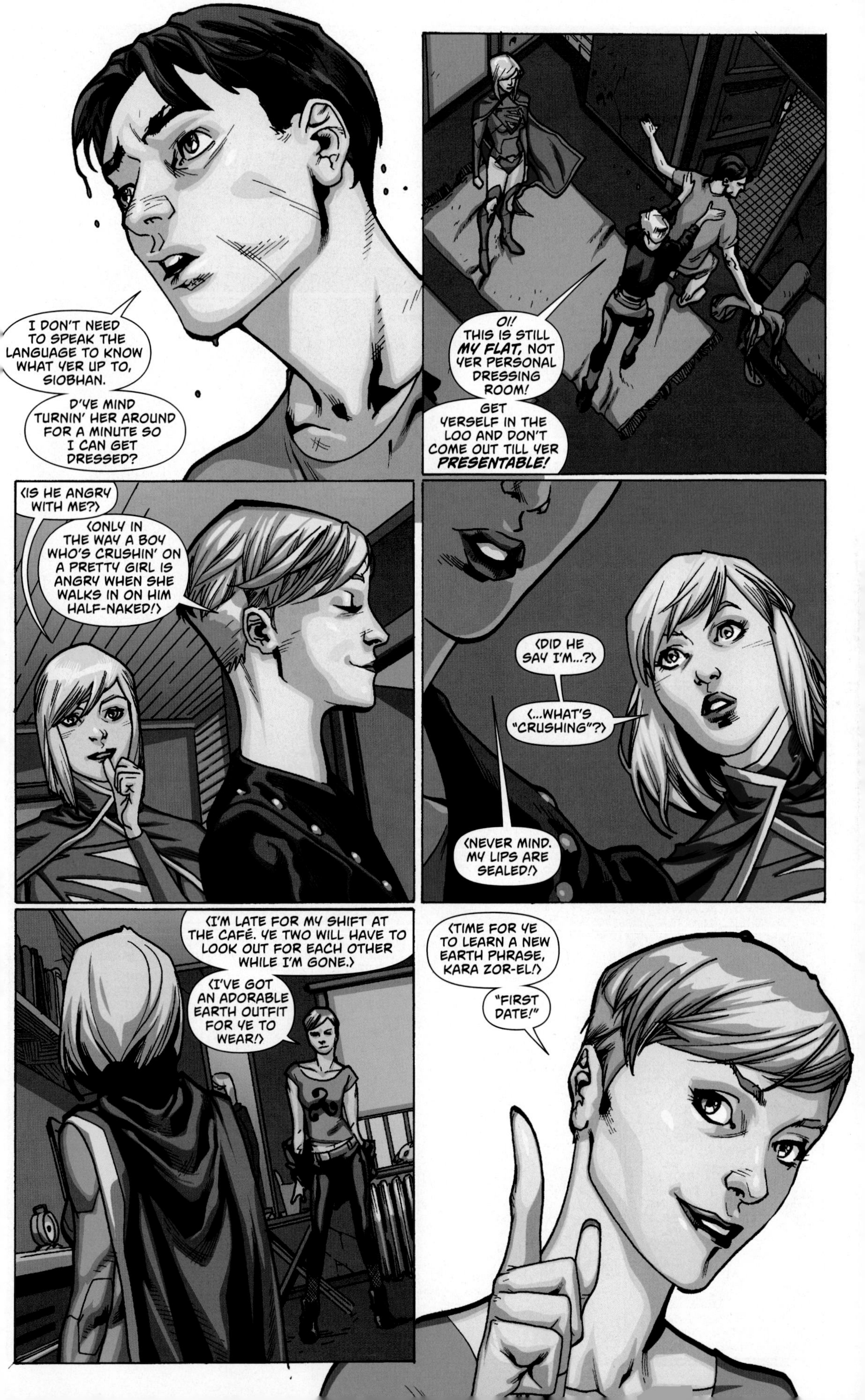
I DON'T NEED TO SPEAK THE LANGUAGE TO KNOW WHAT YER UP TO, SIOBHAN.
D'YE MIND TURNIN' HER AROUND FOR A MINUTE SO I CAN GET DRESSED?
OI! THIS IS STILL MY FLAT, NOT YER PERSONAL DRESSING ROOM!
GET YERSELF IN THE LOO AND DON'T COME OUT TILL YER PRESENTABLE!
<IS HE ANGRY WITH ME?>
<ONLY IN THE WAY A BOY WHO'S CRUSHIN' ON A PRETTY GIRL IS ANGRY WHEN SHE WALKS IN ON HIM HALF-NAKED!>
<DID HE SAY I'M...?>
<...WHAT'S "CRUSHING"?>
<NEVER MIND. MY LIPS ARE SEALED!>
<I'M LATE FOR MY SHIFT AT THE CAFÉ. YE TWO WILL HAVE TO LOOK OUT FOR EACH OTHER WHILE I'M GONE.>
<I'VE GOT AN ADORABLE EARTH OUTFIT FOR YE TO WEAR!>
<TIME FOR YE TO LEARN A NEW EARTH PHRASE, KARA ZOR-EL!>
"FIRST DATE!"

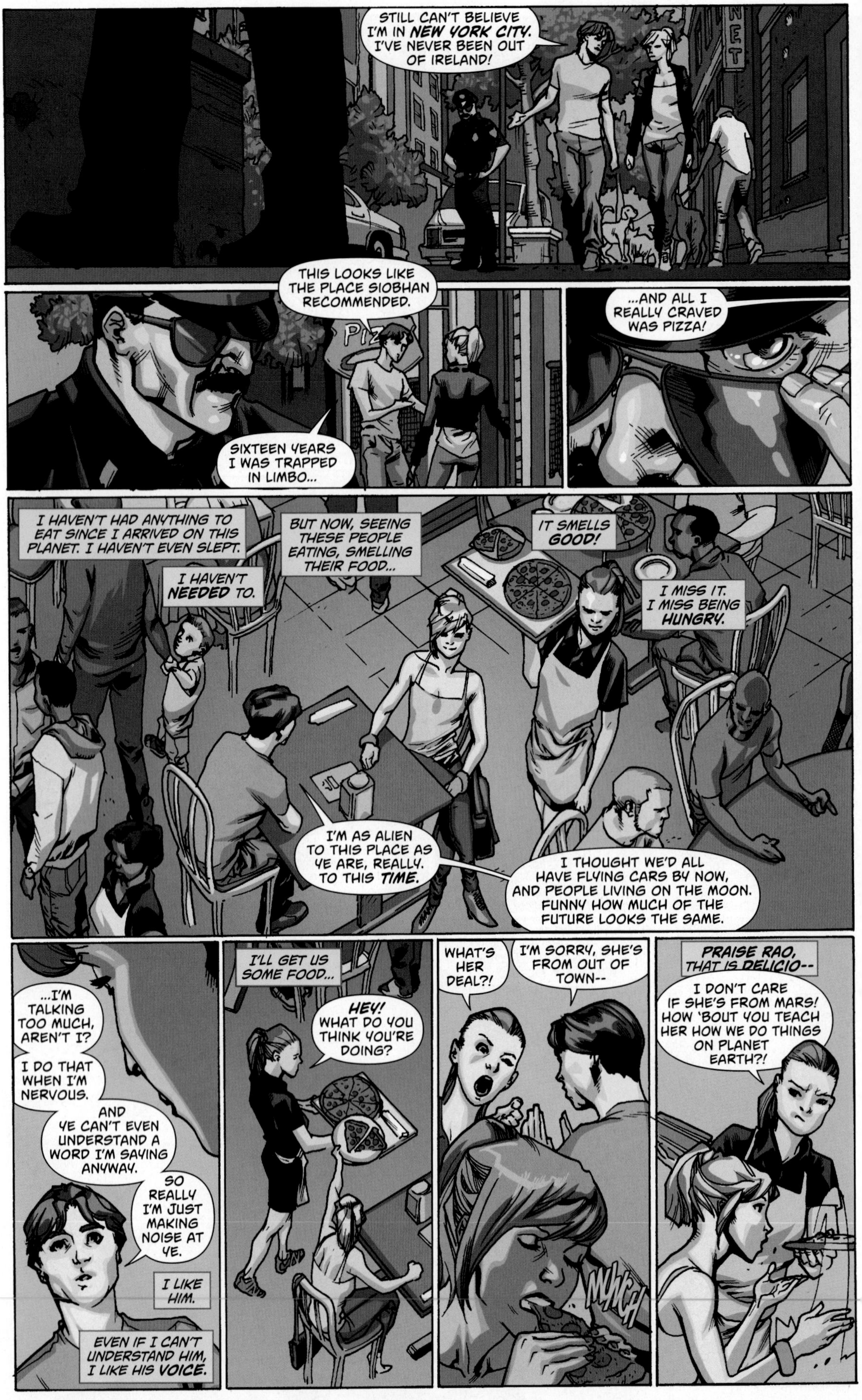
STILL CAN'T BELIEVE I'M IN NEW YORK CITY. I'VE NEVER BEEN OUT OF IRELAND!
THIS LOOKS LIKE THE PLACE SIOBHAN RECOMMENDED.
SIXTEEN YEARS I WAS TRAPPED IN LIMBO...
...AND ALL I REALLY CRAVED WAS PIZZA!
I HAVEN'T HAD ANYTHING TO EAT SINCE I ARRIVED ON THIS PLANET. I HAVEN'T EVEN SLEPT.
I HAVEN'T NEEDED TO.
BUT NOW, SEEING THESE PEOPLE EATING, SMELLING THEIR FOOD...
IT SMELLS GOOD!
I MISS IT. I MISS BEING HUNGRY.
I'M AS ALIEN TO THIS PLACE AS YE ARE, REALLY. TO THIS TIME.
I THOUGHT WE'D ALL HAVE FLYING CARS BY NOW, AND PEOPLE LIVING ON THE MOON. FUNNY HOW MUCH OF THE FUTURE LOOKS THE SAME.
...I'M TALKING TOO MUCH, AREN'T I?
I DO THAT WHEN I'M NERVOUS.
AND YE CAN'T EVEN UNDERSTAND A WORD I'M SAYING ANYWAY.
SO REALLY I'M JUST MAKING NOISE AT YE.
I LIKE HIM.
EVEN IF I CAN'T UNDERSTAND HIM, I LIKE HIS VOICE.
I'LL GET US SOME FOOD...
HEY! WHAT DO YOU THINK YOU'RE DOING?
WHAT'S HER DEAL?!
I'M SORRY, SHE'S FROM OUT OF TOWN--
MUNCH
PRAISE RAO, THAT IS DELICIO--
I DON'T CARE IF SHE'S FROM MARS! HOW 'BOUT YOU TEACH HER HOW WE DO THINGS ON PLANET EARTH?!

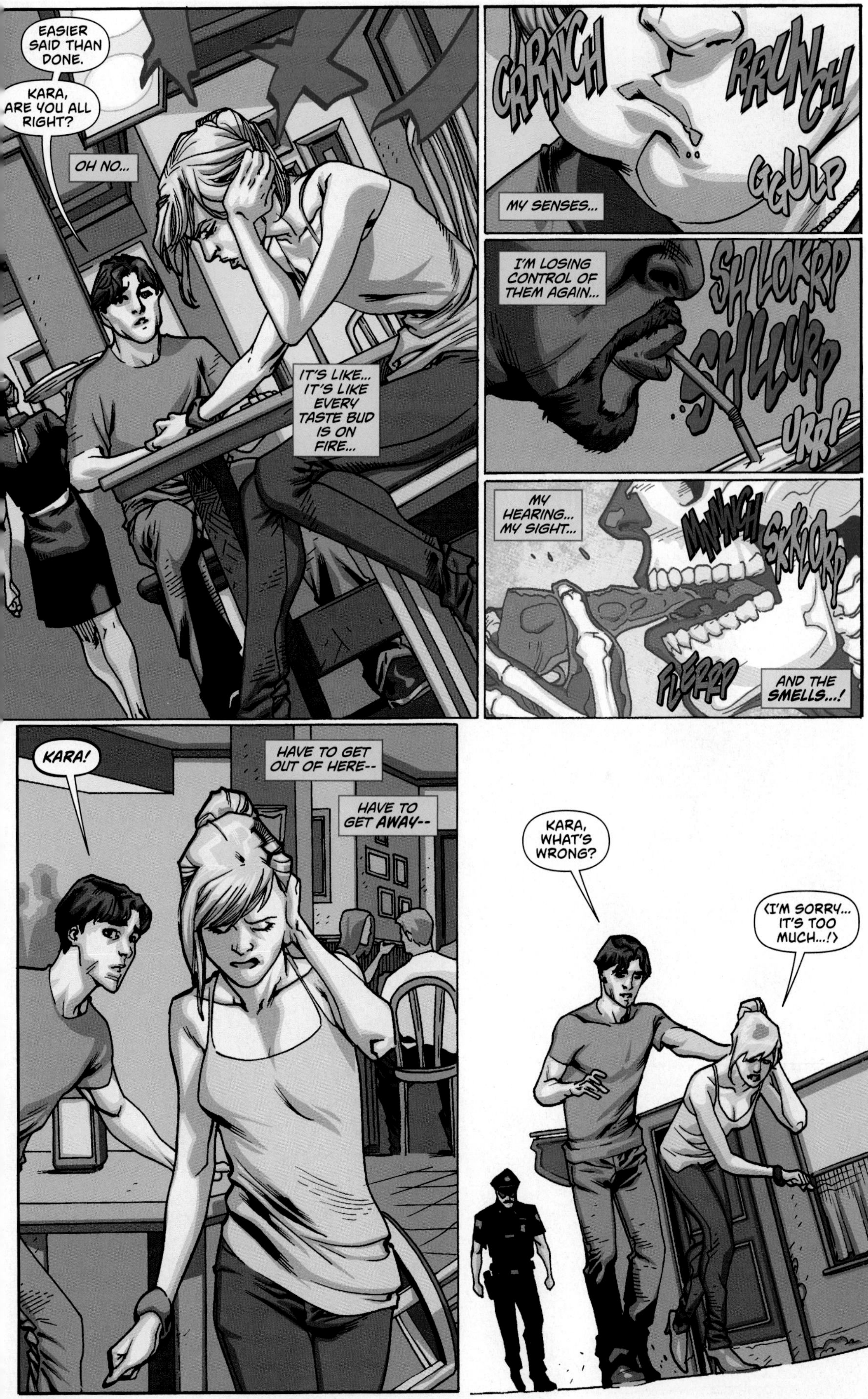
EASIER SAID THAN DONE.
KARA, ARE YOU ALL RIGHT?
OH NO...
IT'S LIKE... IT'S LIKE EVERY TASTE BUD IS ON FIRE...
CRRNCH
RRUNCH
GGULP
MY SENSES...
I'M LOSING CONTROL OF THEM AGAIN...
SHLOKRP
SHLLURP
URRP
MY HEARING... MY SIGHT...
MNNCH
SKRLORP
FLERRP
AND THE SMELLS...!
KARA!
HAVE TO GET OUT OF HERE--
HAVE TO GET AWAY--
KARA, WHAT'S WRONG?
<I'M SORRY... IT'S TOO MUCH...!>

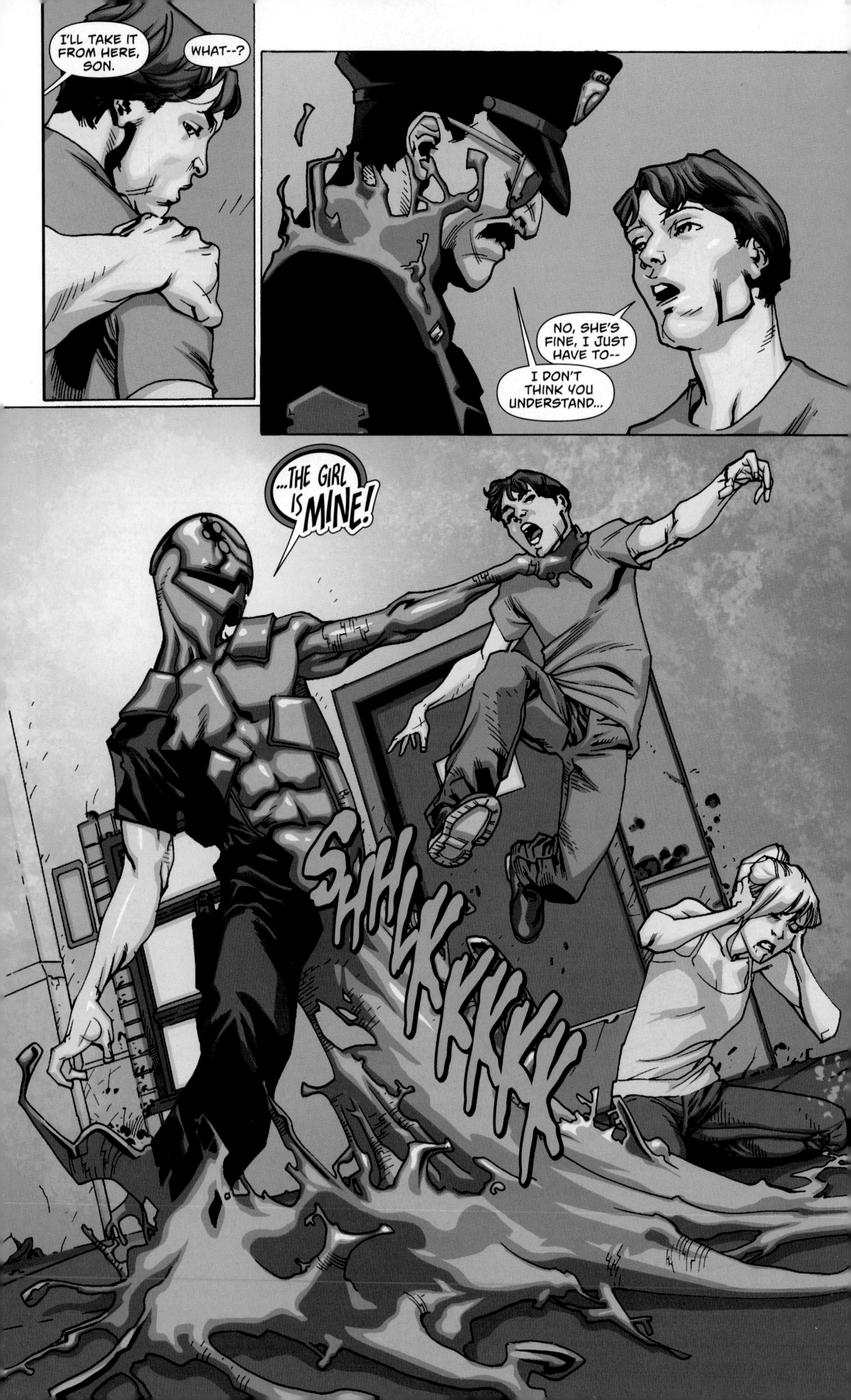
I'LL TAKE IT FROM HERE, SON.
WHAT--?
NO, SHE'S FINE, I JUST HAVE TO--
I DON'T THINK YOU UNDERSTAND...
...THE GIRL IS MINE!
SHHLKKKKK

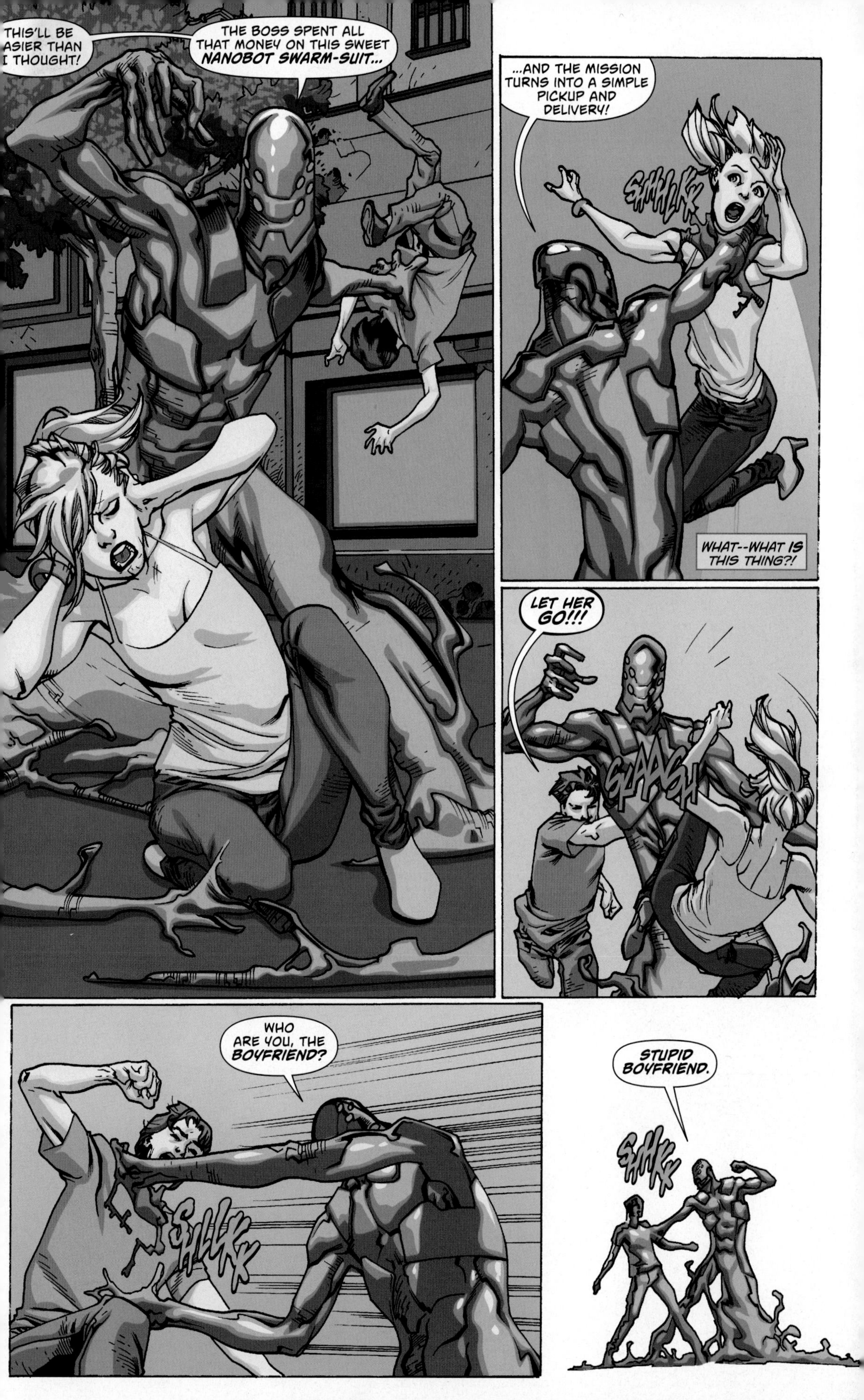
THIS'LL BE
ASIER THAN
I THOUGHT!
THE BOSS SPENT ALL THAT MONEY ON THIS SWEET *NANOBOT SWARM-SUIT...*
...AND THE MISSION TURNS INTO A SIMPLE PICKUP AND DELIVERY!
WHAT--WHAT *IS* THIS THING?!
LET HER *GO!!!*
WHO ARE YOU, THE *BOYFRIEND?*
STUPID BOYFRIEND.

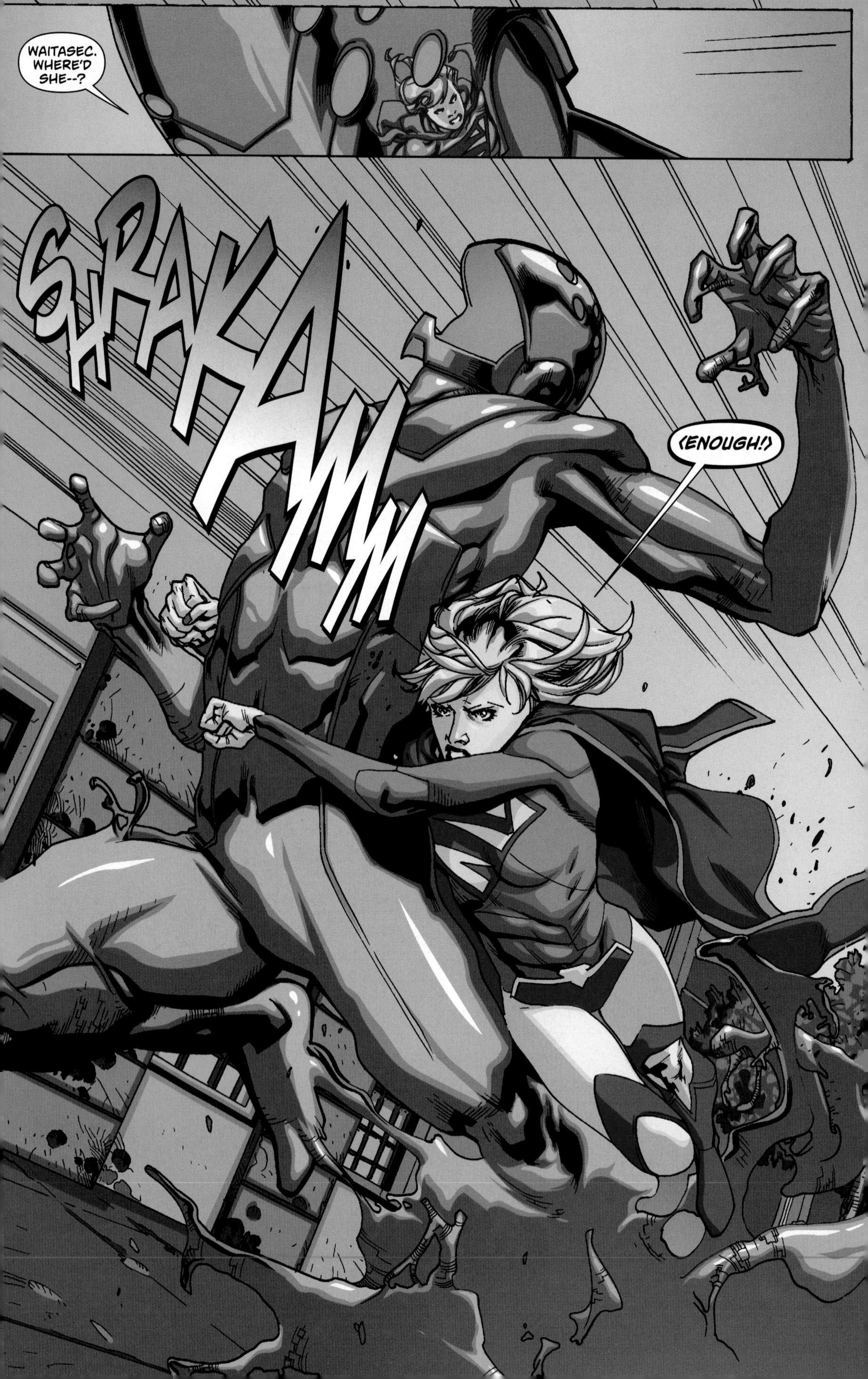
WAITASEC. WHERE'D SHE--?
SHRAKAMM
<ENOUGH!>

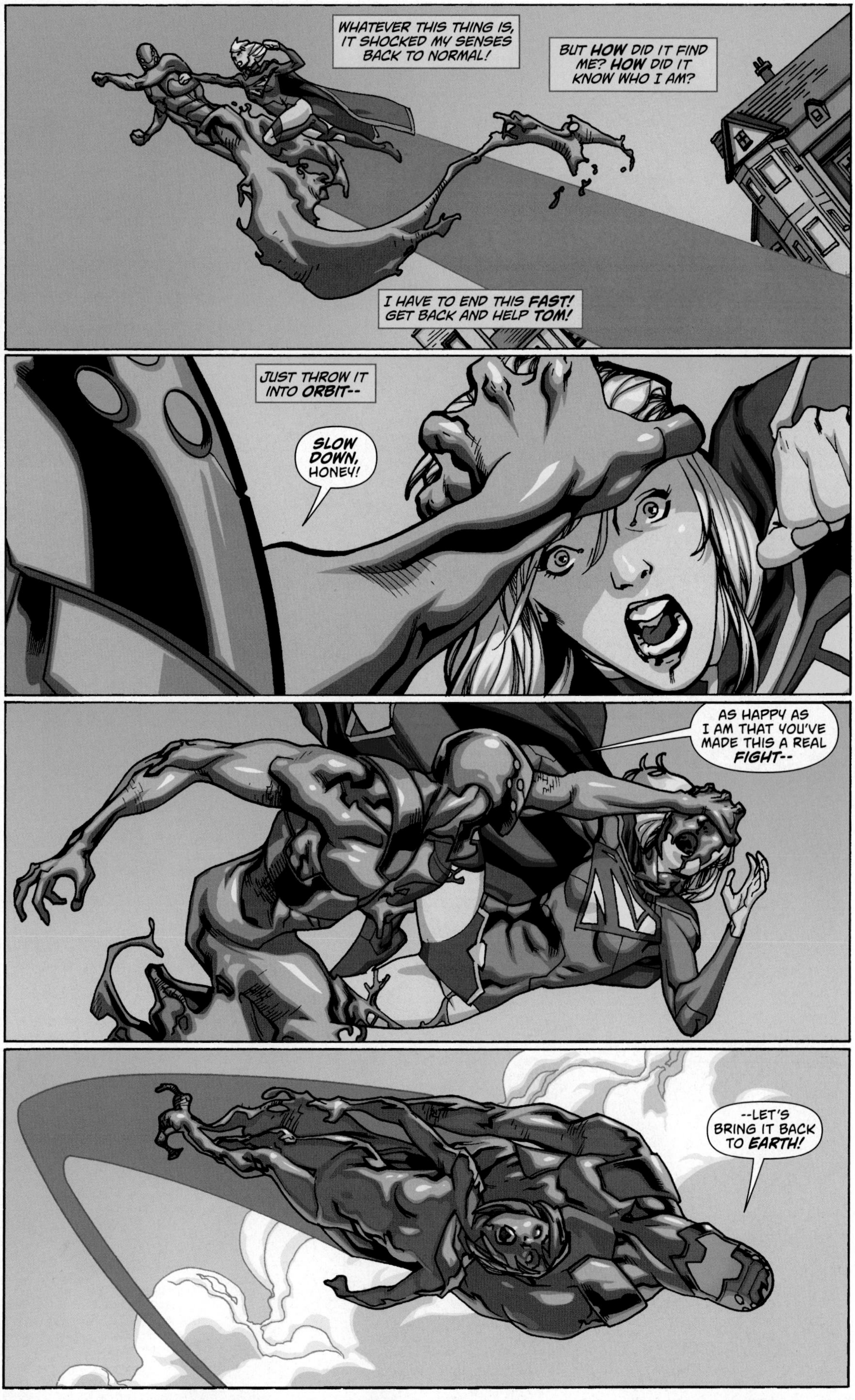
WHATEVER THIS THING IS, IT SHOCKED MY SENSES BACK TO NORMAL!
BUT HOW DID IT FIND ME? HOW DID IT KNOW WHO I AM?
I HAVE TO END THIS FAST! GET BACK AND HELP TOM!
JUST THROW IT INTO ORBIT--
SLOW DOWN, HONEY!
AS HAPPY AS I AM THAT YOU'VE MADE THIS A REAL FIGHT--
--LET'S BRING IT BACK TO EARTH!

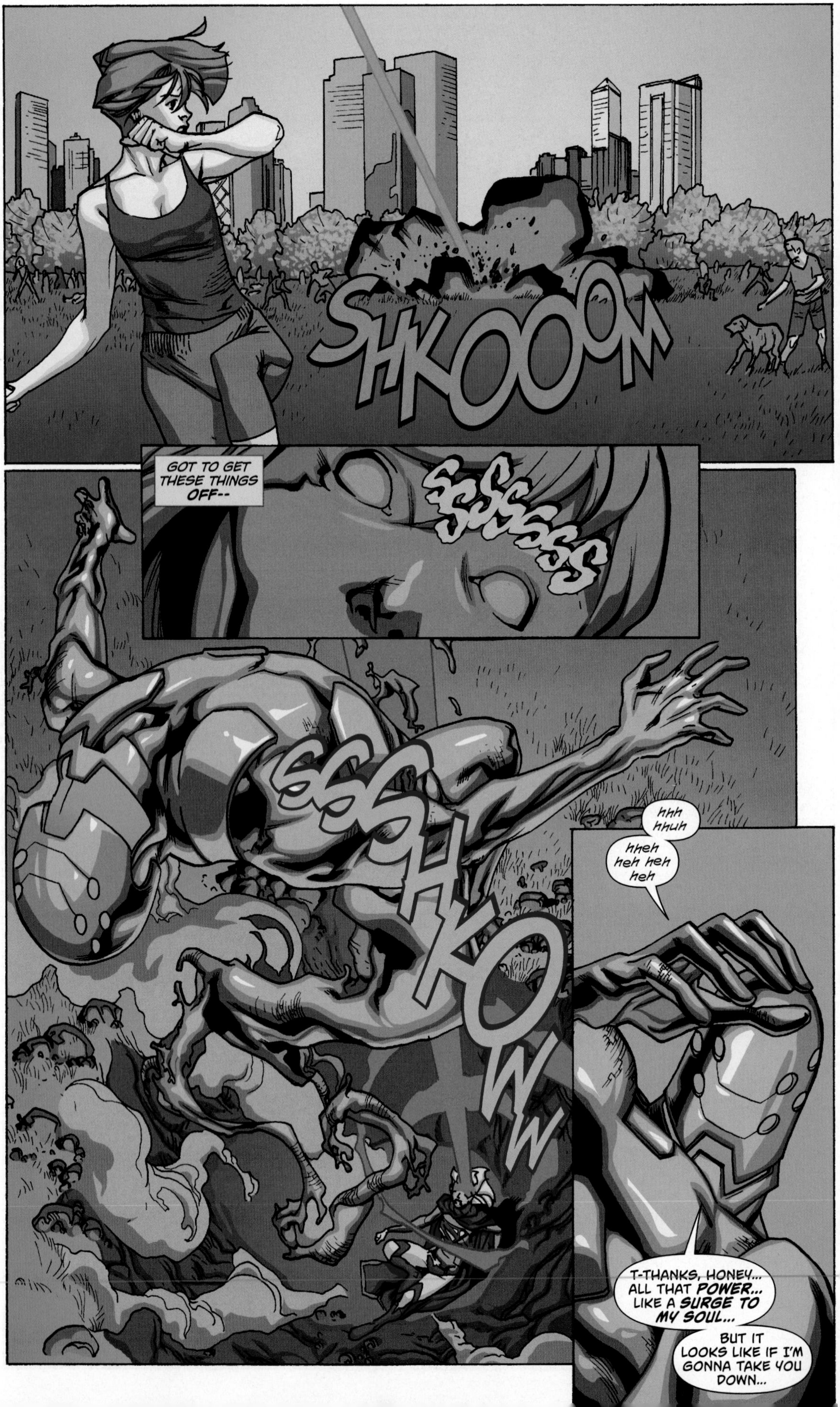
SHKOOOM
GOT TO GET THESE THINGS OFF--
SSSSSSS
SSSHKOWW
hhh hhuh
hheh heh heh heh
T-THANKS, HONEY... ALL THAT POWER... LIKE A SURGE TO MY SOUL...
BUT IT LOOKS LIKE IF I'M GONNA TAKE YOU DOWN...

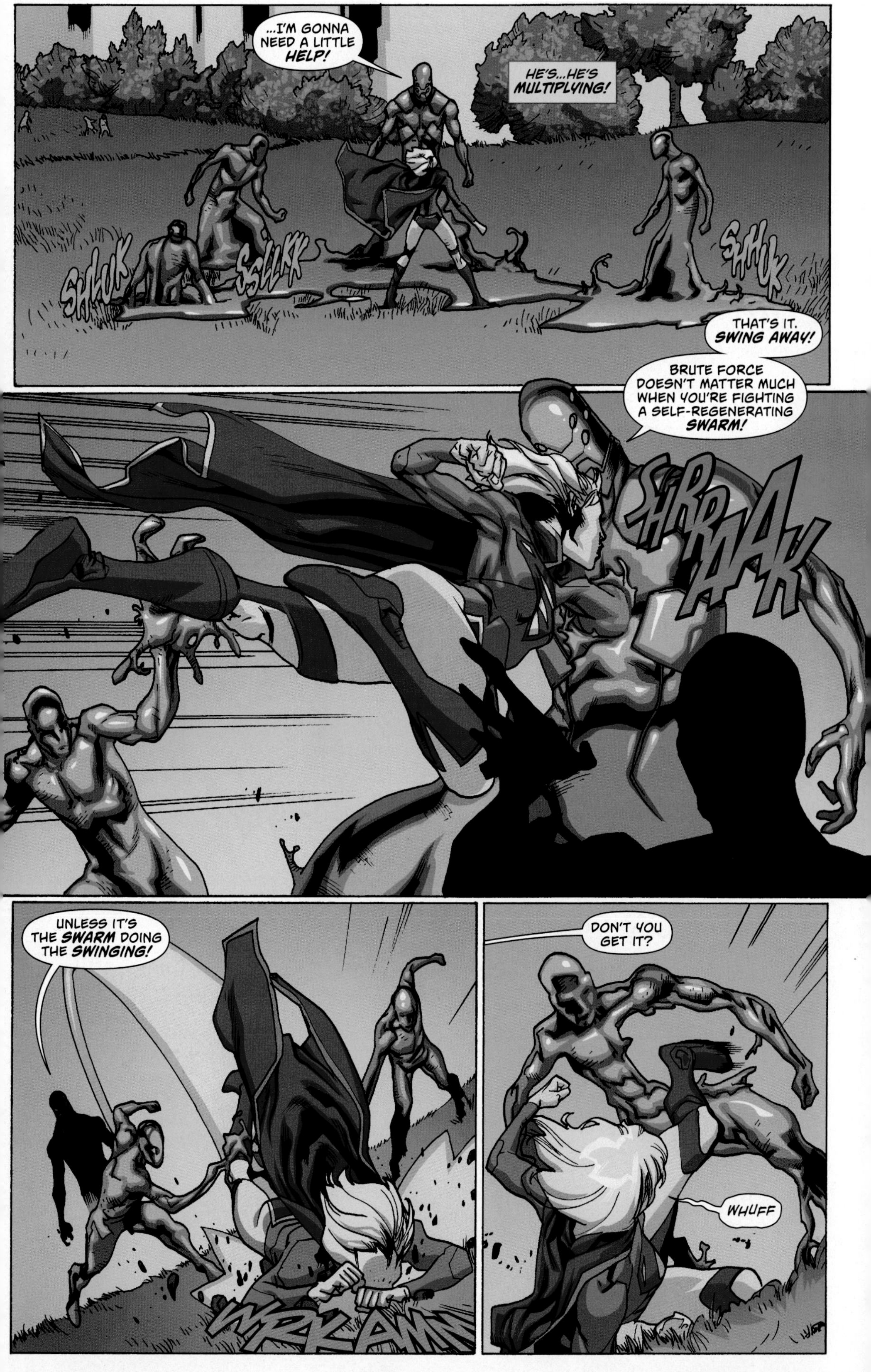
...I'M GONNA NEED A LITTLE HELP!
HE'S...HE'S MULTIPLYING!
SHLUK
SSLLKK
SHLUK
THAT'S IT. SWING AWAY!
BRUTE FORCE DOESN'T MATTER MUCH WHEN YOU'RE FIGHTING A SELF-REGENERATING SWARM!
SHRAAK
UNLESS IT'S THE SWARM DOING THE SWINGING!
WRKAM
DON'T YOU GET IT?
WHUFF

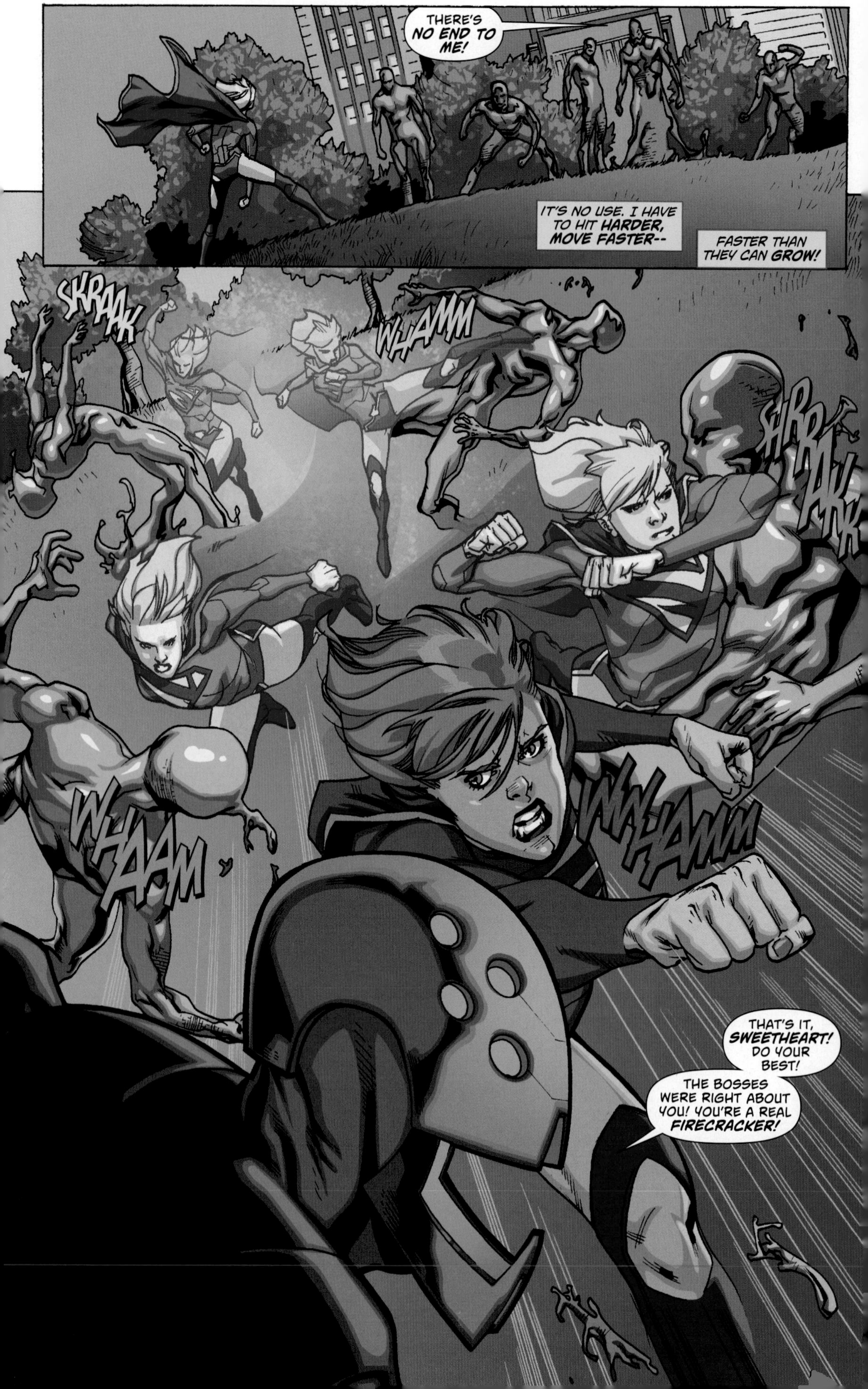
THERE'S NO END TO ME!
IT'S NO USE. I HAVE TO HIT HARDER, MOVE FASTER--
FASTER THAN THEY CAN GROW!
SKRAAAK
WHAMM
SHRRAKK
WHAAM
WHAMM
THAT'S IT, SWEETHEART! DO YOUR BEST!
THE BOSSES WERE RIGHT ABOUT YOU! YOU'RE A REAL FIRECRACKER!

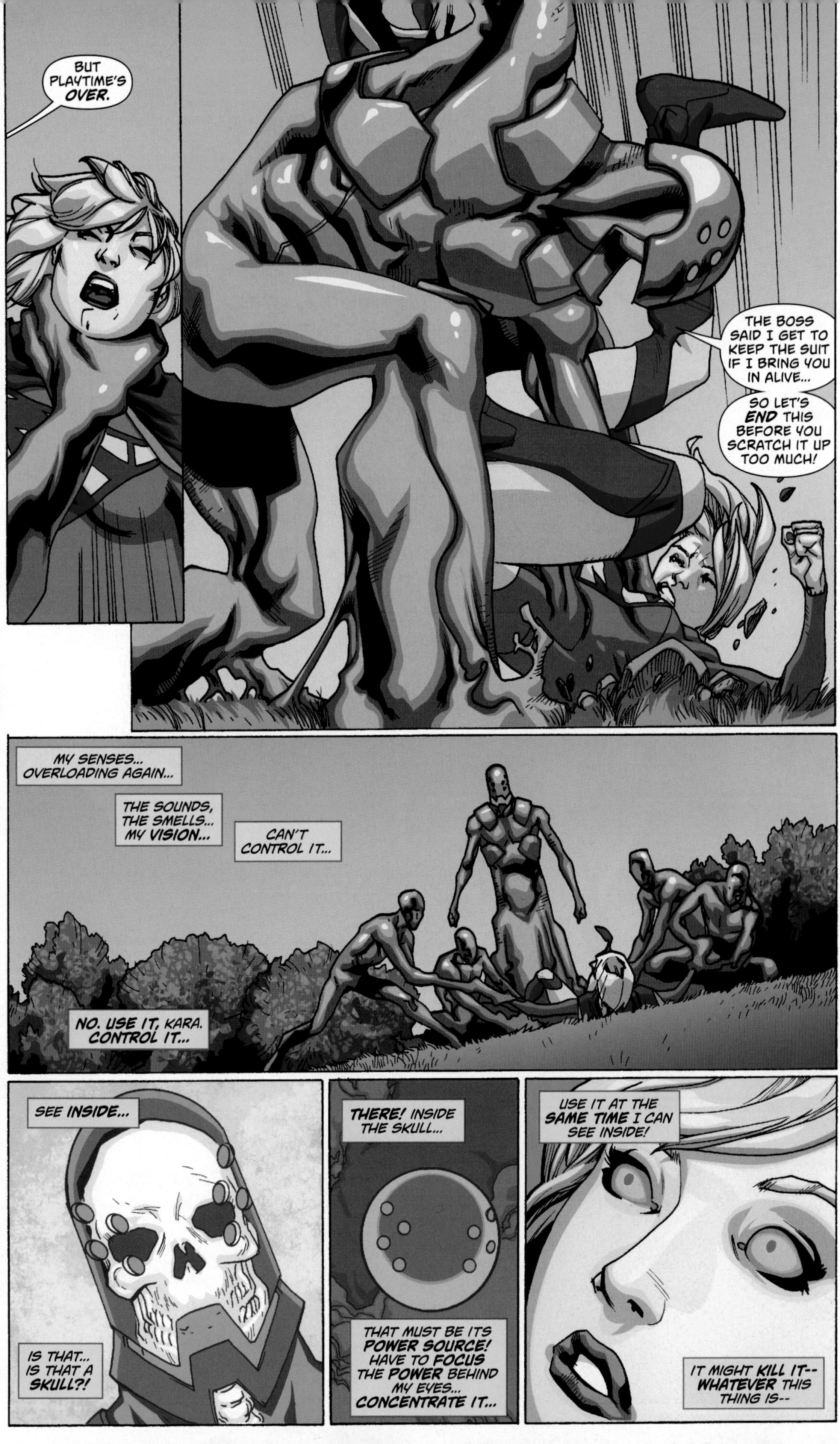
BUT PLAYTIME'S OVER.
THE BOSS SAID I GET TO KEEP THE SUIT IF I BRING YOU IN ALIVE...
SO LET'S END THIS BEFORE YOU SCRATCH IT UP TOO MUCH!
MY SENSES... OVERLOADING AGAIN...
THE SOUNDS, THE SMELLS... MY VISION...
CAN'T CONTROL IT...
NO. USE IT, KARA. CONTROL IT...
SEE INSIDE...
IS THAT... IS THAT A SKULL?!
THERE! INSIDE THE SKULL...
THAT MUST BE ITS POWER SOURCE! HAVE TO FOCUS THE POWER BEHIND MY EYES... CONCENTRATE IT...
USE IT AT THE SAME TIME I CAN SEE INSIDE!
IT MIGHT KILL IT-- WHATEVER THIS THING IS--

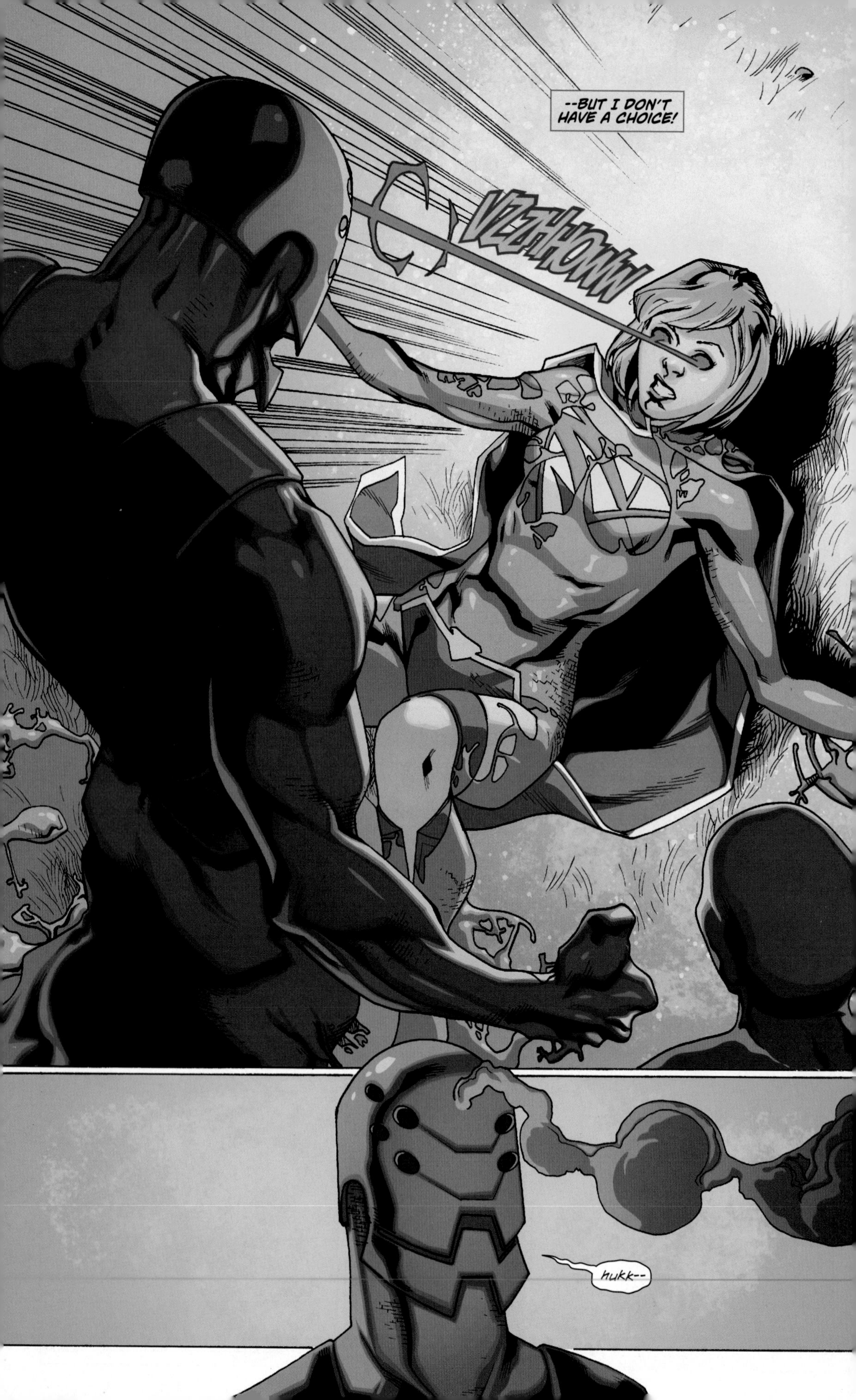
--BUT I DON'T HAVE A CHOICE!
VZZHOWW
hukk--

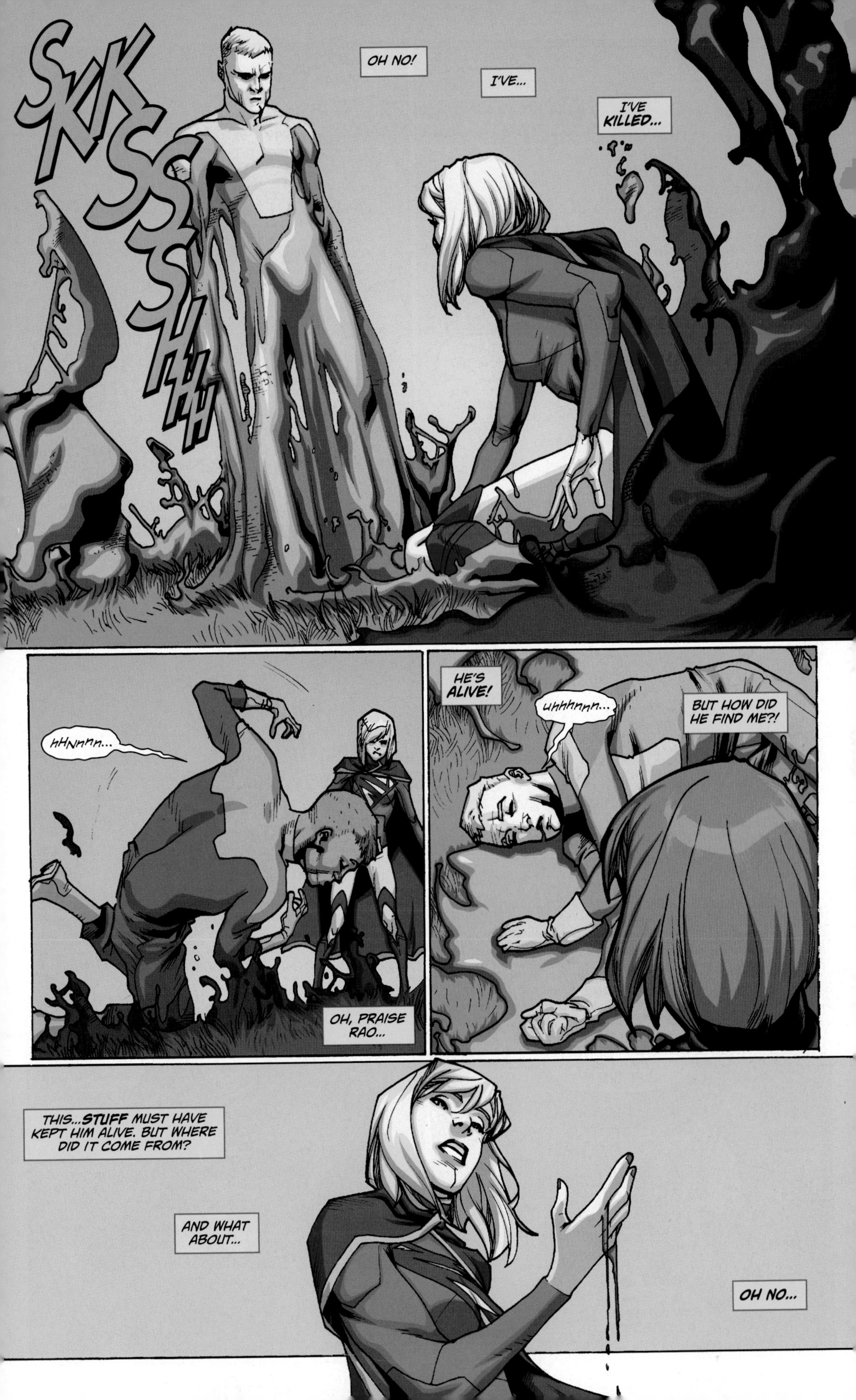
SKKSSSHHH
OH NO!
I'VE...
I'VE KILLED...
hHNnnn...
OH, PRAISE RAO...
HE'S ALIVE!
uhhhhnnn...
BUT HOW DID HE FIND ME?!
THIS...STUFF MUST HAVE KEPT HIM ALIVE. BUT WHERE DID IT COME FROM?
AND WHAT ABOUT...
OH NO...

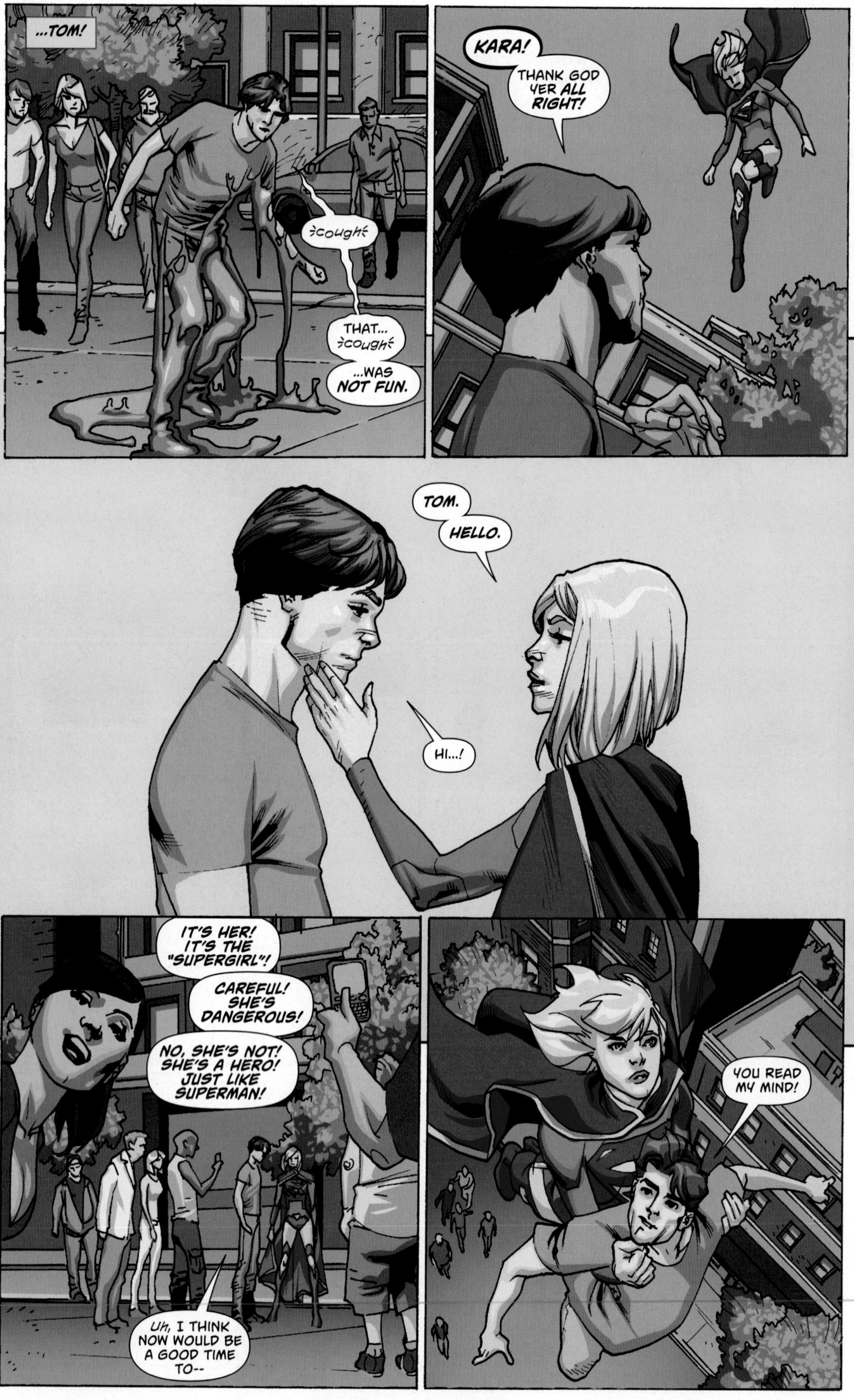
...TOM!
cough
THAT... *cough*
...WAS NOT FUN.
KARA!
THANK GOD YER ALL RIGHT!
TOM.
HELLO.
HI...!
IT'S HER! IT'S THE "SUPERGIRL"!
CAREFUL! SHE'S DANGEROUS!
NO, SHE'S NOT! SHE'S A HERO! JUST LIKE SUPERMAN!
Uh, I THINK NOW WOULD BE A GOOD TIME TO--
YOU READ MY MIND!

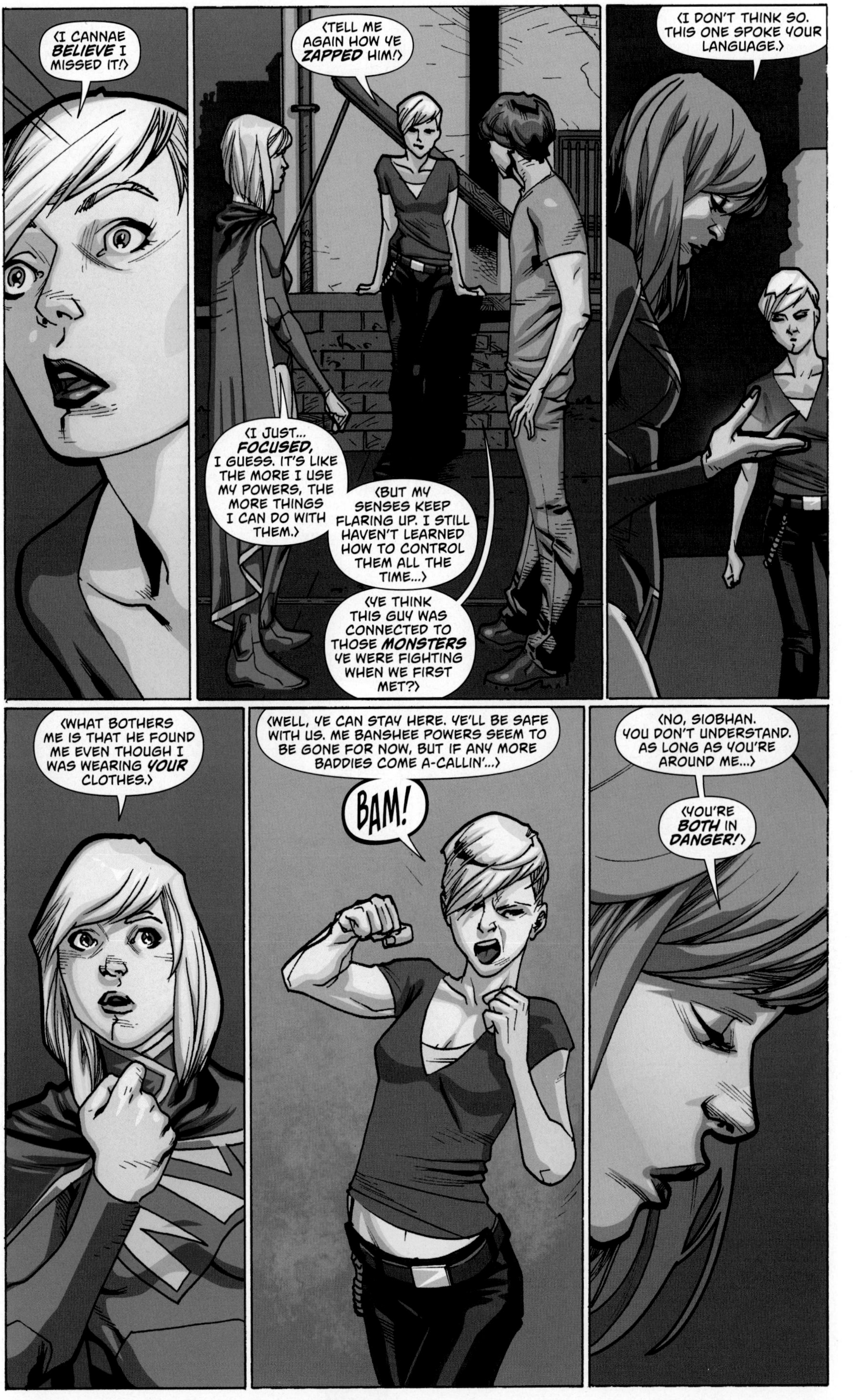

⟨I CANNAE BELIEVE I MISSED IT!⟩
⟨TELL ME AGAIN HOW YE ZAPPED HIM!⟩
⟨I JUST... FOCUSED, I GUESS. IT'S LIKE THE MORE I USE MY POWERS, THE MORE THINGS I CAN DO WITH THEM.⟩
⟨BUT MY SENSES KEEP FLARING UP. I STILL HAVEN'T LEARNED HOW TO CONTROL THEM ALL THE TIME...⟩
⟨YE THINK THIS GUY WAS CONNECTED TO THOSE MONSTERS YE WERE FIGHTING WHEN WE FIRST MET?⟩
⟨I DON'T THINK SO. THIS ONE SPOKE YOUR LANGUAGE.⟩
⟨WHAT BOTHERS ME IS THAT HE FOUND ME EVEN THOUGH I WAS WEARING YOUR CLOTHES.⟩
⟨WELL, YE CAN STAY HERE. YE'LL BE SAFE WITH US. ME BANSHEE POWERS SEEM TO BE GONE FOR NOW, BUT IF ANY MORE BADDIES COME A-CALLIN'...⟩
BAM!
⟨NO, SIOBHAN. YOU DON'T UNDERSTAND. AS LONG AS YOU'RE AROUND ME...⟩
⟨YOU'RE BOTH IN DANGER!⟩

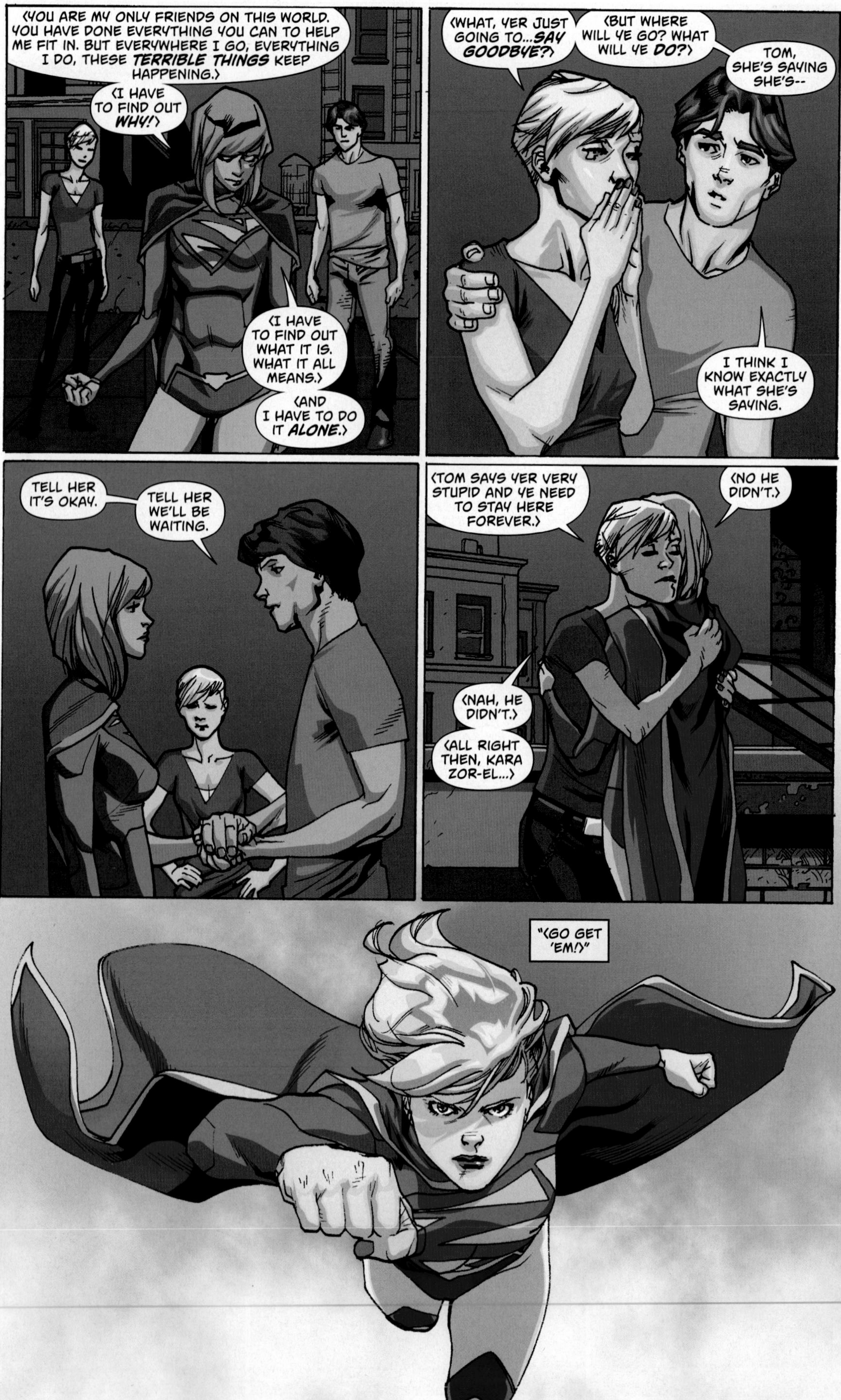

‹YOU ARE MY ONLY FRIENDS ON THIS WORLD. YOU HAVE DONE EVERYTHING YOU CAN TO HELP ME FIT IN. BUT EVERYWHERE I GO, EVERYTHING I DO, THESE TERRIBLE THINGS KEEP HAPPENING.›
‹I HAVE TO FIND OUT WHY!›
‹I HAVE TO FIND OUT WHAT IT IS. WHAT IT ALL MEANS.›
‹AND I HAVE TO DO IT ALONE.›
‹WHAT, YER JUST GOING TO...SAY GOODBYE?›
‹BUT WHERE WILL YE GO? WHAT WILL YE DO?›
TOM, SHE'S SAYING SHE'S--
I THINK I KNOW EXACTLY WHAT SHE'S SAYING.
TELL HER IT'S OKAY.
TELL HER WE'LL BE WAITING.
‹TOM SAYS YER VERY STUPID AND YE NEED TO STAY HERE FOREVER.›
‹NO HE DIDN'T.›
‹NAH, HE DIDN'T.›
‹ALL RIGHT THEN, KARA ZOR-EL...›
"‹GO GET 'EM!›"

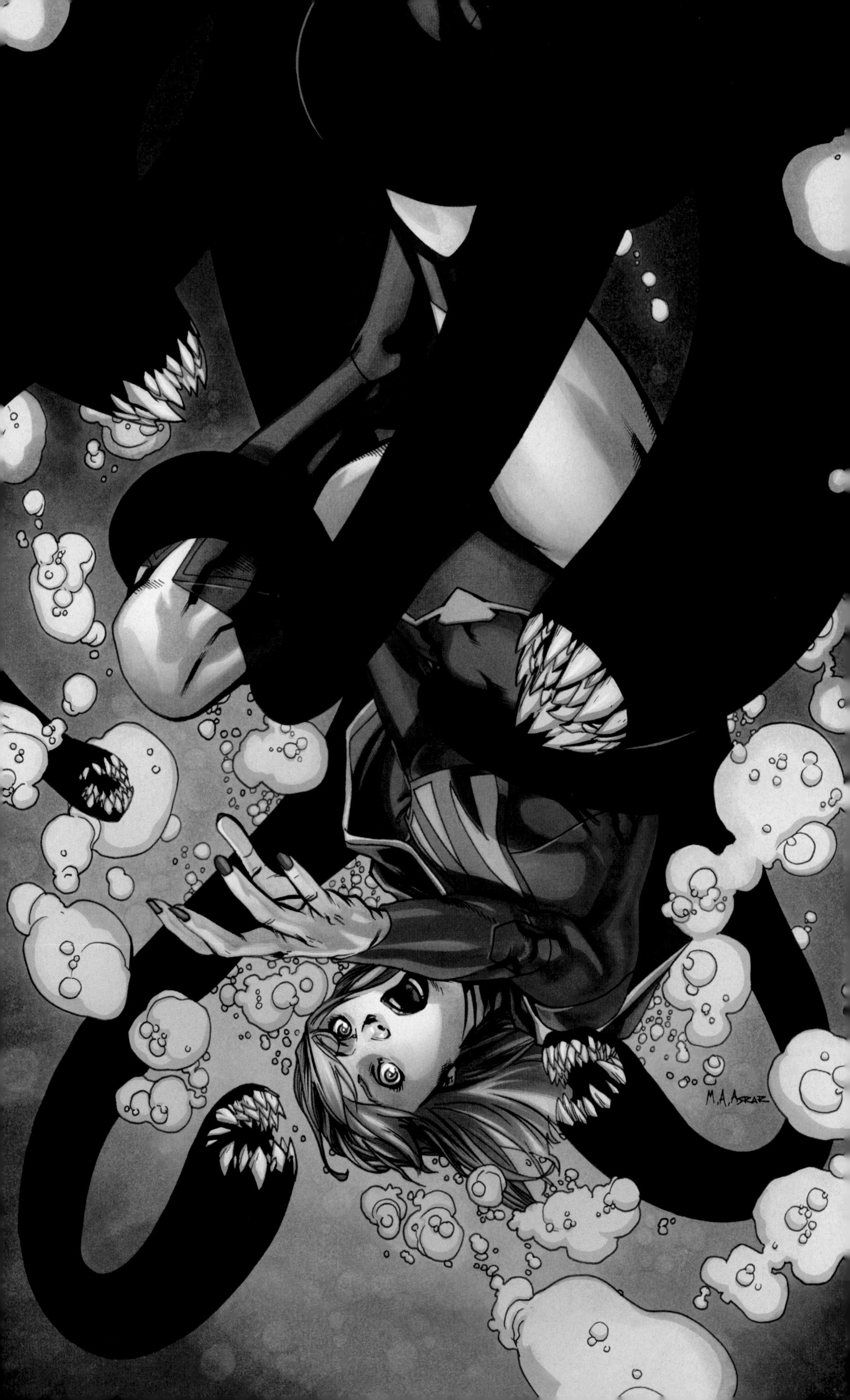
M.A. Asrar

INHERITANCE

MICHAEL GREEN & MIKE JOHNSON writers **MAHMUD ASRAR** penciller **CAM SMITH, MARC DEERING & MAHMUD ASRAR** inkers
cover art by **MAHMUD ASRAR & DAVE McCAIG**

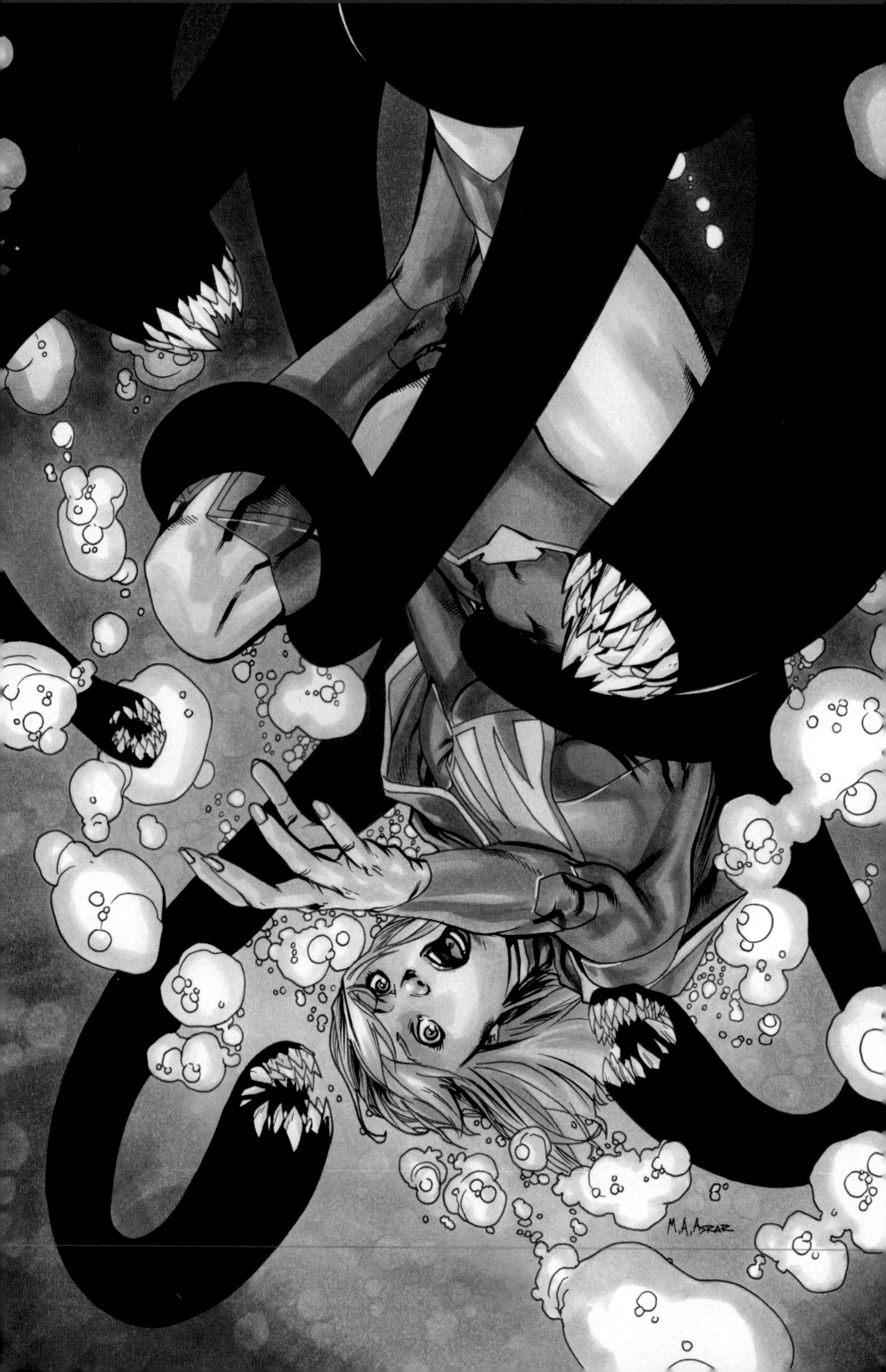
M.A. ASRAR

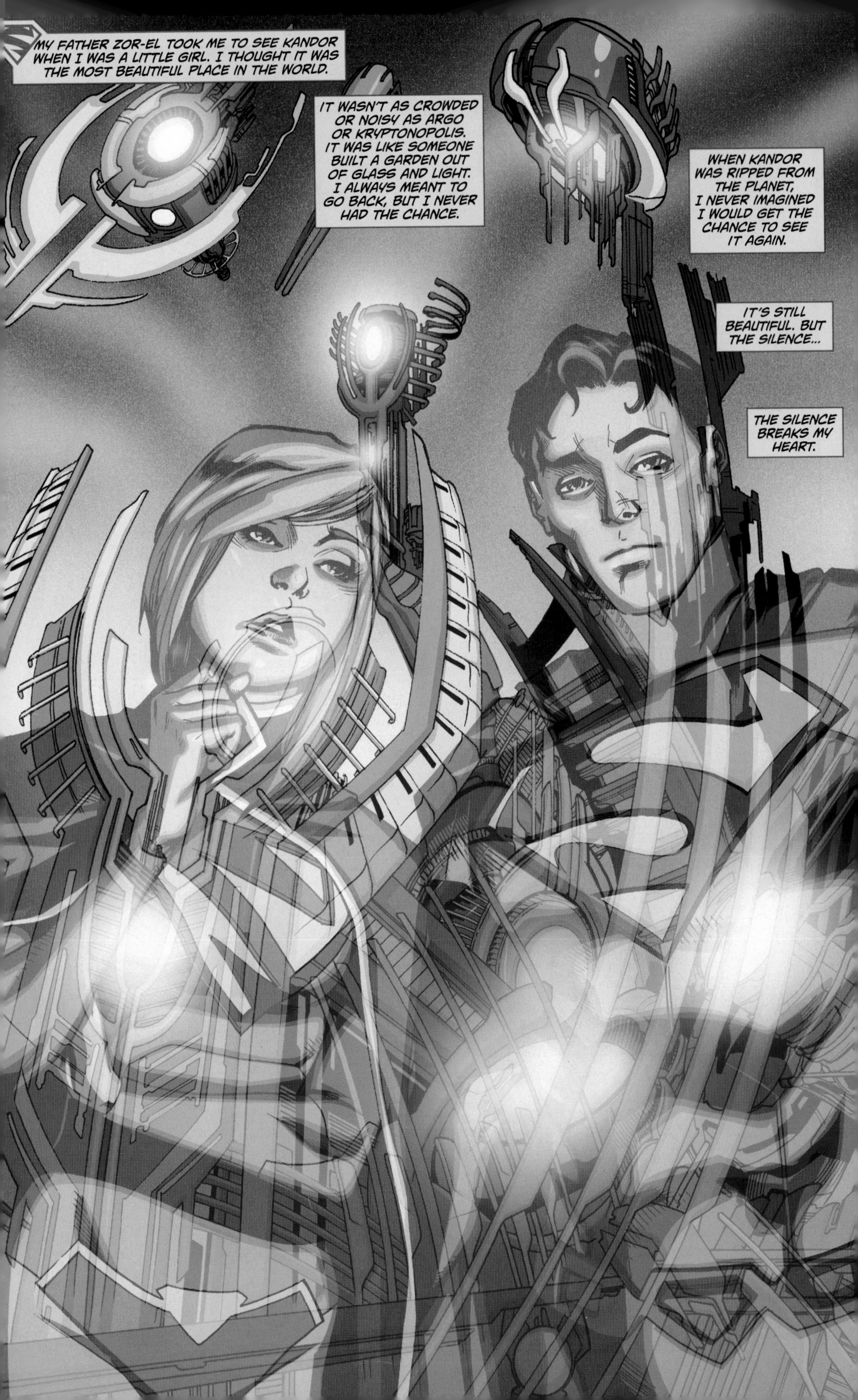
MY FATHER ZOR-EL TOOK ME TO SEE KANDOR WHEN I WAS A LITTLE GIRL. I THOUGHT IT WAS THE MOST BEAUTIFUL PLACE IN THE WORLD.
IT WASN'T AS CROWDED OR NOISY AS ARGO OR KRYPTONOPOLIS. IT WAS LIKE SOMEONE BUILT A GARDEN OUT OF GLASS AND LIGHT. I ALWAYS MEANT TO GO BACK, BUT I NEVER HAD THE CHANCE.
WHEN KANDOR WAS RIPPED FROM THE PLANET, I NEVER IMAGINED I WOULD GET THE CHANCE TO SEE IT AGAIN.
IT'S STILL BEAUTIFUL. BUT THE SILENCE...
THE SILENCE BREAKS MY HEART.

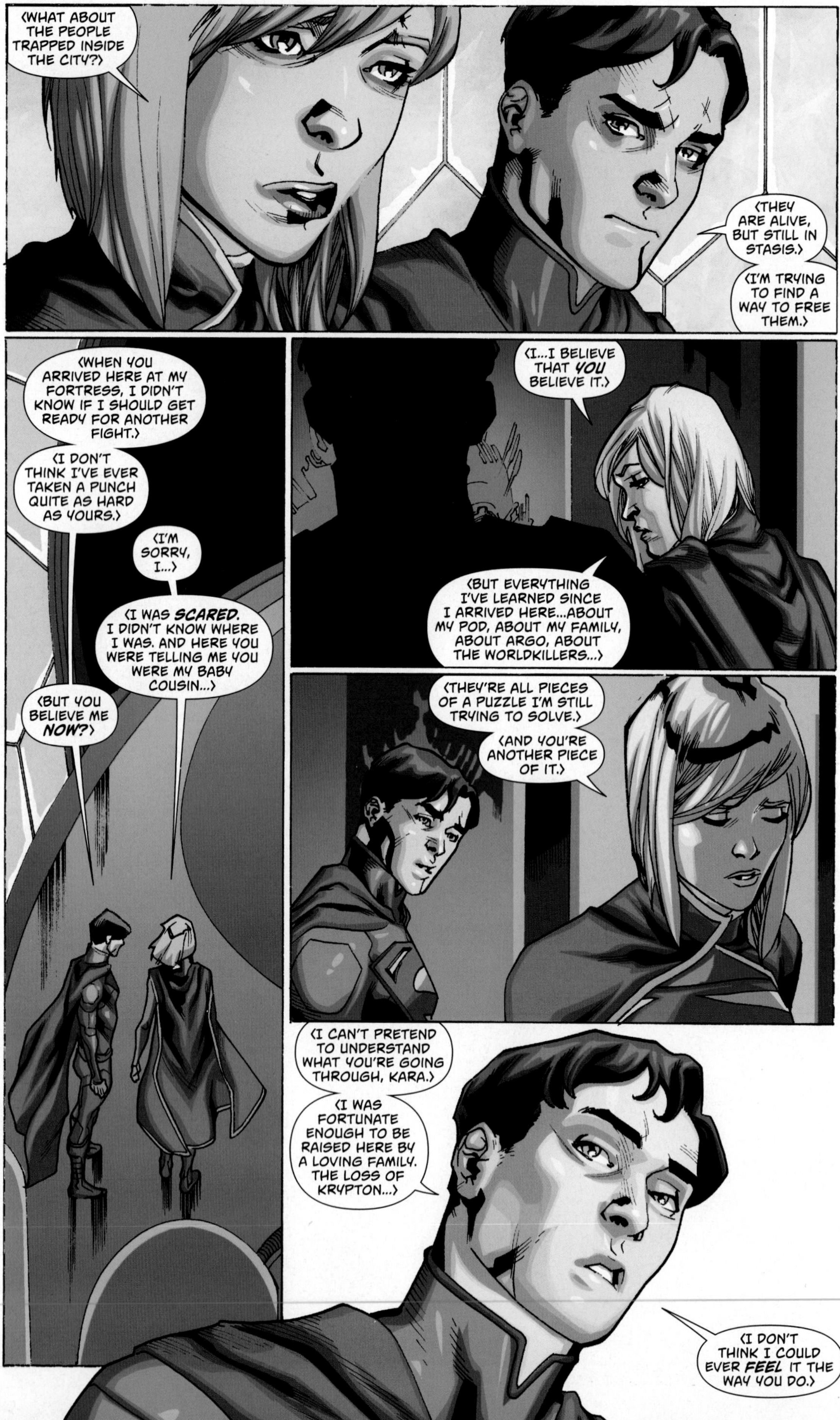

‹WHAT ABOUT THE PEOPLE TRAPPED INSIDE THE CITY?›
‹THEY ARE ALIVE, BUT STILL IN STASIS.›
‹I'M TRYING TO FIND A WAY TO FREE THEM.›
‹WHEN YOU ARRIVED HERE AT MY FORTRESS, I DIDN'T KNOW IF I SHOULD GET READY FOR ANOTHER FIGHT.›
‹I DON'T THINK I'VE EVER TAKEN A PUNCH QUITE AS HARD AS YOURS.›
‹I'M SORRY, I...›
‹I WAS SCARED. I DIDN'T KNOW WHERE I WAS. AND HERE YOU WERE TELLING ME YOU WERE MY BABY COUSIN...›
‹BUT YOU BELIEVE ME NOW?›
‹I...I BELIEVE THAT YOU BELIEVE IT.›
‹BUT EVERYTHING I'VE LEARNED HERE SINCE I ARRIVED HERE...ABOUT MY POD, ABOUT MY FAMILY, ABOUT ARGO, ABOUT THE WORLDKILLERS...›
‹THEY'RE ALL PIECES OF A PUZZLE I'M STILL TRYING TO SOLVE.›
‹AND YOU'RE ANOTHER PIECE OF IT.›
‹I CAN'T PRETEND TO UNDERSTAND WHAT YOU'RE GOING THROUGH, KARA.›
‹I WAS FORTUNATE ENOUGH TO BE RAISED HERE BY A LOVING FAMILY. THE LOSS OF KRYPTON...›
‹I DON'T THINK I COULD EVER FEEL IT THE WAY YOU DO.›

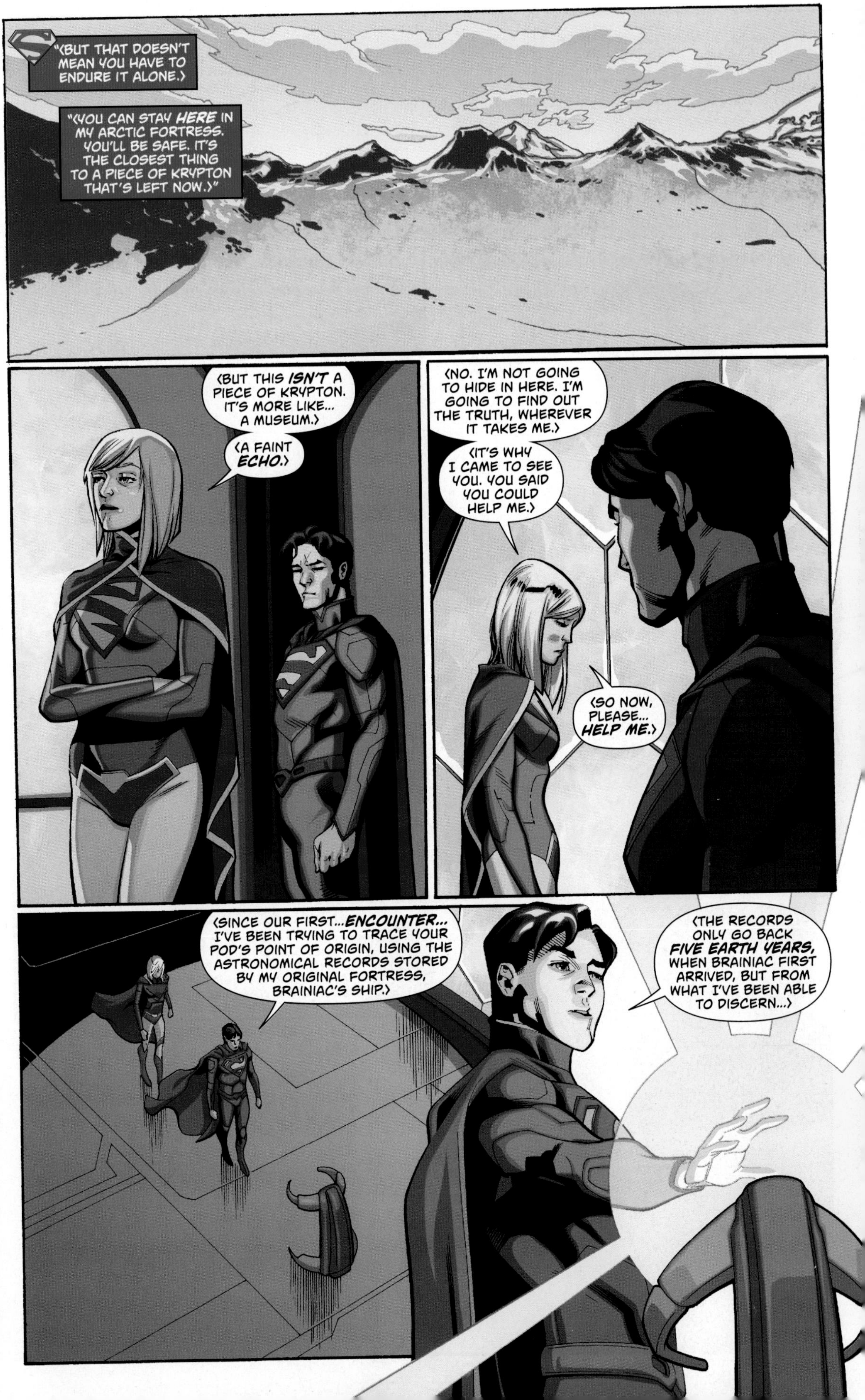
"‹BUT THAT DOESN'T MEAN YOU HAVE TO ENDURE IT ALONE.›
"‹YOU CAN STAY HERE IN MY ARCTIC FORTRESS. YOU'LL BE SAFE. IT'S THE CLOSEST THING TO A PIECE OF KRYPTON THAT'S LEFT NOW.›"
‹BUT THIS ISN'T A PIECE OF KRYPTON. IT'S MORE LIKE... A MUSEUM.›
‹A FAINT ECHO.›
‹NO. I'M NOT GOING TO HIDE IN HERE. I'M GOING TO FIND OUT THE TRUTH, WHEREVER IT TAKES ME.›
‹IT'S WHY I CAME TO SEE YOU. YOU SAID YOU COULD HELP ME.›
‹SO NOW, PLEASE... HELP ME.›
‹SINCE OUR FIRST...ENCOUNTER... I'VE BEEN TRYING TO TRACE YOUR POD'S POINT OF ORIGIN, USING THE ASTRONOMICAL RECORDS STORED BY MY ORIGINAL FORTRESS, BRAINIAC'S SHIP.›
‹THE RECORDS ONLY GO BACK FIVE EARTH YEARS, WHEN BRAINIAC FIRST ARRIVED, BUT FROM WHAT I'VE BEEN ABLE TO DISCERN...›

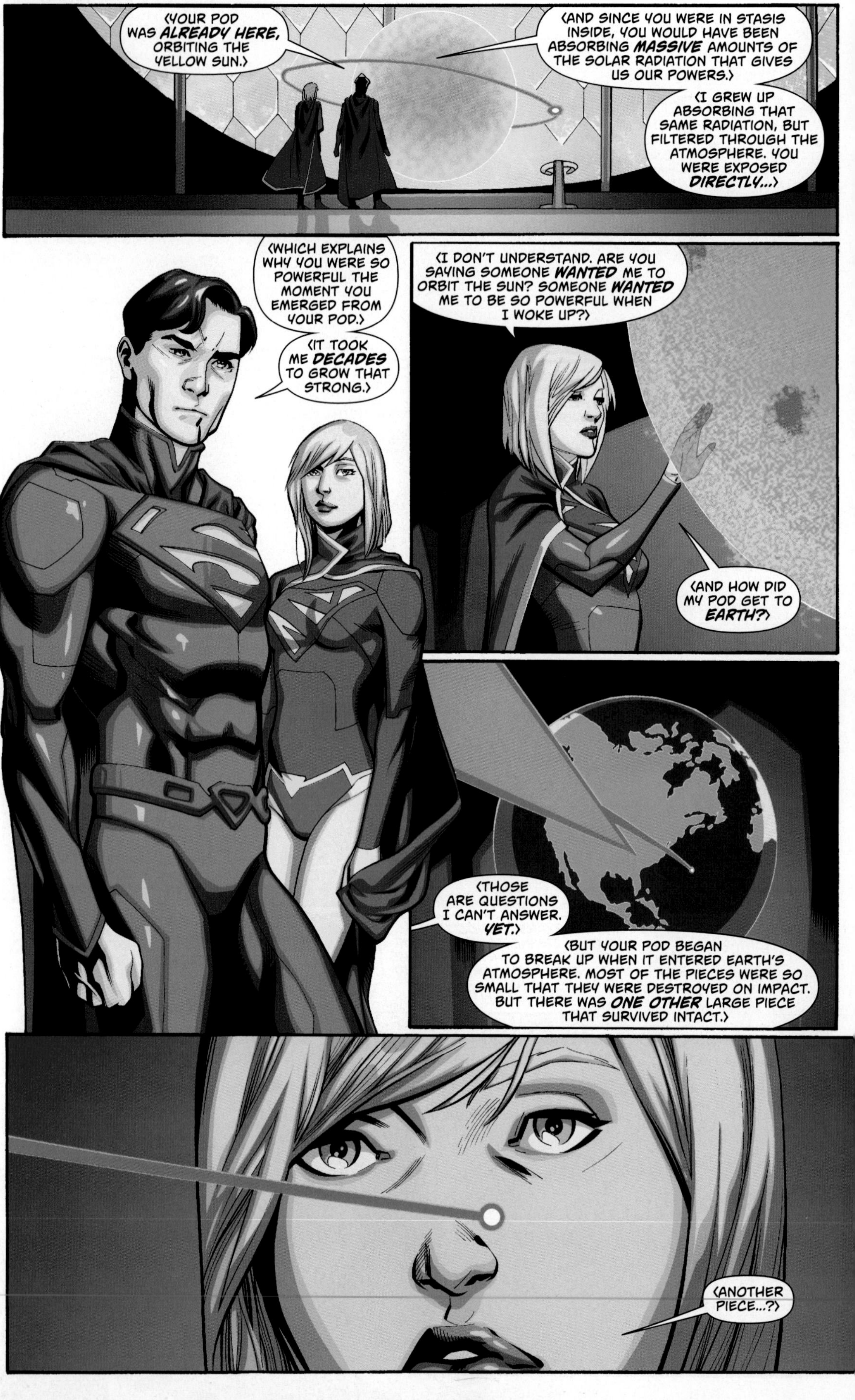
‹YOUR POD WAS ALREADY HERE, ORBITING THE YELLOW SUN.›
‹AND SINCE YOU WERE IN STASIS INSIDE, YOU WOULD HAVE BEEN ABSORBING MASSIVE AMOUNTS OF THE SOLAR RADIATION THAT GIVES US OUR POWERS.›
‹I GREW UP ABSORBING THAT SAME RADIATION, BUT FILTERED THROUGH THE ATMOSPHERE. YOU WERE EXPOSED DIRECTLY...›
‹WHICH EXPLAINS WHY YOU WERE SO POWERFUL THE MOMENT YOU EMERGED FROM YOUR POD.›
‹IT TOOK ME DECADES TO GROW THAT STRONG.›
‹I DON'T UNDERSTAND. ARE YOU SAYING SOMEONE WANTED ME TO ORBIT THE SUN? SOMEONE WANTED ME TO BE SO POWERFUL WHEN I WOKE UP?›
‹AND HOW DID MY POD GET TO EARTH?›
‹THOSE ARE QUESTIONS I CAN'T ANSWER. YET.›
‹BUT YOUR POD BEGAN TO BREAK UP WHEN IT ENTERED EARTH'S ATMOSPHERE. MOST OF THE PIECES WERE SO SMALL THAT THEY WERE DESTROYED ON IMPACT. BUT THERE WAS ONE OTHER LARGE PIECE THAT SURVIVED INTACT.›
‹ANOTHER PIECE...?›

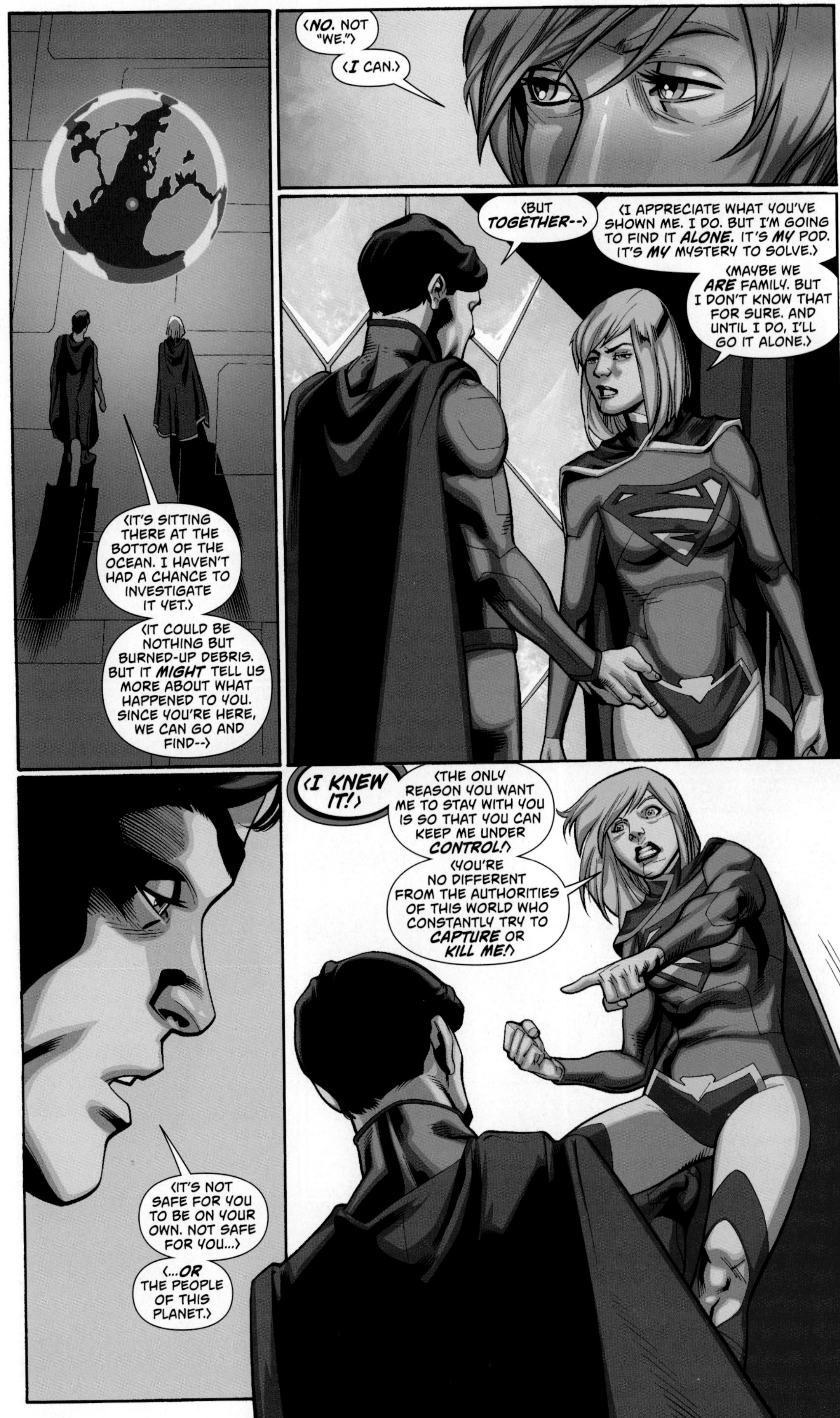

‹IT'S SITTING THERE AT THE BOTTOM OF THE OCEAN. I HAVEN'T HAD A CHANCE TO INVESTIGATE IT YET.›
‹IT COULD BE NOTHING BUT BURNED-UP DEBRIS. BUT IT MIGHT TELL US MORE ABOUT WHAT HAPPENED TO YOU. SINCE YOU'RE HERE, WE CAN GO AND FIND--›
‹NO. NOT "WE."›
‹I CAN.›
‹BUT TOGETHER--›
‹I APPRECIATE WHAT YOU'VE SHOWN ME. I DO. BUT I'M GOING TO FIND IT ALONE. IT'S MY POD. IT'S MY MYSTERY TO SOLVE.›
‹MAYBE WE ARE FAMILY. BUT I DON'T KNOW THAT FOR SURE. AND UNTIL I DO, I'LL GO IT ALONE.›
‹IT'S NOT SAFE FOR YOU TO BE ON YOUR OWN. NOT SAFE FOR YOU...›
‹...OR THE PEOPLE OF THIS PLANET.›
‹I KNEW IT!›
‹THE ONLY REASON YOU WANT ME TO STAY WITH YOU IS SO THAT YOU CAN KEEP ME UNDER CONTROL!›
‹YOU'RE NO DIFFERENT FROM THE AUTHORITIES OF THIS WORLD WHO CONSTANTLY TRY TO CAPTURE OR KILL ME!›

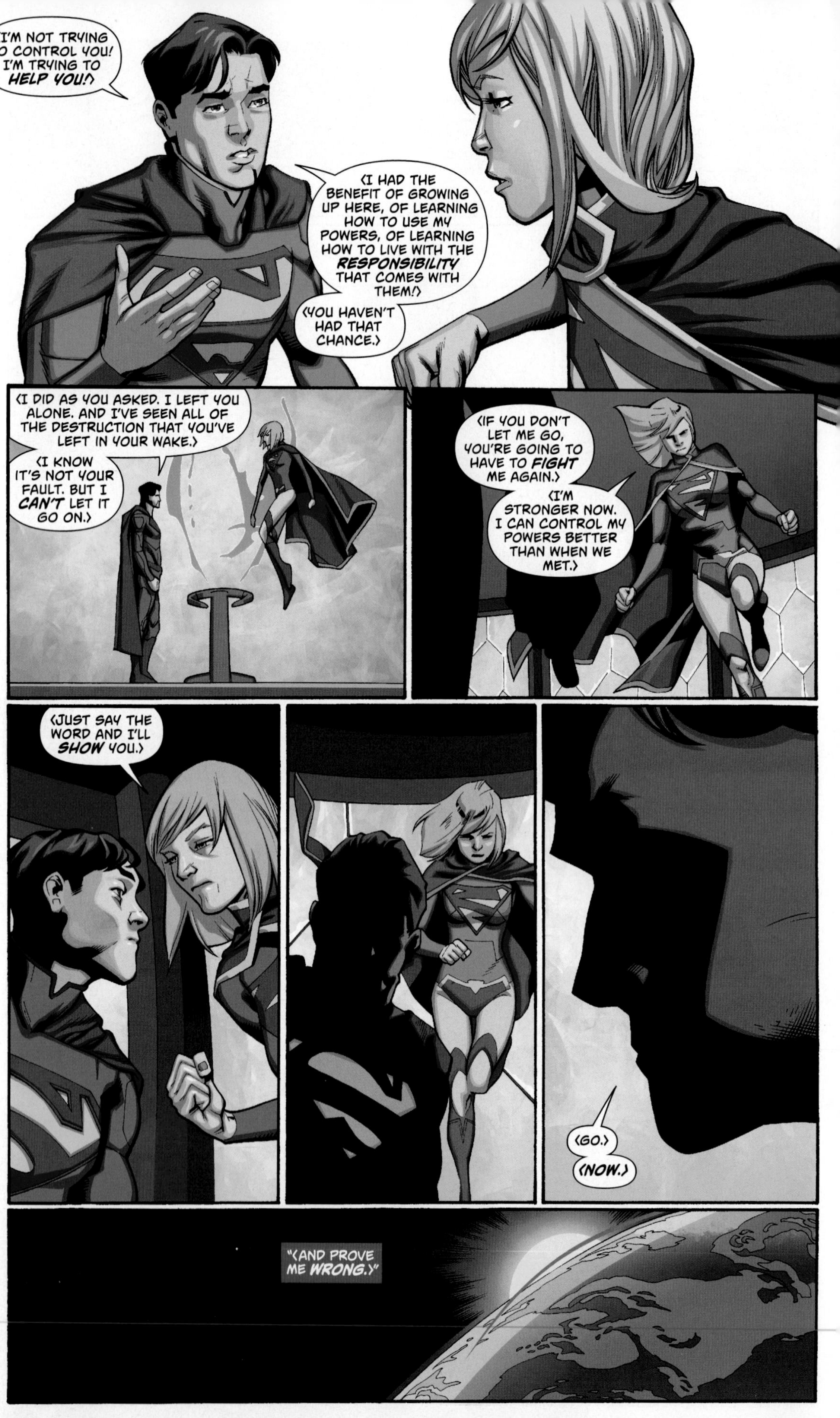
‹I'M NOT TRYING TO CONTROL YOU! I'M TRYING TO HELP YOU!›
‹I HAD THE BENEFIT OF GROWING UP HERE, OF LEARNING HOW TO USE MY POWERS, OF LEARNING HOW TO LIVE WITH THE RESPONSIBILITY THAT COMES WITH THEM!›
‹YOU HAVEN'T HAD THAT CHANCE.›
‹I DID AS YOU ASKED. I LEFT YOU ALONE. AND I'VE SEEN ALL OF THE DESTRUCTION THAT YOU'VE LEFT IN YOUR WAKE.›
‹I KNOW IT'S NOT YOUR FAULT. BUT I CAN'T LET IT GO ON.›
‹IF YOU DON'T LET ME GO, YOU'RE GOING TO HAVE TO FIGHT ME AGAIN.›
‹I'M STRONGER NOW. I CAN CONTROL MY POWERS BETTER THAN WHEN WE MET.›
‹JUST SAY THE WORD AND I'LL SHOW YOU.›
‹GO.›
‹NOW.›
"‹AND PROVE ME WRONG.›"

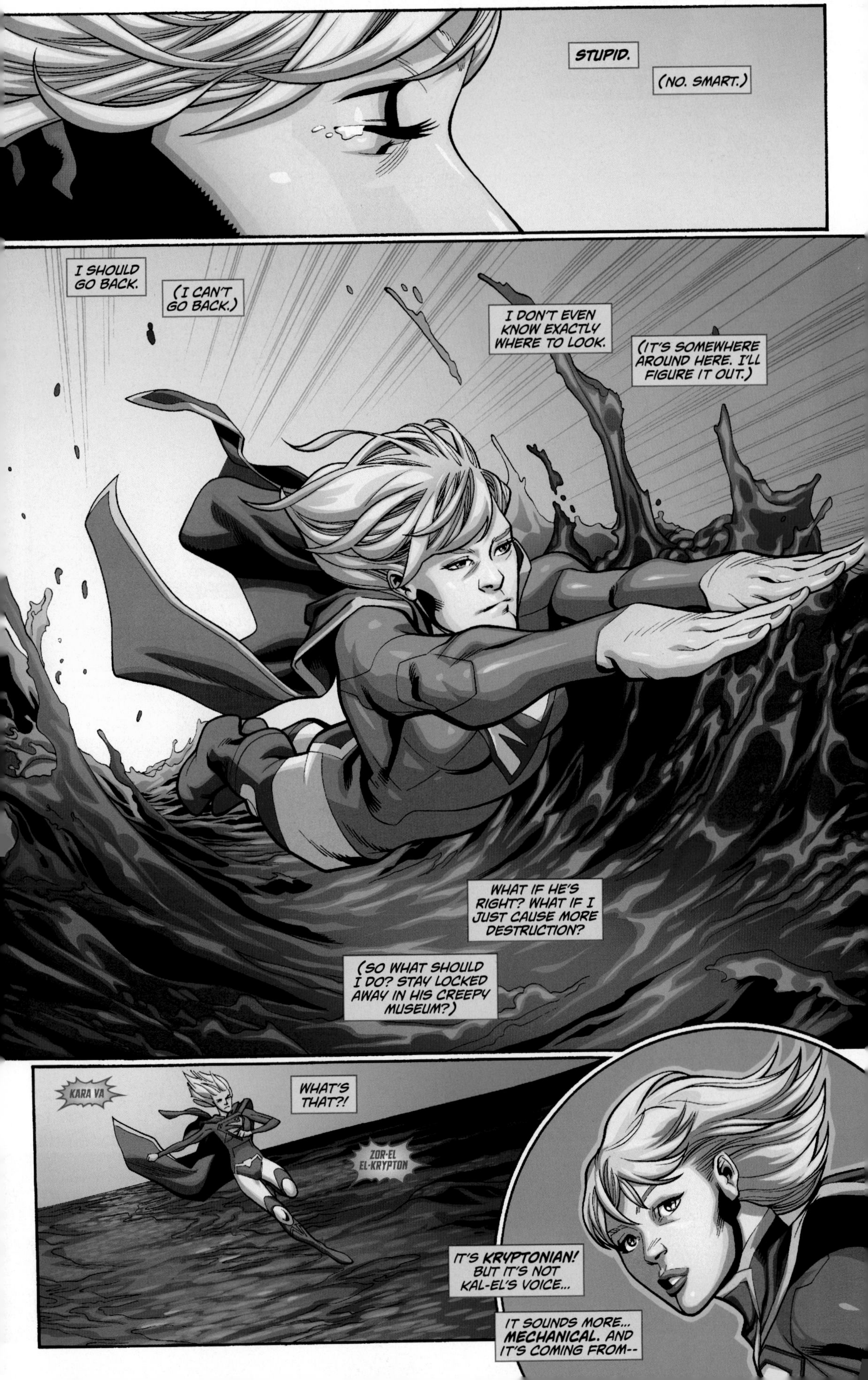
STUPID.
(NO. SMART.)
I SHOULD GO BACK.
(I CAN'T GO BACK.)
I DON'T EVEN KNOW EXACTLY WHERE TO LOOK.
(IT'S SOMEWHERE AROUND HERE. I'LL FIGURE IT OUT.)
WHAT IF HE'S RIGHT? WHAT IF I JUST CAUSE MORE DESTRUCTION?
(SO WHAT SHOULD I DO? STAY LOCKED AWAY IN HIS CREEPY MUSEUM?)
KARA VA
WHAT'S THAT?!
ZOR-EL EL-KRYPTON
IT'S KRYPTONIAN! BUT IT'S NOT KAL-EL'S VOICE...
IT SOUNDS MORE... MECHANICAL. AND IT'S COMING FROM--

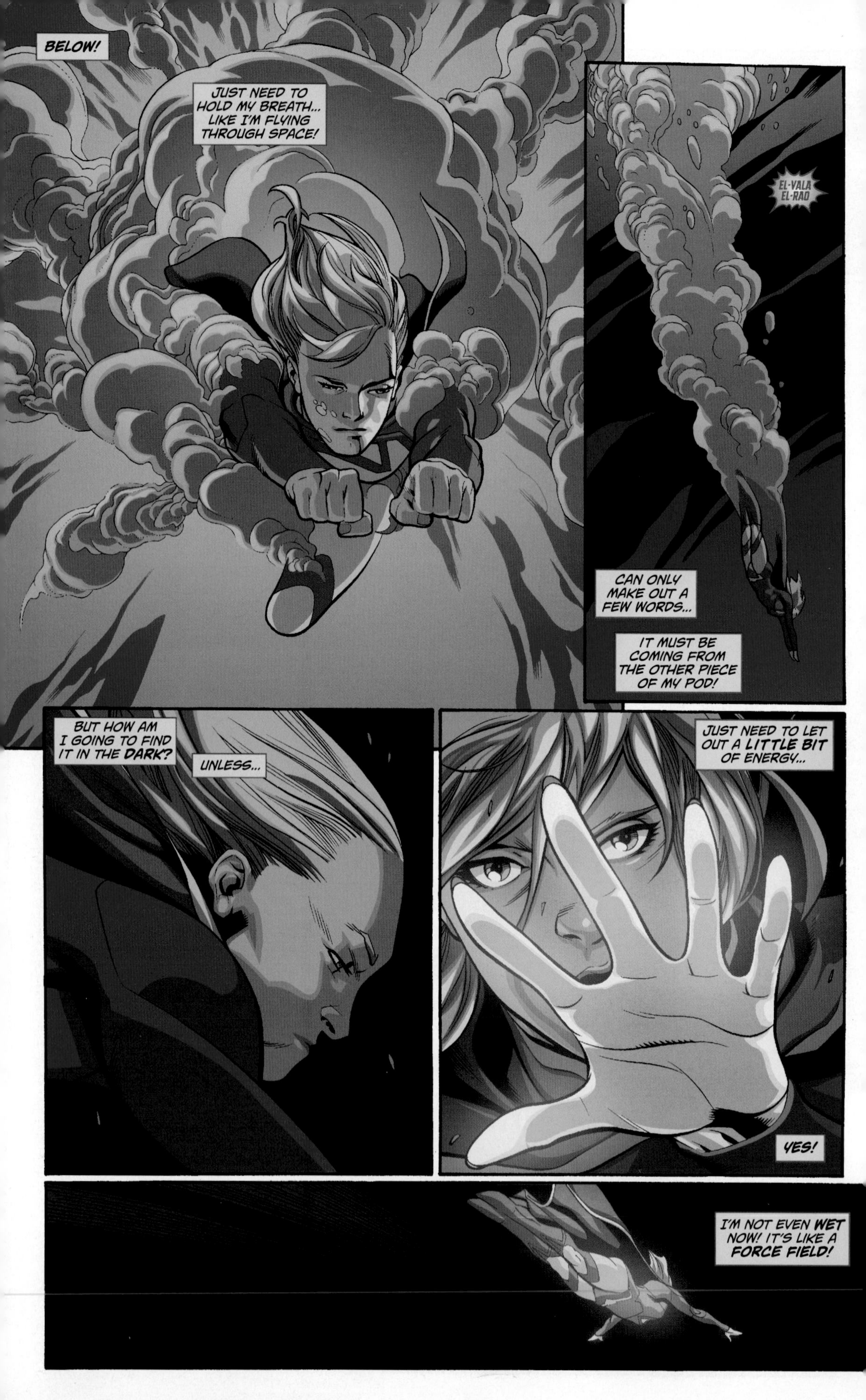
BELOW!
JUST NEED TO HOLD MY BREATH... LIKE I'M FLYING THROUGH SPACE!
EL-VALA EL-RAO
CAN ONLY MAKE OUT A FEW WORDS...
IT MUST BE COMING FROM THE OTHER PIECE OF MY POD!
BUT HOW AM I GOING TO FIND IT IN THE DARK?
UNLESS...
JUST NEED TO LET OUT A LITTLE BIT OF ENERGY...
YES!
I'M NOT EVEN WET NOW! IT'S LIKE A FORCE FIELD!

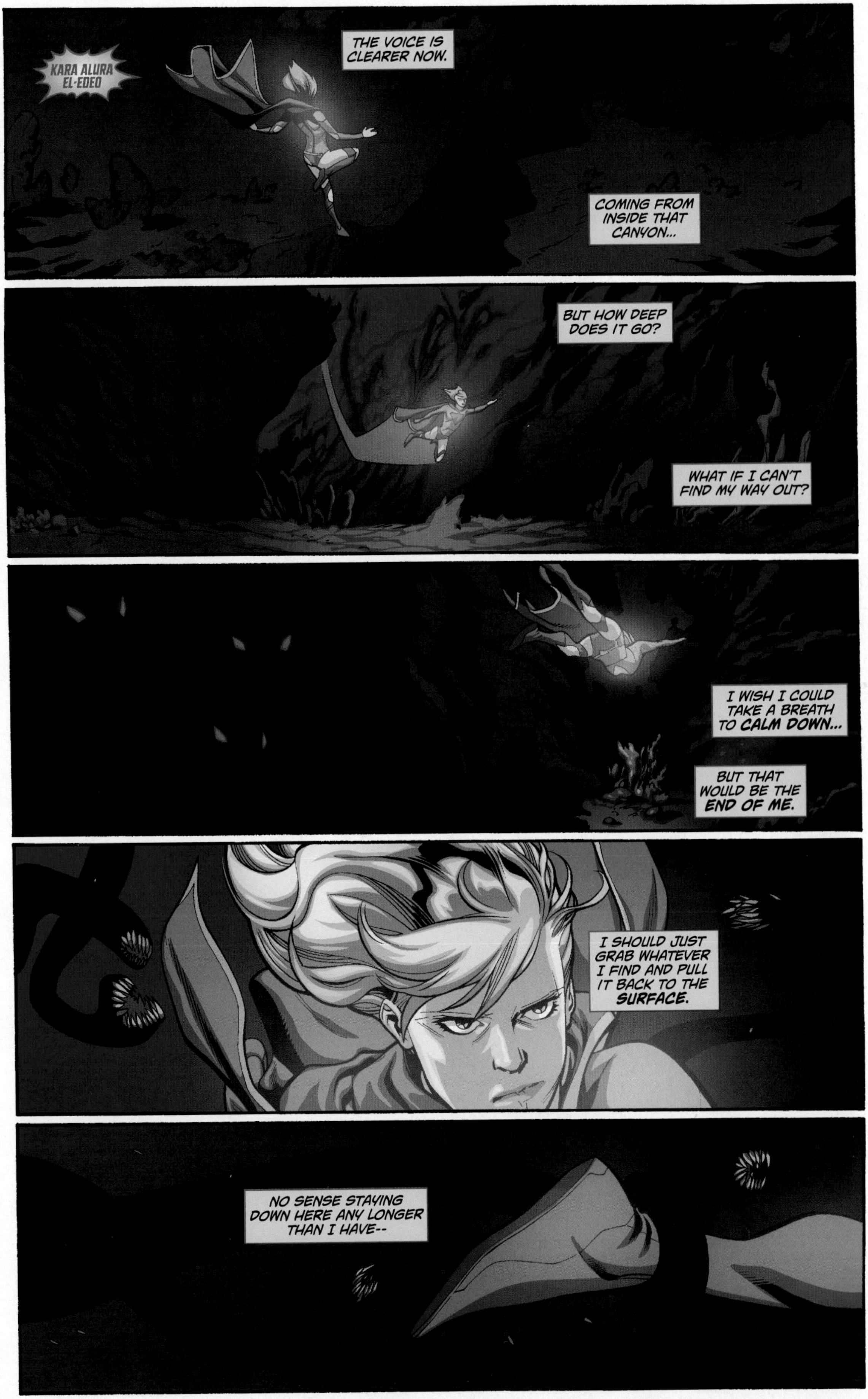
KARA ALURA EL-EDEO
THE VOICE IS CLEARER NOW.
COMING FROM INSIDE THAT CANYON...
BUT HOW DEEP DOES IT GO?
WHAT IF I CAN'T FIND MY WAY OUT?
I WISH I COULD TAKE A BREATH TO CALM DOWN...
BUT THAT WOULD BE THE END OF ME.
I SHOULD JUST GRAB WHATEVER I FIND AND PULL IT BACK TO THE SURFACE.
NO SENSE STAYING DOWN HERE ANY LONGER THAN I HAVE--

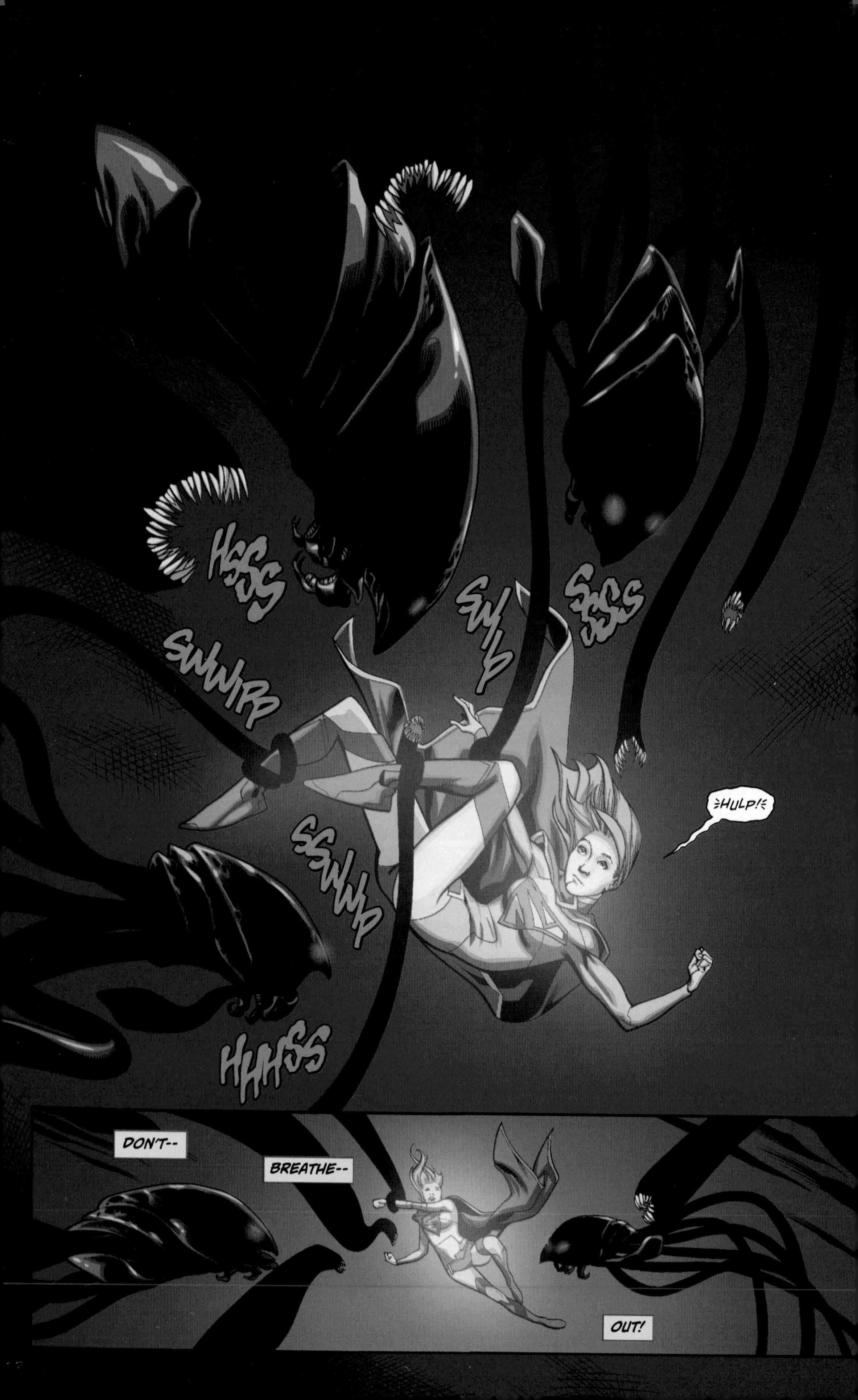

HSSS
SWWIPP
SWIP
SSSS
SSWWIP
HULP!
HHHSS
DON'T--
BREATHE--
OUT!

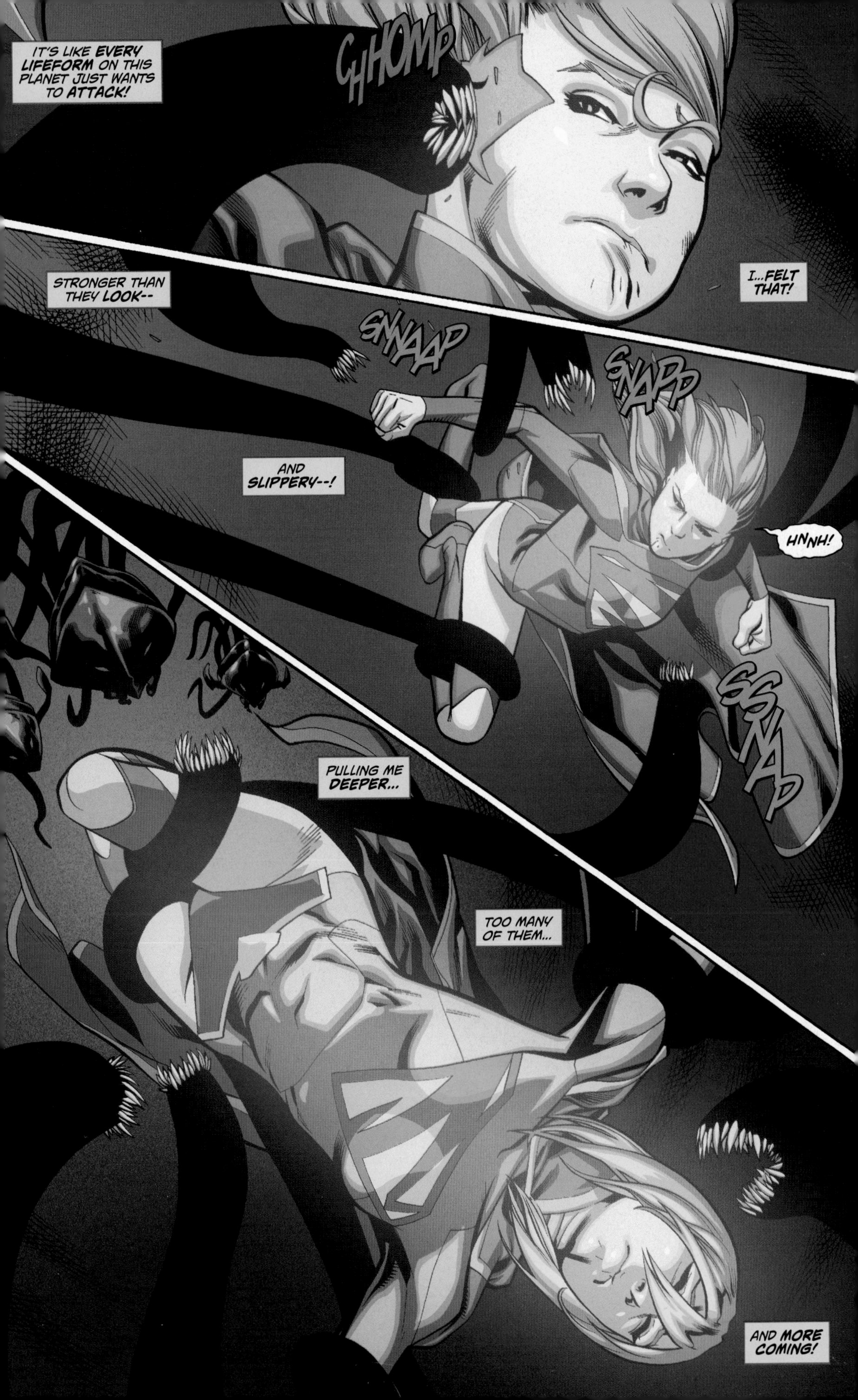

IT'S LIKE EVERY LIFEFORM ON THIS PLANET JUST WANTS TO ATTACK!
CHHOMP
STRONGER THAN THEY LOOK--
I...FELT THAT!
SNNAAP
SNAPP
AND SLIPPERY--!
HNNH!
SSNAPP
PULLING ME DEEPER...
TOO MANY OF THEM...
AND MORE COMING!

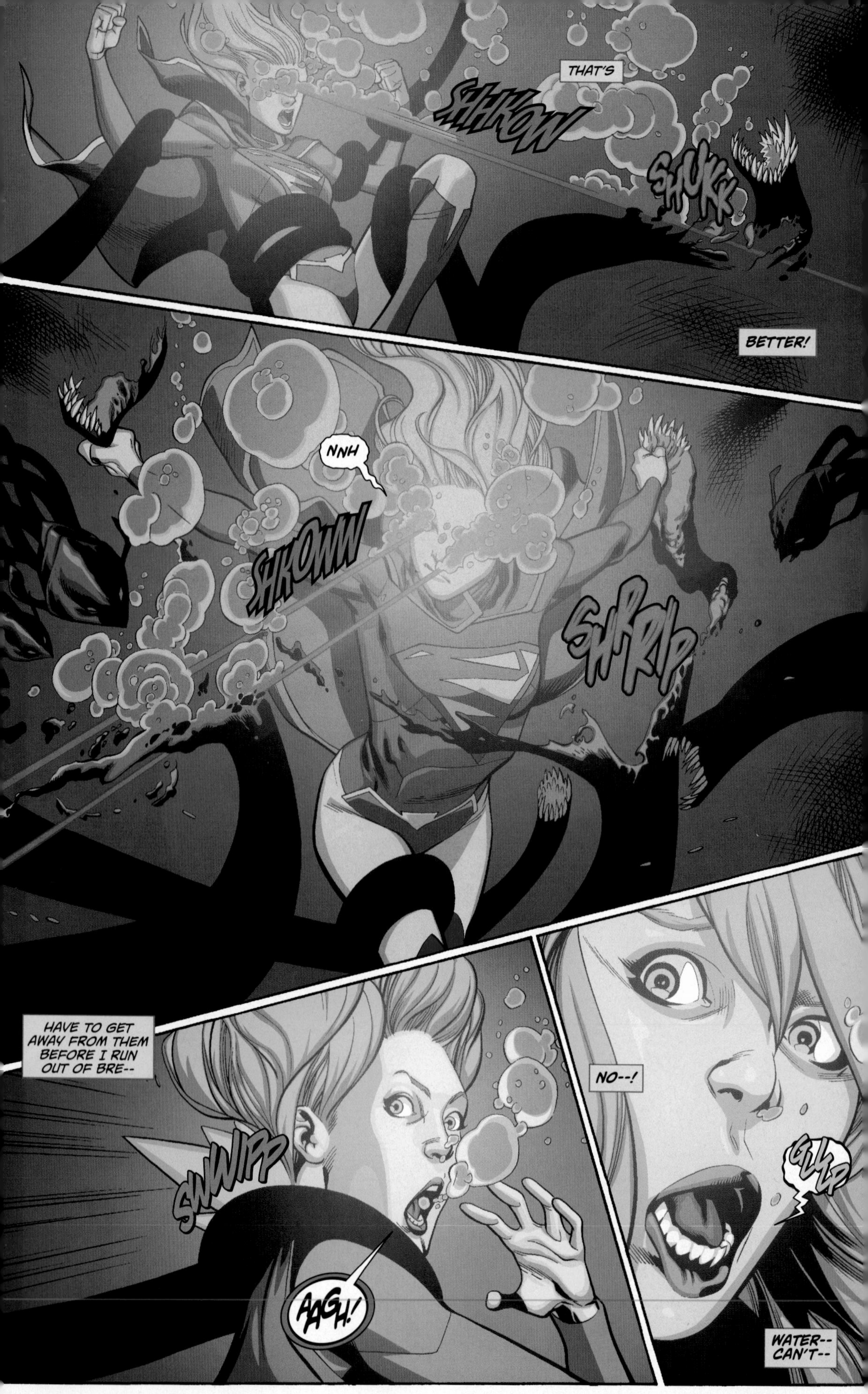
THAT'S
SHKOW
SHUKK
BETTER!
NNH
SHKOWW
SHRIP
HAVE TO GET AWAY FROM THEM BEFORE I RUN OUT OF BRE--
SNWIPP
AAGH!
NO--!
GLULP
WATER-- CAN'T--

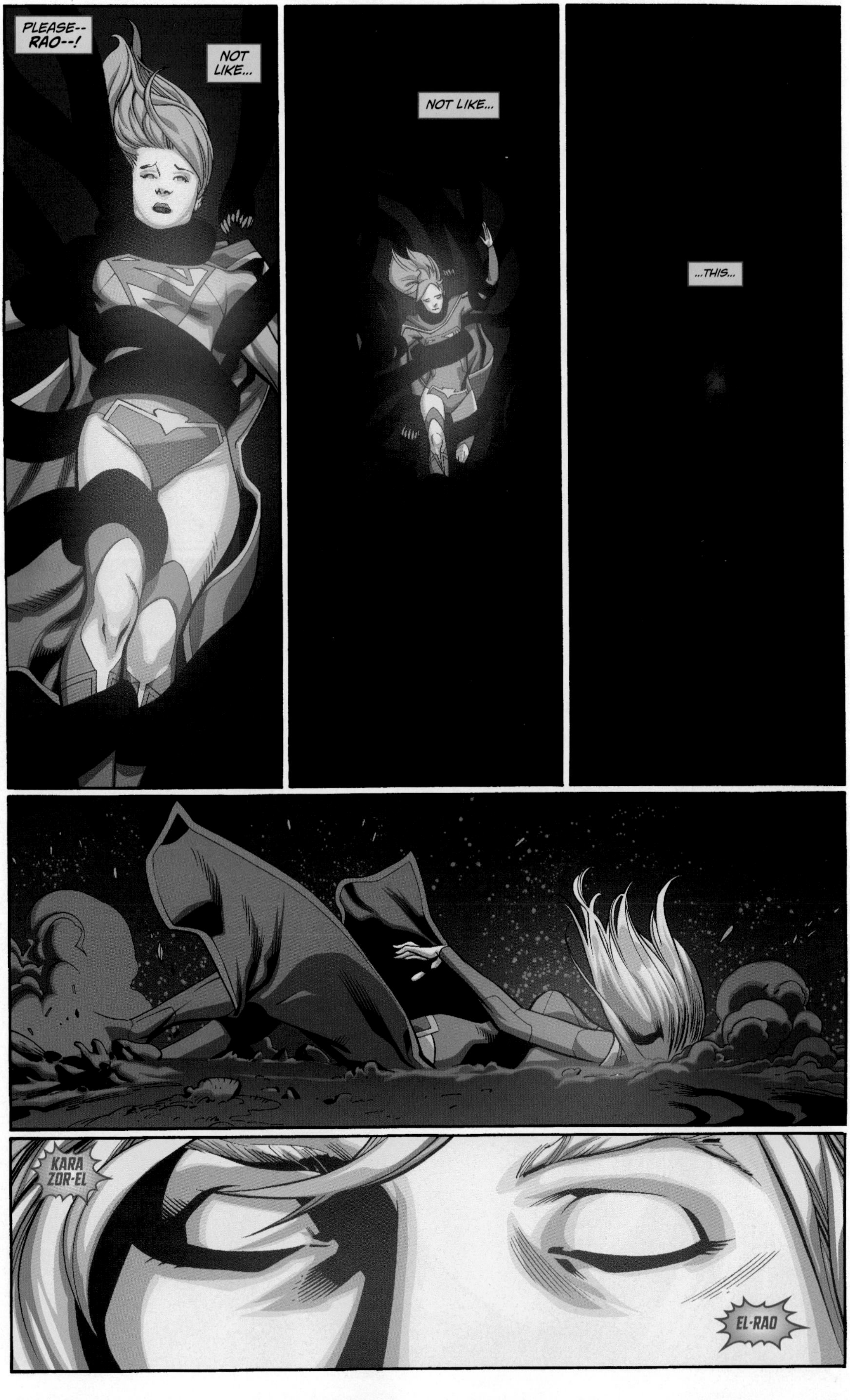
PLEASE--
RAO--!
NOT LIKE...
NOT LIKE...
...THIS...
KARA ZOR-EL
EL-RAO

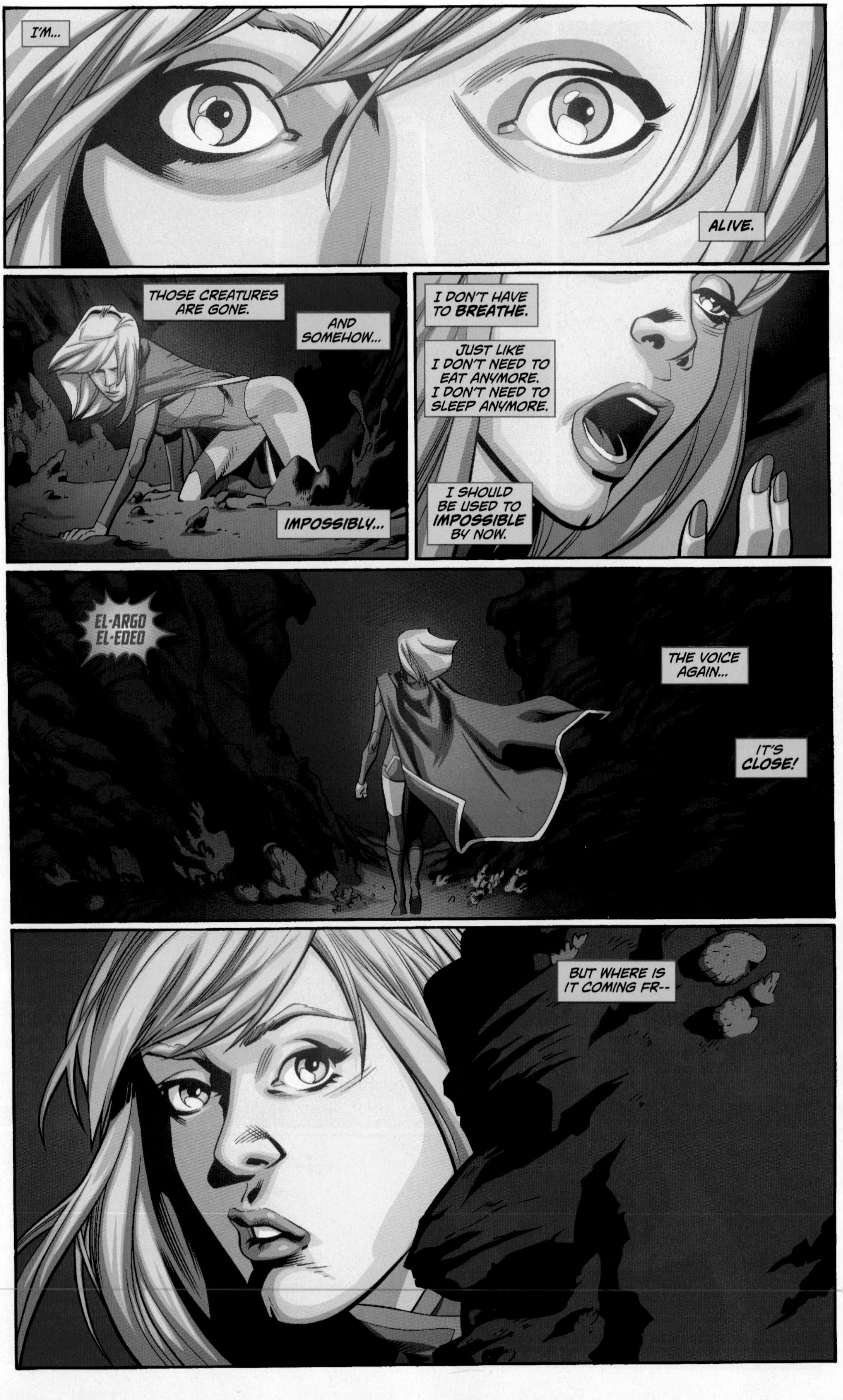
I'M...
ALIVE.
THOSE CREATURES ARE GONE.
AND SOMEHOW...
IMPOSSIBLY...
I DON'T HAVE TO BREATHE.
JUST LIKE I DON'T NEED TO EAT ANYMORE. I DON'T NEED TO SLEEP ANYMORE.
I SHOULD BE USED TO IMPOSSIBLE BY NOW.
EL-ARGO EL-EDEO
THE VOICE AGAIN...
IT'S CLOSE!
BUT WHERE IS IT COMING FR--

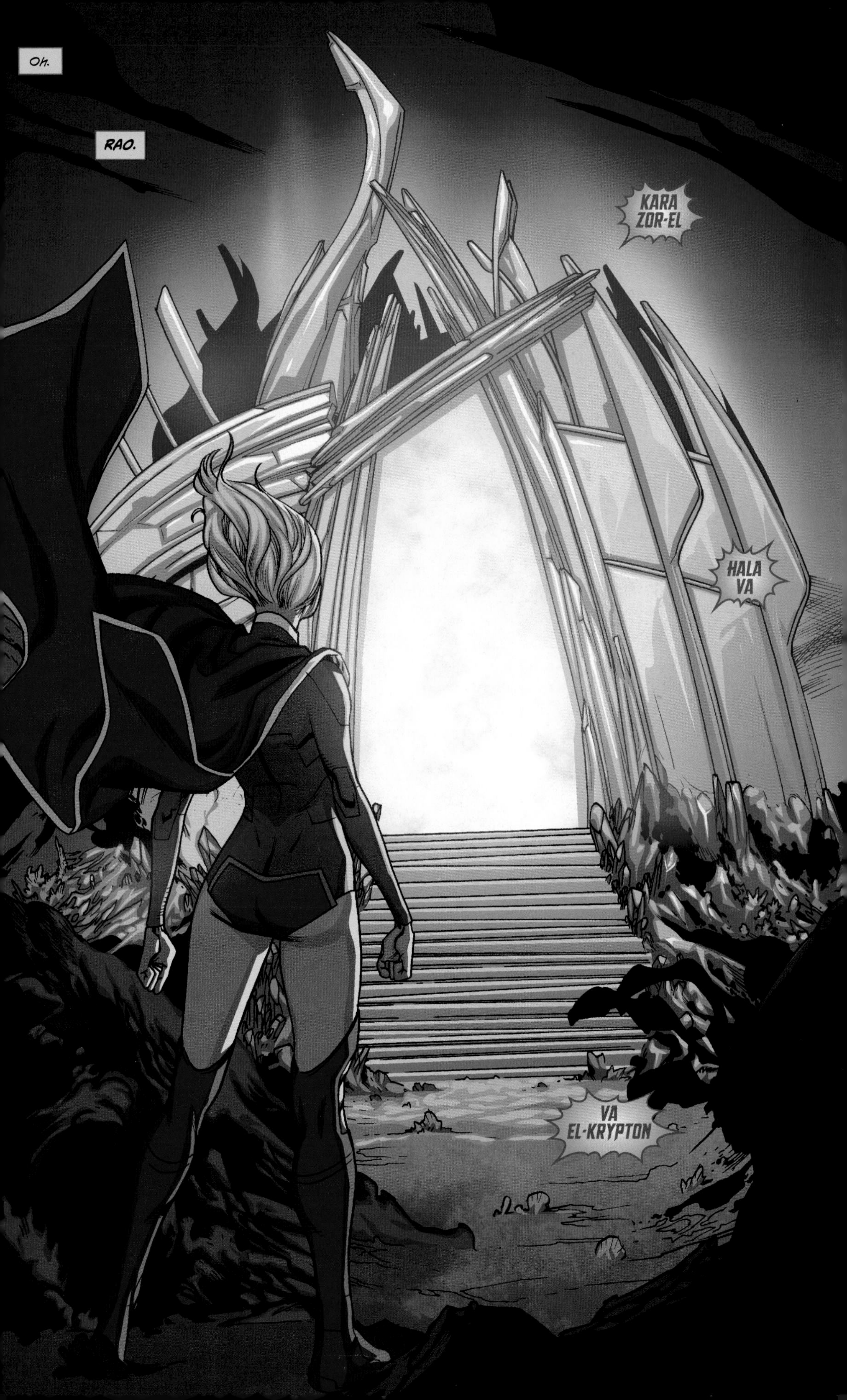
Oh.
RAO.
KARA ZOR-EL
HALA VA
VA EL-KRYPTON

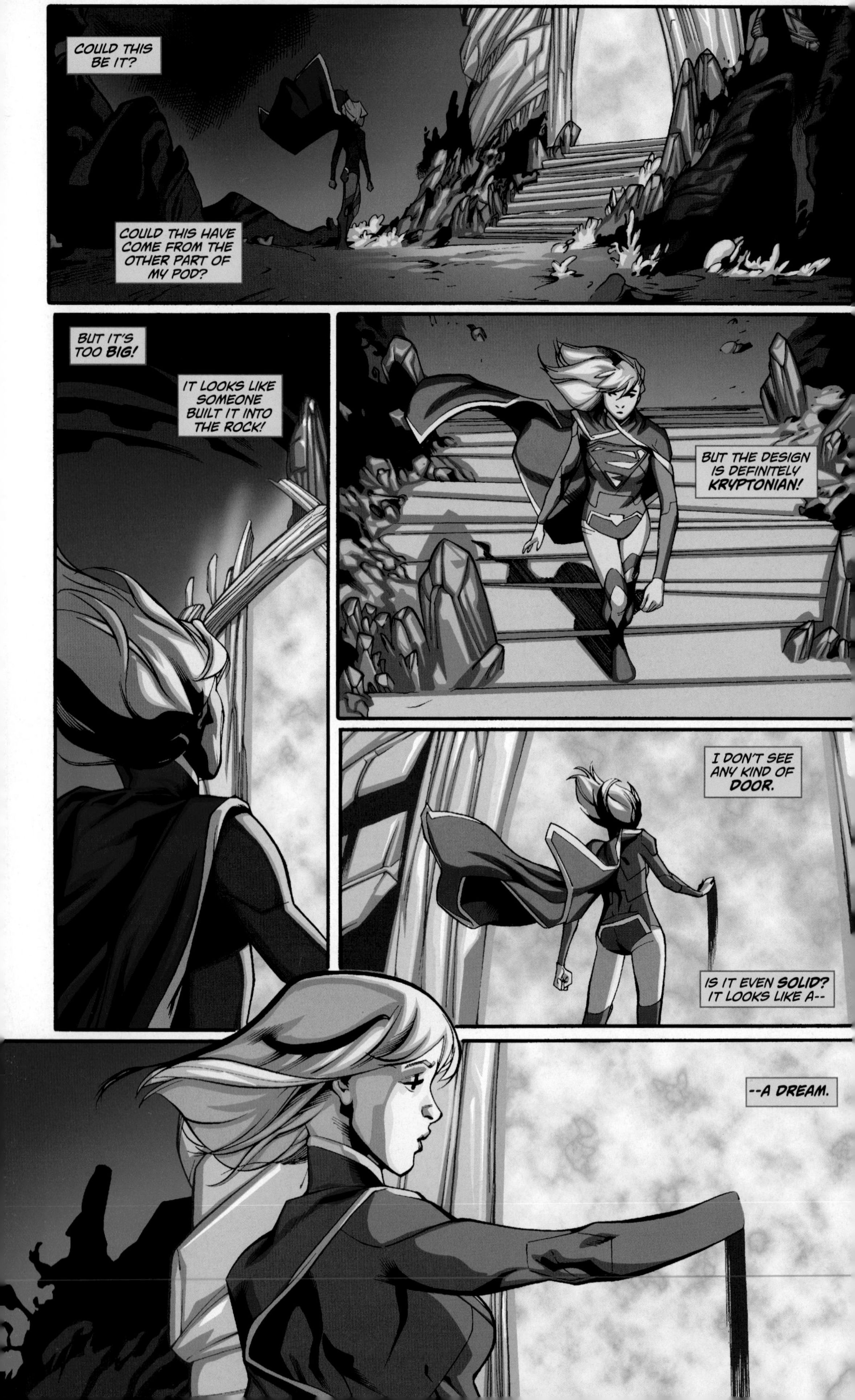
COULD THIS BE IT?
COULD THIS HAVE COME FROM THE OTHER PART OF MY POD?
BUT IT'S TOO BIG!
IT LOOKS LIKE SOMEONE BUILT IT INTO THE ROCK!
BUT THE DESIGN IS DEFINITELY KRYPTONIAN!
I DON'T SEE ANY KIND OF DOOR.
IS IT EVEN SOLID? IT LOOKS LIKE A--
--A DREAM.

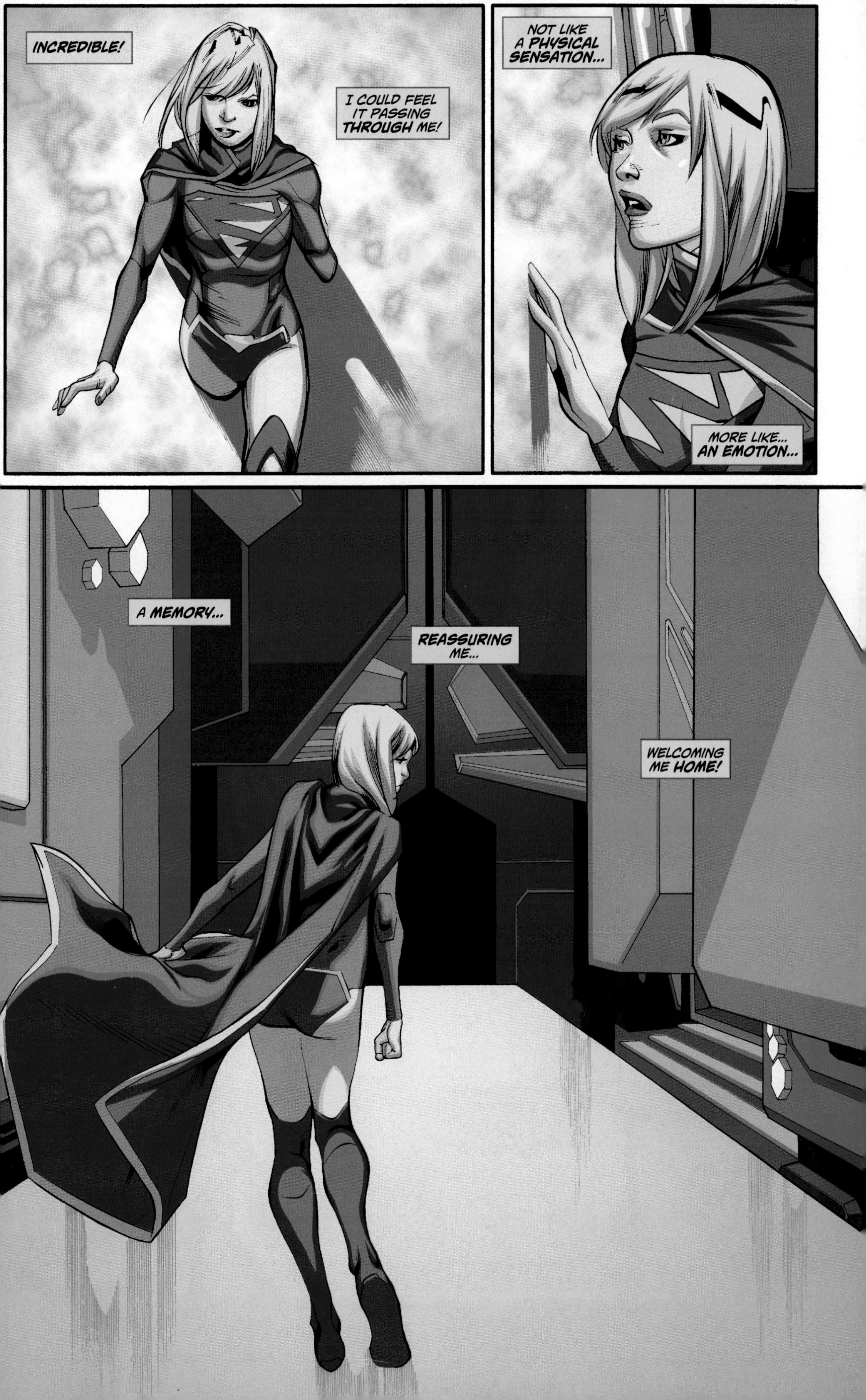
INCREDIBLE!
I COULD FEEL IT PASSING THROUGH ME!
NOT LIKE A PHYSICAL SENSATION...
MORE LIKE... AN EMOTION...
A MEMORY...
REASSURING ME...
WELCOMING ME HOME!

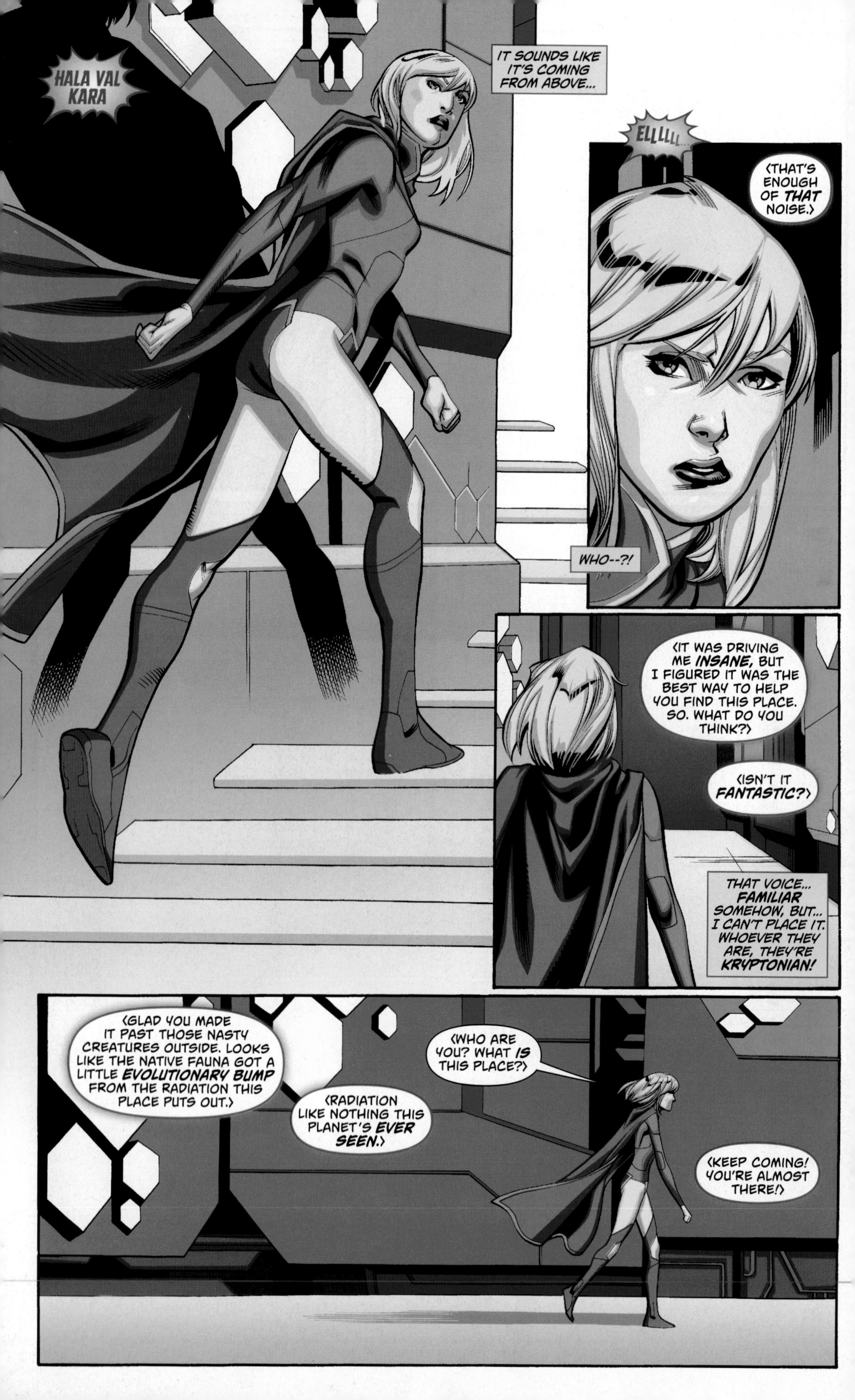
HALA VAL KARA
IT SOUNDS LIKE IT'S COMING FROM ABOVE...
ELLLLLL...
‹THAT'S ENOUGH OF ***THAT*** NOISE.›
WHO--?!
‹IT WAS DRIVING ME ***INSANE,*** BUT I FIGURED IT WAS THE BEST WAY TO HELP YOU FIND THIS PLACE. SO. WHAT DO YOU THINK?›
‹ISN'T IT ***FANTASTIC?***›
*THAT VOICE... **FAMILIAR** SOMEHOW, BUT... I CAN'T PLACE IT. WHOEVER THEY ARE, THEY'RE **KRYPTONIAN!***
‹GLAD YOU MADE IT PAST THOSE NASTY CREATURES OUTSIDE. LOOKS LIKE THE NATIVE FAUNA GOT A LITTLE ***EVOLUTIONARY BUMP*** FROM THE RADIATION THIS PLACE PUTS OUT.›
‹RADIATION LIKE NOTHING THIS PLANET'S ***EVER SEEN.***›
‹WHO ARE YOU? WHAT ***IS*** THIS PLACE?›
‹KEEP COMING! YOU'RE ALMOST THERE!›

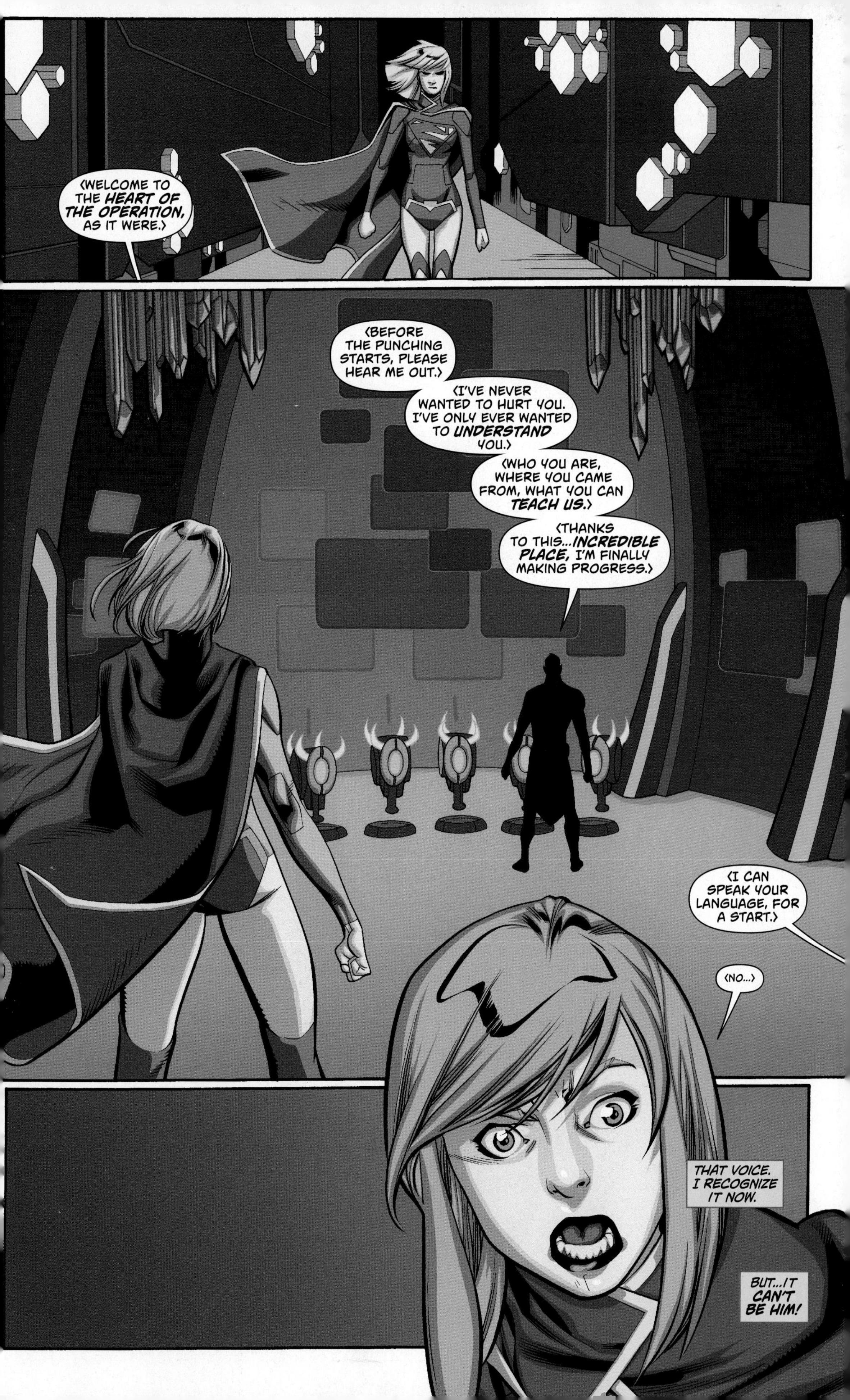

⟨WELCOME TO THE **HEART OF THE OPERATION,** AS IT WERE.⟩
⟨BEFORE THE PUNCHING STARTS, PLEASE HEAR ME OUT.⟩
⟨I'VE NEVER WANTED TO HURT YOU. I'VE ONLY EVER WANTED TO **UNDERSTAND** YOU.⟩
⟨WHO YOU ARE, WHERE YOU CAME FROM, WHAT YOU CAN **TEACH US.**⟩
⟨THANKS TO THIS...**INCREDIBLE PLACE,** I'M FINALLY MAKING PROGRESS.⟩
⟨I CAN SPEAK YOUR LANGUAGE, FOR A START.⟩
⟨NO...⟩
THAT VOICE. I RECOGNIZE IT NOW.
BUT...IT **CAN'T BE HIM!**

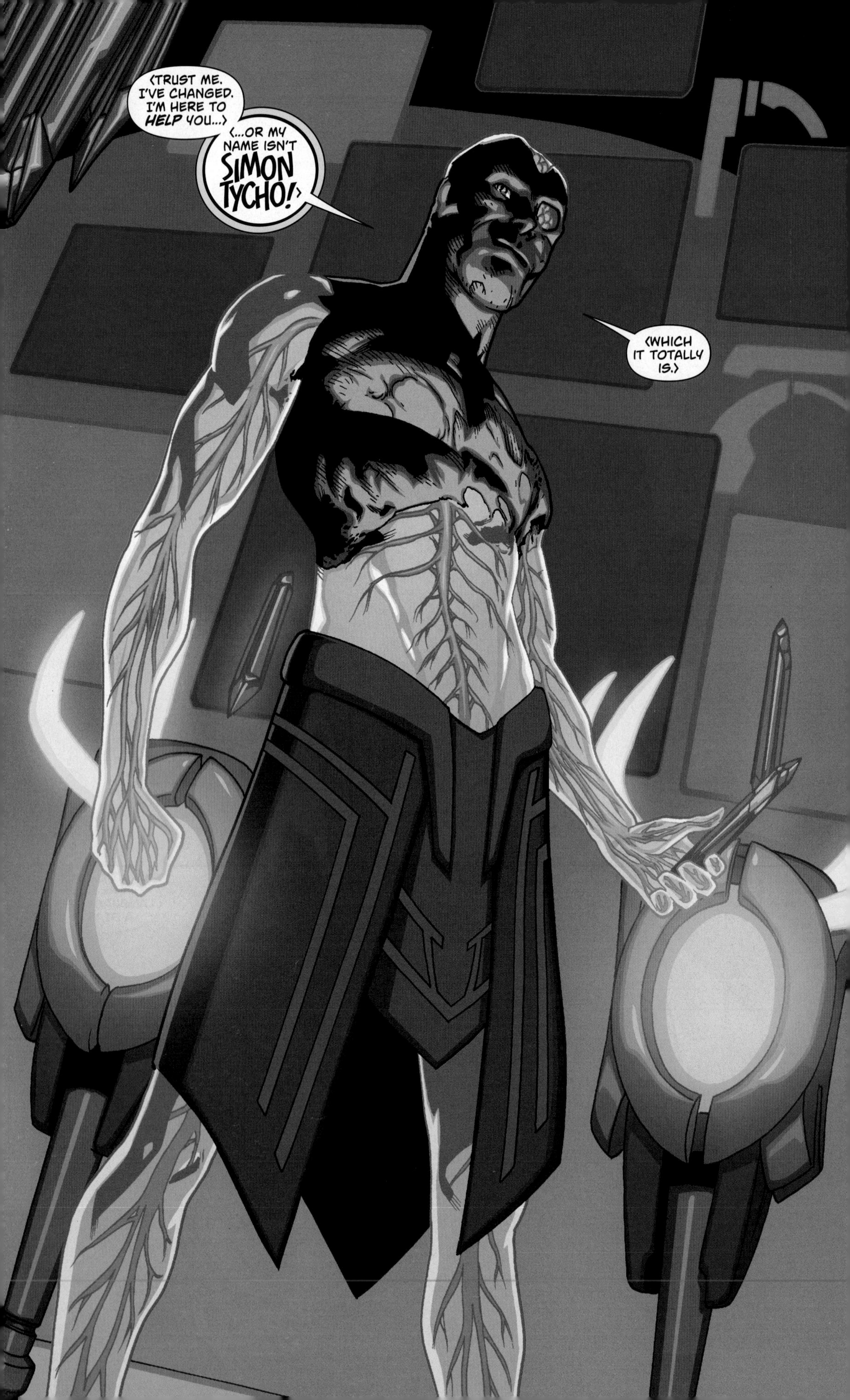
‹TRUST ME. I'VE CHANGED. I'M HERE TO HELP YOU...›
‹...OR MY NAME ISN'T SIMON TYCHO!›
‹WHICH IT TOTALLY IS.›

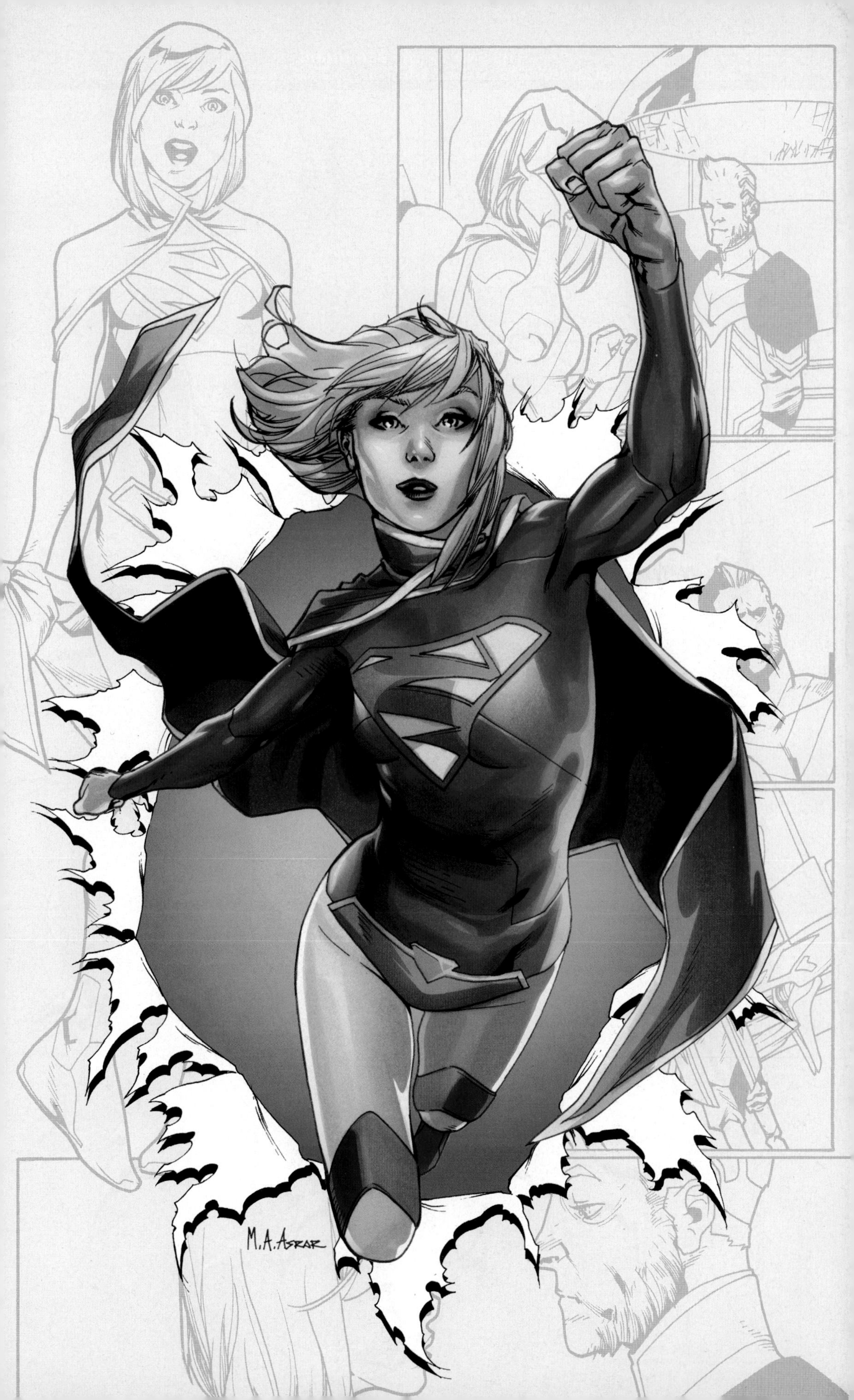
M.A. ASRAR

THE END OF THE BEGINNING

MICHAEL GREEN & MIKE JOHNSON writers **MAHMUD ASRAR** artist cover art by **MAHMUD ASRAR & DAVE McCAIG**

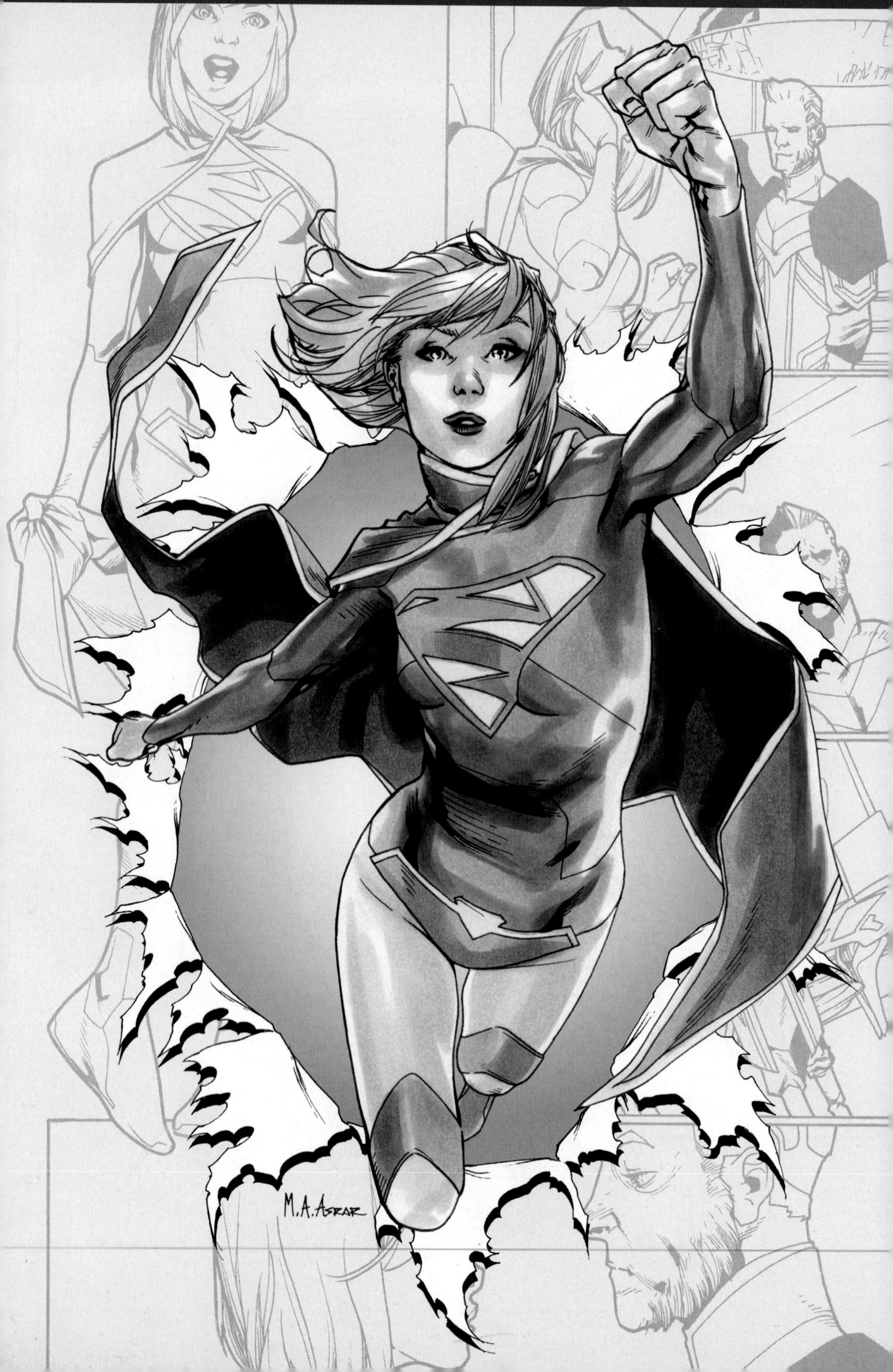
M.A. Asrar

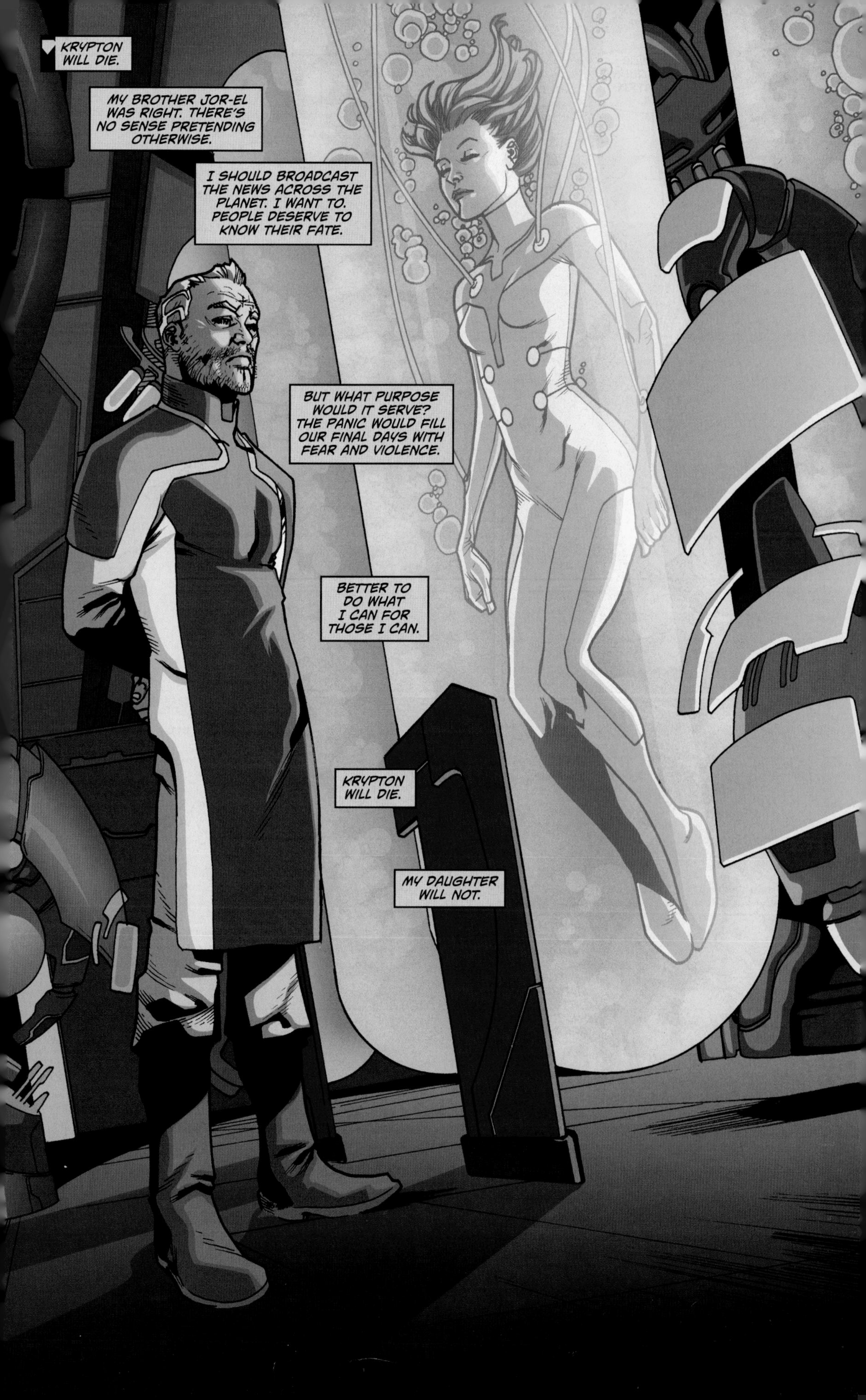
KRYPTON WILL DIE.
MY BROTHER JOR-EL WAS RIGHT. THERE'S NO SENSE PRETENDING OTHERWISE.
I SHOULD BROADCAST THE NEWS ACROSS THE PLANET. I WANT TO. PEOPLE DESERVE TO KNOW THEIR FATE.
BUT WHAT PURPOSE WOULD IT SERVE? THE PANIC WOULD FILL OUR FINAL DAYS WITH FEAR AND VIOLENCE.
BETTER TO DO WHAT I CAN FOR THOSE I CAN.
KRYPTON WILL DIE.
MY DAUGHTER WILL NOT.

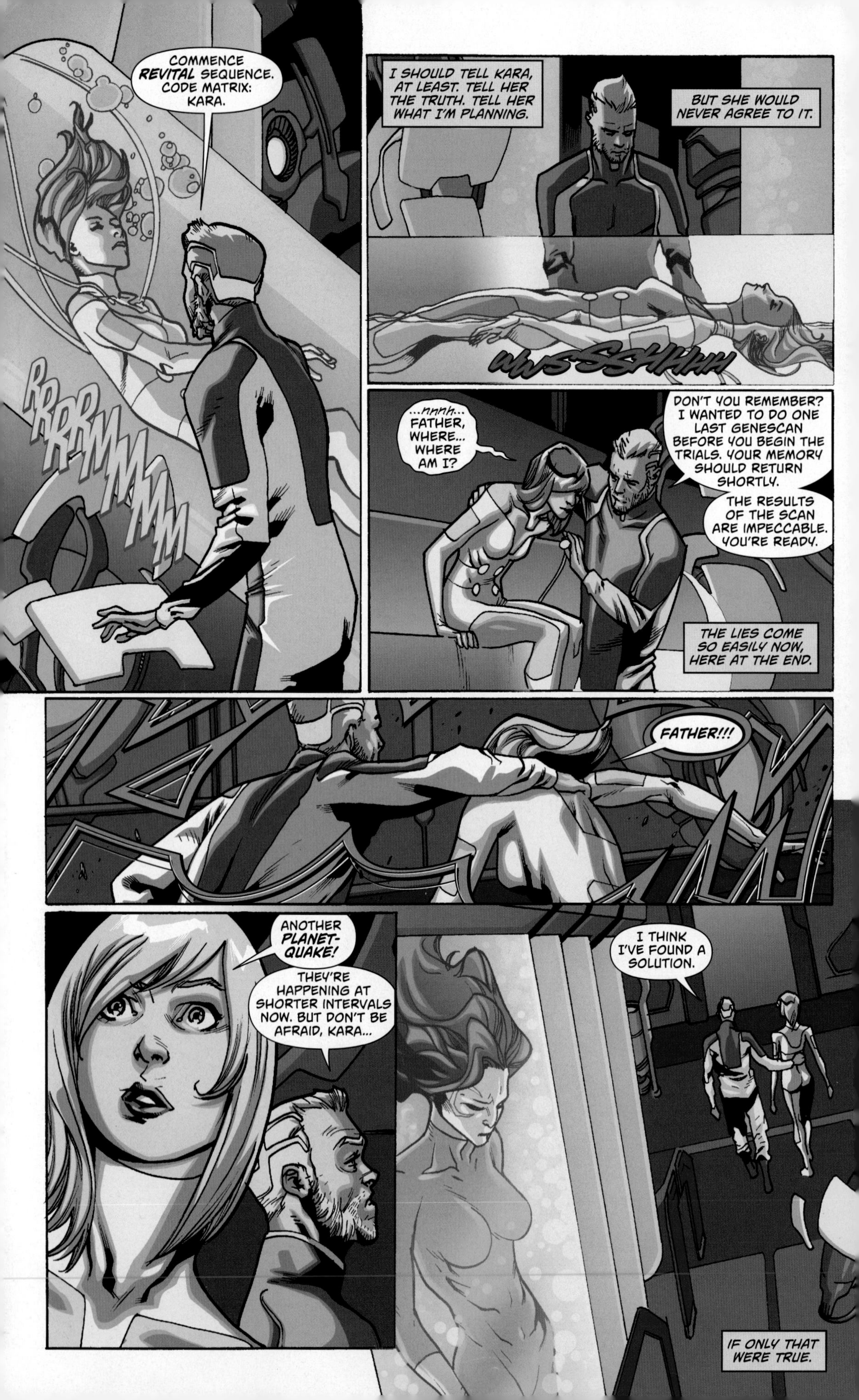
COMMENCE REVITAL SEQUENCE. CODE MATRIX: KARA.
RRRRMMMMMMM
I SHOULD TELL KARA, AT LEAST. TELL HER THE TRUTH. TELL HER WHAT I'M PLANNING.
BUT SHE WOULD NEVER AGREE TO IT.
WWSSSHHHH
...nnnh... FATHER, WHERE... WHERE AM I?
DON'T YOU REMEMBER? I WANTED TO DO ONE LAST GENESCAN BEFORE YOU BEGIN THE TRIALS. YOUR MEMORY SHOULD RETURN SHORTLY.
THE RESULTS OF THE SCAN ARE IMPECCABLE. YOU'RE READY.
THE LIES COME SO EASILY NOW, HERE AT THE END.
FATHER!!!
ANOTHER PLANET-QUAKE!
THEY'RE HAPPENING AT SHORTER INTERVALS NOW. BUT DON'T BE AFRAID, KARA...
I THINK I'VE FOUND A SOLUTION.
IF ONLY THAT WERE TRUE.

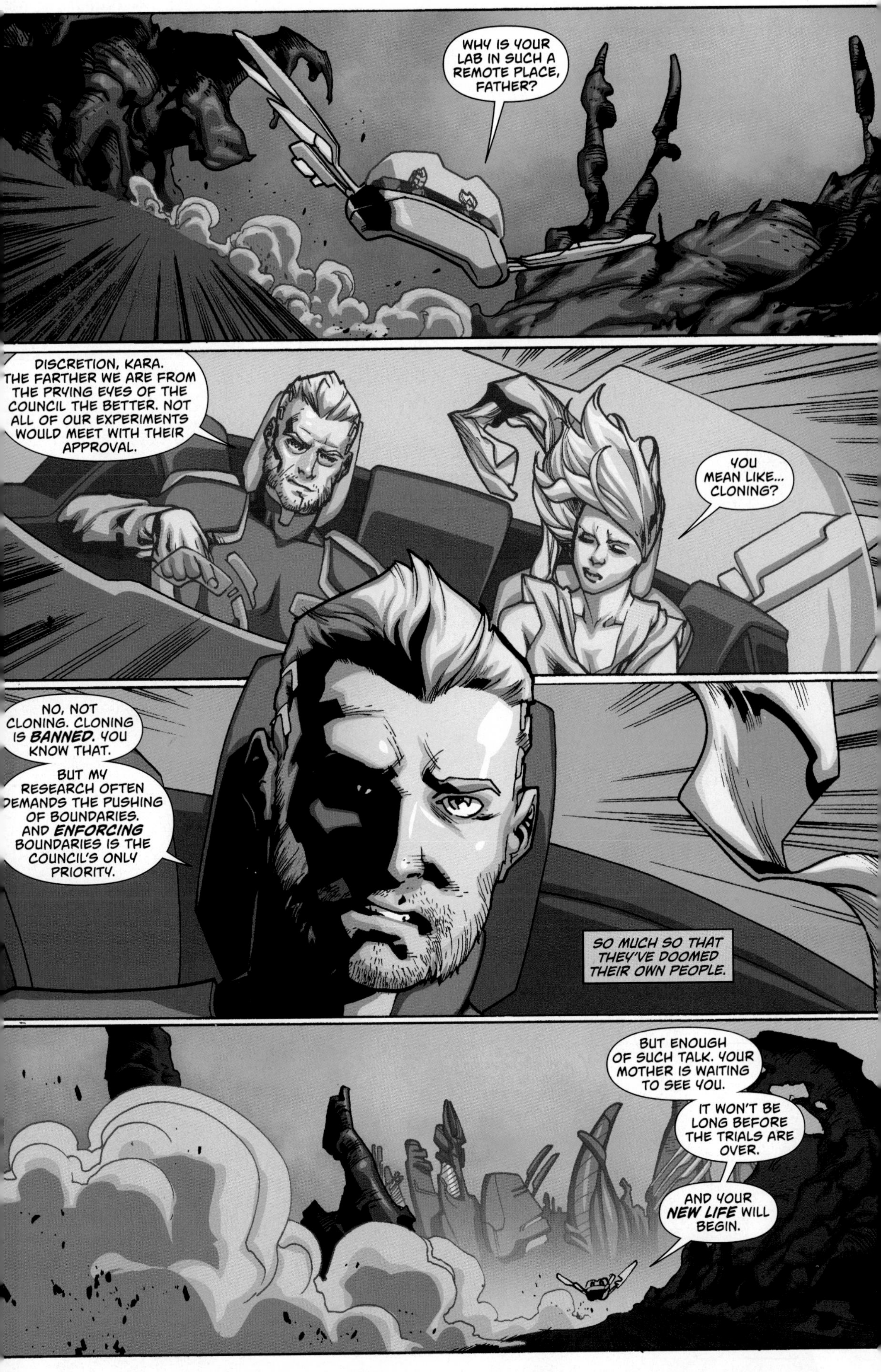
WHY IS YOUR LAB IN SUCH A REMOTE PLACE, FATHER?
DISCRETION, KARA. THE FARTHER WE ARE FROM THE PRYING EYES OF THE COUNCIL THE BETTER. NOT ALL OF OUR EXPERIMENTS WOULD MEET WITH THEIR APPROVAL.
YOU MEAN LIKE... CLONING?
NO, NOT CLONING. CLONING IS ***BANNED***. YOU KNOW THAT.
BUT MY RESEARCH OFTEN DEMANDS THE PUSHING OF BOUNDARIES. AND ***ENFORCING*** BOUNDARIES IS THE COUNCIL'S ONLY PRIORITY.
SO MUCH SO THAT THEY'VE DOOMED THEIR OWN PEOPLE.
BUT ENOUGH OF SUCH TALK. YOUR MOTHER IS WAITING TO SEE YOU.
IT WON'T BE LONG BEFORE THE TRIALS ARE OVER.
AND YOUR ***NEW LIFE*** WILL BEGIN.

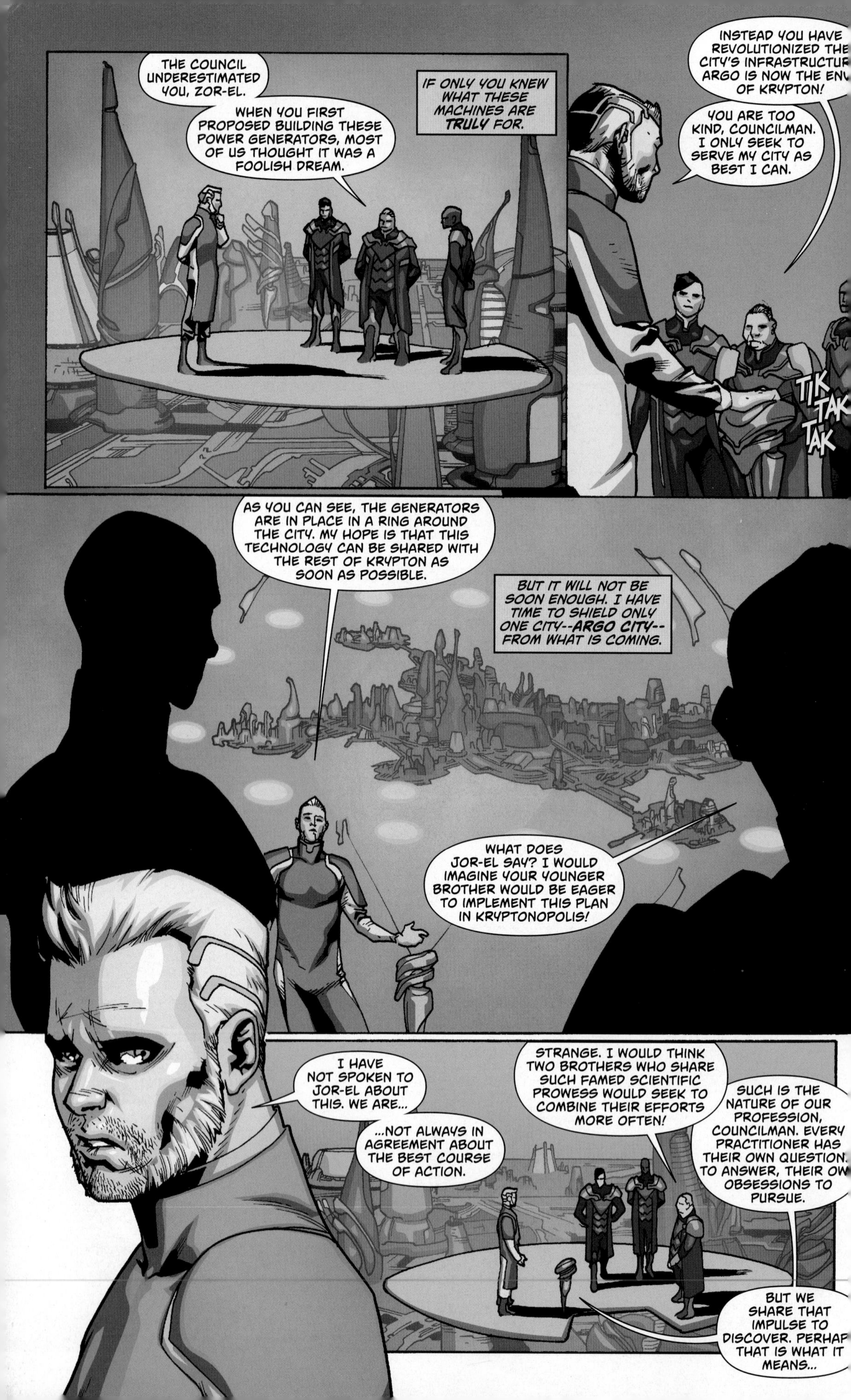
THE COUNCIL UNDERESTIMATED YOU, ZOR-EL.
WHEN YOU FIRST PROPOSED BUILDING THESE POWER GENERATORS, MOST OF US THOUGHT IT WAS A FOOLISH DREAM.
IF ONLY YOU KNEW WHAT THESE MACHINES ARE TRULY FOR.
INSTEAD YOU HAVE REVOLUTIONIZED THE CITY'S INFRASTRUCTUR ARGO IS NOW THE ENV OF KRYPTON!
YOU ARE TOO KIND, COUNCILMAN. I ONLY SEEK TO SERVE MY CITY AS BEST I CAN.
TIK TAK TAK
AS YOU CAN SEE, THE GENERATORS ARE IN PLACE IN A RING AROUND THE CITY. MY HOPE IS THAT THIS TECHNOLOGY CAN BE SHARED WITH THE REST OF KRYPTON AS SOON AS POSSIBLE.
BUT IT WILL NOT BE SOON ENOUGH. I HAVE TIME TO SHIELD ONLY ONE CITY--ARGO CITY--FROM WHAT IS COMING.
WHAT DOES JOR-EL SAY? I WOULD IMAGINE YOUR YOUNGER BROTHER WOULD BE EAGER TO IMPLEMENT THIS PLAN IN KRYPTONOPOLIS!
I HAVE NOT SPOKEN TO JOR-EL ABOUT THIS. WE ARE...
...NOT ALWAYS IN AGREEMENT ABOUT THE BEST COURSE OF ACTION.
STRANGE. I WOULD THINK TWO BROTHERS WHO SHARE SUCH FAMED SCIENTIFIC PROWESS WOULD SEEK TO COMBINE THEIR EFFORTS MORE OFTEN!
SUCH IS THE NATURE OF OUR PROFESSION, COUNCILMAN. EVERY PRACTITIONER HAS THEIR OWN QUESTION TO ANSWER, THEIR OW OBSESSIONS TO PURSUE.
BUT WE SHARE THAT IMPULSE TO DISCOVER. PERHAP THAT IS WHAT IT MEANS...

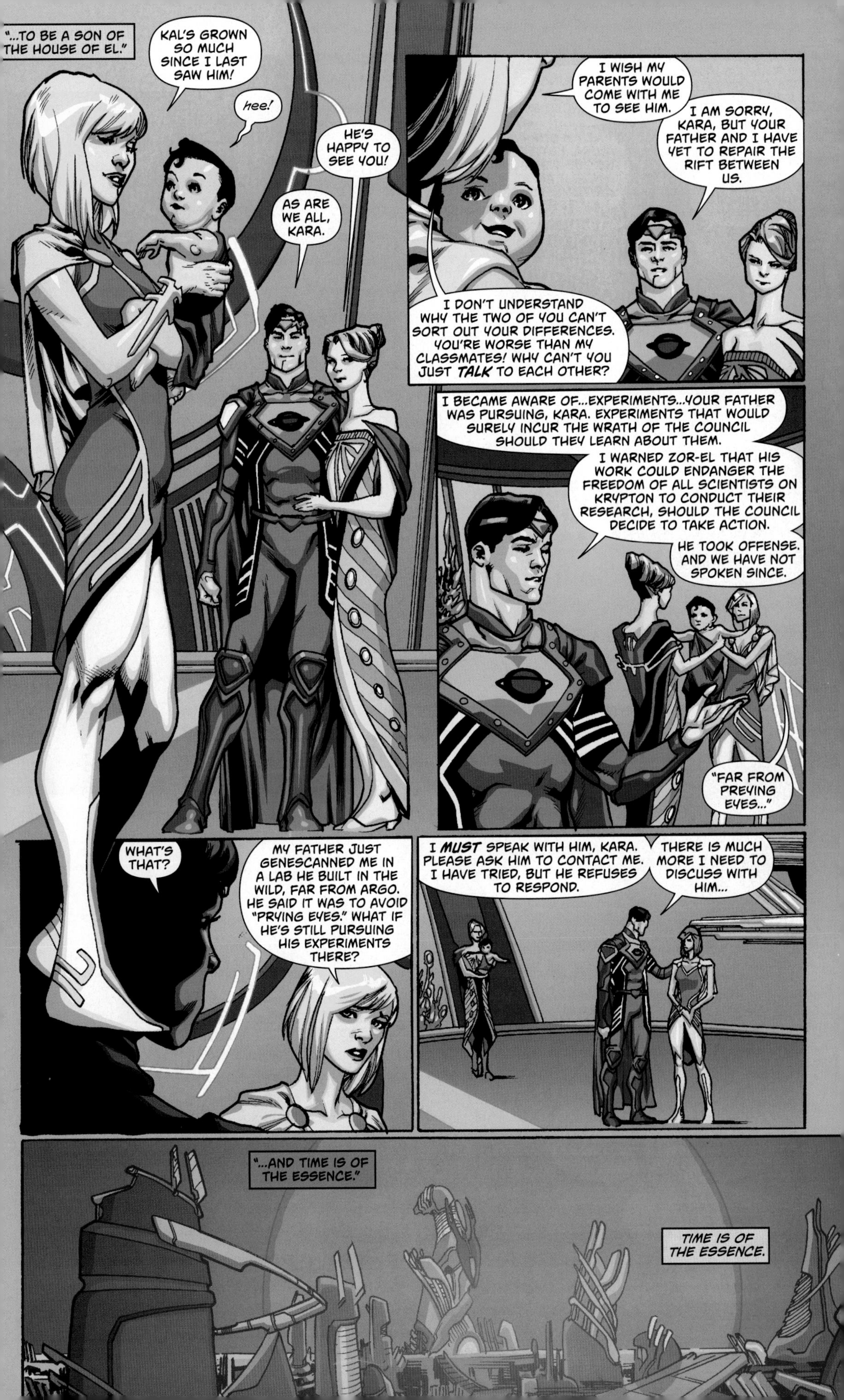
"...TO BE A SON OF THE HOUSE OF EL."
KAL'S GROWN SO MUCH SINCE I LAST SAW HIM!
hee!
HE'S HAPPY TO SEE YOU!
AS ARE WE ALL, KARA.
I WISH MY PARENTS WOULD COME WITH ME TO SEE HIM.
I AM SORRY, KARA, BUT YOUR FATHER AND I HAVE YET TO REPAIR THE RIFT BETWEEN US.
I DON'T UNDERSTAND WHY THE TWO OF YOU CAN'T SORT OUT YOUR DIFFERENCES. YOU'RE WORSE THAN MY CLASSMATES! WHY CAN'T YOU JUST TALK TO EACH OTHER?
I BECAME AWARE OF...EXPERIMENTS...YOUR FATHER WAS PURSUING, KARA. EXPERIMENTS THAT WOULD SURELY INCUR THE WRATH OF THE COUNCIL SHOULD THEY LEARN ABOUT THEM.
I WARNED ZOR-EL THAT HIS WORK COULD ENDANGER THE FREEDOM OF ALL SCIENTISTS ON KRYPTON TO CONDUCT THEIR RESEARCH, SHOULD THE COUNCIL DECIDE TO TAKE ACTION.
HE TOOK OFFENSE. AND WE HAVE NOT SPOKEN SINCE.
"FAR FROM PREYING EYES..."
WHAT'S THAT?
MY FATHER JUST GENESCANNED ME IN A LAB HE BUILT IN THE WILD, FAR FROM ARGO. HE SAID IT WAS TO AVOID "PRYING EYES." WHAT IF HE'S STILL PURSUING HIS EXPERIMENTS THERE?
I MUST SPEAK WITH HIM, KARA. PLEASE ASK HIM TO CONTACT ME. I HAVE TRIED, BUT HE REFUSES TO RESPOND.
THERE IS MUCH MORE I NEED TO DISCUSS WITH HIM...
"...AND TIME IS OF THE ESSENCE."
TIME IS OF THE ESSENCE.

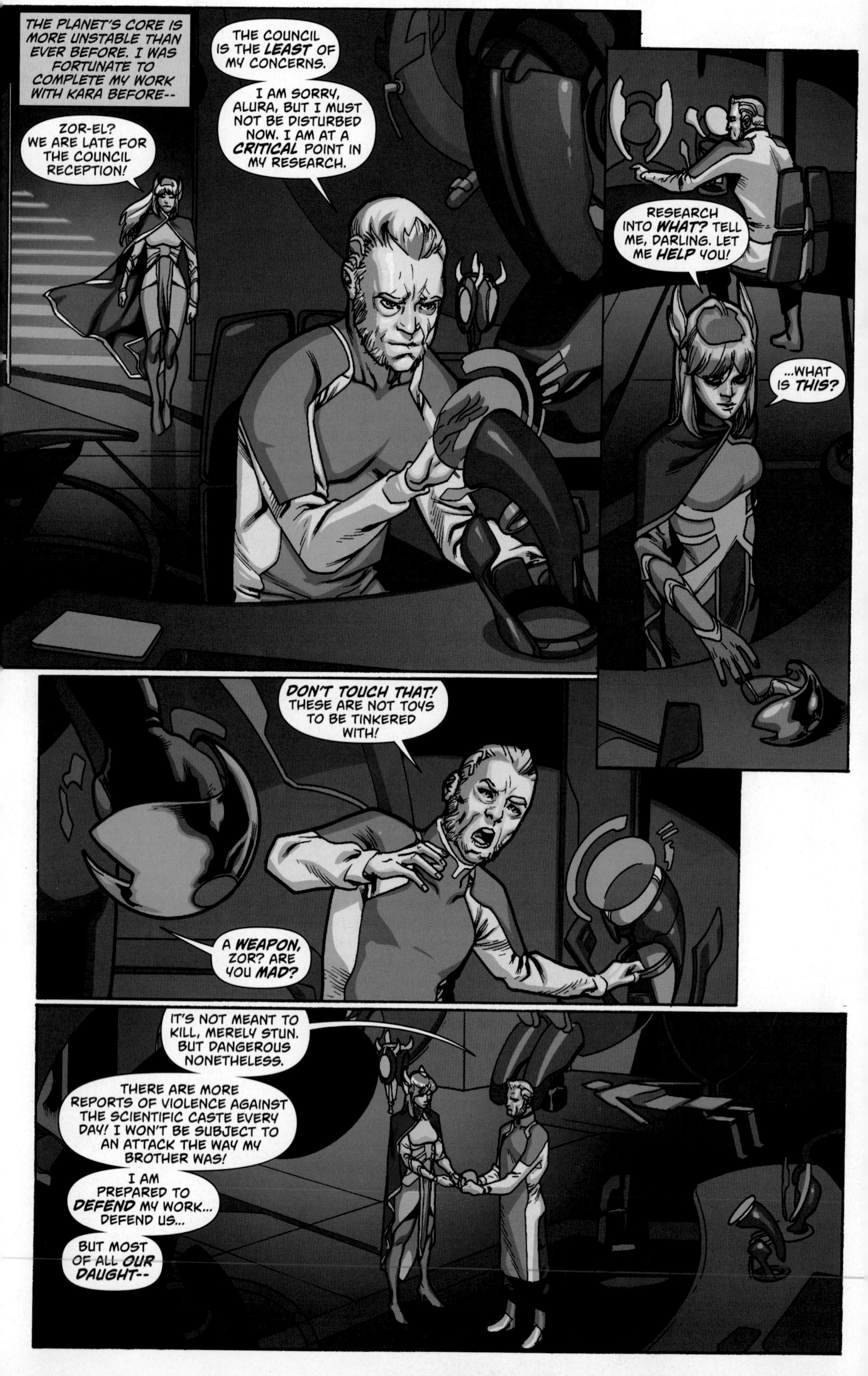
THE PLANET'S CORE IS MORE UNSTABLE THAN EVER BEFORE. I WAS FORTUNATE TO COMPLETE MY WORK WITH KARA BEFORE--
ZOR-EL? WE ARE LATE FOR THE COUNCIL RECEPTION!
THE COUNCIL IS THE LEAST OF MY CONCERNS.
I AM SORRY, ALURA, BUT I MUST NOT BE DISTURBED NOW. I AM AT A CRITICAL POINT IN MY RESEARCH.
RESEARCH INTO WHAT? TELL ME, DARLING. LET ME HELP YOU!
...WHAT IS THIS?
DON'T TOUCH THAT! THESE ARE NOT TOYS TO BE TINKERED WITH!
A WEAPON, ZOR? ARE YOU MAD?
IT'S NOT MEANT TO KILL, MERELY STUN. BUT DANGEROUS NONETHELESS.
THERE ARE MORE REPORTS OF VIOLENCE AGAINST THE SCIENTIFIC CASTE EVERY DAY! I WON'T BE SUBJECT TO AN ATTACK THE WAY MY BROTHER WAS!
I AM PREPARED TO DEFEND MY WORK... DEFEND US...
BUT MOST OF ALL OUR DAUGHT--

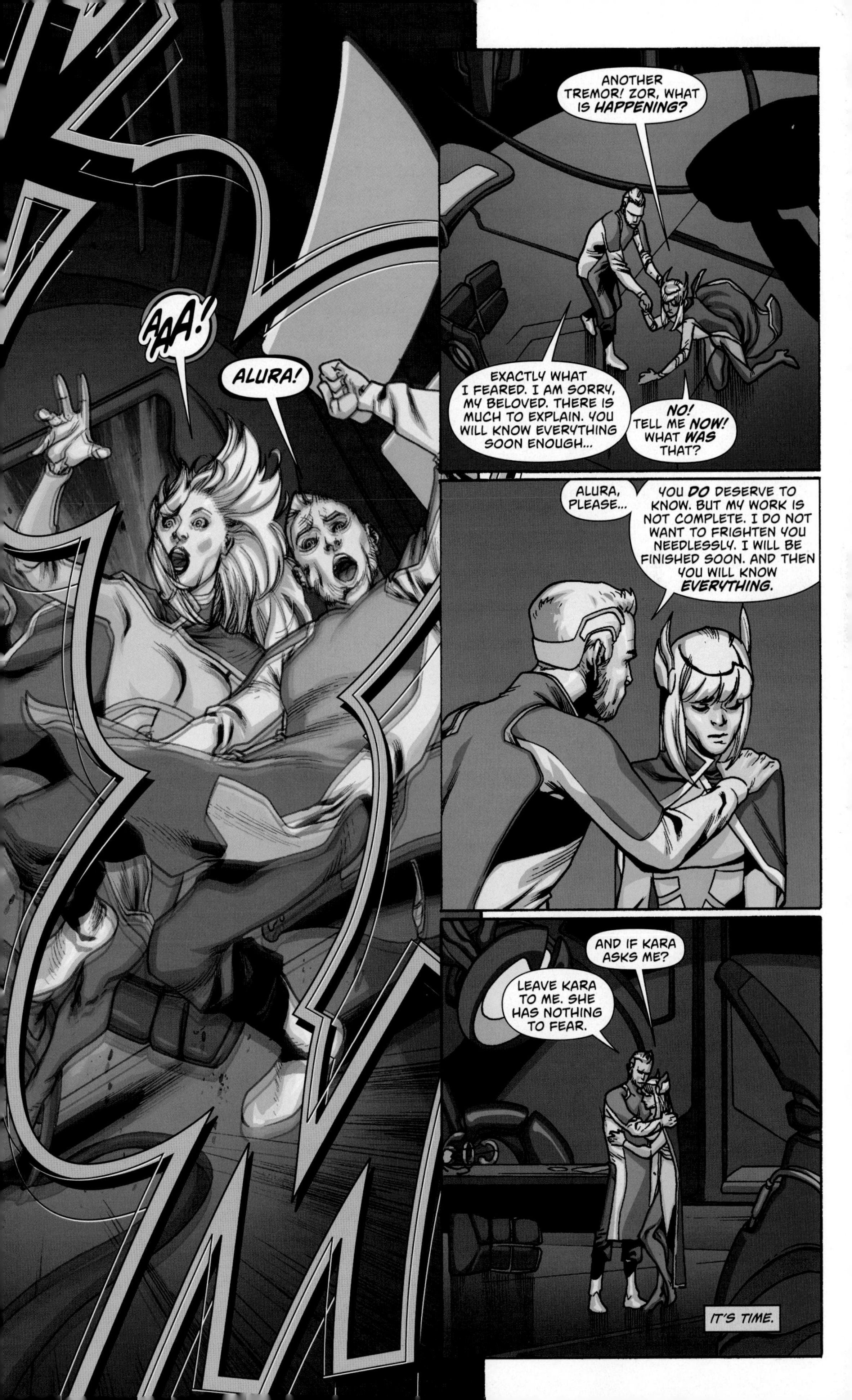
AAA!
ALURA!
ANOTHER TREMOR! ZOR, WHAT IS HAPPENING?
EXACTLY WHAT I FEARED. I AM SORRY, MY BELOVED. THERE IS MUCH TO EXPLAIN. YOU WILL KNOW EVERYTHING SOON ENOUGH...
NO! TELL ME NOW! WHAT WAS THAT?
ALURA, PLEASE...
YOU DO DESERVE TO KNOW. BUT MY WORK IS NOT COMPLETE. I DO NOT WANT TO FRIGHTEN YOU NEEDLESSLY. I WILL BE FINISHED SOON. AND THEN YOU WILL KNOW EVERYTHING.
AND IF KARA ASKS ME?
LEAVE KARA TO ME. SHE HAS NOTHING TO FEAR.
IT'S TIME.

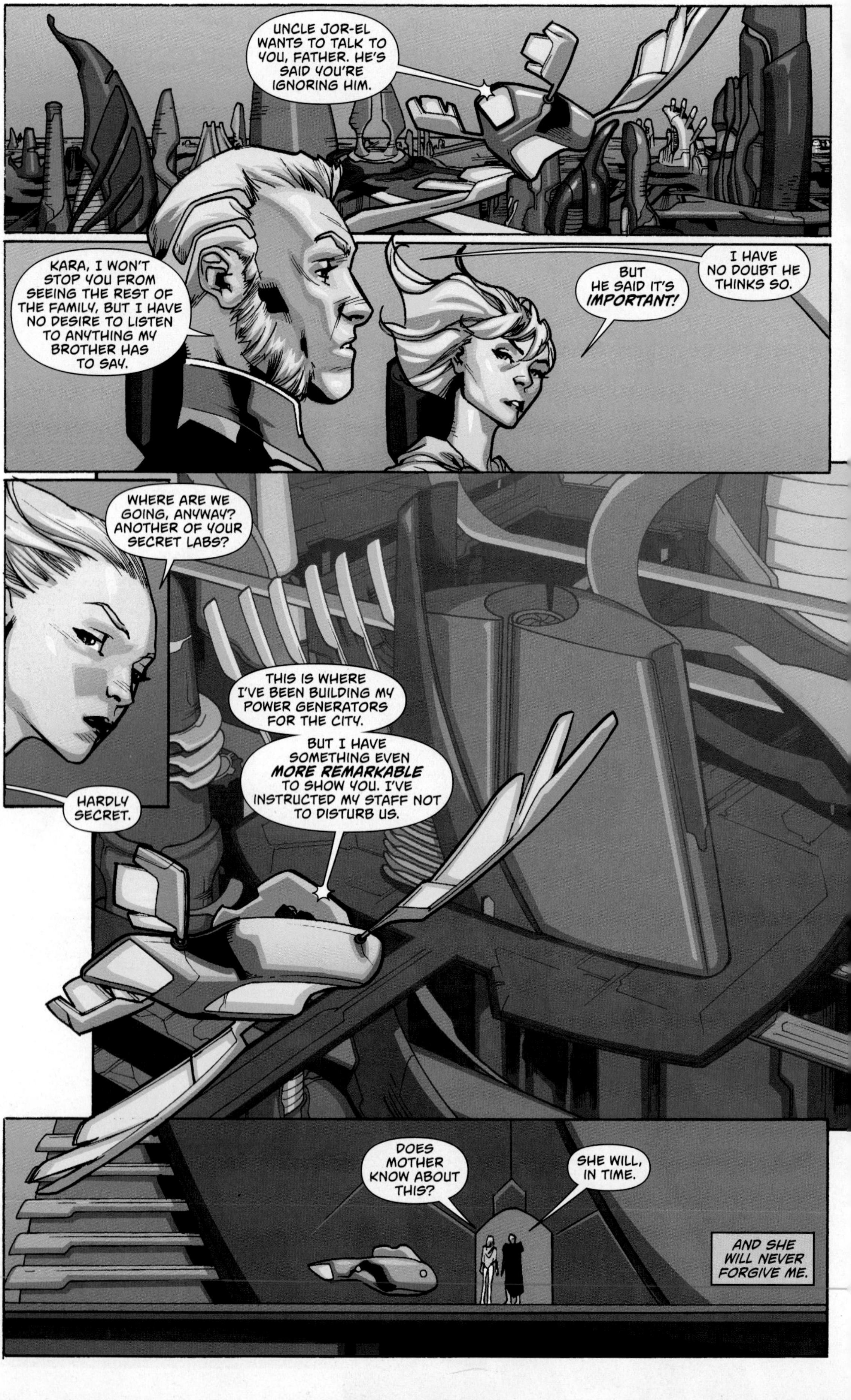
UNCLE JOR-EL WANTS TO TALK TO YOU, FATHER. HE'S SAID YOU'RE IGNORING HIM.
KARA, I WON'T STOP YOU FROM SEEING THE REST OF THE FAMILY, BUT I HAVE NO DESIRE TO LISTEN TO ANYTHING MY BROTHER HAS TO SAY.
BUT HE SAID IT'S *IMPORTANT!*
I HAVE NO DOUBT HE THINKS SO.
WHERE ARE WE GOING, ANYWAY? ANOTHER OF YOUR SECRET LABS?
HARDLY SECRET.
THIS IS WHERE I'VE BEEN BUILDING MY POWER GENERATORS FOR THE CITY.
BUT I HAVE SOMETHING EVEN ***MORE REMARKABLE*** TO SHOW YOU. I'VE INSTRUCTED MY STAFF NOT TO DISTURB US.
DOES MOTHER KNOW ABOUT THIS?
SHE WILL, IN TIME.
AND SHE WILL NEVER FORGIVE ME.

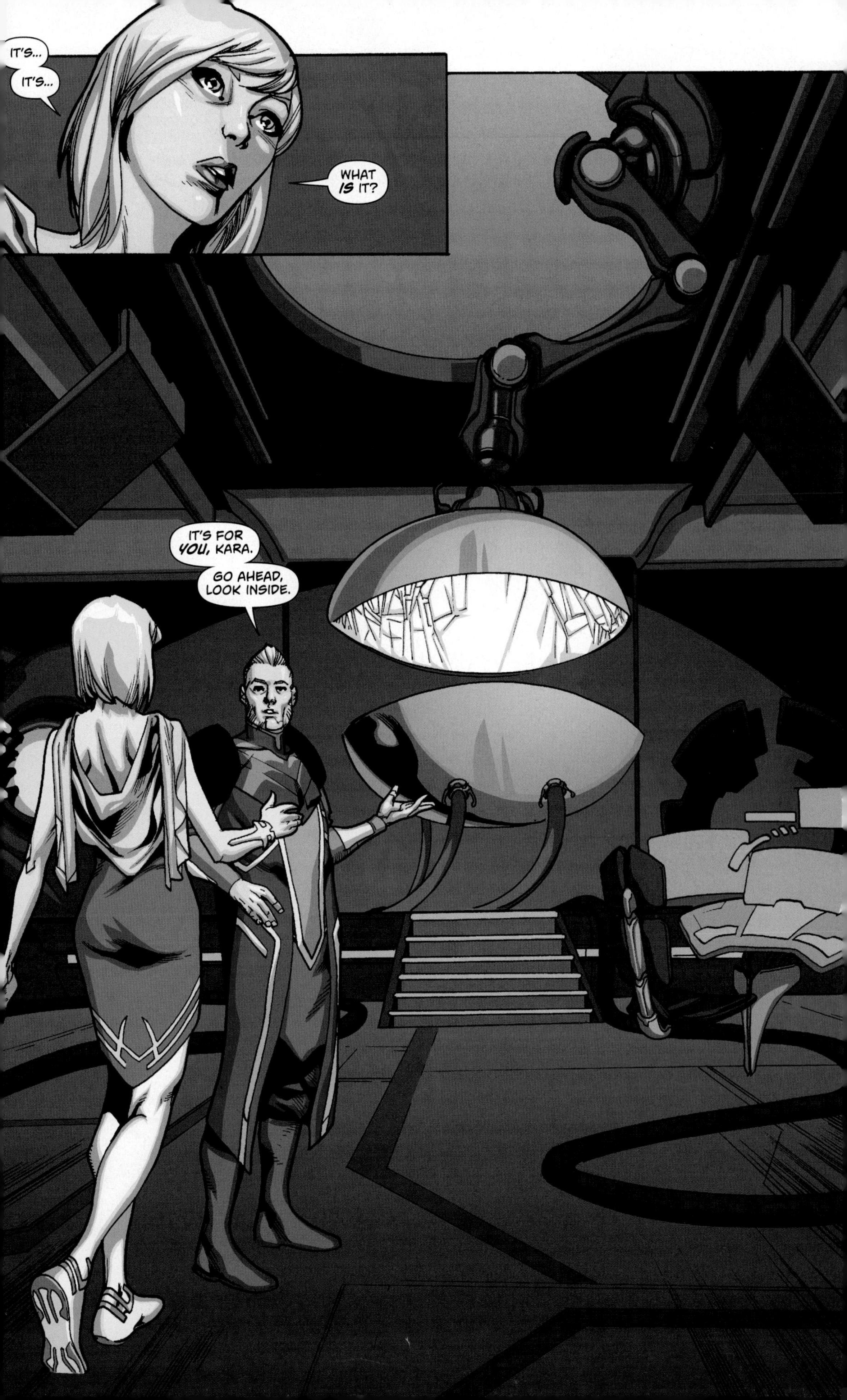
IT'S...
IT'S...
WHAT IS IT?
IT'S FOR YOU, KARA.
GO AHEAD, LOOK INSIDE.

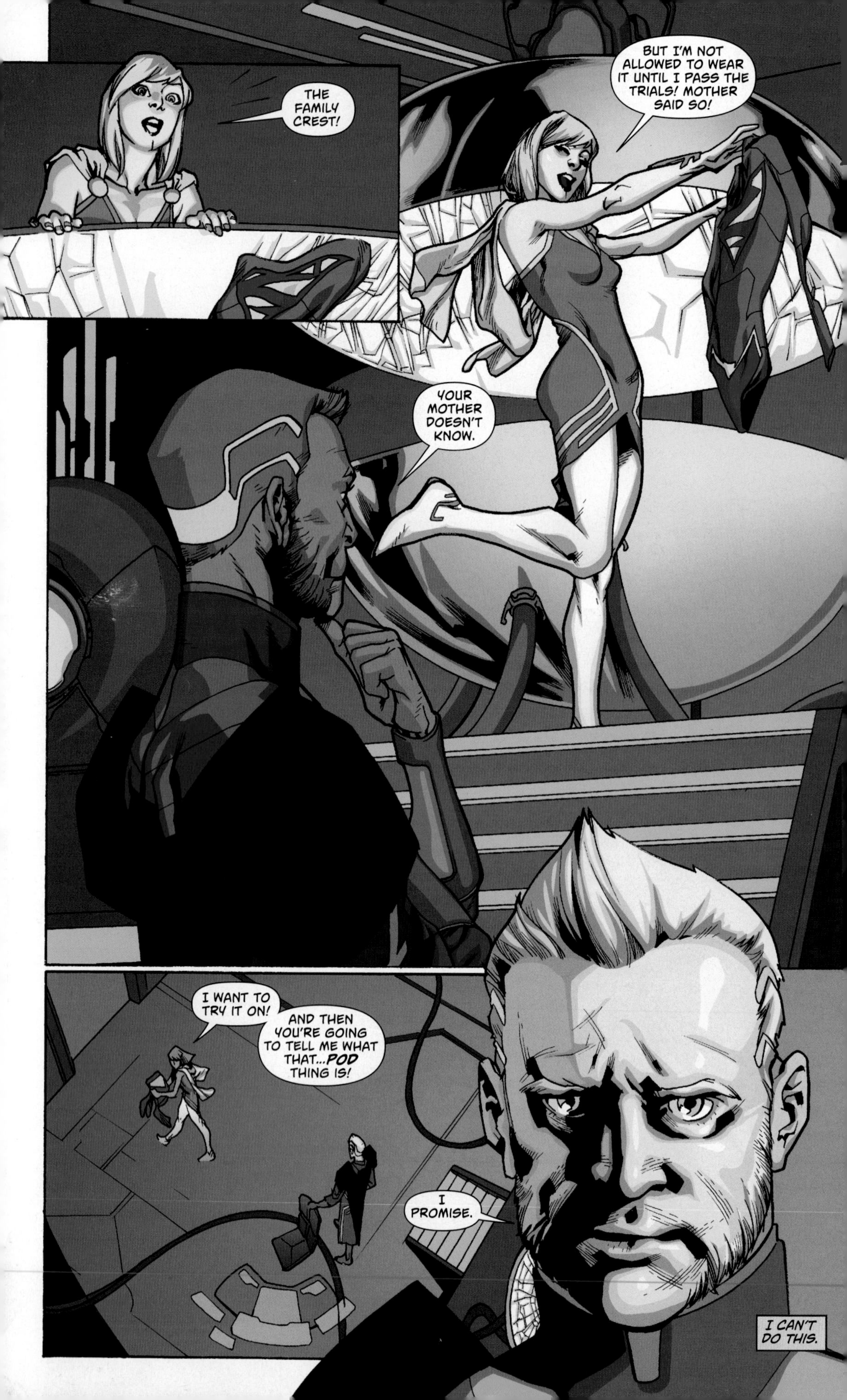
THE FAMILY CREST!
BUT I'M NOT ALLOWED TO WEAR IT UNTIL I PASS THE TRIALS! MOTHER SAID SO!
YOUR MOTHER DOESN'T KNOW.
I WANT TO TRY IT ON!
AND THEN YOU'RE GOING TO TELL ME WHAT THAT...POD THING IS!
I PROMISE.
I CAN'T DO THIS.

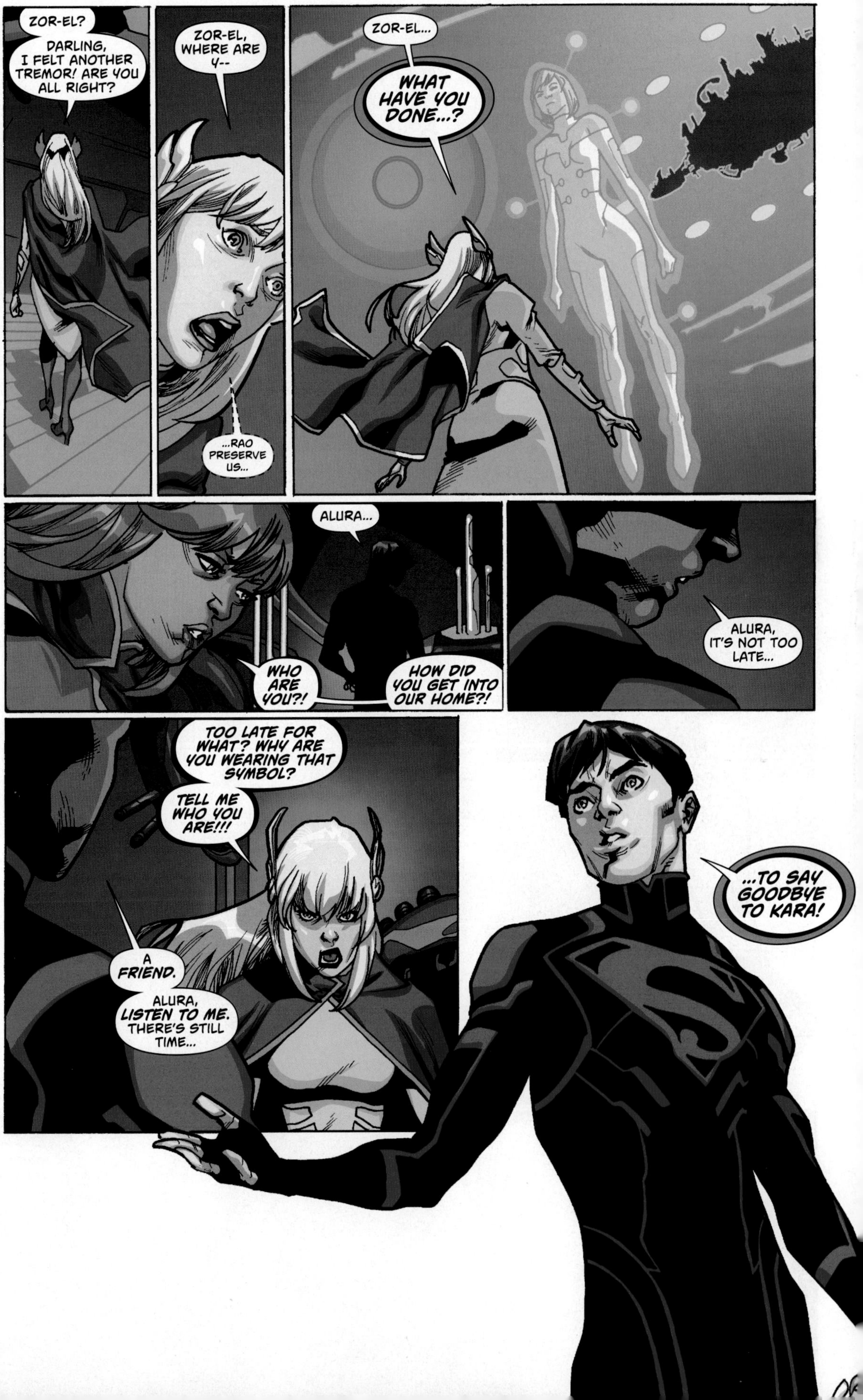
ZOR-EL?
DARLING, I FELT ANOTHER TREMOR! ARE YOU ALL RIGHT?
ZOR-EL, WHERE ARE Y--
...RAO PRESERVE US...
ZOR-EL...
WHAT HAVE YOU DONE...?
ALURA...
WHO ARE YOU?!
HOW DID YOU GET INTO OUR HOME?!
ALURA, IT'S NOT TOO LATE...
TOO LATE FOR WHAT? WHY ARE YOU WEARING THAT SYMBOL?
TELL ME WHO YOU ARE!!!
A FRIEND.
ALURA, LISTEN TO ME. THERE'S STILL TIME...
...TO SAY GOODBYE TO KARA!

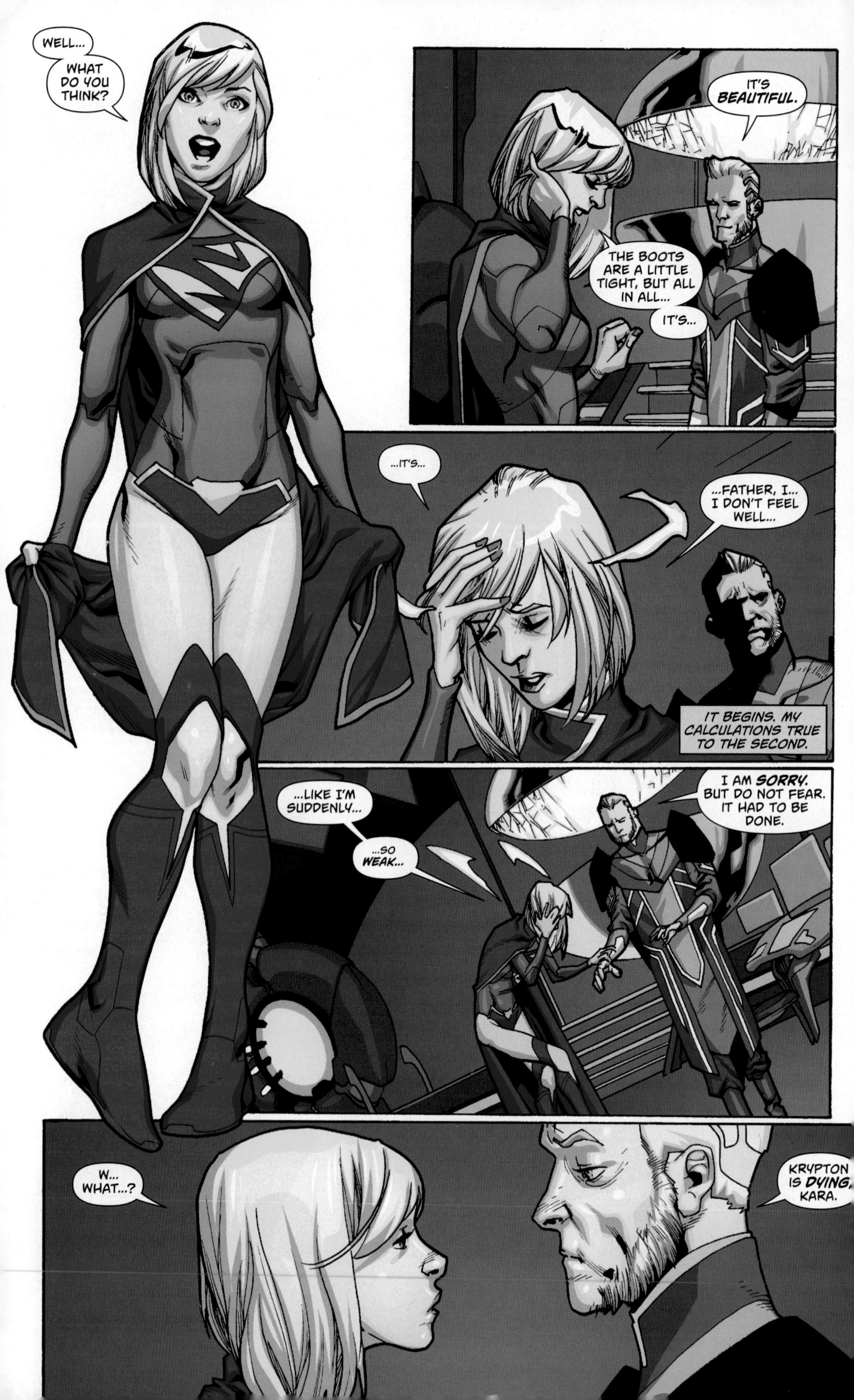
WELL... WHAT DO YOU THINK?
IT'S **BEAUTIFUL.**
THE BOOTS ARE A LITTLE TIGHT, BUT ALL IN ALL...
IT'S...
...IT'S...
...FATHER, I... I DON'T FEEL WELL...
IT BEGINS. MY CALCULATIONS TRUE TO THE SECOND.
...LIKE I'M SUDDENLY...
...SO **WEAK...**
I AM **SORRY.** BUT DO NOT FEAR. IT HAD TO BE DONE.
W... WHAT...?
KRYPTON IS **DYING,** KARA.

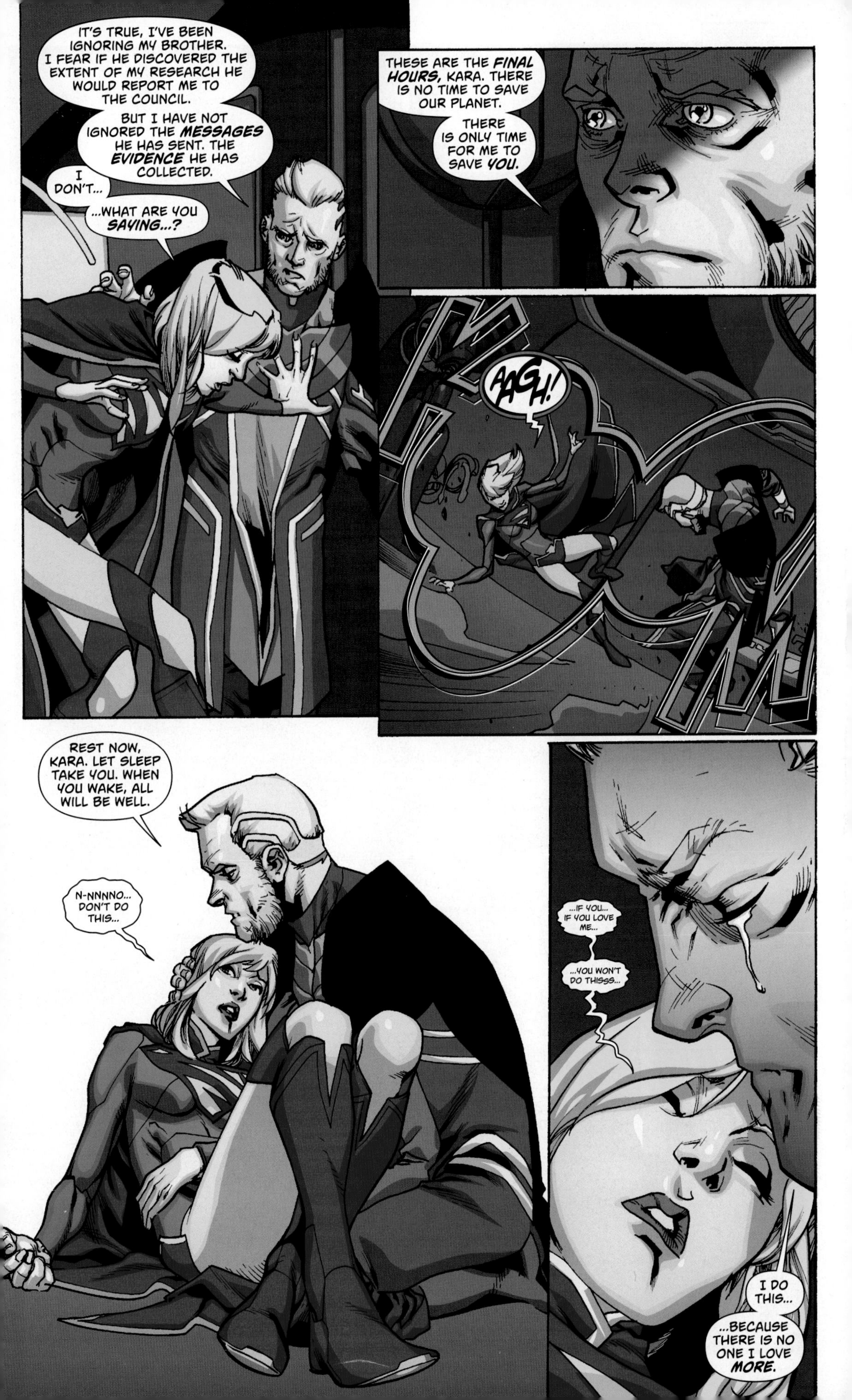
IT'S TRUE, I'VE BEEN IGNORING MY BROTHER. I FEAR IF HE DISCOVERED THE EXTENT OF MY RESEARCH HE WOULD REPORT ME TO THE COUNCIL.
BUT I HAVE NOT IGNORED THE MESSAGES HE HAS SENT. THE EVIDENCE HE HAS COLLECTED.
I DON'T...
...WHAT ARE YOU SAYING...?
THESE ARE THE FINAL HOURS, KARA. THERE IS NO TIME TO SAVE OUR PLANET.
THERE IS ONLY TIME FOR ME TO SAVE YOU.
AAGH!
REST NOW, KARA. LET SLEEP TAKE YOU. WHEN YOU WAKE, ALL WILL BE WELL.
N-NNNNO... DON'T DO THIS...
...IF YOU... IF YOU LOVE ME...
...YOU WON'T DO THISSS...
I DO THIS...
...BECAUSE THERE IS NO ONE I LOVE MORE.

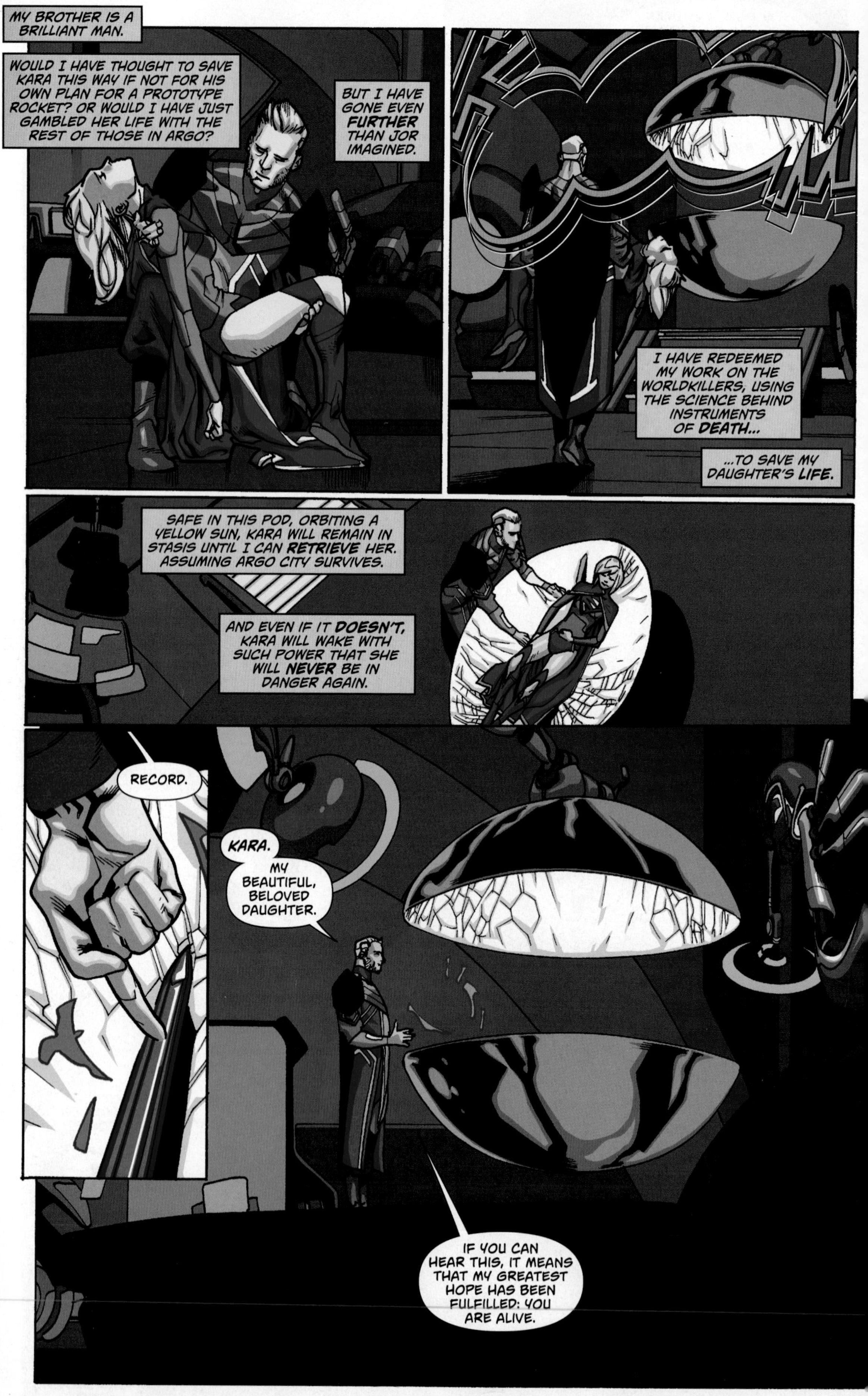

MY BROTHER IS A BRILLIANT MAN.
WOULD I HAVE THOUGHT TO SAVE KARA THIS WAY IF NOT FOR HIS OWN PLAN FOR A PROTOTYPE ROCKET? OR WOULD I HAVE JUST GAMBLED HER LIFE WITH THE REST OF THOSE IN ARGO?
BUT I HAVE GONE EVEN FURTHER THAN JOR IMAGINED.
I HAVE REDEEMED MY WORK ON THE WORLDKILLERS, USING THE SCIENCE BEHIND INSTRUMENTS OF DEATH...
...TO SAVE MY DAUGHTER'S LIFE.
SAFE IN THIS POD, ORBITING A YELLOW SUN, KARA WILL REMAIN IN STASIS UNTIL I CAN RETRIEVE HER. ASSUMING ARGO CITY SURVIVES.
AND EVEN IF IT DOESN'T, KARA WILL WAKE WITH SUCH POWER THAT SHE WILL NEVER BE IN DANGER AGAIN.
RECORD.
KARA.
MY BEAUTIFUL, BELOVED DAUGHTER.
IF YOU CAN HEAR THIS, IT MEANS THAT MY GREATEST HOPE HAS BEEN FULFILLED: YOU ARE ALIVE.

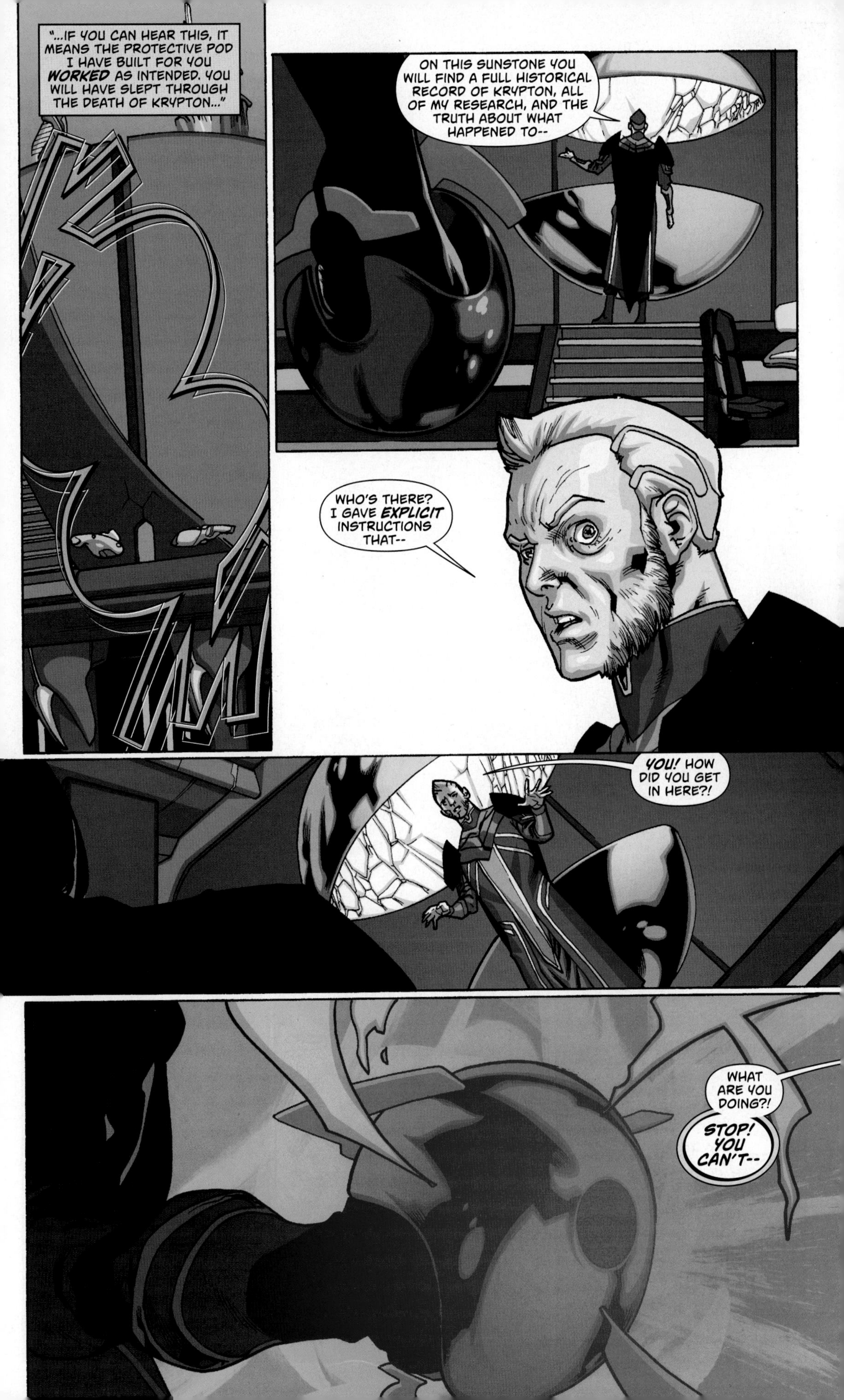
"...IF YOU CAN HEAR THIS, IT MEANS THE PROTECTIVE POD I HAVE BUILT FOR YOU WORKED AS INTENDED. YOU WILL HAVE SLEPT THROUGH THE DEATH OF KRYPTON..."
ON THIS SUNSTONE YOU WILL FIND A FULL HISTORICAL RECORD OF KRYPTON, ALL OF MY RESEARCH, AND THE TRUTH ABOUT WHAT HAPPENED TO--
WHO'S THERE? I GAVE EXPLICIT INSTRUCTIONS THAT--
YOU! HOW DID YOU GET IN HERE?!
WHAT ARE YOU DOING?!
STOP! YOU CAN'T--

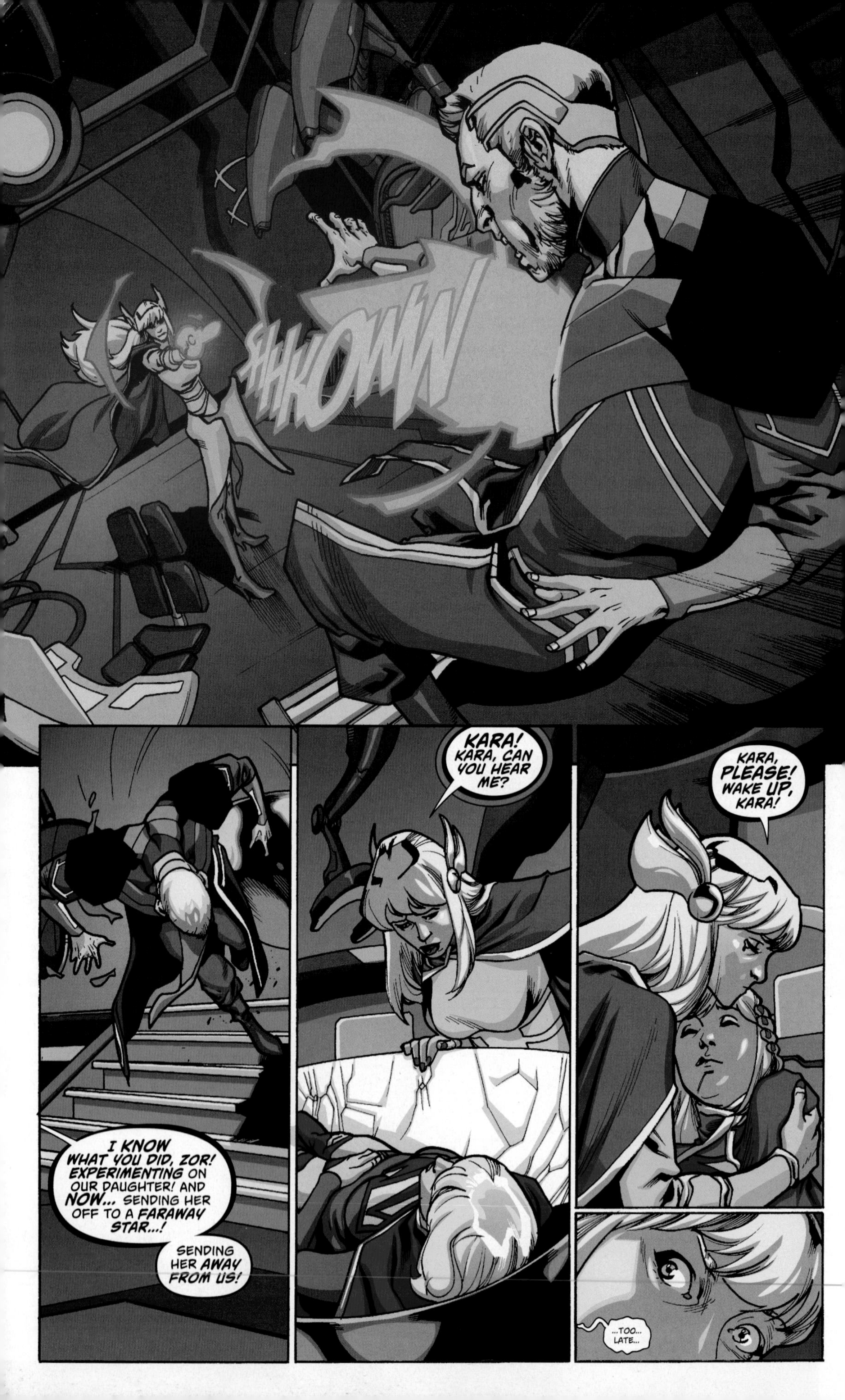
SHHKOWW
I KNOW WHAT YOU DID, ZOR! EXPERIMENTING ON OUR DAUGHTER! AND NOW... SENDING HER OFF TO A FARAWAY STAR...!
SENDING HER AWAY FROM US!
KARA! KARA, CAN YOU HEAR ME?
KARA, PLEASE! WAKE UP, KARA!
...TOO... LATE...

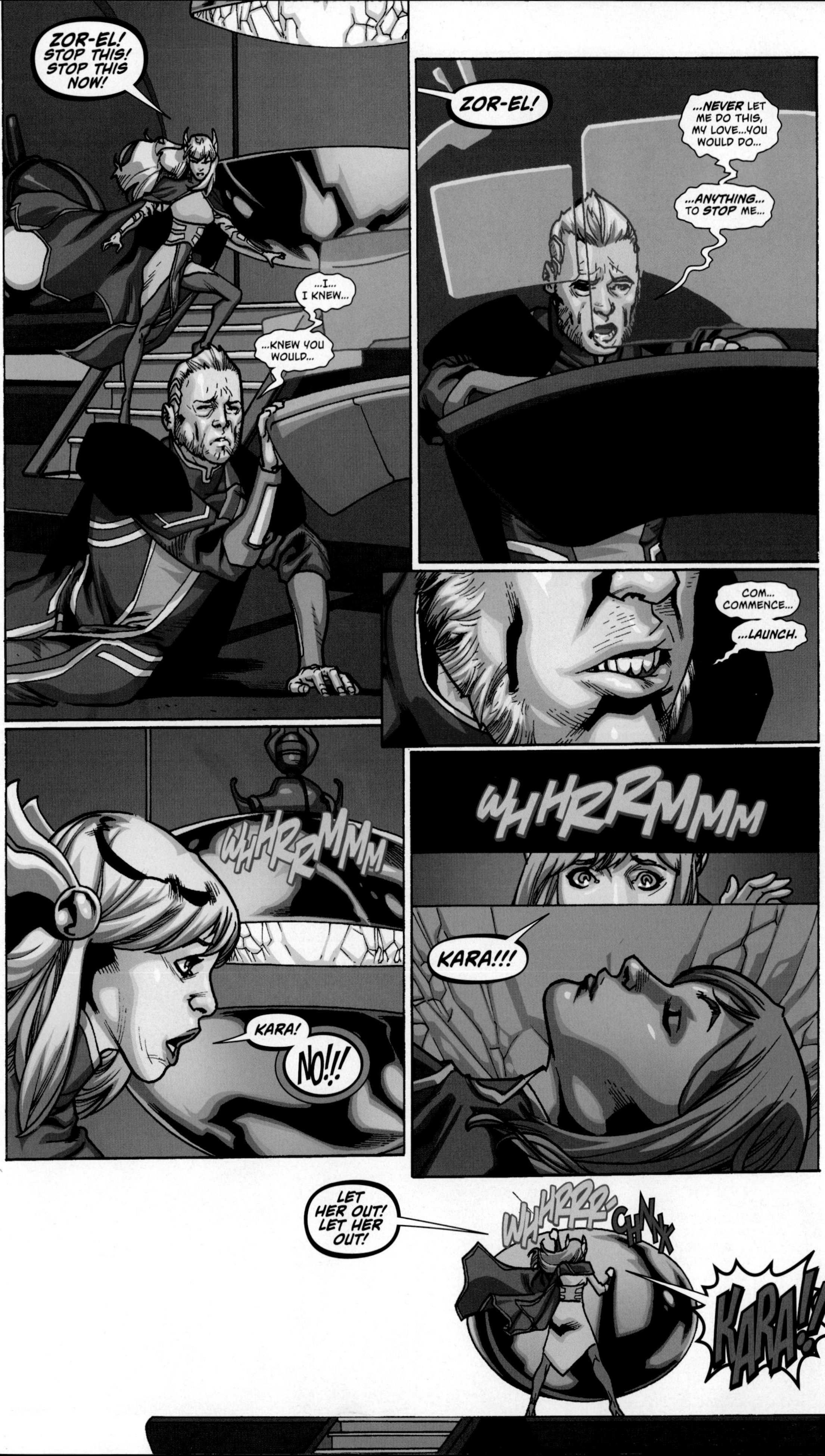
ZOR-EL! STOP THIS! STOP THIS NOW!
ZOR-EL!
...NEVER LET ME DO THIS, MY LOVE...YOU WOULD DO...
...ANYTHING... TO STOP ME...
...I... I KNEW...
...KNEW YOU WOULD...
COM... COMMENCE...
...LAUNCH.
WHHRRMMM
WHHRRMMM
KARA! NO!!!
KARA!!!
LET HER OUT! LET HER OUT!
WHHRRR-CHNK
KARA!!!

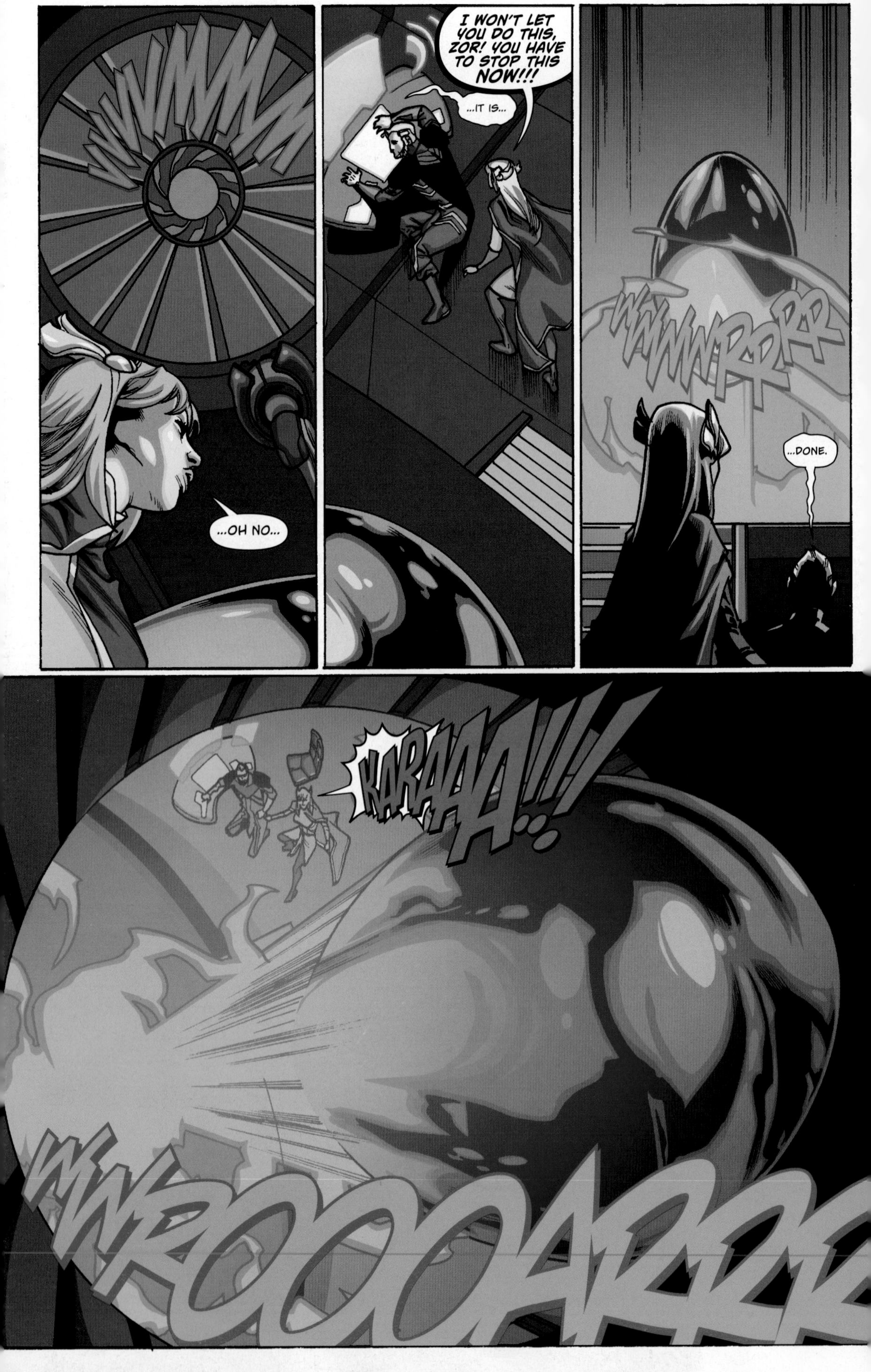
WVVMMMMM
...OH NO...
I WON'T LET YOU DO THIS, ZOR! YOU HAVE TO STOP THIS NOW!!!
...IT IS...
WWWNRRRR
...DONE.
KARAAAA!!!
WWROOOOARRR

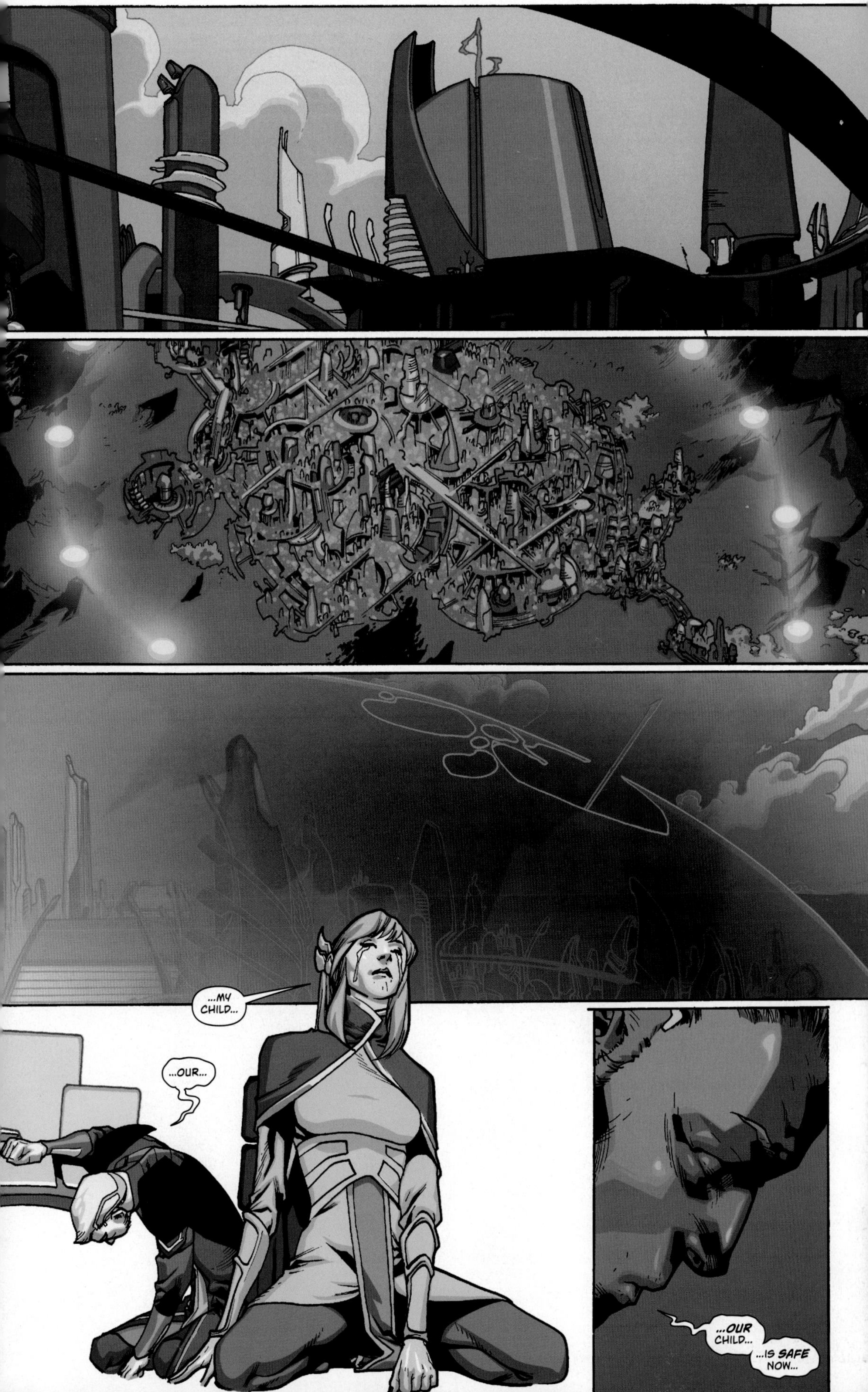
...MY CHILD...
...OUR...
...OUR CHILD...
...IS SAFE NOW...

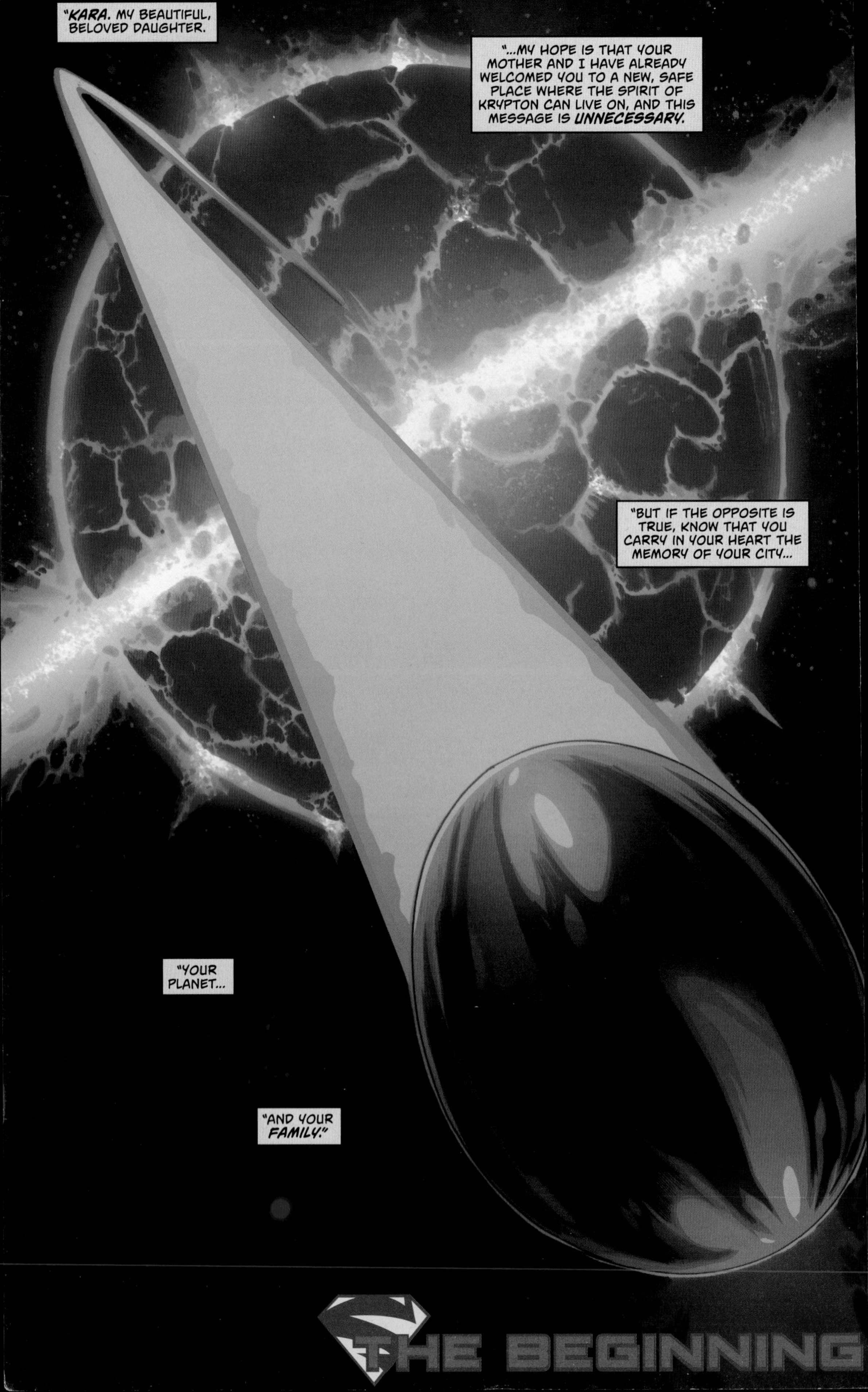
"KARA. MY BEAUTIFUL, BELOVED DAUGHTER.
"...MY HOPE IS THAT YOUR MOTHER AND I HAVE ALREADY WELCOMED YOU TO A NEW, SAFE PLACE WHERE THE SPIRIT OF KRYPTON CAN LIVE ON, AND THIS MESSAGE IS UNNECESSARY.
"BUT IF THE OPPOSITE IS TRUE, KNOW THAT YOU CARRY IN YOUR HEART THE MEMORY OF YOUR CITY...
"YOUR PLANET...
"AND YOUR FAMILY."
THE BEGINNING

SUPERGIRL

SUPERGIRL #12 LAYOUTS BY MAHMUD ASRAR

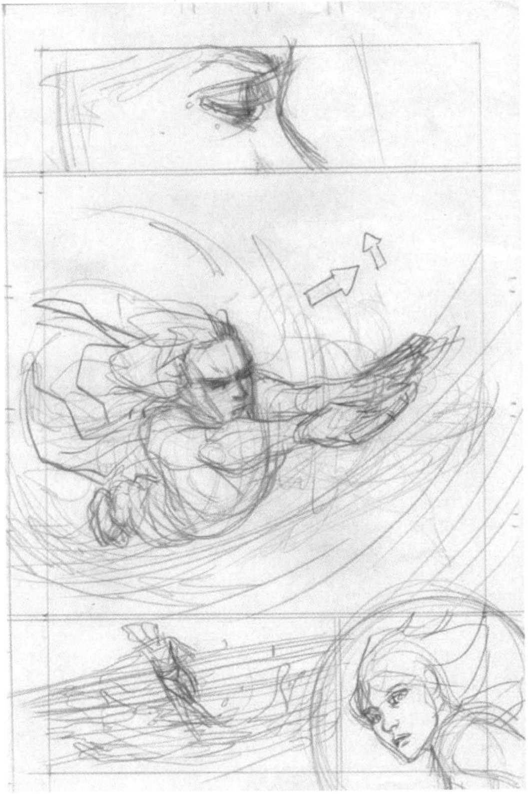

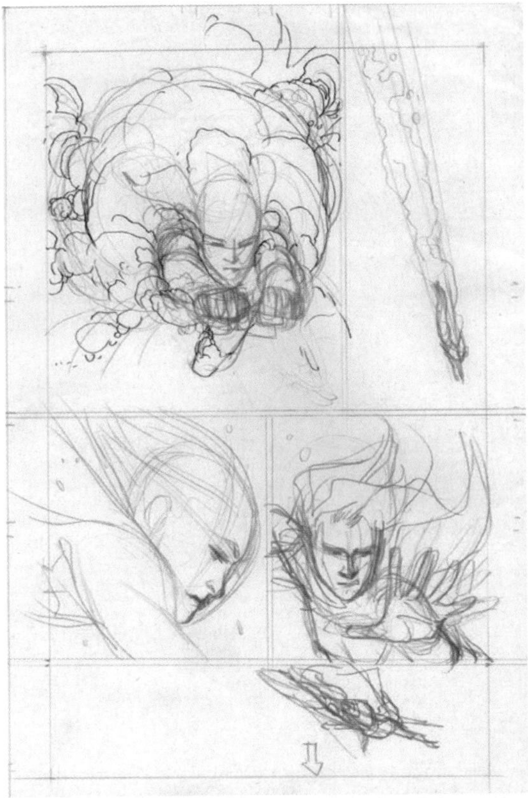

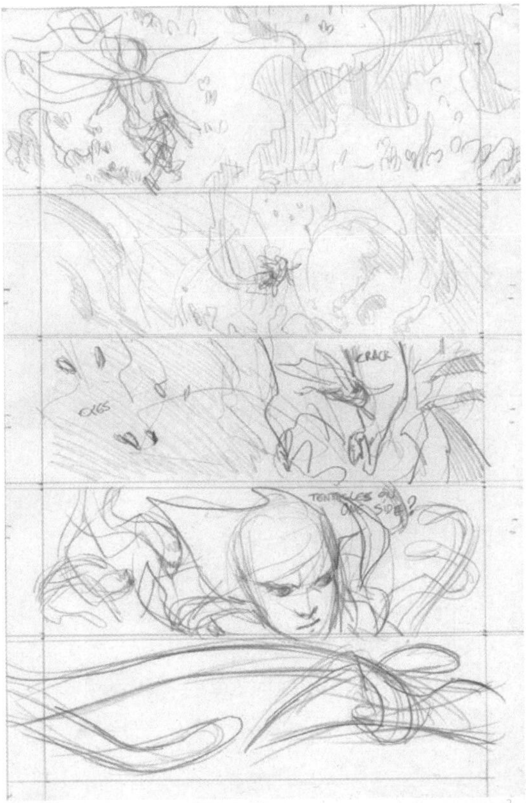
EGGS
CRACK

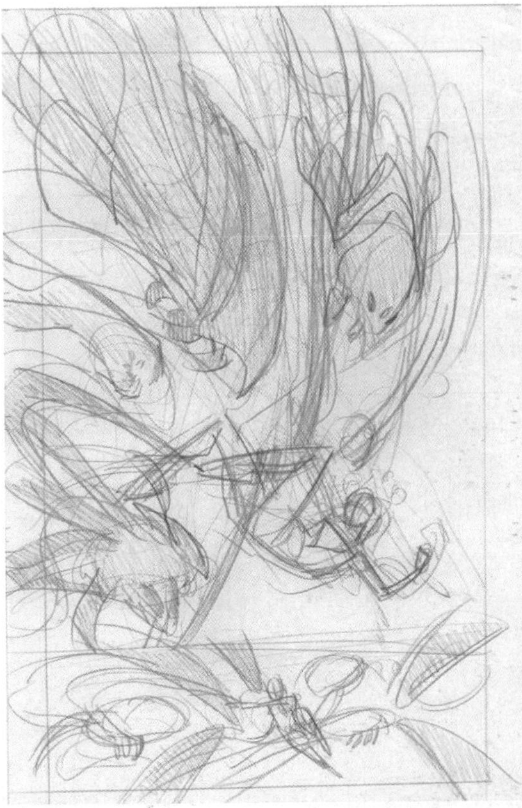

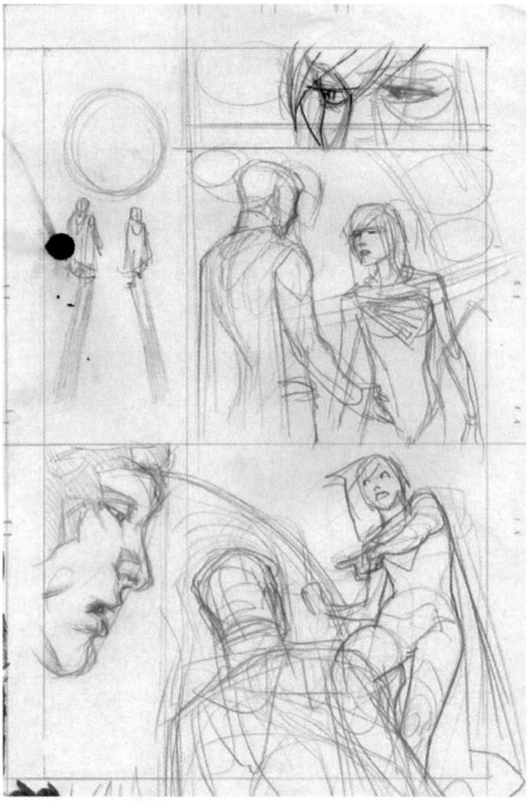
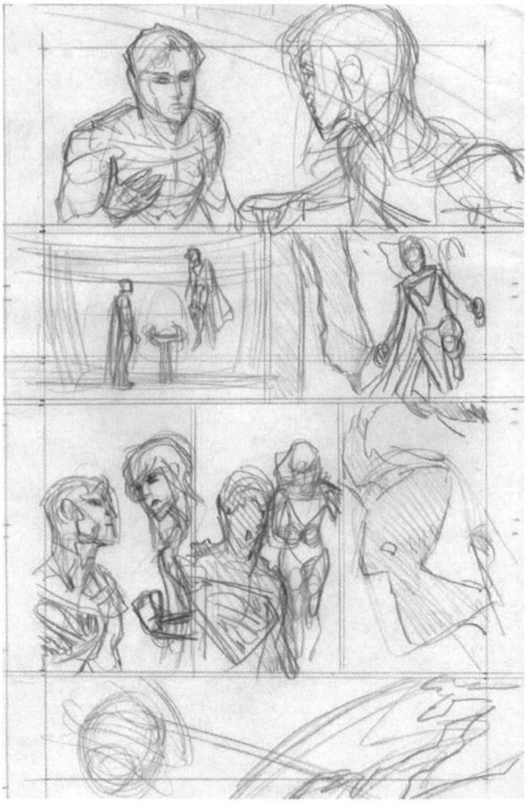
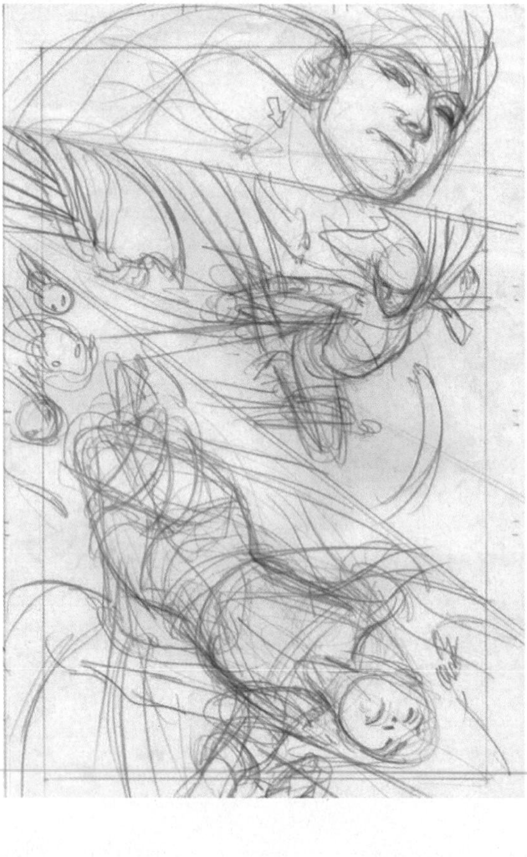
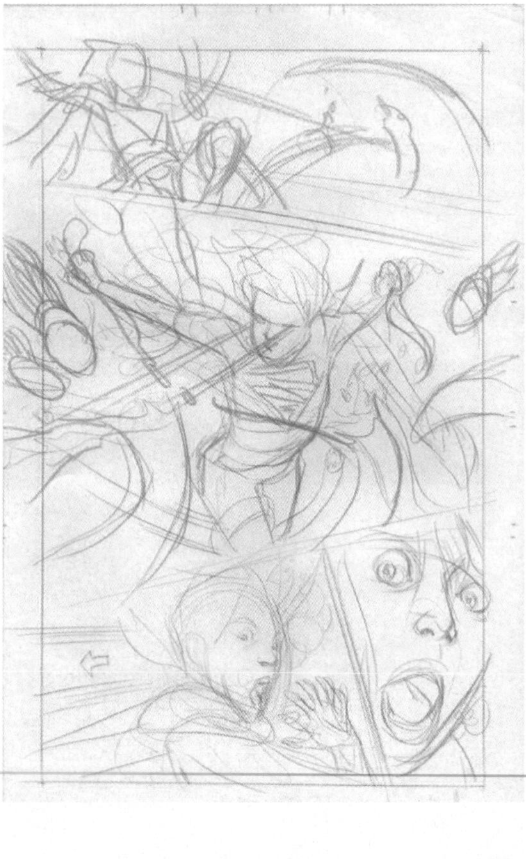

SUPERGIRL
CHARACTER DESIGNS BY MAHMUD ASRAR

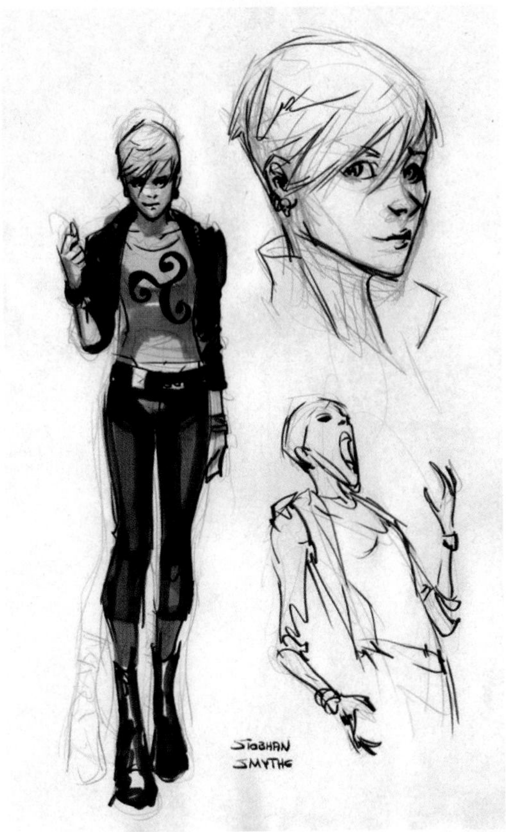
SIOBHAN
SMYTHE

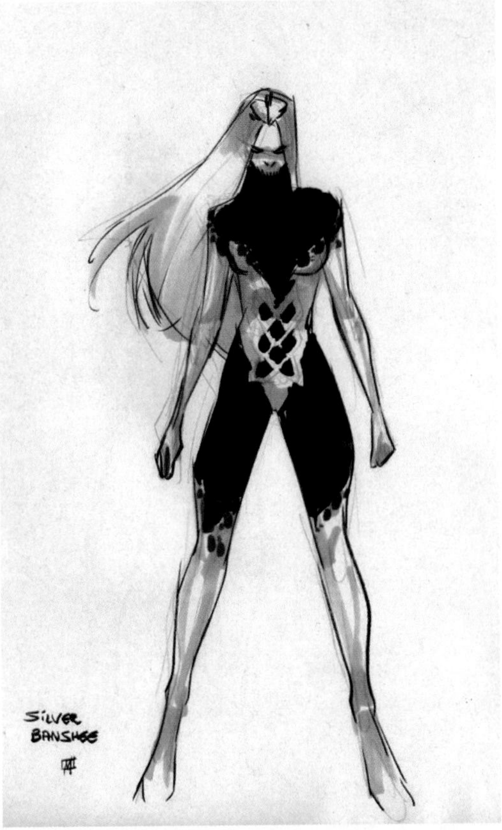
SILVER
BANSHEE

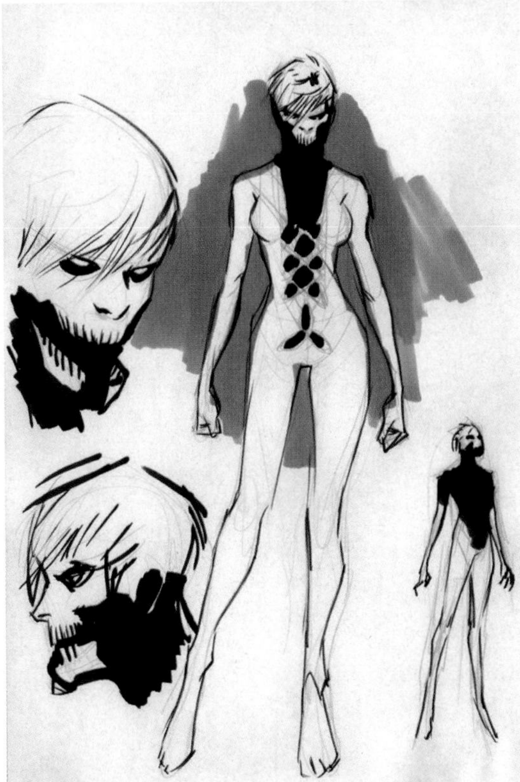

SILVER
BANSHEE

SILVER
BANSHEE

SILVER
BANSHEE

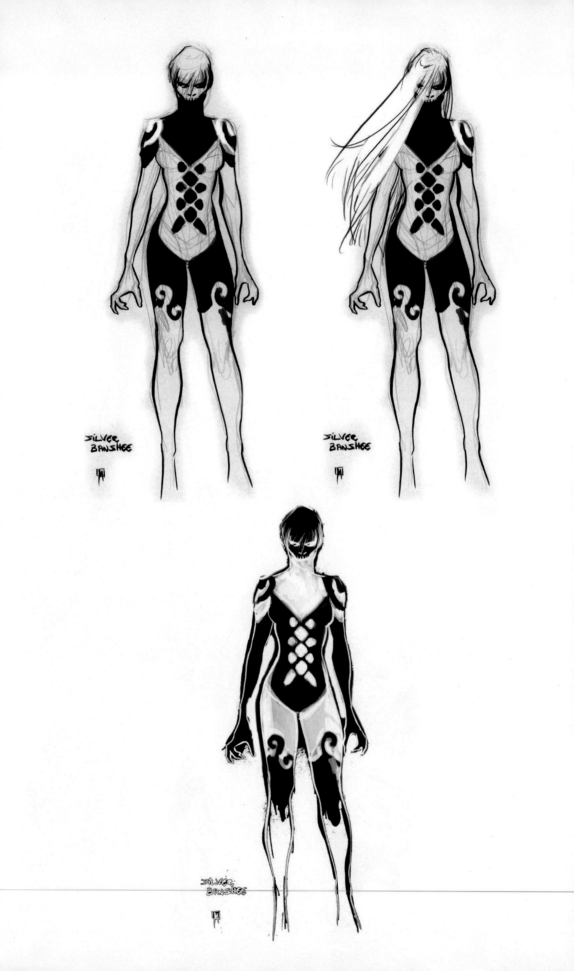

BLACK
BANSHEE

SILVER
BANSHEE

BLACK
BANSHEE

SUPERGIRL
COVER SKETCHES BY MAHMUD ASRAR

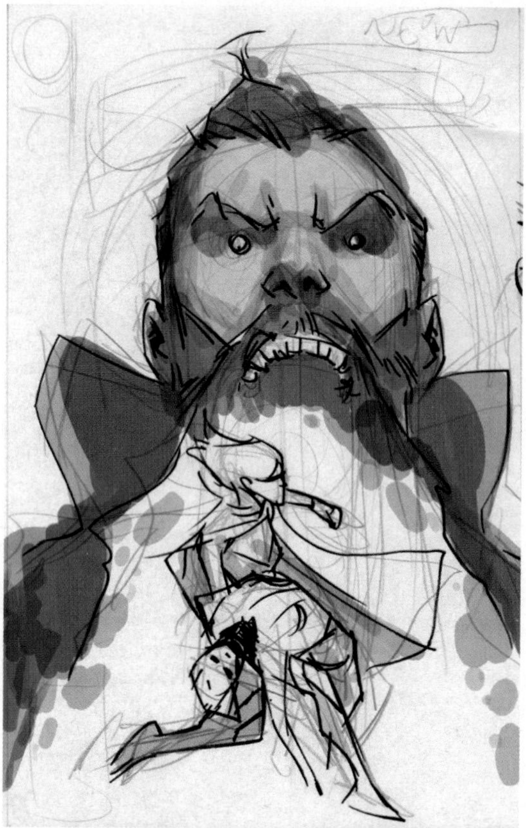

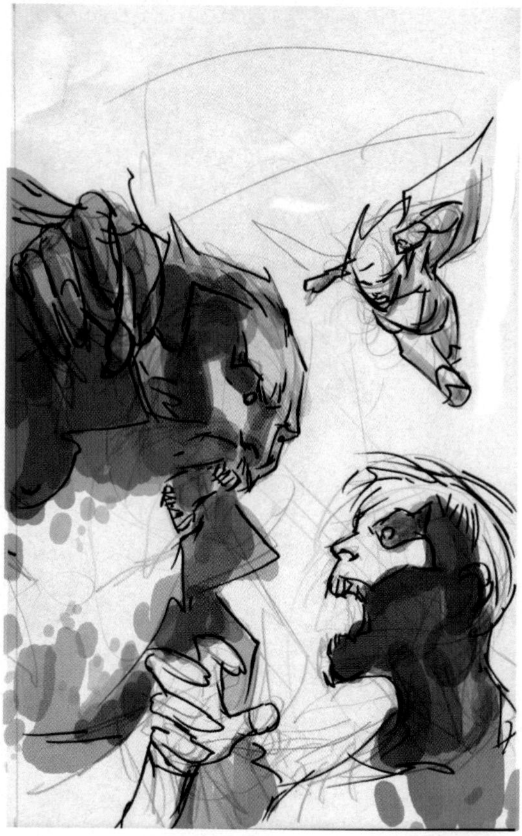

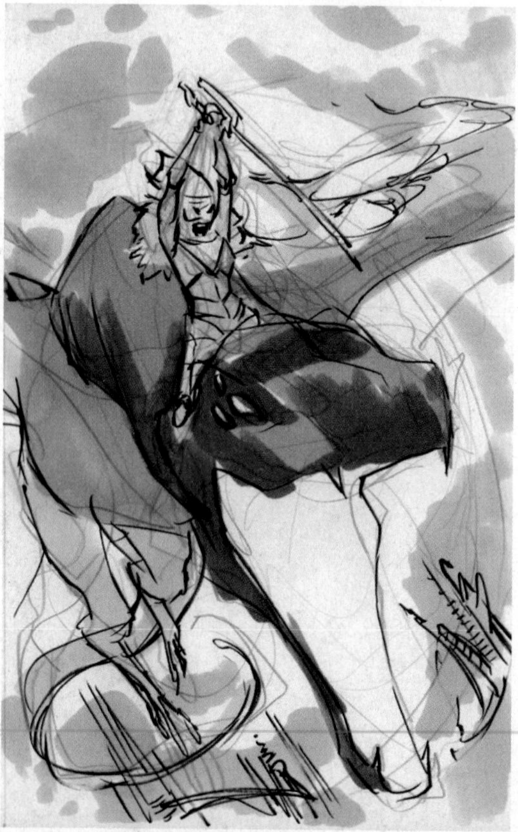

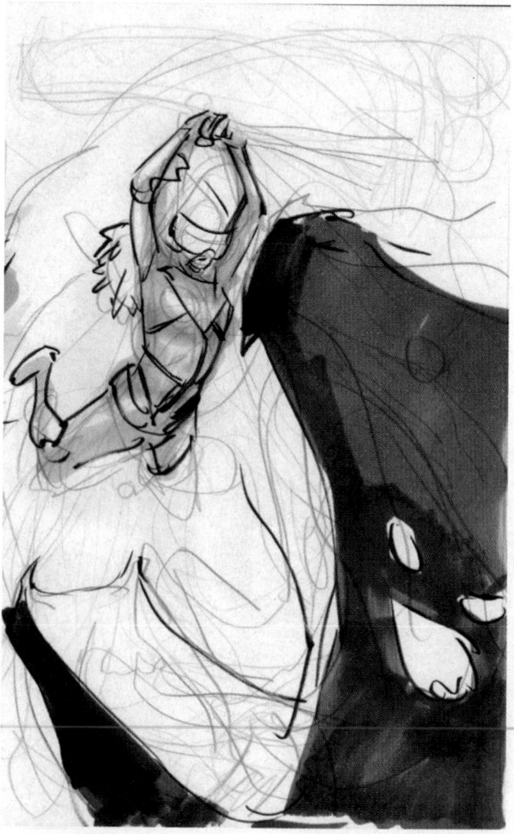

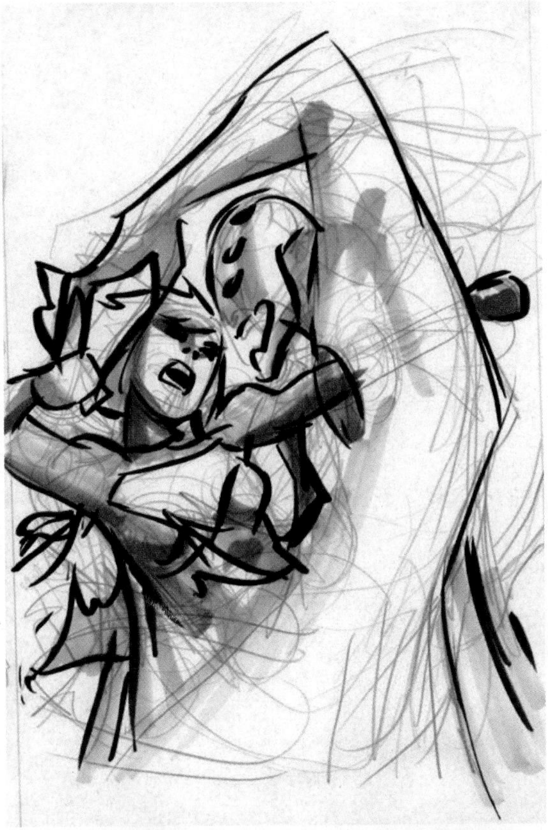
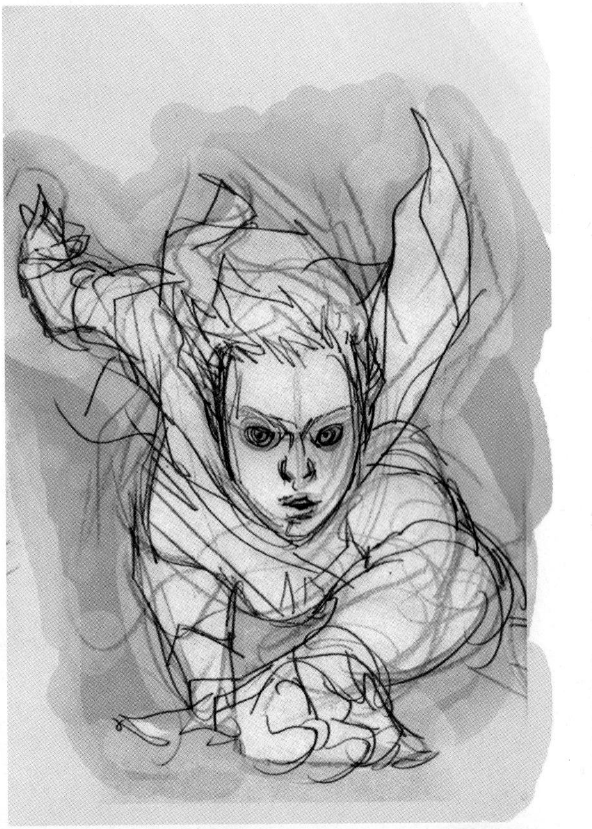
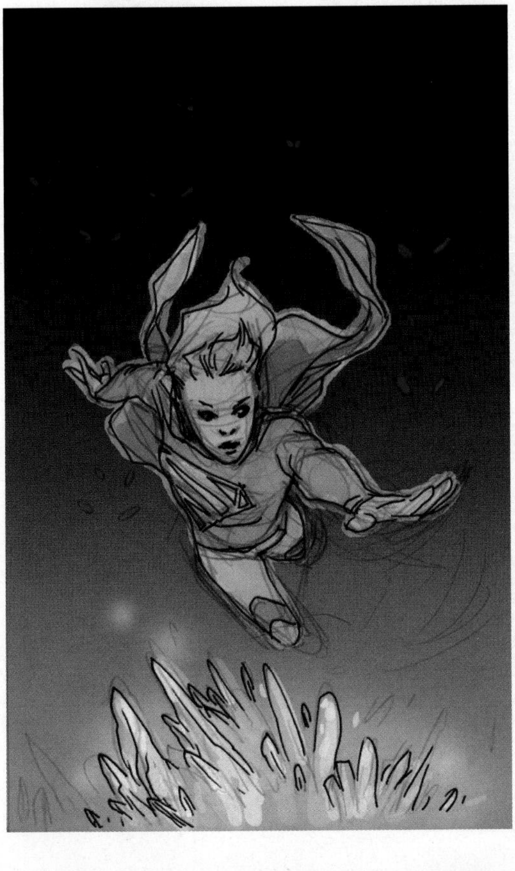
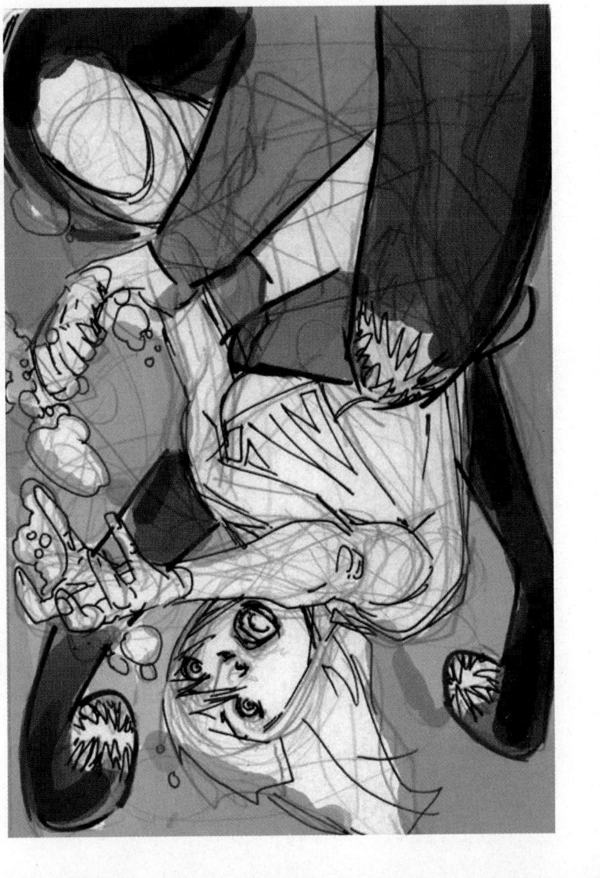

SUPERGIRL

ISSUE #0 UNUSED COVER BY MAHMUD ASRAR

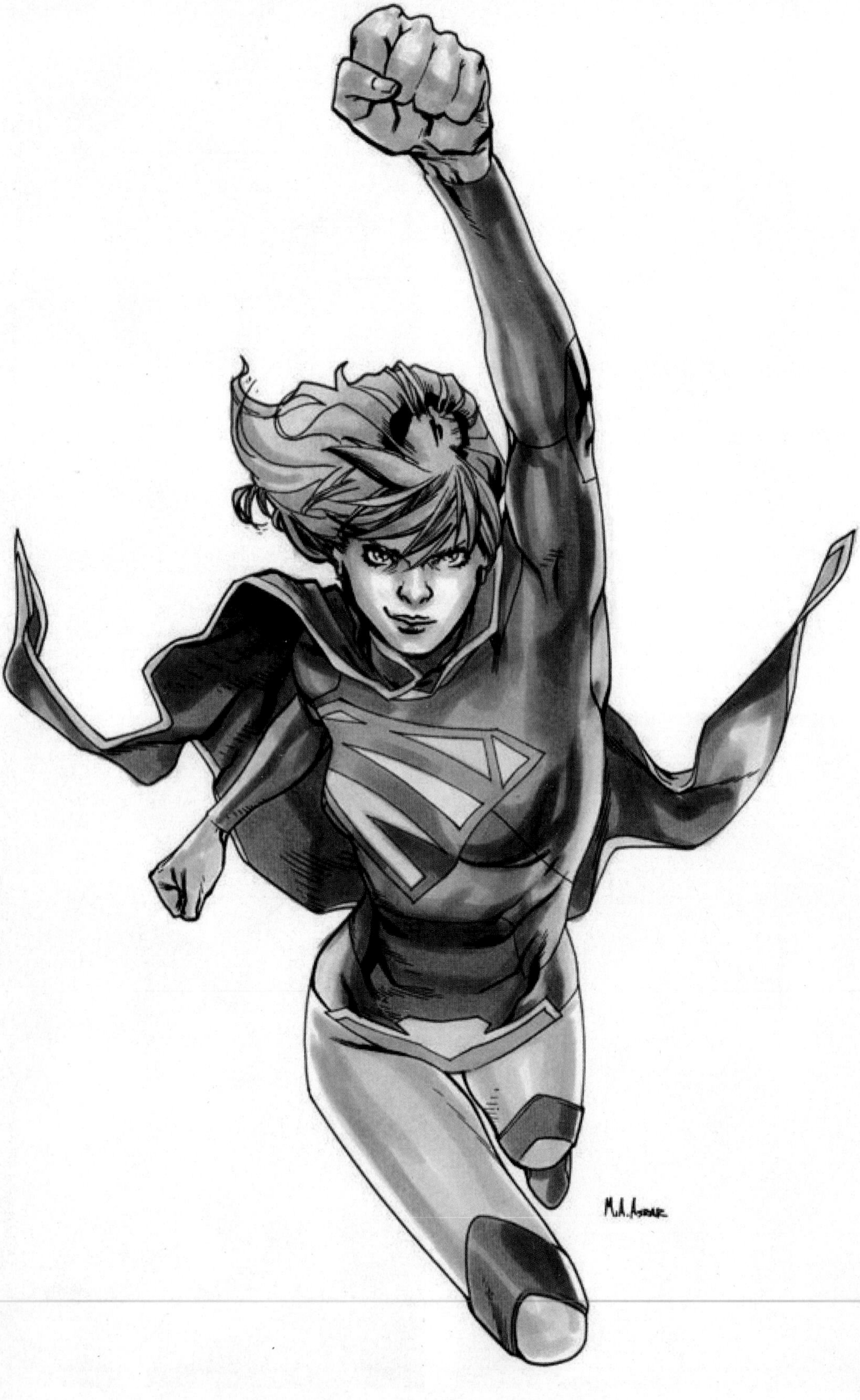

M.A. Asrar